```
ble-pilot $ ansible-playbook -i virtualmachines/demo/invent

[nfs service demo] *******************************************

[Gathering Facts] ********************************      *******
[demo.example.com]

[NFS server installed] *********                        *******
nged: [demo.example.com]

[share directory exists] ************************************
nged: [demo.example.com]

[share in /etc/exports file] ********************************
nged: [demo.example.com]

[export share] **********************************************
nged: [demo.example.com]

[firewall enabled] ****************************************
nged: [demo.example.com] => (item=nfs)
nged: [demo.example.com] => (item=rpc-bind)
nged: [demo.example.com] => (item=mountd)

NING HANDLER [restart NFS server] **************************
nged: [demo.example.com]

Y RECAP ***************************************************
o.example.com                 : ok=7      changed=6      unreachable=0
```


ANSIBLE FOR LINUX BY EXAMPLES

100+ Automation Examples For
Linux System Administrator And DevOps

Luca Berton

Ansible For Linux by Examples

100+ Automation Examples For Linux System Administrator and DevOps

Luca Berton

This book is for sale at
http://leanpub.com/ansibleforlinuxbyexamples

This version was published on 2022-04-08

ISBN 978-80-908536-3-8

Leanpub

This is a Leanpub book. Leanpub empowers authors and publishers with the Lean Publishing process. Lean Publishing is the act of publishing an in-progress ebook using lightweight tools and many iterations to get reader feedback, pivot until you have the right book and build traction once you do.

Contents

CONTENTS

CONTENTS

CONTENTS

Introduction

This book provides an introduction to the Ansible language.

Ansible is a popular open source IT automation technology for scripting applications in a wide variety of domains.

It is free, portable, powerful, and remarkably easy and fun to use.

This book is a tool to learn the Ansible automation technology with some real-life examples.

Whenever you are new to automation or a profession automation engineer, this book's goal is to bring you quickly up to speed on the fundamentals of the core Ansible language.

Every successful IT department needs automation nowadays for bare metal servers, virtual machines, cloud providers, containers, and edge computing. Automate your IT journey with Ansible automation technology.

I'm going to teach you example by example how to accomplish the most common System Administrator tasks.

You are going to start with the installation of Ansible in Red Hat Enterprise Linux, Ubuntu, and macOS using the most command package manager and archives.

Each of the 100+ lessons summarizes a module: from the most important parameter to some live demo of code and real-life usage. Each code is battle proved in the real life. Console interaction and verification are included in every video. A mundane activity like creating a text file, extracting and archiving, fetching a repository using HTTPS or SSH connections could be automated with some lines of code and these are only some of the long lists included in the course.

There are some Ansible codes usable in all the Linux systems, some specific for RedHat-like, Debian-like, and Windows systems.

The 20+ Ansible troubleshooting lesson teaches you how to read the error message, how to reproduce, and the process of troubleshooting and resolution.

Are you ready to automate your day with Ansible?

Whois Luca Berton

I'm Luca Berton and we're going to have a lot of fun together.

First of all, let me introduce myself.

I've been Ansible Technical Support Engineer of Red Hat, based in the Czech Republic, even if I'm Italian.

I've been more than 15 years System Administration, working with infrastructure, either on-premise or on the major cloud providers.

I'm an enthusiast of the Open Source support the community by sharing my knowledge in different events of public access.

I'm also a co-founder of my hometown Linux Users Group, visited by Richard Stallman, the founder of the Free Software Movement.

I consider myself a lazy person so I always try new ways to automate the repetitive task of my work.

After years of Perl, Bash, and python scripting I landed in Ansible technology. I took the certification and worked for more than a year with the Ansible Engineer Team.

I consider Ansible the best infrastructure automation technology nowadays, it's human-readable, the learning curve is accessible, and very requested by the recruiters in the market.

This ultimate guide contains all of the obvious and not-so-obvious solutions using Ansible automation.

In every lesson of this course, I'm going to share with you one specific use case, the possible solution, the code, the execution, and the verification of the target system.

All these solutions are battle-tested and used by me in my everyday automation.

You could easily jump between lessons and review again all the times that you need.

Awards & Recognition

2022

- Ansible Anwendertreffen - From Zero to Hero: How to build the Ansible Pilot Community - by Luca Berton (Red Hat CZ) 15:15 - 16:00[1] 15 Feb 2022
- Red Hat Ansible Playbook included in RHSB-2021-009 Log4Shell - Remote Code Execution - log4j (CVE-2021-44228)[2] 12 Jan 2022
- AWS Tip Set sysctl kernel parameters — Ansible module sysctl[3] 12 Jan 2022
- The Ansible Bullhorn #41 - A Newsletter for the Ansible Developer Community[4] 7 Jan 2022

2021

- The Ansible Bullhorn #34 - A Newsletter for the Ansible Developer Community[5] 17 Sep 2021

The course is going to keep track of the evolution of the Ansible technology adding more content whenever is needed.

---

[1] https://www.ansible-anwender.de/post/2022/01/register/
[2] https://access.redhat.com/security/vulnerabilities/RHSB-2021-009#diagnose
[3] https://awstip.com/set-sysctl-kernel-parameters-ansible-module-sysctl-83fc2b3f77f
[4] https://mailchi.mp/redhat/the-bullhorn-41
[5] https://us19.campaign-archive.com/?u=56d874e027110e35dea0e03c1&id=5f02018283

Are you ready to have fun?

Ansible For Beginners With Examples

In this chapter you're going to discover the Ansible Basics, Architecture and Terminology.

What is Ansible

In this chapter, I'll explain to you what is Ansible and why it is so powerful for your IT department.

Ansible

- Infrastructure Automation tool
- Open Source infrastructure as code

First of all, let's begin our adventure with the fabulous Open Source technology named Ansible. It is classified as an Infrastructure Automation tool, so you could automate your System Administrator tasks very easily. Infrastructure as code is the process of managing and provisioning computer data centers through machine-readable definition files, rather than physical hardware configuration or interactive configuration tools. Ansible follows the DevOps principles. With Ansible you could deploy your infrastructure as code on-premise and on the most well-known public cloud provider.

Ansible three Use Cases

- Provision

- Config management
- Application deployment

The three main use cases of Ansible are provision, configuration management, and app deployment. But after touching the technology I'm sure you could invent some more ways to use it!

Provisioning

- The process of setting up the IT infrastructure

Let's start talking about provisioning: all the System Administrator know how important is to manage a uniform fleet of machines. Some people still rely on software to create workstation images. But there is a drawback, with imaging technology you're only taking a snapshot in time of the machine. So every time you need to reinstall software because of the modern key activation systems or update manually to the latest security patches. Ansible is very powerful to automate this process being able to create a more smooth process.

Configuration management

- The process for maintaining systems and software in a desired and consistent state

The second key use case is "configuration management": maintain up-to-date and in a consistent way all your fleet, coordinating rolling updates and scheduling downtime. With Ansible you could verify the status of your managed hosts and take action in a small group of them. A huge variety of modules is available for the most common use cases. Not to mention the common use case to check the compliance of your fleet to some international standard and apply resolution plans.

Application deployment

- The process to publish your software between testing, staging and production environment

The third key use case where Ansible is useful is Application deployment. It could automate the continuous integration / continuous delivery workflow pipeline of your web application for example. Your DevOps team will be delighted!.

Ansible in DevOps

Ansible is used to apply the DevOps principles in worldwide organizations. Let me quickly summarize.

DevOps is a set of practices that combines software development (Dev) and IT operations (Ops). As DevOps is intended to be a cross-functional mode of working, those who practice the methodology use different sets of tools referred to as "toolchains" rather than a single one. These toolchains are expected to fit into one or more of the following categories, reflective of key aspects of the development and delivery process. The seven categories:

Code: code development and review, source code management tools, code merging.

Build: continuous integration tools, build status.

Test: continuous testing tools that provide quick and timely feedback on business risks.

Release: artifact repository, application pre-deployment staging.

Deploy: change management, release approvals, release automation.

Operate: infrastructure configuration and management, infrastructure as code tools.

Monitor: applications performance monitoring, end-user experience.

Four key tenets of Ansible

1. Declarative
You declare what you want rather than how to get to.

2. Agentless
You don't need to install an agent. It takes advantage of OpenSSH.

3. Idempotent
An operation could be run multiple times without changing beyond the initial operation.

4. Community driven
Published in Ansible Galaxy as collections and roles.

The four key tenets of ansible are: declarative, agentless, idempotent, and community-driven. With "declarative" it means that you could use in a way very similar to a programming language apply sequencing, selection, and iteration to the code flow. With "agentless" it means that you don't need to install and update any agents on the target machine, it uses the SSH connection and python interpreter. The language itself is "idempotent", which means that the code will check a precise status on the managed machine. It means that for example the first time your code will change something, the following runs it only verify that nothing changed and move forward. The last tenet is "community-driven", which means that exists a public archive called "Ansible Galaxy" where you could download the code made by other open source contributors. This code is organized in roles and collections, but we'll see it in the future.

Ansible six values

- Simple

YAML human readable automation.

- Powerful

Configuration management, workflow orchestration, application deployment.

- Cross-platform

Agentless support for all major OS, physical, virtual, cloud and network.

- Work with existing tools

Homogenize existing environment.

- "batteries included"

Come bundled with 750+ modules.

- Community powered

Download \250k/months People \3500 contributors, 1200 users on IRC.

Now let's talk about the six values of Ansible. The first is that is "simple: the code is written in YAML language, that is a human-readable data serialization language. It is well known and easy to learn, it is commonly used for configuration files and in applications where data is being stored or transmitted. Ansible is Powerful, it is battle-tested as Configuration management, workflow orchestration, application deployment. The third value is "cross-platform" by nature, the Agentless support for all major Operating Systems, physical, virtual, cloud, and network provider. Another value of Ansible is that it works with existing tools, it easy to homogenize the existing environment. The "batteries included" means that Ansible included bundled more than 750 modules to automate the most common tasks. The last value is that Ansible is "community-powered", every month has more than 250000 downloads, an average of 3500 contributors, and more than 1200 users on IRC.

Ansible history

- 2012

Developed by Michael DeHaan

- 2015

Acquired by Red Hat

- 2016

AnsibleFest events

- 2020

Red Hat Ansible Automation Platform 1.0

- 2021

Red Hat Ansible Automation Platform 2.1

The main events in Ansible history are the following.

The first release of Ansible was public on the 20th of February 2012. The Ansible tool was developed by Michael DeHaan. Ansible Inc., originally AnsibleWorks Inc., was the company set up to commercially support and sponsor the project.

On the 16th of October 2015 Red Hat acquired Ansible Inc., and evaluate Ansible as a "powerful IT automation solutions" designed to help enterprises move toward friction less IT.

AnsibleFest is an annual conference of the Ansible community of users, contributors since 2016 in London and the USA.

Ansible & Ansible Tower & Ansible Automation Platform

- Ansible

Community driven project fast-moving innovations Open Source but only command line tools.

- Red Hat Ansible Tower / Ansible Automation Platform

It is a framework designed by RedHat. It provides a web UI to manage your infrastructure.

Ansible is a community-driven project with fast-moving innovations Open Source but only command-line tools.

Enterprise needs more services and some stable releases. For example, they need an SLA for support. Red Hat offers this service to companies namely under the Ansible Tower umbrella, now re branded as Ansible Automation Platform.

Ansible Tower is a REST API, web service, and web-based console designed to make Ansible more usable for IT teams with members of different technical proficiency and skill-sets. It is a hub for automation tasks. The tower is a commercial product supported by Red Hat Inc. but derived from AWX upstream project, which is open source since September 2017.

Red Hat maintains also Ansible Engine. With Ansible Engine, organizations can access the tools and innovations available from the underlying Ansible technology in a hardened, enterprise-grade manner. Ansible Engine is developed by Red Hat with the explicit intent of being used as an enterprise IT platform.

Getting Started

In this chapter, I'll explain you how to move the firsts steps with Ansible technology. How to connect to the managed hosts and how to execute some simple tasks using the command line.

Ansible architecture

Let's Begin a talking about Ansible architecture. The node where Ansible is actually installed is called "control node" and it manages all your fleet of nodes. The controlled node on the other hand is called "managed node". The target nodes could be Linux, Mac, Windows and several network equipment. Each target has some specificity like different Linux distribution and module usage. We will discuss of the specificity the in the next sections.

Connection with managed nodes

The connection between "control node" and "managed nodes" is managed by SSH protocol without any requirement of specific client on the target machine. Other competitor require a client software often called "agent". With SSH connection the only requirements are a username and a certificate to access the target machine. There are some way to automate also this first script step. After completing SSH connection another requirement is "python" interpreter, witch come out-of-the-box for modern operating systems. By default Ansible uses SFTP to transfer files but you could switch to SCP in configuration. The Windows target could be connected using WinRM technology and uses PowerShell as interpreter.

Create a basic inventory

- /etc/ansible/hosts

```
1  host1.example.com
```

- default inventory file /etc/ansible/hosts
- "host1.example.com" is a managed host

The list of managed hosts is stored in /etc/ansible/hosts. In this example it contain only one host named host1.example.com.

Run your first Ansible command

```
1  $ ansible all -m ping
2  host1.example.org | SUCCESS => {
3      "ansible_facts": {
4          "discovered_interpreter_python": "/usr/bin/python"
5      },
6      "changed": false,
7      "ping": "pong"
8  }
```

- "ping" module executed on "all" hosts
- "host1.example.com" replied with a success code

Now we're ready to run your first Ansible command. The Ansible command is called module in Ansible slang. The first line executed Ansible ping module on all hosts. The response is a pong. Please note that this means that Ansible is able to connect with SSH username, identify using public key and execute the local python executer. So it's completely different from any ping in networking.

Run ad-hoc command on Ansible

```
1   $ ansible all -a "/bin/echo hello"
2   host1.example.org | CHANGED | rc=0 >>
3   hello
```

- "/bin/echo hello" command executed on "all" hosts
- "host1.example.com" replied with a changed code and print "hello" on standard output

Ansible could also execute some command on the target host and report the status on the console of "control node". In this example "/bin/echo hello" command was executed on "all" hosts. "host1.example.com" replied with a changed code and print "hello" on standard output. Please note that you would receive a "changed" state every time you run a command on the remote machine.

Run ad-hoc command with privilege escalation on Ansible

```
1   $ ansible all -m ping -u devops --become
2   host1.example.org | SUCCESS => {
3       "ansible_facts": {
4           "discovered_interpreter_python": "/usr/bin/python"
5       },
6       "changed": false,
7       "ping": "pong"
8   }
```

- "ping" module executed on "all" host as user "root" after login with user "devops"
- "host1.example.com" replied with a changed code and print "hello" on standard output

In this example I run the "ping" module against "all" host as user "root" after login with user "devops". "host1.example.com" replied with a changed code and print "hello" on standard output.

Recap

In this module we learned the basic concept of Ansible architecture, how to write the list of managed hosts and how to execute some simple commands against it.

Inventory

In this chapter, I'll explain to you what is an Ansible inventory, why do you need, the different types how to edit and use it in your day to day journey.

```
1  An inventory is the set of hosts Ansible could work again\
2  st.
3  They could be categorized as groups/patterns.
```

The list of multiple hosts managed by Ansible is called "inventory". It is fundamentally the list of nodes or hosts in your infrastructure at the same time, using a list or group of lists known as inventory. You could organize your inventory with "groups" or "patterns" to select the hosts or group you want Ansible to run against.

- "all" keyword

```
1  the keyword all includes all hosts of the inventory, exce\
2  pt localhost
```

The special keyword "all" include all the hosts of the inventory used. It will be very useful in the following lessons. The only exception is localhost that you need to specify.

Simple INI inventory

- `./ini_simple_inventory`

```
1   one.example.com
2
3   [webservers]
4   two.example.com
5   three.example.com
```

- file name: ini_simple_inventory
- "one.example.com" is ungrouped
- "two.example.com" and "three.example.com" are grouped as "webserver"

The simplest inventory type is the INI inventory, by the type of the file. The default location is "/etc/ansible/hosts" but you could use your customized with "-i" parameter. In this example host "one.example.com" is ungrouped and "two.example.com" and "three.example.com" are grouped as "webserver".

Simple YAML inventory

- `./simple_yaml_inventory.yml`

```
1   ---
2   all:
3     hosts:
4       one.example.com:
5     children:
6       webservers:
7         hosts:
8           two.example.com:
9           three.example.com:
```

- file name: inventory.yml
- "one.example.com" is ungrouped
- "two.example.com" and "three.example.com" are grouped as "webserver"

You could express the same inventory using YAML syntax In this example In this example host "one.example.com" is ungrouped and "two.example.com" and "three.example.com" are grouped as "webserver".

Add ranges of hosts

- ./ini_range_inventory

```
1   [webservers]
2   www[01:99].example.com
3
4   [databases]
5   db-[a-f].example.com
```

- "webservers" group contains all hosts from wwww01.example.com to www99.example.com

- "Databases" group contains all hosts from db-a.example.com to db-f.example.com,

Group members could be defined also using ranges by numbers or letters. In the range by numbers you could also specify a stride the increment between a sequence of number. In this INI example "webservers" group contains all hosts from "www01.example.com" to "www99.example.com". "databases" group contains all hosts from "db-a.example.com" to "db-f.example.com".

Host in multiple groups

- ./ini_groupsmultiple_inventory

```
1   one.example.com
2
3   [webservers]
4   two.example.com
5   three.example.com
6
7   [prod]
8   two.example.com
9
10  [dev]
11  three.example.com
```

- hosts "two.example.com" and "three.example.com" are present in multiple groups

Hosts could be present in multiple groups. In this INI example hosts "two.example.com" and "three.example.com" are grouped as "webserver". "two.example.com" is present in "webserver" as well as "prod" group.
"three.example.com" is present in "webserver" and "dev" group.

Host variables

- `./ini_hostinventory`

```
1    [webservers]
2    localhost  ansible_connection=local
3    one.example.com ansible_connection=ssh ansible_user=devops
4    two.example.com ansible_connection=ssh ansible_user=ansib\
5    le
```

- Customization of "ansible_connection" and "ansible_user" variables

In inventory you might would like to store variable values that relate to a specific host or group. This example scenario is common because it defines different connection with different hosts. For example to use "local" connection for the localhost and "ssh", default, for all the other hosts. For each hosts you could customize also the login user "devops for "one.example.com" and "ansible" for "two.example.com".

Group variables

- `./ini_groupsvariables_inventory`

```
1    [webservers]
2    one.example.com
3    two.example.com
4
5    [webservers:vars]
6    ntp_server=europe.pool.ntp.org
```

- `./inventory.yml`

```
1    ---
2    webservers:
3      hosts:
4        two.example.com:
5        three.example.com:
6      vars:
7        ntp_server: europe.pool.ntp.org
```

As well as per single host is possible to define group variables. This two inventory files in the example (INI and YAML format) the variables "ntp_server" has assigned the value "europe.pool.ntp.org" for all the hosts of the group.

Inheriting variable values

- ./ini_variableinheriting_inventory

```
1    [asia]
2    host1.example.com
3
4    [europe]
5    host2.example.com
6
7    [webserver:children]
8    asia
9    europe
10
11   [webservers:vars]
12   ntp_server=europe.pool.ntp.org
```

- ./variableinheriting_inventory.yml

```
1   ---
2   children:
3     webservers:
4       children:
5         asia:
6           hosts:
7             host1.example.com:
8         europe:
9           hosts:
10            host2.example.com:
11      vars:
12        ntp_server: europe.pool.ntp.org
```

Hosts and group could be combined together. In this example the group "webserver" has two members "asia" and "europe". This two elements are defined as a single host "host1.example.com" and "host2.example.com", respectively, but could contains more hosts as well. "ntp_server" variables is defined at "webservers" level. So in the end "ntp_server" variable is available for "webserver", "asia" and "europe" group. "ntp_server" variable is available as well in "host1.example.com" and "host2.example.com" hosts.

Use multiple inventory sources

```
1   $ ansible-playbook playbook.yml -i production -i developm\
2   ent
```

- Execute ansible playbook named "playbook.yml" against "production" and "development"

Is possible to use multiple inventory files for each execution. In this example is going to be executed ansible playbook named "playbook.yml" against "production" and "development" inventories.

localhost inventory

- `./ini_local_inventory`

```
1   localhost ansible_connection="local"
```

- file name: inventory
- /etc/ansible/hosts default

One special case in inventory is with localhost. You need to specify the connection type as "local", otherwise Ansible presume to use the default SSH connection.

Recap

Now you know more about Ansible INI and YAML inventory files, host and group variable.

Playbook

In this chapter, I'll explain to you what is an Ansible Playbook and why do you need. We'll cover how to start with a simple playbook, from the basic syntax and how to add more tasks.

```
1   A playbook is a set of play to be executed against an inv\
2   entory.
```

YAML syntax

```
 1  # This is a YAML comment
 2  some data # This is also a YAML comment
 3
 4  this is a string
 5  'this is another string'
 6  "this is yet another a string"
 7
 8  with_newlines: |
 9  Example Company
10  123 Main Street
11  New York, NY 10001
12
13  without_newlines: >
14  This is an example
15  of a long string,
16  that will become
17  a single sentence.
18
19  yaml_dictionary: {name1: value1, name2: value2}
20
21  yaml_list1:
22  - value1
23  - value2
24  yaml_list2: [value1, value2]
```

Every playbook is based on YAML syntax so the file is easy and human readable. YAML is a text format and you could easy recognize by the presence of the three dash symbols at the beginning and three dots in the end. The three dots are not mandatory so a lot of people simply omit them. This file type is very sensitive to spacing between elements. It's strictly important that elements of the same level are in the same indentation, despite some programming languages. You could use the symbol "#" for comments, even on the lines with some previous code. String are very important and you could specify directly or with single or double quote. I recommend you to use a double quote as a general rule. Using the pipe and major statement you could define multi-line strings. The first statement will keep the newlines, the second not. Others useful data structures are dictionaries and lists that you could see in action in the grayboard.

helloworld.yml

- helloworld.yml

```
1   ---
2   - name: Hello World sample
3     hosts: all
4     tasks:
5       - name: Hello message
6         ansible.builtin.debug:
7           msg: "Hello World!"
8   ...
```

```
1   file name: helloworld.yml
2   Name of the playbook
3   Hosts of execution
4   List of tasks
5   One task named "Hello message"
6   Module ansible.builtin.debug
7   Argument "msg" of module debug
```

This is the output of the execution of the "helloworld.yml". I'd like you to note the command used is "ansible-playbook". The first parameter is the inventory file and the second is the playbook.
In this execution the play is executed against the "host1.example.com" node. The output is very clear of the step by step execution. When the command is successful the output

is highlighted with green color. A warning will be presented in orange and an error in red. The most attent of you have noticed an extra task executed called "Gathering Facts" that is performed by Ansible to acquire some information of the managed node. We'll discuss more about facts gathering in the following lesson. Try by yourself the execution of this code and become confident with this output summary. It will be very useful. Two tasks are being executed.

Tip1: ansible-playbook –check option

```
$ ansible-playbook -i inventory  --check  helloworld.yml
PLAY [Hello World sample] *******************************\
*******************************************************\
**********
TASK [Gathering Facts] *********************************\
*******************************************************\
********
ok: [host1.example.com]
TASK [Hello message] ***********************************\
*******************************************************\
******
ok: [host1.example.com] => {
    "msg": "Hello World!"
}
PLAY RECAP *********************************************\
****************************************************
host1.example.com          : ok=2    changed=0    unreachabl\
e=0    failed=0    skipped=1    rescued=0    ignored=0
```

A very useful option of "–check" for ansible-playbook command. This option to perform a dry run on the playbook execution. This causes Ansible to report what changes would have occurred if the playbook were executed, but does not make any actual changes to managed hosts.

Tip2: debug day-to-day usage

- helloworld_debug.yml

```
1   ---
2   - name: Hello World sample
3     hosts: all
4     tasks:
5       - name: Hello message
6         debug:
7           msg: "Hello World!"
8           verbosity: 2
9   ...
```

```
1   file name: helloworld_debug.yml
2   Name of the playbook
3   Hosts of execution
4   List of tasks
5   One task named "Hello message"
6   Module debug
7   Argument "msg" of module debug
8   Argument "varbosity" is "2"
```

This tip allow you to keep the debug code in your playbook and enable the execution only when you need. For example the message is printed only when Ansible is invoked with output level two.

helloworld_debug.yml - execution - part 1

```
ansible-playbook -i inventory helloworld_debug.yml
PLAY [Hello World sample] *****************************\
*******************************************************\
**********

TASK [Gathering Facts] *******************************\
*******************************************************\
********
ok: [host1.example.com]

TASK [Hello message] *********************************\
*******************************************************\
******
skipping: [host1.example.com]

PLAY RECAP *******************************************\
****************************************************
host1.example.com          : ok=1      changed=0      unreachabl\
e=0     failed=0     skipped=1     rescued=0     ignored=0
```

This is the output of "helloworld_debug.yml" when is executed normally, which means not in debug mode. As you could notice the hello message is skipped.

helloworld_debug.yml - execution - part 2

```
1   $ ansible-playbook -i inventory -vv helloworld_debug.yml
2   PLAY [Hello World sample] ******************************\
3   *******************************************************\
4   **********
5   TASK [Gathering Facts] *********************************\
6   *******************************************************\
7   ********
8   ok: [host1.example.com]
9   TASK [Hello message] ***********************************\
10  *******************************************************\
11  ******
12  ok: [host1.example.com] => {
13      "msg": "Hello World!"
14  }
15  PLAY RECAP *********************************************\
16  *****************************************************
17  host1.example.com          : ok=2    changed=0    unreachabl\
18  e=0    failed=0    skipped=1    rescued=0    ignored=0
```

This is the output of "helloworld_debug.yml" when is executed in debug level two mode, please notice the two "V" in the command line. As you could notice the hello message is printed.

Idempotency

```
1   idempotency
2   modules check the desired final state has already been ac\
3   hieved, otherwise apply
```

One important characteristics of most of Ansible modules is to be "idempotent". It means that before executing any actions on the target node, the module is going to check the actual status. If the actual status match the desired once, no action is going to be performed. If the current status divert from the expected once an action will take place. Please note that if you execute another time the playbook the desired status will be found and no further actions will be performed. This property is called "idempotency" and you're young to take advantage of it.

multipleplays.yml

```
1    ---
2    - name: first play
3      hosts: web.example.com
4      tasks:
5        - name: first task
6          ansible.builtin.yum:
7            name: httpd
8            status: present
9        - name: second task
10         ansible.builtin.service:
11           name: httpd
12           enabled: true
13   - name: second play
14     hosts: database.example.com
15     tasks:
16       - name: first task
17         ansible.builtin.service:
18           name: mariadb
19           enabled: true
```

- file name: multipleplays.yml

Two plays inside to be execute against of web.example.com and database.example.com

The "multipleplays.yml" playbook contains two plays. The first play is executed against the "web.example.com" host and install and apache web server and enable on boot. The second play is going to be executed against "database.example.com" and enable on boot the execution of "madiadb" database management system. As you could see using multiple play is very powerful to execute different tasks in different hosts. Now the definition of playbook make more sense.

privilege_escalation.yml

```
 1  ---
 2  - name: install httpd
 3    hosts: web.example.com
 4    become: true
 5    become_method: sudo
 6    become_user: root
 7    tasks:
 8      - name: install httpd
 9        ansible.builtin.yum:
10          name: httpd
11          status: present
```

- privilege_escalation.yml

"become" specify that privilege escalation is necessary
"become_method" specify the escalation method
"become_user" specify the destination user (default "root")

Some action need to be taken by a user with administrative power. In Linux typically is the "root" user. Some distribution allow the privilege escalation using "sudo" command using the "wheel" group. In this example I'm going to install a software so I need the privilege escalation. The "yum" module need to perform some action on the managed node. In playbook when is not necessary you could disable.

Most common Ansible modules

- Files modules

copy: copy a local file to the managed host
fetch: copy files from remote nodes to local
file: set permissions and other properties of files
lineinfile: ensure a particular line is or is not in a file
synchronize: synchronize content using rsync

- Software package modules

package: manage packages using autodetected package manager native to the operating system
yum: manage packages using the YUM package manager
apt: manage packages using the APT package manager
dnf: manage packages using the DNF package manager
gem: manage Ruby gems
pip: manage Python packages from PyPI

- System modules

firewalld: manage arbitrary ports and services using firewalld
reboot: reboot a machine
service: manage services
user: add, remove, and manage user accounts

- Net tools modules

get_url: Download files in HTTP, HTTPS, and FTP
nmcli: Manage networking
uri: Interact with web services

Recap

In this module we put the foundation of the following operation on Ansible Playbook. Keep going and soon you will be able to automate all your System Administrator tasks.

Variables

In this chapter, I'll explain to you what are Ansible variables, why do you need, the different types how to edit and use it in your day to day journey.

```
1   variable store dynamic value for a given environment.
```

In your Playbook is a good practice to use Variables to store all the dynamic value that you need. Editing variables you could reuse your code in the future only parameterize accordingly your business needs.

Not permitted variables names

- no white spaces my var
- no dots my.var
- don't starts with number 1stvar
- don't contain special character myvar$1

Ansible allow all the combination of letters and numbers in variables names. If you plan to use numbers be aware that you can't use at the beginning, but this is a general rule in information technology world.

The four main limitations in variable names are: no white spaces are allowed, no dots, don't starts with numbers, don't contain special characters. So on the right you see some example of invalid variables names.

variableprint.yml

- ./variableprint.yml

```
1   ---
2   - name: Variable print sample
3     hosts: all
4     vars:
5       fruit: "apple"
6     tasks:
7       - name: Print variable
8         ansible.builtin.debug:
9           msg: "Print the value of variable {{ fruit }}"
```

```
1   file name: variableprint.yml
2   Name of the playbook
3   Hosts of execution
4   List of tasks
5   One task named "Print variable"
6   Module debug
7   Argument "msg" of module debug
```

The "variableprint.yml" playbook is similar to "helloworlds.yml" playbook. The syntax and the structure of the element is very similar except for the presence of the variable "fruit". Variables store information like strings, numbers and more complex data structures like lists, dictionaries, etc. In this case the variable has name "fruit" and value "apple". The "debug" module in this case will concatenate the text "Print the value of variable" with the value of the variable "fruit". Please note the double bracket that means the values of the variable. It's a best practice always to include the double brackets within double quote in the code.

variableprint.yml - execution

```
1   $ ansible-playbook -i inventory variableprint.yml
2   PLAY [Variable print sample] ***************************\
3   *********************
4
5   TASK [Gathering Facts] *********************************\
6   *********************
7   ok: [host1.example.com]
8
9   TASK [Print variable] **********************************\
10  *********************
11  ok: [host1.example.com] => {
12      "msg": "Print the value of variable apple"
13  }
14
15  PLAY RECAP *********************************************\
16  *********************
17  host1.example.com          : ok=2    changed=0    unreachable=0    \
18   failed=0    skipped=0    rescued=0    ignored=0
```

This is the output of the execution of the "variableprint.yml" is very similar to the one of "helloworld.yml" file. Please note print of the message "Print the value of variable apple" obtained combining the string with the value of the variable. Also this execution is successful as you could see in the play recap area and the green color. Two tasks are being executed.

variableprint.yml - extra variables

```
1   $ ansible-playbook -i inventory  -e fruit=banana  variabl\
2   eprint.yml
3   PLAY [Variable print sample] ***************************\
4   ********************
5
6   TASK [Gathering Facts] ********************************\
7   ********************
8   ok: [host1.example.com]
9
10  TASK [Print variable] *********************************\
11  ********************
12  ok: [host1.example.com] => {
13      "msg": "Print the value of variable banana"
14  }
15
16  PLAY RECAP ********************************************\
17  ********************
18  host1.example.com          : ok=2    changed=0    unreachable=0    \
19   failed=0     skipped=0     rescued=0    ignored=0
```

You could override the playbook variables specify the value from
the command line. Variables set on the command line are called
extra variables.

This is the output of the execution of the "variableprint.yml" is very
similar to the previous one. Please note print of the message "Print
the value of variable banana" obtained combining the string with
the value of the variable. The value passed from the command line
override any playbook value.

Host Variables and Group Variables

- inventory_host_variables

```
1  [servers]
2  host1.example.com ansible_user=devops
```

- inventory_group_variables

```
1  [servers]
2  host1.example.com
3  host2.example.com
4
5  [servers:vars]
6  user=alice
```

Host and group variables could be defined in your inventory file. In the left column you could see an example of host variable. The variable "ansible_user" is assigned the value "devops". This host variable is available for host1.example.com. On the right column you see an example of group variable. The variable "user" is assigned the value "alice". This group variable will be available for host1.example.com and host2.example.com with the same value.

- inventory_host_dir

```
1  [servers]
2  host1.example.com
```

- host_vars/demo1.example.com

```
1   ansible_user=devops
```

- inventory_group_dir

```
1   [servers]
2   host1.example.com
3   host2.example.com
```

- group_vars/servers

```
1   user=alice
```

You can achieve the same result also using using directories to populate host and group variables. As you could see the result will be the same of the previous slide but using more files. In the left column you could see an example of host variable. The variable "ansible_user" is assigned the value "devops". This host variable is available for host1.example.com. On the right column you see an example of group variable. The variable "user" is assigned the value "alice". This group variable will be available for host1.example.com and host2.example.com with the same value.

Array variables

- array.yml

```
 1   ---
 2   - name: Array sample
 3     hosts: all
 4     vars:
 5       users:
 6         alice:
 7           firstname: Alice
 8           homedir: /users/alice
 9         bob:
10           firstname: Bob
11           homedir: /users/bob
```

```
1   file name: array.yml
2   Users are organized in a hierarchical data structure.
3
4   Returns 'Alice'
5   users.alice.firstname
6   Returns 'Alice'
7   users['alice']['firstname']
```

A very useful data structure is the Array. You could organize the information in a hierarchical data structure. In the example it's easy readable the list of users: alice and bob. Each element of the list has some two properties: firstname and homedir. You could access to the data with dot notation or square brackets. In both cases you obtain the same result as you could see in the slide.

array.yml - execution

```
$ ansible-playbook -i inventory array.yml
PLAY [Array sample] *********************************\
****************************************************\
*****
TASK [Gathering Facts] *****************************\
****************************************************\
********
ok: [host1.example.com]
TASK [Print Alice's firstname] *********************\
****************************************************\
***************ok: [host1.example.com] => {
    "msg": "Print Alice's firstname: Alice"
}
PLAY RECAP *****************************************\
***********************************************host\
1.example.com                 : ok=2    changed=0    unr\
eachable=0    failed=0    skipped=0    rescued=0    ignor\
ed=0
```

This is the output of the execution of the "array.yml" is very similar to the previous one. You could notice the output of "Print Alice's firstname: Alice". Ansible accessed the array variable value and show in the output message as expected.

Registered Variables

- registeredvariables.yml

```
1    ---
2    - name: Installs a package and prints the result
3      hosts: all
4      become: true
5      tasks:
6        - name: Install the package
7          ansible.builtin.yum:
8            name: wget
9            state: installed
10         register: install_result
11
12       - name: debug
13         ansible.builtin.debug:
14           var: install_result
```

```
1    file name: registeredvariables.yml
2
3    Store the standard output in variable install_result
4    that could be printed as well
```

Another very useful data structure are registered variables. You could save inside registered variables the output of any commands. In this example will be printed on screen.

registeredvariables.yml - execution

```
$ ansible-playbook -i inventory registeredvariables.yml
PLAY [Installs a package and prints the result] *********\
*******************************************************\
*********************************************
TASK [Gathering Facts] *********************************\
*********************************************************
ok: [host1.example.com]
TASK [Install the package] *****************************\
*********************************************************
ok: [host1.example.com]
TASK [debug] *******************************************\
*********************************************************
ok: [host1.example.com] => {
    "install_result": {
        "changed": false,
        "failed": false,
        "msg": "Nothing to do",
        "rc": 0,
        "results": []
    }
}
PLAY RECAP *********************************************\
*********************************************************
host1.example.com          : ok=3    changed=0    unreach\
able=0    failed=0    skipped=0    rescued=0    ignored=0
```

This is the output of the execution of the "registeredvariables.yml"
is like expected. At first the yum module verify the presence of the
package, if missing proceed with the installation. The output of the
setup process is stored inside a registered variable that is printed on
screen.

Recap

In this module we explored the variable usage inside the Ansible Playbook. You now are aware about the use of tools like the user defined, Host, Group and registered variables.

Facts and Magic Variables

In this chapter, I'll explain to you what are Ansible facts and magic variables, why do you need, the different types how to edit and use it in your day to day journey.

Ansible Facts

```
1   facts are variables related to remote hosts.
```

Variables related to remote systems are called facts. With facts, you can use the behavior or state of one system as configuration on other systems. They are so powerful because you could obtain a very comprehensive vision of the current host, the operating system, the distribution used, the ip address, the networking configuration, the storage configuration, etc.

List all facts of a machine ad-hoc

```
$ ansible -m setup hostname
    "ansible_all_ipv4_addresses": [
        "REDACTED IP ADDRESS"
    ],
    "ansible_all_ipv6_addresses": [
        "REDACTED IPV6 ADDRESS"
    ],
    "ansible_apparmor": {
        "status": "disabled"
    },
    "ansible_architecture": "x86_64",
    "ansible_bios_date": "11/28/2013",
    "ansible_bios_version": "4.1.5",
    "ansible_cmdline": {
        "BOOT_IMAGE": "/boot/vmlinuz-3.10.0-862.14.4.el7.\
x86_64",
        "console": "ttyS0,115200",
        "no_timer_check": true,
        "nofb": true,
        "nomodeset": true,
        "ro": true,
        "root": "LABEL=cloudimg-rootfs",
        "vga": "normal"
    "ansible_date_time": {
        "date": "2018-10-25",
        "day": "25",
        "epoch": "1540469324",
        "hour": "12",
        "iso8601": "2018-10-25T12:08:44Z",
        "iso8601_basic": "20181025T120844109754",
        "iso8601_basic_short": "20181025T120844",
        "iso8601_micro": "2018-10-25T12:08:44.109968Z",
        "minute": "08",
        "month": "10",
        "second": "44",
```

```
36          "time": "12:08:44",
37          "tz": "UTC",
38          "tz_offset": "+0000",
39          "weekday": "Thursday",
40          "weekday_number": "4",
41          ""weeknumber": "43",
42          "year": "2018"
43      },
44      "ansible_default_ipv4": {
45          "address": "REDACTED",
46          "alias": "eth0",
47      [...]
```

The best way to understand Ansible facts is to list by yourself using this simple ad-hoc command. You will be surprised by the amount of information you're going to obtain by the host. For example the current hardware configuration: architecture, processor, ram, available memory, storage configuration, etc. There are also more information about the software configuration: operating system, the distribution used, the ip address, the networking configuration, the storage configuration, etc.

List all facts of a machine playbook

- facts_printall.yml

```
1   ---
2   - name: facts_printall
3     hosts: all
4     tasks:
5     - name: Print all facts
6       ansible.builtin.debug:
7         var: ansible_facts
```

You could access the same amount of data from the Ansible playbook. In this simple example you're going to list all the ansible facts for all the hosts of the inventory. The expected result will be the same of the previous ad-hoc execution.

facts_printall.yml - execution

```
ansible-playbook -i inventory facts_printall.yml
PLAY [facts_printall] *********************************\
*******************************************************\
*******
TASK [Gathering Facts] *******************************\
*******************************************************\
********
ok: [host1.example.com]
TASK [Print all facts] *******************************\
*******************************************************\
********
ok: [host1.example.com] => {
    "ansible_facts": {
        "architecture": "x86_64",
        "bios_date": "10/12/2020",
        "bios_version": "N22ET66W (1.43 )",
        "br_4332d8483447": {
            "active": false,
            "device": "br-4332d8483447",
            "features": {
                "esp_hw_offload": "off [fixed]",
                "esp_tx_csum_hw_offload": "off [fixed]",
                "fcoe_mtu": "off [fixed]",
```

This is the output of the execution of the "facts_printall.yml". In this execution the play is executed against the "host1.example.com" node. The output is very long with all the facts re obtained in automatically by Ansible in the task "Gathering Facts". I encourage you to run this code and be confident with Ansible Facts.

Reference a fact

- facts_printone.yml

```
1   ---
2   - name: facts_printone
3     hosts: all
4     tasks:
5     - name: Print a fact
6       ansible.builtin.debug:
7         var: "{{ ansible_facts['ansible_architecture'] }}"
```

You could easily interact with facts specifying the fact name. In this example we're listing the architecture of all the managed nodes. Feel free to customize the code to the ansible facts that better fit your needs.

Magic variables

```
1   Magic variables are variables related to Ansible.
```

Variables related to remote systems are called facts. With facts, you can use the behavior or state of one system as configuration on other systems.

Most common magic variables

- hostvars
- groups
- group_names
- inventory_hostname
- ansible_version

The most common magic variables are "hostvars", "groups", "group_names", "inventory_hostname" and "ansible_version". With "hostvars" magic variable you could access variables defined for any host in the play. It is very useful when you would like to access the property of one host from another one. You could combine "hostvars" with ansible facts to access property of another hosts. "groups" magic variable list all the groups in the inventory. You could use "groups" and "hostvars" magic variables together to list all the IP addresses of the hosts in a group. "group_names" is a list of which groups is the current host part of. "Inventory_hostname" magic variable contains the name of the host configured in the inventory. "ansible_version" magic variable contains the version information about Ansible.

Recap

Ansible Facts and Magic Variables are very useful in your Ansible Playbook especially when you need to execute some operations that impacts all hosts in the inventory. For example to generate a custom `/etc/hosts` file for all hosts involved in the inventory. You could apply loop or other statements that you're going to explore in the next lessons.

Vault

In this module, we are going to talk about how to store in a secure way encrypted any sensitive data such as passwords or API keys using Ansible Vault.

```
1   Ansible Vault encrypts variables and files to protect sen\
2   sitive content and let you use in playbooks or roles
```

Ansible Vault stores variables and files in an encrypted way and let you use in playbooks or roles. The cipher used to protect files is AES 256 in recent versions of Ansible.

Creating an encrypted file

```
1  $ ansible-vault create secret.yml
2  New Vault password: password
3  Confirm New Vault password: password
4
5  $ ansible-vault create --vault-password-file=vault-passwo\
6  rd.txt secret1.yml
```

To create a new encrypted file, use the `ansible-vault create filename` command. The command prompts for the new vault password and then opens a file using the default editor. In this example the password used is **password** but I strongly encourage you to use one more secure as possible.

Viewing an encrypted file

```
1  $ ansible-vault view secret1.yml
2  Vault password: password
3  INFERNO.
4  I.
5  Nel mezzo del cammin di nostra vita
6  mi ritrovai per una selva oscura
7  ché la diritta via era smarrita.
8  Ahi quanto a dir qual era è cosa dura
9  esta selva selvaggia e aspra e forte
10 che nel pensier rinova la paura!
11 Tant'è amara che poco è più morte;
12 ma per trattar del ben ch'i' vi trovai,
13 dirò de l'altre cose ch'i' v'ho scorte.
```

You can use the ansible-vault view filename command to view an Ansible Vault-encrypted file without opening it for editing.

Editing an existing encrypted file

```
1   $ ansible-vault edit secret.yml
2   Vault password: password
```

To edit an existing encrypted file, Ansible Vault provides the ansible-vault edit filename command. This command decrypts the file to a temporary file and allows you to edit it. When saved, it copies the content and removes the temporary file.

Encrypting an existing file

```
1   $ ansible-vault encrypt cleartext1.yml --output=vault1.yml
2   New Vault password: password
3   Confirm New Vault password: password
4   Encryption successful
```

To encrypt a file that already exists, use the ansible-vault encrypt filename command. The --output option save the encrypted file with a new name. If you omit this option the original file will be overwritten with the encrypted one.

Decrypting an existing file

```
1   $ ansible-vault decrypt vault1.yml --output=decrypted.yml
2   Vault password: password
3   Decryption successful
```

An existing encrypted file can be permanently decrypted by using the ansible-vault decrypt filename command. When decrypting a single file, you can use the `--output` option to save the decrypted file under a different name.

Changing password of an encrypted file

```
1  $ ansible-vault rekey secret.yml
2  Vault password: password1
3  New Vault password: password
4  Confirm New Vault password: password
5  Rekey successful
```

You can use the `ansible-vault rekey filename` command to change the password of an encrypted file. This command can rekey multiple data files at once. It prompts for the original password and then the new password.

Playbooks and Ansible Vault

```
1   $ ansible-playbook playbook.yml
2   TASK [include_vars] ************************************\
3   *******************************fatal: [localhost]: FAIL\
4   ED! => {"ansible_facts": {}, "ansible_included_var_files"\
5   : [], "changed": false, "message": "Attempting to decrypt\
6    but no vault secrets found"}
7
8   $ ansible-playbook --vault-id @prompt playbook.yml
9   Vault password (default): password
10
11  $ ansible-playbook --vault-password-file=vault-password.t\
12  xt playbook.yml
```

To run a playbook that accesses files encrypted with Ansible Vault, you need to provide the encryption password to the `ansible-playbook` command. If you do not provide the password, the playbook returns an error. To provide the vault password to the playbook, use the `--vault-id` option. For example, to provide the vault password interactively, use `--vault-id @prompt` as illustrated. Alternatively you could use a password file.

Recap

In this module we explored the Ansible Vault security storage to save secrets and confidential information inside Ansible. As we saw this tools are robust and completely integrated inside Ansible Technology.

Conditional

In this module, I'll explain to you what are Ansible conditionals operations and how you could use every day in your Ansible Playbook.

```
1  Conditional statement check a condition and change the be\
2  havior of the program accordingly
```

Let's start! In order to write useful code, we almost always need the ability to check conditions and change the behavior of the program accordingly. Conditional statements give us this ability. The Ansible form is the "when" statement. Ansible uses Jinja2 tests and filters in conditionals. Ansible supports all the standard tests and filters, and adds some unique ones as well.

Basic conditionals with "when"

- conditional_basic_false.yml

```
1   ---
2   - name: conditional_basic
3     hosts: all
4     vars:
5       configure_nginx: false
6     tasks:
7       - name: reload nginx
8         ansible.builtin.service:
9           name: nginx
10          state: reloaded
11        when: configure_nginx
```

This is the basic example of usage of "when" statement in your Ansible playbook. The task "reload ngnix" is going to be executed only when the "configure_nginx" boolean variable is set to "true". In this example is not so we expect this task to be skipped. Let's see the output of the executed code.

Execution:

```
1   $ ansible-playbook -i inventory conditional_basic_false.y\
2   ml
3   PLAY [conditional_basic] *******************************\
4   **********************************************************\
5   *********
6   TASK [Gathering Facts] *********************************\
7   **********************************************************\
8   *******
9   ok: [host1.example.com]
10  TASK [reload nginx] ************************************\
11  **********************************************************\
12  *****
13  skipping: [host1.example.com]
14  PLAY RECAP ********************************************\
15  ****************************************************
```

```
16  host1.example.com          : ok=1     changed=0     unreachabl\
17  e=0     failed=0    skipped=1    rescued=0    ignored=0
```

This is the output of the execution of the "conditional_basic_false.yml". In this execution the play is executed against the "host1.example.com" node. The output is highlighted with green and blue colors. As you could see the task of the task "reload nginx" is read by Ansible but skipped based on our conditional statement.

- conditional_basic_true.yml

```
1   ---
2   - name: conditional_basic
3     hosts: all
4     vars:
5       configure_nginx: true
6     tasks:
7       - name: reload nginx
8         ansible.builtin.service:
9           name: nginx
10          state: reloaded
11        when: configure_nginx
```

This is the same basic example of usage of "when" statement in your Ansible playbook but we changed the variable value from "false" to "true". The task "reload ngnix" is now going to be executed because the "configure_nginx" boolean variable is set to "true". Let's see the output of this code execution.

Execution:

```
$ ansible-playbook -i inventory conditional_basic_true.yml
PLAY [conditional_basic] *******************************\
*******************************************************\
*********
TASK [Gathering Facts] ********************************\
*******************************************************\
********
ok: [host1.example.com]
TASK [reload nginx] ***********************************\
*******************************************************\
*****
ok: [host1.example.com]
PLAY RECAP ********************************************\
***************************************************
host1.example.com         : ok=2    changed=0    unreachabl\
e=0    failed=0    skipped=0    rescued=0    ignored=0
```

This is the output of the execution of the "conditional_basic_-true.yml". In this execution the play is executed against the "host1.example.com" node. The output is highlighted with green color. As you could see the task of the task "reload ngnx" is read by Ansible and executed successfully in our conditional statement.

Conditionals based on ansible_facts

- conditional_facts.yml

```
1   ---
2   - name: conditional_facts
3     hosts: all
4     tasks:
5     - name: Shut down Debian-like systems
6       ansible.builtin.command: /sbin/shutdown -t now
7       when: ansible_facts['os_family'] == "Debian"
```

It is very useful combine conditional and facts. So you're able to adapt the execution of your code based on individual hosts conditions, IP address, operating system, the status of a filesystem, and many more. In this example we're going to execute the shutdown if the target system in Debian-like so Debian and Ubuntu managed hosts.

Execution:

```
1   $ ansible-playbook -i inventory conditional_facts.yml
2   PLAY [conditional_facts] ********************************\
3   **********************************************************\
4   **********
5   TASK [Gathering Facts] *********************************\
6   **********************************************************\
7   ********
8   ok: [host1.example.com]
9   TASK [Shut down Debian-like systems] *******************\
10  **********************************************************\
11  ********************
12  skipping: [host1.example.com]
13  PLAY RECAP *********************************************\
14  *****************************************************
15  host1.example.com                      : ok=1     changed=0    \
16   unreachable=0    failed=0    skipped=1    rescued=0      i\
17  gnored=0
```

This is the output of the execution of the "conditional_facts.yml". In this execution the play is executed against the "host1.example.com" node. The target host is not a Debian-like system because you could notice that the task named "Shut down Debian-like systems" is in the "skipped" status.

Recap

Conditionals are very important because enable us to create Ansible Playbook that respond to some events, conditions or Ansible Facts. This statements is the foundation of the smart Ansible Playbook.

Loop

In this chapter, I'll explain to you what are Ansible loop operations and how you could use every day in your Ansible Playbook.

```
1   Loop automate repetitive tasks
```

Computers are great in automation of repetitive tasks. Repeating identical or similar tasks without making errors is something that computers do well and people do poorly.
Repeated execution of a set of statements is called iteration. Ansible has several statements for iteration – the "loop" statement, and the "with_items" statements. The with statement rely on plugins.

- loop_simple.yml

```
 1    ---
 2    - name: Check services
 3      hosts: all
 4      tasks:
 5      - name: httpd and mariadb are running
 6        ansible.builtin.service:
 7          name: "{{ item }}"
 8          state: started
 9        loop:
10          - httpd
11          - mariadb
```

A simple loop iterates a task over a list of items. The "loop" statement is added to the task, and takes as a value the list of items over which the task should be iterated. The loop variable item iterate the current value during each iteration.

- loop_hash_or_dict.yml

```
 1    ---
 2    - name: Users exist and are in the correct groups
 3      hosts: all
 4      tasks:
 5      - name: Users exist and are in the correct groups
 6        ansible.builtin.user:
 7          name: "{{ item.name }}"
 8          state: present
 9          groups: "{{ item.group }}"
10        loop:
11          - name: alice
12            group: wheel
13          - name: bob
14            group: root
```

The loop list could does not need to be a list of simple values. In the following example, each item in the list is actually a hash or a dictionary. Each hash or dictionary in the example has two keys, name
and groups, and the value of each key in the current item loop variable can be retrieved with the "item.name" and "item.group" variables, respectively.

with_* statement

- with_items

Like "loop" for simple lists, list of strings or a list of hashes/dictionaries.
Flatter to list if lists of lists are provided

- with_file

This keyword requires a list of control node file names. The loop variable item holds the content of the file

- with_sequence

requires parameters to generate a list of values based on a numeric sequence

loop_with_items.yml

```
 1   ---
 2   - name: Example with_items
 3     hosts: all
 4     vars:
 5       data:
 6           - alice
 7           - bob
 8     tasks:
 9     - name: Print values of data
10       ansible.builtin.debug:
11         msg: "{{ item }}"
12       with_items: "{{ data }}"
```

In the "loop_with_items.yml" playbook the variable "data" is a list of strings. The task "Print values of data" uses the "with_items" to iterate item by item and print onscreen.

Recap

Loops statement are very useful to automate repetitive tasks. Loops are the foundation of a successful Ansible Playbook.

Handler

In this chapter, I'll explain to you what are Ansible Handler statement and how you could use every day in your Ansible Playbook.

```
 1   Handler run operations on change
```

Handlers are very important for idempotency. They allow to execute some steps only if necessary and to save computer cycles when there is no need to be executed.

rollingupdate.yml

```
1    ---
2    - name: Rolling update
3      hosts: all
4      become: true
5      tasks:
6        - name: latest apache httpd package is installed
7          ansible.builtin.yum:
8            name: httpd
9            state: latest
10         notify: restart apache
11
12     handlers:
13       - name: restart apache
14         ansible.builtin.service:
15           name: httpd
16           state: restarted
```

The "rollingupdate.yml" is composed by one task and one handler. The handler code is executed only if necessary. Please note the "notify" statement mention the name of the handler to run. This playbook check the version of apache http web server on all hosts, if an update is available, the yum module provide the upgrade process and restart the daemon at the end. If an upgrade is not necessary the handler code is not necessary.

A more complex playbook could have multiple handlers and you could reference by name.

Role

In this chapter, I'll explain to you what are Ansible role about code re usage how you could use every day in your Ansible Playbook.

```
1   Role enable code reuse to Ansible
```

Roles are like function in traditional programming world. Use Ansible roles to develop playbooks more quickly and to reuse Ansible code.

Role tree directories

```
1   $ tree user.example
2   user.example/
3   ├── defaults
4   │
5   └── main.yml
6   ├── files
7   ├── handlers
8   │
9   └── main.yml
10  ├── meta
11  │
12  └── main.yml
13  ├── README.md
14  ├── tasks
15  │
16  └── main.yml
17  ├── templates
18  ├── tests
19  │
20  ├── inventory
21  │
22  └── test.yml
23  └── vars
24  └── main.yml
```

Directory description:

- `defaults` the main.yml file in this directory contains the default values of role variables that can be overwritten when the role is used. These variables have low precedence and are intended to be changed and customized in

plays.

- `files` This directory contains static files that are referenced by role tasks.
- `handlers` The main.yml file in this directory contains the role's handler definitions.
- `meta` The main.yml file in this directory contains information about the role, including author, license, platforms, and optional role dependencies.

tasks The main.yml file in this directory contains the role's task definitions.

- `templates` This directory contains Jinja2 templates that are referenced by role tasks.
- `tests` This directory can contain an inventory and test.yml playbook that can be used to test the role.
- `vars` The main.yml file in this directory defines the role's variable values. Often these variables are used for internal purposes within the role. These variables have high precedence, and are not intended to be changed when

used in a playbook.
Not every role will have all of these directories.

Using Ansible roles in a playbook

- ./role_simple.yml

```
1    ---
2    - name: role example
3      hosts: all
4      roles:
5         - role1
6         - role2
```

```
1    file name: role_simple.yml
2    Apply the "role1" and "role2" to the "all" managed hosts
```

- ./role_vars.yml

```
1    ---
2    - name: role example
3      hosts: all
4      roles:
5      - role: role1
6      - role: role2
7        var1: value
8        var2: value
```

```
1    file name: role_vars.yml
2    Apply the "role1" and "role2" to the "all" managed hosts
3
4    "Role2" has two variables parameters
```

Order of execution

- ./role_vars.yml

```
1    ---
2    - name: order of execution example
3      hosts: all
4      pre_tasks:
5        - debug:
6            msg: 'pre-task'
7          notify: my handler
8      roles:
9        - role1
10     tasks:
11       - debug:
12           msg: 'first task'
13         notify: my handler
14     post_tasks:
15       - debug:
16           msg: 'post-task'
17         notify: my handler
18     handlers:
19       - name: my handler
20         debug:
21           msg: Running my handler
```

For each play in a playbook, tasks execute as ordered in the tasks
list. After all tasks execute, any notified handlers are executed.
When a role is added to a play, role tasks are added to the beginning
of the tasks list. If a second role is included in a play, its tasks list is
added after the first role.
Role handlers are added to plays in the same manner that role tasks
are added to plays. Each play defines a handlers list. Role handlers
are added to the handlers list first, followed by any handlers
defined in the handlers section of the play. In certain scenarios, it
may be necessary to execute some play tasks before the roles. To
support such scenarios, plays can be configured with a pre_tasks
section. Any task listed in this section executes before any roles are
executed. If any of these tasks notify a handler, those handler tasks

execute before the roles or normal tasks.

Plays also support a post_tasks keyword. These tasks execute after the play's normal tasks, and any handlers they notify, are run.

Ansible Galaxy

- https://galaxy.ansible.com/[6]

Installing Roles from Ansible Galaxy manually

```
$ ansible-galaxy install geerlingguy.redis -p roles/
```

Installing Roles from Ansible Galaxy requirements.yml

- ./requirements.yml

```
- src: geerlingguy.redis
  version: "1.5.0"
```

```
$ ansible-galaxy install -r roles/requirements.yml  -p ro\
les
```

Ansible Best Practices

Follow the Ansible Best Practices allows you to have a successful execution of your code, simplify the troubleshooting, and impact positively on your automation journey.

---

[6]https://galaxy.ansible.com/

Use whitespaces

Use spaces and not tabs for your YAML code. Adding a new line before each block or task makes a playbook easy to read.

For example:

- WRONG

```
1   ---
2   - hosts: all
3     tasks:
4     - ansible.builtin.yum:
5         name: httpd
6         state: latest
7     - name: end message
8       ansible.builtin.debug:
9         msg: "httpd succesfully installed"
```

- CORRECT

```
1   ---
2   - hosts: all
3     tasks:
4     - ansible.builtin.yum:
5         name: httpd
6         state: latest
7
8     - name: end message
9       ansible.builtin.debug:
10        msg: "httpd succesfully installed"
```

Assign a "name" to every step

Always set the "name" parameter for every Ansible statements of your code: Ansible Plays, Tasks, Blocks.

For example:

- WRONG

```
1   ---
2   - hosts: all
3     tasks:
4     - ansible.builtin.yum:
5         name: httpd
6         state: latest
```

- CORRECT

```
1   ---
2   - name: install apache
3     hosts: all
4     tasks:
5       - name: install apache packages
6         ansible.builtin.yum:
7           name: httpd
8           state: latest
```

Use human-readable and meaningful names for variables

Variables are very important to store parameters or save the result of a previous task.
Using human-readable and meaningful names increases your code

reuse and readability between your team.

It's also easy to use the "ansible-playbook" command "–extra-vars" extra variable parameter to override a variable at execution.

For example:

- WRONG

```
1    httpkeepalive: 25
2    webpo: 80
3    aaaa: 8080
```

- CORRECT

```
1    apache_max_keepalive: 25
2    apache_port: 80
3    tomcat_port: 8080
```

Use native YAML

The usage of native YAML improves code readability and allows you to find faster and easier the mistakes. It also allows using some YAML linter and parser to validate.

For example:

- WRONG

```
1  - name: install apache
2    ansible.builtin.yum:
3      name: apache-{{ apache_version }} state=present updat\
4  e_cache=yes disable_gpg_check=yes enablerepo=apache
5    notify: restart apache
```

- CORRECT

```
1  - name: install apache
2    ansible.builtin.yum: apache-{{ apache_version }}
3      state: present
4      update_cache: yes
5      disable_gpg_check: yes
6      enablerepo: apache
7    notify: restart apache
```

Use native modules against run commands

Always prefer to use native modules to command modules.
Native modules are built for idempotency and have business logic
inside to validate parameters before execution.
Commands module ("command", "shell", "raw", and "script") are
great should be used as a last resort.

For example:

- WRONG

```
1   - name: Add repository into repo.d list
2     become: true
3     ansible.builtin.shell: 'echo -e "[google-chrome]\nname=\
4   google-chrome\nbaseurl=http://dl.google.com/linux/chrome/\
5   rpm/stable/x86_64\nenabled=1\ngpgcheck=1\ngpgkey=https://\
6   dl.google.com/linux/linux_signing_key.pub" > /etc/yum.rep\
7   os.d/google-chrome.repo'
8     args:
9       creates: /etc/yum.repos.d/google-chrome.repo
10    when: ansible_os_family == 'RedHat'
```

- CORRECT

```
1   - name: Add repository into repo.d list
2     ansible.builtin.yum_repository:
3       name: google-chrome
4       description: google-chrome repository
5       baseurl: http://dl.google.com/linux/chrome/rpm/stable\
6   /x86_64
7       enabled: true
8       gpgcheck: true
9       gpgkey: https://dl.google.com/linux/linux_signing_key\
10  .pub
```

Configure debug messages

When developing Ansible code is very useful to rely on "debug" tasks to display the content of a variable while your playbook runs. However, could be considered annoying to read too much at the production level.

Set the "verbosity" parameter set to "2" allows you to see the messages only when you want.

For example:

- WRONG

```
1  - name: message output
2    ansible.builtin.debug:
3      msg: "This text always displays"
```

- CORRECT

```
1  - name: message output
2    ansible.builtin.debug:
3      msg: "This text displays with ansible-playbook -vv"
4      verbosity: 2
```

Execute your task with less possible privilege

This is a piece of general advice for any security best practice to execute a task with less possible privilege.
In Ansible you could implement specifying the "become: true" at the task level and not for all the playbook if not all the tasks need to execute as root/administrator user.

For example:

- WRONG

```
1    ---
2    - name: install apache
3      hosts: all
4      become: true
5      tasks:
6        - name: message output
7          ansible.builtin.debug:
8            msg: "This text always displays"
9
10       - name: install apache packages
11         ansible.builtin.yum:
12           name: httpd
13           state: latest
```

- CORRECT

```
1    ---
2    - name: install apache
3      hosts: all
4      tasks:
5        - name: message output
6          ansible.builtin.debug:
7            msg: "This text always displays"
8
9        - name: install apache packages
10         ansible.builtin.yum:
11           name: httpd
12           state: latest
13         become: true
```

Use version control

The use of Source Code Management is used to track modifications
to a source code repository such as GitHub, GitLab, BitBucket is a

must if you're a team and allow you to track your progress in time. It enables also code sharing between others colleagues and guarantees that your execution nodes are always up-to-date.

Always mention the "state" parameter

Many modules have optional "state" parameters with some implicit value.
The default value could vary between different modules for "state", and some modules support several "state" settings. Explicitly setting state: present or state: absent makes playbooks and roles clearer.

Use comments

Add a comment (a line starting with "#") that helps others (and possibly yourself in the future) understand what a statement play or task (or variable setting) does, how it does it, and why.

Install Ansible

In this chapter you're going to discover how to install Ansible in the most common Operating Systems nowadays.

Ansible terminology - ansible vs ansible-core packages

What is ansible-core? What is the ansible community package? What happened to the Ansible project after version 2.9? An overview of the ansible community and ansible-core packages and use-cases nowadays.

What is ansible-core? What is the ansible community package?

What happened to the Ansible project after version 2.9?
Today we're going to talk about ansible community and ansible-core packages released since 2021.

ansible vs ansible-core

What happened to ansible after version 2.9?
Starting with version 2.10, Ansible distributes two deliverable: a community package called `ansible` and a minimalist language and run time called `ansible-core` (called `ansible-base` in version 2.10). Choose the Ansible style and version that matches your particular needs.
The ansible package includes the Ansible language and run time

plus a range of community curated Collections. It recreates and expands on the functionality that was included in Ansible 2.9.

You can choose any of the following ways to install the Ansible community package:

- Install the latest release with your OS package manager (for Red Hat Enterprise Linux, CentOS, Fedora, Debian, or Ubuntu).
- Install with pip (the Python package manager).

Ansible community package release cycle

The Ansible community team typically releases two major versions of the community package per year, on a flexible release cycle that trails the release of ansible-core. This cycle can be extended to allow for larger changes to be properly implemented and tested before a new release is made available. See Ansible Road map for upcoming release details. Between major versions, the Ansible team releases a new minor version of the Ansible community package every three weeks. Minor releases include new backward-compatible features, modules, and plugins, as well as bug fixes.

Starting with version 2.10, the Ansible community team guarantees maintenance for only one major community package release at a time. For example, when Ansible 5.0.0 gets released, the team will stop making new 4.x releases. Community members may maintain older versions if desired.

ansible community

- Uses new versioning (2.10, then 3.0.0)
- Follows semantic versioning rules
- Does not use semantic versioning
- Maintains only one version at a time
- Includes language, run time, and selected Collections
- Developed and maintained in Collection repositories

ansible-core (was ansible-base 2.10)

- Continues "classic Ansible" versioning (2.11, then 2.12)
- Does not use semantic versioning
- Maintains the latest version plus two older versions
- Includes language, run time, and builtin plugins
- Developed and maintained in ansible/ansible repository

ansible-core

The ansible-core package is primarily for developers and users who want to install only the collections they need.

What is the ansible-core package?

Ansible Core is the command-line tool that is primarily for developers and users who want to install only the collections they need. It contains a minimal amount of modules and plugins and allows other Collections to be installed. Similar to Ansible 2.9 though without any content that has since moved into a Collection.
Ansible core or ansible-core is the main building block and architecture for Ansible and includes:

- CLI tools such as ansible-playbook, ansible-doc. and others for driving and interacting with automation.
- The Ansible language uses YAML to create a set of rules for developing Ansible Playbooks and includes functions such as conditionals, blocks, includes loops, and other Ansible imperatives.
- An architectural framework that allows extensions through Ansible collections.

ansible-core releases a new major release approximately twice a year.

ansible community

The Ansible community package offers the functionality of Ansible 2.9, with 85+ collections containing thousands of modules and plugins.

What is the ansible community package?

Each major release of the Ansible community package accepts the latest released version of each included Collection and the latest released version of ansible-core.
Major releases of the Ansible community package can contain breaking changes in the modules and other plugins within the included Collections and/or in core features.
The Ansible package depends on ansible-base (soon ansible-core). So when you do pip install ansible, pip installs ansible-core automatically.
Ansible 3.0.0 and following contains more Collections thanks to the wider Ansible community reviewing Collections against the community checklist.
The Ansible community team typically releases two major versions of the community package per year, on a flexible release cycle that trails the release of ansible-core.

Links

- Ansible 3.0.0 Q&A[7]
- Releases and maintenance[8]
- Installing Ansible[9]
- Ansible community change logs[10]

---

[7] https://www.ansible.com/blog/ansible-3.0.0-qa

[8] https://docs.ansible.com/ansible/devel/reference_appendices/release_and_maintenance.html

[9] https://docs.ansible.com/ansible/latest/installation_guide/intro_installation.html

[10] https://docs.ansible.com/ansible/devel/reference_appendices/release_and_maintenance.html#ansible-community-changelogs

- Ansible Core Documentation[11]
- pip install ansible-core[12]
- pip install ansible[13]

How to install Ansible in RedHat Enterprise Linux (RHEL) 8 with Ansible Engine

How to install the latest version of Ansible in Red Hat Enterprise version 8 using Ansible Engine software collection.

I'll show you the easier way to install and maintain Ansible inside RHEL 8 with the distribution tools.

How to install Ansible in RHEL 8

The easier way to install and maintain Ansible inside Red Hat Enterprise Linux version 8 with the distribution tools.
The repository that contains Ansible is called the Ansible Engine software collection `ansible-2.9-for-rhel-8-x86_64-rpms`.
The main advantage of using software collection is that you don't require any external repository such as EPEL for this content.
Software Collections are fully supported by Red Hat and included in your subscription plan.

Demo

How to install the latest version of Ansible in RHEL8.

---

[11]https://docs.ansible.com/ansible-core/devel/index.html
[12]https://pypi.org/project/ansible-core/
[13]https://pypi.org/project/ansible/

```
1   #!/bin/bash
2   sudo subscription-manager register
3   sudo subscription-manager repos --enable ansible-2.9-for-\
4   rhel-8-x86_64-rpms
5   sudo yum install ansible
```

How to install Ansible in Ubuntu 20.04

How to install Ansible in Ubuntu 20.04 LTS using the **universe** and **PPA** repositories.

Today we're going to talk about the easier way to install and maintain Ansible inside ubuntu 20.04 with the distribution tools.

How to install Ansible in Ubuntu 20.04

We're going to see the easy way to install and maintain Ansible inside Ubuntu with the distribution tools.

We are going to see how to install Ansible in two different ways.

The first method to install Ansible is using the universe repository, the default that you get after installation.

The main advantage of using the universe repository is that you don't require any external repository.

And the second method to install Ansible is using the PPA repository. Please bear in mind that adding additional repositories have different quality assurance of software.

Demo

How to install Ansible in Ubuntu 20.04 LTS with universe and PPA repositories.

code Universe

```bash
#!/bin/bash
sudo apt update
sudo apt install ansible
```

code PPA

```bash
#!/bin/bash
sudo apt update
sudo apt install software-properties-common
sudo add-apt-repository --yes --update ppa:ansible/ansible
sudo apt remove ansible
sudo apt install ansible-base
```

How to install Ansible in Fedora 35

How to install and maintain the latest version of Ansible inside Fedora 35 using the default repository with a practical demo.

How to install Ansible in Fedora 35

Let's install Ansible in Fedora 35.
The good news is that Ansible is included in the default repository so you could install it simply with your usual package manager.
You could expect the latest version of Ansible in the updates repository.
At the moment is available the latest 2.9.

demo

How to install the latest version of Ansible in Fedora.

code

- install-Ansible-Fedora.sh

```
1  #!/bin/bash
2  $ sudo dnf list available ansible
3  $ sudo dnf install ansible
4  $ sudo "rpm -qa | grep ansible"
5  $ sudo dnf list ansible
```

execution

```
1   $ ssh devops@fedora.example.com
2   [devops@demo ~]$ sudo su
3   [root@demo devops]# cat /etc/redhat-release
4   Fedora release 35 (Thirty Five)
5   [root@demo devops]# hostnamectl
6    Static hostname: demo.example.com
7          Icon name: computer-vm
8            Chassis: vm
9         Machine ID: 1894b60f7c1a45b9a6fc87cf8a4bed54
10           Boot ID: 68bfe9b366c34c8d95df1a3774cf5641
11    Virtualization: oracle
12  Operating System: Fedora Linux 35 (Cloud Edition)
13       CPE OS Name: cpe:/o:fedoraproject:fedora:35
14            Kernel: Linux 5.14.10-300.fc35.x86_64
15      Architecture: x86-64
16   Hardware Vendor: innotek GmbH
17    Hardware Model: VirtualBox
18  [root@demo devops]# dnf list available ansible
19  Fedora 35 - x86_64                                          \
20              3.3 MB/s |  61 MB      00:18
21  Fedora 35 openh264 (From Cisco) - x86_64                    \
22              2.7 kB/s |  2.5 kB     00:00
23  Fedora Modular 35 - x86_64                                  \
```

```
24            1.6 MB/s | 2.6 MB        00:01
25 Fedora 35 - x86_64 - Updates                                      \
26            1.1 MB/s |  15 MB        00:12
27 Fedora Modular 35 - x86_64 - Updates                              \
28            400 kB/s | 736 kB        00:01
29 Available Packages
30 ansible.noarch                                        2.9.27-1.fc\
31 35                                      updates
32 [root@demo devops]# dnf install ansible
33 Last metadata expiration check: 0:00:14 ago on Fri 03 Dec\
34  2021 03:42:34 PM UTC.
35 Dependencies resolved.
36 ================================================================\
37 ===========================================
38  Package                       Architecture       Version\
39                    Repository       Size
40 ================================================================\
41 ===========================================
42 Installing:
43  ansible                       noarch             2.9.27-\
44 1.fc35              updates         15 M
45 Installing dependencies:
46  libsodium                     x86_64             1.0.18-\
47 8.fc35              fedora         161 k
48  python3-bcrypt                x86_64             3.2.0-1\
49 .fc35               fedora          43 k
50  python3-jmespath              noarch             0.10.0-\
51 4.fc35              fedora          46 k
52  python3-ntlm-auth             noarch             1.5.0-4\
53 .fc35               fedora          53 k
54  python3-pynacl                x86_64             1.4.0-4\
55 .fc35               fedora         108 k
56  python3-requests_ntlm         noarch             1.1.0-1\
57 6.fc35              fedora          18 k
58  python3-xmltodict             noarch             0.12.0-\
```

```
13.fc35                 fedora                  22 k
 sshpass                                x86_64           1.09-2.\
fc35                    fedora                  27 k
Installing weak dependencies:
 python3-paramiko                       noarch           2.7.2-6\
.fc35                   fedora                 288 k
 python3-pyasn1                         noarch           0.4.8-7\
.fc35                   fedora                 134 k
 python3-winrm                          noarch           0.4.1-4\
.fc35                   fedora                  80 k

Transaction Summary
================================================================\
============================================
Install  12 Packages

Total download size: 16 M
Installed size: 100 M
Is this ok [y/N]: y
Downloading Packages:
(1/12): python3-bcrypt-3.2.0-1.fc35.x86_64.rpm                    \
        317 kB/s |  43 kB      00:00
(2/12): python3-jmespath-0.10.0-4.fc35.noarch.rpm                \
        323 kB/s |  46 kB      00:00
(3/12): libsodium-1.0.18-8.fc35.x86_64.rpm                       \
        704 kB/s | 161 kB      00:00
(4/12): python3-ntlm-auth-1.5.0-4.fc35.noarch.rpm                \
        566 kB/s |  53 kB      00:00
(5/12): python3-pyasn1-0.4.8-7.fc35.noarch.rpm                   \
        1.5 MB/s | 134 kB      00:00
(6/12): python3-paramiko-2.7.2-6.fc35.noarch.rpm                 \
        1.4 MB/s | 288 kB      00:00
(7/12): python3-requests_ntlm-1.1.0-16.fc35.noarch.rpm          \
        827 kB/s |  18 kB      00:00
(8/12): python3-pynacl-1.4.0-4.fc35.x86_64.rpm                   \
```

```
 94             935 kB/s |  108 kB     00:00
 95  (9/12): python3-xmltodict-0.12.0-13.fc35.noarch.rpm        \
 96             848 kB/s |   22 kB     00:00
 97  (10/12): sshpass-1.09-2.fc35.x86_64.rpm                    \
 98             580 kB/s |   27 kB     00:00
 99  (11/12): python3-winrm-0.4.1-4.fc35.noarch.rpm            \
100             1.3 MB/s |   80 kB     00:00
101  (12/12): ansible-2.9.27-1.fc35.noarch.rpm                  \
102             1.4 MB/s |   15 MB     00:11
103  ---------------------------------------------------------\
104  -----------------------------------------
105  Total                                                      \
106             1.3 MB/s |   16 MB     00:12
107  Running transaction check
108  Transaction check succeeded.
109  Running transaction test
110  Transaction test succeeded.
111  Running transaction
112    Preparing        :                                       \
113                                           1/1
114    Installing       : sshpass-1.09-2.fc35.x86_64            \
115                                          1/12
116    Installing       : python3-xmltodict-0.12.0-13.fc35.noa\
117  rch                                     2/12
118    Installing       : python3-pyasn1-0.4.8-7.fc35.noarch   \
119                                          3/12
120    Installing       : python3-ntlm-auth-1.5.0-4.fc35.noarc\
121  h                                       4/12
122    Installing       : python3-requests_ntlm-1.1.0-16.fc35.\
123  noarch                                  5/12
124    Installing       : python3-winrm-0.4.1-4.fc35.noarch    \
125                                          6/12
126    Installing       : python3-jmespath-0.10.0-4.fc35.noarc\
127  h                                       7/12
128    Installing       : python3-bcrypt-3.2.0-1.fc35.x86_64   \
```

```
129                                        8/12
130    Installing       : libsodium-1.0.18-8.fc35.x86_64         \
131                                        9/12
132    Installing       : python3-pynacl-1.4.0-4.fc35.x86_64    \
133                                        10/12
134    Installing       : python3-paramiko-2.7.2-6.fc35.noarch\
135                                        11/12
136    Installing       : ansible-2.9.27-1.fc35.noarch           \
137                                        12/12
138    Running scriptlet: ansible-2.9.27-1.fc35.noarch           \
139                                        12/12
140    Verifying        : libsodium-1.0.18-8.fc35.x86_64          \
141                                        1/12
142    Verifying        : python3-bcrypt-3.2.0-1.fc35.x86_64    \
143                                        2/12
144    Verifying        : python3-jmespath-0.10.0-4.fc35.noarc\
145  h                                     3/12
146    Verifying        : python3-ntlm-auth-1.5.0-4.fc35.noarc\
147  h                                     4/12
148    Verifying        : python3-paramiko-2.7.2-6.fc35.noarch\
149                                        5/12
150    Verifying        : python3-pyasn1-0.4.8-7.fc35.noarch   \
151                                        6/12
152    Verifying        : python3-pynacl-1.4.0-4.fc35.x86_64    \
153                                        7/12
154    Verifying        : python3-requests_ntlm-1.1.0-16.fc35.\
155  noarch                               8/12
156    Verifying        : python3-winrm-0.4.1-4.fc35.noarch     \
157                                        9/12
158    Verifying        : python3-xmltodict-0.12.0-13.fc35.noa\
159  rch                                  10/12
160    Verifying        : sshpass-1.09-2.fc35.x86_64            \
161                                        11/12
162    Verifying        : ansible-2.9.27-1.fc35.noarch           \
163                                        12/12
```

```
164
165  Installed:
166    ansible-2.9.27-1.fc35.noarch                        libs\
167  odium-1.0.18-8.fc35.x86_64
168    python3-bcrypt-3.2.0-1.fc35.x86_64                  pyth\
169  on3-jmespath-0.10.0-4.fc35.noarch
170    python3-ntlm-auth-1.5.0-4.fc35.noarch               pyth\
171  on3-paramiko-2.7.2-6.fc35.noarch
172    python3-pyasn1-0.4.8-7.fc35.noarch                  pyth\
173  on3-pynacl-1.4.0-4.fc35.x86_64
174    python3-requests_ntlm-1.1.0-16.fc35.noarch          pyth\
175  on3-winrm-0.4.1-4.fc35.noarch
176    python3-xmltodict-0.12.0-13.fc35.noarch             sshp\
177  ass-1.09-2.fc35.x86_64
178
179  Complete!
180  [root@demo devops]# rpm -qa | grep ansible
181  ansible-2.9.27-1.fc35.noarch
182  [root@demo devops]# ansible --version
183  ansible 2.9.27
184    config file = /etc/ansible/ansible.cfg
185    configured module search path = ['/root/.ansible/plugin\
186  s/modules', '/usr/share/ansible/plugins/modules']
187    ansible python module location = /usr/lib/python3.10/si\
188  te-packages/ansible
189    executable location = /usr/bin/ansible
190    python version = 3.10.0 (default, Oct  4 2021, 00:00:00\
191  ) [GCC 11.2.1 20210728 (Red Hat 11.2.1-1)]
192  [root@demo devops]# yum list installed google-chrome-stab\
193  le
194  Error: No matching Packages to list
195  [root@demo devops]# yum list installed ansible
196  Installed Packages
197  ansible.noarch                              2.9.27-1.fc\
198  35                              @updates
```

```
199  [root@demo devops]# dnf list installed ansible
200  Installed Packages
201  ansible.noarch                                    2.9.27-1.fc\
202  35                              @updates
203  [root@demo devops]#
```

before execution

```
1   $ ssh devops@fedora.example.com
2   [devops@demo ~]$ sudo su
3   [root@demo devops]# cat /etc/redhat-release
4   Fedora release 35 (Thirty Five)
5   [root@demo devops]# hostnamectl
6     Static hostname: demo.example.com
7           Icon name: computer-vm
8             Chassis: vm
9          Machine ID: 1894b60f7c1a45b9a6fc87cf8a4bed54
10            Boot ID: 68bfe9b366c34c8d95df1a3774cf5641
11      Virtualization: oracle
12   Operating System: Fedora Linux 35 (Cloud Edition)
13        CPE OS Name: cpe:/o:fedoraproject:fedora:35
14             Kernel: Linux 5.14.10-300.fc35.x86_64
15       Architecture: x86-64
16    Hardware Vendor: innotek GmbH
17     Hardware Model: VirtualBox
18   [root@demo devops]# dnf list installed ansible
19   Error: No matching Packages to list
20   [root@demo devops]# dnf list ansible
21   Last metadata expiration check: 0:03:45 ago on Fri 03 Dec\
22    2021 03:42:34 PM UTC.
23   Available Packages
24   ansible.noarch                                    2.9.27-1.f\
25   c35                              updates
26   [root@demo devops]#
```

after execution

```
1   [root@demo devops]# rpm -qa | grep ansible
2   ansible-2.9.27-1.fc35.noarch
3   [root@demo devops]# ansible --version
4   ansible 2.9.27
5     config file = /etc/ansible/ansible.cfg
6     configured module search path = ['/root/.ansible/plugin\
7   s/modules', '/usr/share/ansible/plugins/modules']
8     ansible python module location = /usr/lib/python3.10/si\
9   te-packages/ansible
10    executable location = /usr/bin/ansible
11    python version = 3.10.0 (default, Oct  4 2021, 00:00:00\
12  ) [GCC 11.2.1 20210728 (Red Hat 11.2.1-1)]
13  [root@demo devops]# yum list installed google-chrome-stab\
14  le
15  Error: No matching Packages to list
16  [root@demo devops]# yum list installed ansible
17  Installed Packages
18  ansible.noarch                                  2.9.27-1.fc\
19  35                               @updates
20  [root@demo devops]# dnf list installed ansible
21  Installed Packages
22  ansible.noarch                                  2.9.27-1.fc\
23  35                               @updates
24  [root@demo devops]#
```

How to install Ansible in CentOS 9 Stream

The easier way to install the latest version of Ansible and maintain up-to-date in CentOS 9 Stream using DNF and the "AppStream" system repository.

How to install Ansible in CentOS Stream 9

- "ansible-core" in system AppStream repository
- use Extra Packages for Enterprise Linux - EPEL Next additional packages for CentOS Stream

The easier way to install and maintain Ansible inside CentOS Stream version 9 is using the system **AppStream** repository.
Another way is to use the additional EPEL Next repository. This repository is maintained by the Fedora Special Interest Group and that manages a high-quality set of additional packages for CentOS Stream, similar to Extra Packages for Enterprise Linux (EPEL) additional packages target for Red Hat Enterprise Linux (RHEL), CentOS, and Scientific Linux (SL) and Oracle Linux (OL).

Links

- CentOS Stream Download[14]
- EPEL 9 is now available[15]
- Introducing CentOS Stream 9[16]
- Extra Packages for Enterprise Linux (EPEL)[17]

demo

How to install Ansible in CentOS Stream version 9 via AppStream system repository.

code

- Install-Ansible-CentOS-Stream9.sh

---

[14]https://www.centos.org/centos-stream/
[15]https://communityblog.fedoraproject.org/epel-9-is-now-available/
[16]https://blog.centos.org/2021/12/introducing-centos-stream-9/
[17]https://docs.fedoraproject.org/en-US/epel/

```
1  #!/bin/bash
2  sudo dnf install ansible-core
```

execution

```
1  $ ssh devops@centos-stream.example.com
2  [devops@centos-stream ~]$ sudo su
3  [root@centos-stream devops]# cat /etc/redhat-release
4  CentOS Stream release 9
5  [root@centos-stream devops]# cat /etc/os-release
6  NAME="CentOS Stream"
7  VERSION="9"
8  ID="centos"
9  ID_LIKE="rhel fedora"
10  VERSION_ID="9"
11  PLATFORM_ID="platform:el9"
12  PRETTY_NAME="CentOS Stream 9"
13  ANSI_COLOR="0;31"
14  CPE_NAME="cpe:/o:centos:centos:9"
15  HOME_URL="https://centos.org/"
16  BUG_REPORT_URL="https://bugzilla.redhat.com/"
17  REDHAT_SUPPORT_PRODUCT="Red Hat Enterprise Linux 9"
18  REDHAT_SUPPORT_PRODUCT_VERSION="CentOS Stream"
19  [root@centos-stream devops]# hostnamectl
20    Static hostname: centos-stream.example.com
21          Icon name: computer-vm
22            Chassis: vm
23          Machine ID: 27ac33d81e2a400cbdaf6ae0b2b82e1d
24            Boot ID: 4060493b76fc4cc680defa0ffe99af41
25      Virtualization: oracle
26  Operating System: CentOS Stream 9
27        CPE OS Name: cpe:/o:centos:centos:9
28             Kernel: Linux 5.14.0-17.el9.x86_64
29       Architecture: x86-64
30    Hardware Vendor: innotek GmbH
31     Hardware Model: VirtualBox
```

```
[root@centos-stream devops]# dnf search ansible
Updating Subscription Management repositories.
Unable to read consumer identity
This system is not registered with an entitlement server.\
 You can use subscription-manager to register.
CentOS Stream 9 - BaseOS                                         \
              1.2 MB/s | 1.6 MB       00:01
CentOS Stream 9 - AppStream                                      \
              2.7 MB/s | 8.8 MB       00:03
Last metadata expiration check: 0:00:01 ago on Mon 06 Dec\
 2021 11:55:34 AM UTC.
==================================== Name & Summary Matched:\
 ansible ====================================
ansible-collection-microsoft-sql.noarch : The Ansible col\
lection for Microsoft SQL Server
                                        : management
ansible-freeipa-tests.noarch : ansible-freeipa tests
ansible-pcp.noarch : Ansible Metric collection for Perfor\
mance Co-Pilot
ansible-test.x86_64 : Tool for testing ansible plugin and\
 module code
========================================= Name Matched: ansi\
ble ========================================
ansible-core.x86_64 : SSH-based configuration management,\
 deployment, and task execution system
ansible-freeipa.noarch : Roles and playbooks to deploy Fr\
eeIPA servers, replicas and clients
[root@centos-stream devops]# dnf info ansible-core
Updating Subscription Management repositories.
Unable to read consumer identity
This system is not registered with an entitlement server.\
 You can use subscription-manager to register.
Last metadata expiration check: 0:00:55 ago on Mon 06 Dec\
 2021 11:55:34 AM UTC.
Available Packages
```

```
Name           : ansible-core
Version        : 2.12.0
Release        : 1.el9
Architecture   : x86_64
Size           : 2.4 M
Source         : ansible-core-2.12.0-1.el9.src.rpm
Repository     : appstream
Summary        : SSH-based configuration management, deploy\
ment, and task execution system
URL            : http://ansible.com
License        : GPLv3+
Description    : Ansible is a radically simple model-driven\
  configuration management,
               : multi-node deployment, and remote task exe\
cution system. Ansible works
               : over SSH and does not require any software\
  or daemons to be installed
               : on remote nodes. Extension modules can be \
written in any language and
               : are transferred to managed machines automa\
tically.
[root@centos-stream devops]# dnf install ansible-core
Updating Subscription Management repositories.
Unable to read consumer identity
This system is not registered with an entitlement server.\
  You can use subscription-manager to register.
Last metadata expiration check: 0:01:13 ago on Mon 06 Dec\
  2021 11:55:34 AM UTC.
Dependencies resolved.
================================================================\
================================================
 Package                        Architecture    Version    \
                 Repository          Size
================================================================\
================================================
```

```
102  Installing:
103   ansible-core                    x86_64              2.12.0-1.e\
104  19                appstream        2.4 M
105  Installing dependencies:
106   emacs-filesystem                noarch              1:27.1-3.e\
107  19                appstream        9.2 k
108   git                             x86_64              2.31.1-2.e\
109  19.2              appstream        124 k
110   git-core                        x86_64              2.31.1-2.e\
111  19.2              appstream        3.6 M
112   git-core-doc                    noarch              2.31.1-2.e\
113  19.2              appstream        2.5 M
114   perl-Error                      noarch              1:0.17029-\
115  7.el9             appstream         42 k
116   perl-Git                        noarch              2.31.1-2.e\
117  19.2              appstream         43 k
118   python3-babel                   noarch              2.9.1-2.el\
119  9                 appstream        6.0 M
120   python3-cffi                    x86_64              1.14.5-4.e\
121  19                appstream        254 k
122   python3-cryptography            x86_64              3.4.7-5.el\
123  9                 appstream        780 k
124   python3-jinja2                  noarch              2.11.3-4.e\
125  19                appstream        249 k
126   python3-markupsafe              x86_64              1.1.1-12.e\
127  19                appstream         35 k
128   python3-packaging               noarch              20.9-4.el9\
129                    appstream         78 k
130   python3-ply                     noarch              3.11-13.el\
131  9                 appstream        107 k
132   python3-pycparser               noarch              2.20-5.el9\
133                    appstream        135 k
134   python3-pytz                    noarch              2021.1-4.e\
135  19                appstream         52 k
136   python3-resolvolib              noarch              0.5.4-5.el\
```

```
9                          appstream                34 k
 sshpass                                 x86_64              1.09-4.el9\
                           appstream                28 k
Transaction Summary
=================================================================\
================================================
Install  18 Packages
Total download size: 16 M
Installed size: 75 M
Is this ok [y/N]: y
Downloading Packages:
(1/18): emacs-filesystem-27.1-3.el9.noarch.rpm                  \
         38 kB/s | 9.2 kB     00:00
(2/18): git-2.31.1-2.el9.2.x86_64.rpm                          \
         302 kB/s | 124 kB     00:00
(3/18): git-core-2.31.1-2.el9.2.x86_64.rpm                     \
         763 kB/s | 3.6 MB     00:04
(4/18): perl-Error-0.17029-7.el9.noarch.rpm                    \
         375 kB/s |  42 kB     00:00
(5/18): ansible-core-2.12.0-1.el9.x86_64.rpm                   \
         450 kB/s | 2.4 MB     00:05
(6/18): perl-Git-2.31.1-2.el9.2.noarch.rpm                     \
         182 kB/s |  43 kB     00:00
(7/18): python3-cffi-1.14.5-4.el9.x86_64.rpm                   \
         655 kB/s | 254 kB     00:00
(8/18): git-core-doc-2.31.1-2.el9.2.noarch.rpm                 \
         473 kB/s | 2.5 MB     00:05
(9/18): python3-jinja2-2.11.3-4.el9.noarch.rpm                 \
         410 kB/s | 249 kB     00:00
(10/18): python3-markupsafe-1.1.1-12.el9.x86_64.rpm            \
         194 kB/s |  35 kB     00:00
(11/18): python3-packaging-20.9-4.el9.noarch.rpm               \
         321 kB/s |  78 kB     00:00
(12/18): python3-cryptography-3.4.7-5.el9.x86_64.rpm           \
         640 kB/s | 780 kB     00:01
```

```
(13/18): python3-ply-3.11-13.el9.noarch.rpm              \
        397 kB/s | 107 kB        00:00
(14/18): python3-pycparser-2.20-5.el9.noarch.rpm         \
        533 kB/s | 135 kB        00:00
(15/18): python3-pytz-2021.1-4.el9.noarch.rpm            \
        313 kB/s |  52 kB        00:00
(16/18): sshpass-1.09-4.el9.x86_64.rpm                   \
        236 kB/s |  28 kB        00:00
(17/18): python3-resolvelib-0.5.4-5.el9.noarch.rpm       \
        236 kB/s |  34 kB        00:00
(18/18): python3-babel-2.9.1-2.el9.noarch.rpm            \
        730 kB/s | 6.0 MB        00:08
----------------------------------------------------------\
----------------------------------------
Total                                                    \
        1.2 MB/s |  16 MB        00:14
Running transaction check
Transaction check succeeded.
Running transaction test
Transaction test succeeded.
Running transaction
  Preparing        :                                     \
                                1/1
  Installing       : git-core-2.31.1-2.el9.2.x86_64      \
                                1/18
  Installing       : git-core-doc-2.31.1-2.el9.2.noarch  \
                                2/18
  Installing       : sshpass-1.09-4.el9.x86_64           \
                                3/18
  Installing       : python3-resolvelib-0.5.4-5.el9.noarc\
h                               4/18
  Installing       : python3-pytz-2021.1-4.el9.noarch     \
                                5/18
  Installing       : python3-babel-2.9.1-2.el9.noarch    \
                                6/18
```

```
207     Installing        : python3-ply-3.11-13.el9.noarch          \
208                                          7/18
209     Installing        : python3-pycparser-2.20-5.el9.noarch \
210                                          8/18
211     Installing        : python3-cffi-1.14.5-4.el9.x86_64        \
212                                          9/18
213     Installing        : python3-cryptography-3.4.7-5.el9.x86\
214 _64                                     10/18
215     Installing        : python3-packaging-20.9-4.el9.noarch \
216                                         11/18
217     Installing        : python3-markupsafe-1.1.1-12.el9.x86_\
218 64                                      12/18
219     Installing        : python3-jinja2-2.11.3-4.el9.noarch  \
220                                         13/18
221     Installing        : perl-Error-1:0.17029-7.el9.noarch    \
222                                         14/18
223     Installing        : emacs-filesystem-1:27.1-3.el9.noarch\
224                                         15/18
225     Installing        : perl-Git-2.31.1-2.el9.2.noarch        \
226                                         16/18
227     Installing        : git-2.31.1-2.el9.2.x86_64             \
228                                         17/18
229     Installing        : ansible-core-2.12.0-1.el9.x86_64      \
230                                         18/18
231   Running scriptlet: ansible-core-2.12.0-1.el9.x86_64       \
232                                         18/18
233     Verifying         : ansible-core-2.12.0-1.el9.x86_64      \
234                                          1/18
235     Verifying         : emacs-filesystem-1:27.1-3.el9.noarch\
236                                          2/18
237     Verifying         : git-2.31.1-2.el9.2.x86_64             \
238                                          3/18
239     Verifying         : git-core-2.31.1-2.el9.2.x86_64        \
240                                          4/18
241     Verifying         : git-core-doc-2.31.1-2.el9.2.noarch  \
```

```
                                        5/18
    Verifying          : perl-Error-1:0.17029-7.el9.noarch    \
                                        6/18
    Verifying          : perl-Git-2.31.1-2.el9.2.noarch       \
                                        7/18
    Verifying          : python3-babel-2.9.1-2.el9.noarch     \
                                        8/18
    Verifying          : python3-cffi-1.14.5-4.el9.x86_64     \
                                        9/18
    Verifying          : python3-cryptography-3.4.7-5.el9.x86\
_64                                    10/18
    Verifying          : python3-jinja2-2.11.3-4.el9.noarch   \
                                       11/18
    Verifying          : python3-markupsafe-1.1.1-12.el9.x86_\
64                                     12/18
    Verifying          : python3-packaging-20.9-4.el9.noarch \
                                       13/18
    Verifying          : python3-ply-3.11-13.el9.noarch       \
                                       14/18
    Verifying          : python3-pycparser-2.20-5.el9.noarch \
                                       15/18
    Verifying          : python3-pytz-2021.1-4.el9.noarch     \
                                       16/18
    Verifying          : python3-resolvelib-0.5.4-5.el9.noarc\
h                                      17/18
    Verifying          : sshpass-1.09-4.el9.x86_64            \
                                       18/18
Installed products updated.
Installed:
  ansible-core-2.12.0-1.el9.x86_64                    emacs-f\
ilesystem-1:27.1-3.el9.noarch
  git-2.31.1-2.el9.2.x86_64                           git-cor\
e-2.31.1-2.el9.2.x86_64
  git-core-doc-2.31.1-2.el9.2.noarch                 perl-Er\
ror-1:0.17029-7.el9.noarch
```

```
perl-Git-2.31.1-2.el9.2.noarch                        python3\
-babel-2.9.1-2.el9.noarch
python3-cffi-1.14.5-4.el9.x86_64                       python3\
-cryptography-3.4.7-5.el9.x86_64
python3-jinja2-2.11.3-4.el9.noarch                    python3\
-markupsafe-1.1.1-12.el9.x86_64
python3-packaging-20.9-4.el9.noarch                   python3\
-ply-3.11-13.el9.noarch
python3-pycparser-2.20-5.el9.noarch                   python3\
-pytz-2021.1-4.el9.noarch
python3-resolvelib-0.5.4-5.el9.noarch                  sshpass\
-1.09-4.el9.x86_64
Complete!
[root@centos-stream devops]# ansible --version
ansible [core 2.12.0]
  config file = /etc/ansible/ansible.cfg
  configured module search path = ['/root/.ansible/plugin\
s/modules', '/usr/share/ansible/plugins/modules']
  ansible python module location = /usr/lib/python3.9/sit\
e-packages/ansible
  ansible collection location = /root/.ansible/collection\
s:/usr/share/ansible/collections
  executable location = /bin/ansible
  python version = 3.9.8 (main, Nov  8 2021, 00:00:00) [G\
CC 11.2.1 20211019 (Red Hat 11.2.1-6)]
  jinja version = 2.11.3
  libyaml = True
[root@centos-stream devops]# dnf info ansible-core
Updating Subscription Management repositories.
Unable to read consumer identity
This system is not registered with an entitlement server.\
 You can use subscription-manager to register.
Last metadata expiration check: 0:02:00 ago on Mon 06 Dec\
 2021 11:55:34 AM UTC.
Installed Packages
```

```
Name          : ansible-core
Version       : 2.12.0
Release       : 1.el9
Architecture  : x86_64
Size          : 9.3 M
Source        : ansible-core-2.12.0-1.el9.src.rpm
Repository    : @System
From repo     : appstream
Summary       : SSH-based configuration management, deploy\
ment, and task execution system
URL           : http://ansible.com
License       : GPLv3+
Description   : Ansible is a radically simple model-driven\
  configuration management,
              : multi-node deployment, and remote task exe\
cution system. Ansible works
              : over SSH and does not require any software\
  or daemons to be installed
              : on remote nodes. Extension modules can be \
written in any language and
              : are transferred to managed machines automa\
tically.
[root@centos-stream devops]#
```

before execution

```
# dnf info ansible-core
Updating Subscription Management repositories.
Unable to read consumer identity
This system is not registered with an entitlement server.\
 You can use subscription-manager to register.
Last metadata expiration check: 0:00:55 ago on Mon 06 Dec\
 2021 11:55:34 AM UTC.
Available Packages
Name         : ansible-core
Version      : 2.12.0
Release      : 1.el9
Architecture : x86_64
Size         : 2.4 M
Source       : ansible-core-2.12.0-1.el9.src.rpm
Repository   : appstream
Summary      : SSH-based configuration management, deploy\
ment, and task execution system
URL          : http://ansible.com
License      : GPLv3+
Description  : Ansible is a radically simple model-driven\
 configuration management,
             : multi-node deployment, and remote task exe\
cution system. Ansible works
             : over SSH and does not require any software\
 or daemons to be installed
             : on remote nodes. Extension modules can be \
written in any language and
             : are transferred to managed machines automa\
tically.
[root@centos-stream devops]#
```

after execution

```
# dnf info ansible-core
Updating Subscription Management repositories.
Unable to read consumer identity
This system is not registered with an entitlement server.\
 You can use subscription-manager to register.
Last metadata expiration check: 0:02:00 ago on Mon 06 Dec\
 2021 11:55:34 AM UTC.
Installed Packages
Name          : ansible-core
Version       : 2.12.0
Release       : 1.el9
Architecture : x86_64
Size          : 9.3 M
Source        : ansible-core-2.12.0-1.el9.src.rpm
Repository    : @System
From repo     : appstream
Summary       : SSH-based configuration management, deploy\
ment, and task execution system
URL           : http://ansible.com
License       : GPLv3+
Description   : Ansible is a radically simple model-driven\
 configuration management,
              : multi-node deployment, and remote task exe\
cution system. Ansible works
              : over SSH and does not require any software\
 or daemons to be installed
              : on remote nodes. Extension modules can be \
written in any language and
              : are transferred to managed machines automa\
tically.
[root@centos-stream devops]#
```

How to install Ansible in SUSE Linux Enterprise Server (SLES) 15 SP3

How to install and maintain up-to-date Ansible inside SUSE Linux Enterprise Server (SLES) 15 SP3 using the **SUSE Package Hub** repository.

How to install Ansible in SLES 15 SP3

- use SUSE Package Hub repository

The easier way to install and maintain Ansible inside SUSE Linux Enterprise version 15 SP 3 is using the **SUSE Package Hub** repository maintained by the SUSE community.

Links

- SUSE Package Hub - Community Packages for SUSE Linux Enterprise Server / Desktop[18]
- How to register SLES using the SUSEConnect command line tool[19]
- Adding SUSE Package Hub repositories to SUSE Linux Enterprise Server[20]

demo

How to install the latest version of ansible in SUSE Linux Enterprise Server 15 SP3.

---

[18]https://packagehub.suse.com/
[19]https://www.suse.com/support/kb/doc/?id=000018564
[20]https://www.suse.com/support/kb/doc/?id=000018789

code

- Install-Ansible-SLES-15-SP3.sh

```
1  #!/bin/bash
2  SUSEConnect --status
3  SUSEConnect --list-extensions
4  SUSEConnect -p PackageHub/15.3/x86_64
5  zypper install ansible
6  zypper info ansible
7  ansible --version
```

execution

```
1  $ ssh devops@sles.example.com
2  devops@sles:~> sudo su
3  sles:/home/devops # cat /etc/os-release
4  NAME="SLES"
5  VERSION="15-SP3"
6  VERSION_ID="15.3"
7  PRETTY_NAME="SUSE Linux Enterprise Server 15 SP3"
8  ID="sles"
9  ID_LIKE="suse"
10 ANSI_COLOR="0;32"
11 CPE_NAME="cpe:/o:suse:sles:15:sp3"
12 DOCUMENTATION_URL="https://documentation.suse.com/"
13 sles:/home/devops # hostnamectl
14     Static hostname: sles.example.com
15  Transient hostname: sles
16           Icon name: computer-vm
17             Chassis: vm
18          Machine ID: 4a241aac39fa4e75b13748c714c05c47
19             Boot ID: 150e32975f4d4fdd801eb605f7e35393
20      Virtualization: oracle
21    Operating System: SUSE Linux Enterprise Server 15 SP3
```

```
22             CPE OS Name: cpe:/o:suse:sles:15:sp3
23                  Kernel: Linux 5.3.18-57-default
24            Architecture: x86-64
25 sles:/home/devops # uname -a
26 Linux sles 5.3.18-57-default #1 SMP Wed Apr 28 10:54:41 U\
27 TC 2021 (ba3c2e9) x86_64 x86_64 x86_64 GNU/Linux
28 sles:/home/devops # SUSEConnect --status
29 [{"identifier":"sle-module-basesystem","version":"15.3","\
30 arch":"x86_64","status":"Registered"},{"identifier":"SLES\
31 ","version":"15.3","arch":"x86_64","status":"Registered",\
32 "regcode":"***************","starts_at":"2021-12-07 00:0\
33 0:00 UTC","expires_at":"2022-02-07 00:00:00 UTC","subscri\
34 ption_status":"ACTIVE","type":"evaluation"},{"identifier"\
35 :"sle-module-server-applications","version":"15.3","arch"\
36 :"x86_64","status":"Registered"}]
37 sles:/home/devops # zypper refresh
38 Repository 'SLE-Module-Basesystem15-SP3-Pool' is up to da\
39 te.
40 Repository 'SLE-Module-Basesystem15-SP3-Updates' is up to\
41  date.
42 Repository 'SLE-Product-SLES15-SP3-Pool' is up to date.  \
43
44 Repository 'SLE-Product-SLES15-SP3-Updates' is up to date\
45 .
46 Repository 'SLE-Module-Server-Applications15-SP3-Pool' is\
47  up to date.
48 Repository 'SLE-Module-Server-Applications15-SP3-Updates'\
49  is up to date.
50 All repositories have been refreshed.
51 sles:/home/devops # zypper search ansible
52 Refreshing service 'Basesystem_Module_15_SP3_x86_64'.
53 Refreshing service 'SUSE_Linux_Enterprise_Server_15_SP3_x\
54 86_64'.
55 Refreshing service 'Server_Applications_Module_15_SP3_x86\
56 _64'.
```

```
Loading repository data...
Reading installed packages...
No matching items found.
sles:/home/devops # zypper install ansible
Refreshing service 'Basesystem_Module_15_SP3_x86_64'.
Refreshing service 'SUSE_Linux_Enterprise_Server_15_SP3_x\
86_64'.
Refreshing service 'Server_Applications_Module_15_SP3_x86\
_64'.
Loading repository data...
Reading installed packages...
'ansible' not found in package names. Trying capabilities.
No provider of 'ansible' found.
Resolving package dependencies...
Nothing to do.
sles:/home/devops # SUSEConnect --list-extensions
AVAILABLE EXTENSIONS AND MODULES
Basesystem Module 15 SP3 x86_64 (Activated)
    Deactivate with: SUSEConnect -d -p sle-module-basesys\
tem/15.3/x86_64
Containers Module 15 SP3 x86_64
        Activate with: SUSEConnect -p sle-module-containe\
rs/15.3/x86_64
Desktop Applications Module 15 SP3 x86_64
        Activate with: SUSEConnect -p sle-module-desktop-\
applications/15.3/x86_64
Development Tools Module 15 SP3 x86_64
            Activate with: SUSEConnect -p sle-module-deve\
lopment-tools/15.3/x86_64
NVIDIA Compute Module 15 x86_64
                Activate with: SUSEConnect -p sle-module-\
NVIDIA-compute/15/x86_64
SUSE Linux Enterprise Workstation Extension 15 SP3 x86_64
            Activate with: SUSEConnect -p sle-we/15.3/x86\
_64 -r ADDITIONAL REGCODE
```

```
 92    Python 2 Module 15 SP3 x86_64
 93            Activate with: SUSEConnect -p sle-module-python2/\
 94    15.3/x86_64
 95    SUSE Cloud Application Platform Tools Module 15 SP3 x86_64
 96            Activate with: SUSEConnect -p sle-module-cap-tool\
 97    s/15.3/x86_64
 98    SUSE Linux Enterprise Live Patching 15 SP3 x86_64
 99            Activate with: SUSEConnect -p sle-module-live-pat\
100    ching/15.3/x86_64 -r ADDITIONAL REGCODE
101    SUSE Package Hub 15 SP3 x86_64
102            Activate with: SUSEConnect -p PackageHub/15.3/x86\
103    _64
104    Server Applications Module 15 SP3 x86_64 (Activated)
105            Deactivate with: SUSEConnect -d -p sle-module-ser\
106    ver-applications/15.3/x86_64
107    Legacy Module 15 SP3 x86_64
108            Activate with: SUSEConnect -p sle-module-lega\
109    cy/15.3/x86_64
110    Public Cloud Module 15 SP3 x86_64
111            Activate with: SUSEConnect -p sle-module-publ\
112    ic-cloud/15.3/x86_64
113    SUSE Linux Enterprise High Availability Extension 15 SP3 \
114    x86_64
115            Activate with: SUSEConnect -p sle-ha/15.3/x86\
116    _64 -r ADDITIONAL REGCODE
117    Web and Scripting Module 15 SP3 x86_64
118            Activate with: SUSEConnect -p sle-module-web-\
119    scripting/15.3/x86_64
120    Transactional Server Module 15 SP3 x86_64
121            Activate with: SUSEConnect -p sle-module-transact\
122    ional-server/15.3/x86_64
123    REMARKS
124    (Not available) The module/extension is not enabled on yo\
125    ur RMT/SMT
126    (Activated)     The module/extension is activated on your\
```

```
 system
MORE INFORMATION
You can find more information about available modules her\
e:
https://www.suse.com/documentation/sles-15/singlehtml/art\
_modules/art_modules.html
sles:/home/devops # SUSEConnect -p PackageHub/15.3/x86_64
Registering system to SUSE Customer Center
Updating system details on https://scc.suse.com ...
Activating PackageHub 15.3 x86_64 ...
-> Adding service to system ...
-> Installing release package ...
Successfully registered system
sles:/home/devops # zypper search ansible
Refreshing service 'Basesystem_Module_15_SP3_x86_64'.
Refreshing service 'SUSE_Linux_Enterprise_Server_15_SP3_x\
86_64'.
Refreshing service 'SUSE_Package_Hub_15_SP3_x86_64'.
Refreshing service 'Server_Applications_Module_15_SP3_x86\
_64'.
The gpg key signing file 'repomd.xml' will expire in 2 da\
ys.
  Repository:       SUSE-PackageHub-15-SP3-Backports-Pool
  Key Name:         openSUSE:Backports OBS Project <openS\
USE:Backports@build.opensuse.org>
  Key Fingerprint:  637B32FF 3D83F07A 7AE1C40A 9C214D40 6\
5176565
  Key Created:      Wed Oct  2 15:17:53 2019
  Key Expires:      Fri Dec 10 14:17:53 2021 (expires in \
2 days)
  Rpm Name:         gpg-pubkey-65176565-5d94a381
Building repository 'SUSE-PackageHub-15-SP3-Backports-Poo\
l' cache ..........................[done]
Loading repository data...
Reading installed packages...
```

```
S | Name          | Summary                                      \
                                        | Type
--+--------------+---------------------------------------------\
-------------------------------+--------
  | ansible      | SSH-based configuration management, de\
ployment, and task execution s-> | package
  | ansible-cmdb | Ansible Configuration Management Datab\
ase                              | package
  | ansible-doc  | Documentation for Ansible                    \
                                        | package
  | ansible-test | Tool for testing ansible plugin and mo\
dule code                        | package
sles:/home/devops # zypper info ansible
Refreshing service 'Basesystem_Module_15_SP3_x86_64'.
Refreshing service 'SUSE_Linux_Enterprise_Server_15_SP3_x\
86_64'.
Refreshing service 'SUSE_Package_Hub_15_SP3_x86_64'.
Refreshing service 'Server_Applications_Module_15_SP3_x86\
_64'.
Loading repository data...
Reading installed packages...
Information for package ansible:
---------------------------------
Repository      : SUSE-PackageHub-15-SP3-Backports-Pool
Name            : ansible
Version         : 2.9.6-bp153.1.20
Arch            : noarch
Vendor          : openSUSE
Support Level   : unknown
Installed Size  : 96.0 MiB
Installed       : No
Status          : not installed
Source package  : ansible-2.9.6-bp153.1.20.src
Summary         : SSH-based configuration management, depl\
oyment, and task execution system
```

```
197  Description    :
198      Ansible is a radically simple model-driven configurat\
199  ion management, multi-node
200      deployment, and remote task execution system. Ansible\
201   works over SSH and does
202      not require any software or daemons to be installed o\
203  n remote nodes. Extension
204      modules can be written in any language and are transf\
205  erred to managed machines
206      automatically.
207  sles:/home/devops # zypper install ansible
208  Refreshing service 'Basesystem_Module_15_SP3_x86_64'.
209  Refreshing service 'SUSE_Linux_Enterprise_Server_15_SP3_x\
210  86_64'.
211  Refreshing service 'SUSE_Package_Hub_15_SP3_x86_64'.
212  Refreshing service 'Server_Applications_Module_15_SP3_x86\
213  _64'.
214  Loading repository data...
215  Reading installed packages...
216  Resolving package dependencies...
217  Problem: nothing provides python3-coverage needed by ansi\
218  ble-2.9.6-bp153.1.20.noarch
219   Solution 1: do not install ansible-2.9.6-bp153.1.20.noar\
220  ch
221   Solution 2: break ansible-2.9.6-bp153.1.20.noarch by ign\
222  oring some of its dependencies
223  Choose from above solutions by number or cancel [1/2/c/d/\
224  ?] (c): 2
225  Resolving dependencies...
226  Resolving package dependencies...
227  The following 25 NEW packages are going to be installed:
228    ansible libsodium23 python3-Babel python3-Jinja2 python\
229  3-MarkupSafe python3-PyNaCl python3-PyYAML
230    python3-appdirs python3-asn1crypto python3-bcrypt pytho\
231  n3 cffi python3-cryptography
```

```
  python3-jmespath python3-packaging python3-paramiko pyt\
hon3-passlib python3-ply python3-pyasn1
  python3-pycparser python3-pycryptodome python3-pyparsin\
g python3-pytz python3-setuptools
  python3-simplejson python3-six
The following package has no support information from its\
 vendor:
  ansible
25 new packages to install.
Overall download size: 28.3 MiB. Already cached: 0 B. Aft\
er the operation, additional 168.8 MiB
will be used.
Continue? [y/n/v/...? shows all options] (y): y
Retrieving package libsodium23-1.0.16-4.3.18.x86_64      \
    (1/25), 153.5 KiB (335.6 KiB unpacked)
Retrieving: libsodium23-1.0.16-4.3.18.x86_64.rpm ........\
...................................[done]
Retrieving package python3-MarkupSafe-1.0-1.29.x86_64    \
    (2/25),  29.1 KiB ( 72.6 KiB unpacked)
Retrieving: python3-MarkupSafe-1.0-1.29.x86_64.rpm ......\
...................................[done]
Retrieving package python3-PyYAML-5.4.1-1.1.x86_64       \
    (3/25), 106.6 KiB (555.8 KiB unpacked)
Retrieving: python3-PyYAML-5.4.1-1.1.x86_64.rpm .........\
..................................[done]
Retrieving package python3-appdirs-1.4.3-1.21.noarch     \
    (4/25),  22.5 KiB ( 83.5 KiB unpacked)
Retrieving: python3-appdirs-1.4.3-1.21.noarch.rpm .......\
..................................[done]
Retrieving package python3-ply-3.10-1.27.noarch          \
    (5/25), 100.6 KiB (456.2 KiB unpacked)
Retrieving: python3-ply-3.10-1.27.noarch.rpm ...........\
..................................[done]
Retrieving package python3-pyparsing-2.4.7-1.24.noarch   \
    (6/25), 187.4 KiB (877.1 KiB unpacked)
```

```
267  Retrieving: python3-pyparsing-2.4.7-1.24.noarch.rpm .....\
268  .................................[done]
269  Retrieving package python3-simplejson-3.17.2-1.10.x86_64 \
270      (7/25),  73.1 KiB (274.3 KiB unpacked)
271  Retrieving: python3-simplejson-3.17.2-1.10.x86_64.rpm ...\
272  .................................[done]
273  Retrieving package python3-jmespath-0.9.3-1.21.noarch    \
274      (8/25),  48.3 KiB (177.5 KiB unpacked)
275  Retrieving: python3-jmespath-0.9.3-1.21.noarch.rpm ......\
276  .................................[done]
277  Retrieving package python3-asn1crypto-0.24.0-3.2.1.noarch\
278      (9/25), 176.2 KiB (  1.2 MiB unpacked)
279  Retrieving: python3-asn1crypto-0.24.0-3.2.1.noarch.rpm ..\
280  .................................[done]
281  Retrieving package python3-pyasn1-0.4.2-3.2.1.noarch     \
282     (10/25), 150.2 KiB (823.2 KiB unpacked)
283  Retrieving: python3-pyasn1-0.4.2-3.2.1.noarch.rpm .......\
284  .................................[done]
285  Retrieving package python3-pycparser-2.17-3.2.1.noarch   \
286     (11/25), 189.9 KiB (  1.1 MiB unpacked)
287  Retrieving: python3-pycparser-2.17-3.2.1.noarch.rpm .....\
288  .................................[done]
289  Retrieving package python3-pytz-2021.1-3.3.1.noarch      \
290     (12/25),  56.6 KiB (244.6 KiB unpacked)
291  Retrieving: python3-pytz-2021.1-3.3.1.noarch.rpm ........\
292  .................................[done]
293  Retrieving package python3-six-1.14.0-10.1.noarch        \
294     (13/25),  34.9 KiB ( 99.2 KiB unpacked)
295  Retrieving: python3-six-1.14.0-10.1.noarch.rpm ..........\
296  .................................[done]
297  Retrieving package python3-cffi-1.13.2-3.2.5.x86_64      \
298     (14/25), 307.1 KiB (  1.2 MiB unpacked)
299  Retrieving: python3-cffi-1.13.2-3.2.5.x86_64.rpm ........\
300  ......................[done (80.0 KiB/s)]
301  Retrieving package python3-Babel-2.8.0-3.3.1.noarch      \
```

```
302     (15/25),    5.0 MiB ( 26.4 MiB unpacked)
303  Retrieving: python3-Babel-2.8.0-3.3.1.noarch.rpm ........\
304  ......................[done (3.3 MiB/s)]
305  Retrieving package python3-pycryptodome-3.9.0-6.1.x86_64 \
306     (16/25),    7.1 MiB ( 25.3 MiB unpacked)
307  Retrieving: python3-pycryptodome-3.9.0-6.1.x86_64.rpm ...\
308  ......................[done (2.9 MiB/s)]
309  Retrieving package python3-packaging-20.3-1.9.noarch     \
310     (17/25),   67.5 KiB (263.1 KiB unpacked)
311  Retrieving: python3-packaging-20.3-1.9.noarch.rpm .......\
312  ...................................[done]
313  Retrieving package python3-bcrypt-3.2.0-1.10.x86_64      \
314     (18/25),   41.4 KiB ( 79.8 KiB unpacked)
315  Retrieving: python3-bcrypt-3.2.0-1.10.x86_64.rpm ........\
316  ...................................[done]
317  Retrieving package python3-PyNaCl-1.2.1-3.3.1.x86_64     \
318     (19/25),   75.6 KiB (423.4 KiB unpacked)
319  Retrieving: python3-PyNaCl-1.2.1-3.3.1.x86_64.rpm .......\
320  ...................................[done]
321  Retrieving package python3-Jinja2-2.10.1-3.10.2.noarch   \
322     (20/25), 237.4 KiB (   1.2 MiB unpacked)
323  Retrieving: python3-Jinja2-2.10.1-3.10.2.noarch.rpm .....\
324  ...................................[done]
325  Retrieving package python3-setuptools-40.5.0-6.3.1.noarch\
326     (21/25), 616.0 KiB (   3.3 MiB unpacked)
327  Retrieving: python3-setuptools-40.5.0-6.3.1.noarch.rpm ..\
328  ...................................[done]
329  Retrieving package python3-cryptography-2.8-10.1.x86_64  \
330     (22/25), 426.4 KiB (   2.5 MiB unpacked)
331  Retrieving: python3-cryptography-2.8-10.1.x86_64.rpm ....\
332  ...................................[done]
333  Retrieving package python3-paramiko-2.4.2-6.9.1.noarch   \
334     (23/25), 278.9 KiB (   1.6 MiB unpacked)
335  Retrieving: python3-paramiko-2.4.2-6.9.1.noarch.rpm .....\
336  ...................................[done]
```

```
Retrieving package python3-passlib-1.7.4-1.10.noarch     \
   (24/25), 696.2 KiB (   4.2 MiB unpacked)
Retrieving: python3-passlib-1.7.4-1.10.noarch.rpm .......\
......................[done (80.0 KiB/s)]
Retrieving package ansible-2.9.6-bp153.1.20.noarch       \
   (25/25),  12.2 MiB ( 96.0 MiB unpacked)
Retrieving: ansible-2.9.6-bp153.1.20.noarch.rpm .........\
......................[done (3.3 MiB/s)]
Checking for file conflicts: ...........................\
..............................[done]
( 1/25) Installing: libsodium23-1.0.16-4.3.18.x86_64 ....\
..............................[done]
( 2/25) Installing: python3-MarkupSafe-1.0-1.29.x86_64 ..\
..............................[done]
( 3/25) Installing: python3-PyYAML-5.4.1-1.1.x86_64 .....\
..............................[done]
( 4/25) Installing: python3-appdirs-1.4.3-1.21.noarch ...\
..............................[done]
( 5/25) Installing: python3-ply-3.10-1.27.noarch ........\
..............................[done]
( 6/25) Installing: python3-pyparsing-2.4.7-1.24.noarch .\
..............................[done]
( 7/25) Installing: python3-simplejson-3.17.2-1.10.x86_64\
 .............................[done]
( 8/25) Installing: python3-jmespath-0.9.3-1.21.noarch ..\
..............................[done]
Additional rpm output:
update-alternatives: using /usr/bin/jp-3.6 to provide /us\
r/bin/jp (jp) in auto mode
( 9/25) Installing: python3-asn1crypto-0.24.0-3.2.1.noarc\
h .............................[done]
(10/25) Installing: python3-pyasn1-0.4.2-3.2.1.noarch ...\
..............................[done]
(11/25) Installing: python3-pycparser-2.17-3.2.1.noarch .\
..............................[done]
```

```
(12/25) Installing: python3-pytz-2021.1-3.3.1.noarch ....\
.................................[done]
(13/25) Installing: python3-six-1.14.0-10.1.noarch ......\
.................................[done]
(14/25) Installing: python3-cffi-1.13.2-3.2.5.x86_64 ....\
.................................[done]
(15/25) Installing: python3-Babel-2.8.0-3.3.1.noarch ....\
.................................[done]
Additional rpm output:
update-alternatives: using /usr/bin/pybabel-3.6 to provid\
e /usr/bin/pybabel (pybabel) in auto mode
(16/25) Installing: python3-pycryptodome-3.9.0-6.1.x86_64\
.................................[done]
(17/25) Installing: python3-packaging-20.3-1.9.noarch ...\
.................................[done]
(18/25) Installing: python3-bcrypt-3.2.0-1.10.x86_64 ....\
.................................[done]
(19/25) Installing: python3-PyNaCl-1.2.1-3.3.1.x86_64 ...\
.................................[done]
(20/25) Installing: python3-Jinja2-2.10.1-3.10.2.noarch .\
.................................[done]
(21/25) Installing: python3-setuptools-40.5.0-6.3.1.noarc\
h .................................[done]
Additional rpm output:
update-alternatives: using /usr/bin/easy_install-3.6 to p\
rovide /usr/bin/easy_install (easy_install) in auto mode
(22/25) Installing: python3-cryptography-2.8-10.1.x86_64 \
.................................[done]
(23/25) Installing: python3-paramiko-2.4.2-6.9.1.noarch .\
.................................[done]
(24/25) Installing: python3-passlib-1.7.4-1.10.noarch ...\
.................................[done]
(25/25) Installing: ansible-2.9.6-bp153.1.20.noarch .....\
.................................[done]
sles:/home/devops # ansible --version
```

```
ansible 2.9.6
  config file = /etc/ansible/ansible.cfg
  configured module search path = ['/root/.ansible/plugin\
s/modules', '/usr/share/ansible/plugins/modules']
  ansible python module location = /usr/lib/python3.6/sit\
e-packages/ansible
  executable location = /usr/bin/ansible
  python version = 3.6.13 (default, Mar 10 2021, 18:30:35\
) [GCC]
sles:/home/devops # zypper info ansible
Refreshing service 'Basesystem_Module_15_SP3_x86_64'.
Refreshing service 'SUSE_Linux_Enterprise_Server_15_SP3_x\
86_64'.
Refreshing service 'SUSE_Package_Hub_15_SP3_x86_64'.
Refreshing service 'Server_Applications_Module_15_SP3_x86\
_64'.
Loading repository data...
Reading installed packages...
Information for package ansible:
--------------------------------
Repository      : SUSE-PackageHub-15-SP3-Backports-Pool
Name            : ansible
Version         : 2.9.6-bp153.1.20
Arch            : noarch
Vendor          : openSUSE
Support Level   : unknown
Installed Size  : 96.0 MiB
Installed       : Yes
Status          : up-to-date
Source package  : ansible-2.9.6-bp153.1.20.src
Summary         : SSH-based configuration management, depl\
oyment, and task execution system
Description     :
    Ansible is a radically simple model-driven configurat\
ion management, multi-node
```

```
442        deployment, and remote task execution system. Ansible\
443    works over SSH and does
444        not require any software or daemons to be installed o\
445    n remote nodes. Extension
446        modules can be written in any language and are transf\
447    erred to managed machines
448        automatically.
449    sles:/home/devops #
450    before execution
451    sles:/home/devops # zypper search ansible
452    Refreshing service 'Basesystem_Module_15_SP3_x86_64'.
453    Refreshing service 'SUSE_Linux_Enterprise_Server_15_SP3_x\
454    86_64'.
455    Refreshing service 'Server_Applications_Module_15_SP3_x86\
456    _64'.
457    Loading repository data...
458    Reading installed packages...
459    No matching items found.
460    sles:/home/devops # zypper install ansible
461    Refreshing service 'Basesystem_Module_15_SP3_x86_64'.
462    Refreshing service 'SUSE_Linux_Enterprise_Server_15_SP3_x\
463    86_64'.
464    Refreshing service 'Server_Applications_Module_15_SP3_x86\
465    _64'.
466    Loading repository data...
467    Reading installed packages...
468    'ansible' not found in package names. Trying capabilities.
469    No provider of 'ansible' found.
470    Resolving package dependencies...
471    Nothing to do.
472    sles:/home/devops # zypper info ansible
473    Refreshing service 'Basesystem_Module_15_SP3_x86_64'.
474    Refreshing service 'SUSE_Linux_Enterprise_Server_15_SP3_x\
475    86_64'.
476    Refreshing service 'SUSE_Package_Hub_15_SP3_x86_64'.
```

```
477   Refreshing service 'Server_Applications_Module_15_SP3_x86\
478   _64'.
479   Loading repository data...
480   Reading installed packages...
481   Information for package ansible:
482   -------------------------------
483   Repository      : SUSE-PackageHub-15-SP3-Backports-Pool
484   Name            : ansible
485   Version         : 2.9.6-bp153.1.20
486   Arch            : noarch
487   Vendor          : openSUSE
488   Support Level   : unknown
489   Installed Size  : 96.0 MiB
490   Installed       : No
491   Status          : not installed
492   Source package  : ansible-2.9.6-bp153.1.20.src
493   Summary         : SSH-based configuration management, depl\
494   oyment, and task execution system
495   Description     :
496       Ansible is a radically simple model-driven configurat\
497   ion management, multi-node
498       deployment, and remote task execution system. Ansible\
499    works over SSH and does
500       not require any software or daemons to be installed o\
501   n remote nodes. Extension
502       modules can be written in any language and are transf\
503   erred to managed machines
504       automatically.
```

before execution

```
1   # zypper search ansible
2   Refreshing service 'Basesystem_Module_15_SP3_x86_64'.
3   Refreshing service 'SUSE_Linux_Enterprise_Server_15_SP3_x\
4   86_64'.
5   Refreshing service 'Server_Applications_Module_15_SP3_x86\
6   _64'.
7   Loading repository data...
8   Reading installed packages...
9   No matching items found.
10  sles:/home/devops # zypper install ansible
11  Refreshing service 'Basesystem_Module_15_SP3_x86_64'.
12  Refreshing service 'SUSE_Linux_Enterprise_Server_15_SP3_x\
13  86_64'.
14  Refreshing service 'Server_Applications_Module_15_SP3_x86\
15  _64'.
16  Loading repository data...
17  Reading installed packages...
18  'ansible' not found in package names. Trying capabilities.
19  No provider of 'ansible' found.
20  Resolving package dependencies...
21  Nothing to do.
22  sles:/home/devops #
```

after execution

```
1   # zypper info ansible
2   Refreshing service 'Basesystem_Module_15_SP3_x86_64'.
3   Refreshing service 'SUSE_Linux_Enterprise_Server_15_SP3_x\
4   86_64'.
5   Refreshing service 'SUSE_Package_Hub_15_SP3_x86_64'.
6   Refreshing service 'Server_Applications_Module_15_SP3_x86\
7   _64'.
8   Loading repository data...
9   Reading installed packages...
10  Information for package ansible:
11  --------------------------------
```

```
12   Repository         : SUSE-PackageHub-15-SP3-Backports-Pool
13   Name               : ansible
14   Version            : 2.9.6-bp153.1.20
15   Arch               : noarch
16   Vendor             : openSUSE
17   Support Level      : unknown
18   Installed Size : 96.0 MiB
19   Installed          : Yes
20   Status             : up-to-date
21   Source package : ansible-2.9.6-bp153.1.20.src
22   Summary            : SSH-based configuration management, depl\
23   oyment, and task execution system
24   Description    :
25       Ansible is a radically simple model-driven configurat\
26   ion management, multi-node
27       deployment, and remote task execution system. Ansible\
28    works over SSH and does
29       not require any software or daemons to be installed o\
30   n remote nodes. Extension
31       modules can be written in any language and are transf\
32   erred to managed machines
33       automatically.
34   sles:/home/devops #
```

How to install Ansible with PIP

How to install Ansible with PIP, the Python package manager?
PIP is the Python package manager and is going to take care of all
the processes and manage the necessary dependency. It takes care
of the download and installs process of packages directly from PyPI.
PIP is designed to be OS-independent.
It could be a solution for developers that always want the latest up-
to-date release.
The alternative approach is to use the Operating System specific

Package Manager.

For example for Linux yum, DNF, and apt and for macOS Homebrew.

This second approach put more emphasis on stability so the latest release could be not available.

So if you really need the latest release of Ansible I'd suggest you use PIP.

Demo install Ansible with PIP

How to install the latest of Ansible with PIP, the Python package manager.

code PIP user

- install-pip-user.sh

```
1   #!/bin/bash
2   python3 -m pip install --upgrade -user pip
3   python3 -m pip install --user ansible
4   install-pip-global.sh
```

code PIP global

- install-pip-global.sh

```
1   #!/bin/bash
2   python3 -m pip install --upgrade pip
3   python3 -m pip install ansible
```

How to install Ansible in RedHat Enterprise Linux 9 Beta

How to install Ansible Core (ansible-core) in RedHat Enterprise Linux 9 Beta included in the RHEL 9 AppStream repository.

How to install Ansible in RHEL 9 Beta

- The Ansible Core package (ansible-core) included in the RHEL 9 AppStream repository

The good news is that the Ansible Core package (ansible-core) is included out-of-the-box in the RHEL 9 AppStream repository.
No more additional repository (Ansible Engine or EPEL) like previous versions for basic automation.
However, for additional support for the underlying platform and Core-maintained modules is required the Ansible Automation Platform subscription.

Link

- Scope of support for the Ansible Core package included in the RHEL 9 AppStream[21]
- Using Ansible in RHEL 9[22]

demo

How to install the latest version of Ansible-Core in Red Hat Enterprise Linux (RHEL) 9.

---

[21]https://access.redhat.com/articles/6325611
[22]https://access.redhat.com/articles/6393321

code

- Install-Ansible-RHEL9.sh

```
1   #!/bin/bash
2   sudo dnf install ansible-core
```

execution

```
1    $ ssh devops@rhel9.example.com
2    Last login: Fri Jan 21 17:32:05 2022 from 192.168.0.101
3    [devops@localhost ~]$ sudo su
4    [root@localhost devops]# cat /etc/redhat-release
5    Red Hat Enterprise Linux release 9.0 Beta (Plow)
6    [root@localhost devops]# cat /etc/os-release
7    NAME="Red Hat Enterprise Linux"
8    VERSION="9.0 (Plow)"
9    ID="rhel"
10   ID_LIKE="fedora"
11   VERSION_ID="9.0"
12   PLATFORM_ID="platform:el9"
13   PRETTY_NAME="Red Hat Enterprise Linux 9.0 Beta (Plow)"
14   ANSI_COLOR="0;31"
15   CPE_NAME="cpe:/o:redhat:enterprise_linux:9::baseos"
16   HOME_URL="https://www.redhat.com/"
17   DOCUMENTATION_URL="https://access.redhat.com/documentatio\
18   n/red_hat_enterprise_linux/9/"
19   BUG_REPORT_URL="https://bugzilla.redhat.com/"
20   REDHAT_BUGZILLA_PRODUCT="Red Hat Enterprise Linux 9"
21   REDHAT_BUGZILLA_PRODUCT_VERSION=9.0
22   REDHAT_SUPPORT_PRODUCT="Red Hat Enterprise Linux"
23   REDHAT_SUPPORT_PRODUCT_VERSION="9.0 Beta"
24   [root@localhost devops]# hostnamectl
25      Static hostname: n/a                                      \
26
```

```
27   Transient hostname: localhost
28           Icon name: computer-vm
29             Chassis: vm
30          Machine ID: e095682a704549189f7f89473724bc21
31             Boot ID: ab4c4523b571418fad3bd0c754e6063d
32      Virtualization: oracle
33    Operating System: Red Hat Enterprise Linux 9.0 Beta (Pl\
34   ow)
35         CPE OS Name: cpe:/o:redhat:enterprise_linux:9::bas\
36   eos
37              Kernel: Linux 5.14.0-39.el9.x86_64
38        Architecture: x86-64
39     Hardware Vendor: innotek GmbH
40      Hardware Model: VirtualBox
41   [root@localhost devops]# uname -a
42   Linux localhost.localdomain 5.14.0-39.el9.x86_64 #1 SMP P\
43   REEMPT Fri Dec 24 00:07:58 EST 2021 x86_64 x86_64 x86_64 \
44   GNU/Linux
45   [root@localhost devops]# dnf search ansible
46   Updating Subscription Management repositories.
47   Last metadata expiration check: 1:40:46 ago on Fri 21 Jan\
48    2022 04:15:49 PM CET.
49   ================================== Name & Summary Matched:\
50    ansible ===================================
51   ansible-collection-microsoft-sql.noarch : The Ansible col\
52   lection for Microsoft SQL Server
53                                            : management
54   ansible-freeipa-tests.noarch : ansible-freeipa tests
55   ansible-pcp.noarch : Ansible Metric collection for Perfor\
56   mance Co-Pilot
57   ansible-test.x86_64 : Tool for testing ansible plugin and\
58    module code
59   ======================================= Name Matched: ansi\
60   ble ==========================================
61   ansible-core.x86_64 : SSH-based configuration management,\
```

```
deployment, and task execution system
ansible-freeipa.noarch : Roles and playbooks to deploy Fr\
eeIPA servers, replicas and clients
====================================== Summary Matched: ans\
ible ==========================================
rhc-worker-playbook.x86_64 : Python worker for Red Hat co\
nnector that launches Ansible Runner
[root@localhost devops]# dnf info ansible-core
Updating Subscription Management repositories.
Last metadata expiration check: 1:41:06 ago on Fri 21 Jan\
 2022 04:15:49 PM CET.
Available Packages
Name         : ansible-core
Version      : 2.12.1
Release      : 1.el9
Architecture : x86_64
Size         : 2.4 M
Source       : ansible-core-2.12.1-1.el9.src.rpm
Repository   : rhel-9-for-x86_64-appstream-beta-rpms
Summary      : SSH-based configuration management, deploy\
ment, and task execution system
URL          : http://ansible.com
License      : GPLv3+
Description  : Ansible is a radically simple model-driven\
 configuration management,
             : multi-node deployment, and remote task exe\
cution system. Ansible works
             : over SSH and does not require any software\
 or daemons to be installed
             : on remote nodes. Extension modules can be \
written in any language and
             : are transferred to managed machines automa\
tically.
[root@localhost devops]# dnf install ansible-core
Updating Subscription Management repositories.
```

```
 97  Last metadata expiration check: 1:41:25 ago on Fri 21 Jan\
 98   2022 04:15:49 PM CET.
 99  Dependencies resolved.
100  ====================================================================\
101  ==========================================
102   Package                  Arch    Version              Rep\
103  ository                                Size
104  ====================================================================\
105  ==========================================
106  Installing:
107   ansible-core             x86_64  2.12.1-1.el9               rhe\
108  l-9-for-x86_64-appstream-beta-rpms  2.4 M
109  Installing dependencies:
110   git                      x86_64  2.31.1-2.el9.2             rhe\
111  l-9-for-x86_64-appstream-beta-rpms  128 k
112   git-core                 x86_64  2.31.1-2.el9.2             rhe\
113  l-9-for-x86_64-appstream-beta-rpms  3.6 M
114   git-core-doc             noarch  2.31.1-2.el9.2             rhe\
115  l-9-for-x86_64-appstream-beta-rpms  2.5 M
116   perl-AutoLoader          noarch  5.74-479.el9               rhe\
117  l-9-for-x86_64-appstream-beta-rpms   31 k
118   perl-B                   x86_64  1.80-479.el9               rhe\
119  l-9-for-x86_64-appstream-beta-rpms  193 k
120   perl-Carp                noarch  1.50-460.el9               rhe\
121  l-9-for-x86_64-appstream-beta-rpms   31 k
122   perl-Class-Struct        noarch  0.66-479.el9               rhe\
123  l-9-for-x86_64-appstream-beta-rpms   32 k
124   perl-Data-Dumper         x86_64  2.174-462.el9              rhe\
125  l-9-for-x86_64-appstream-beta-rpms   58 k
126   perl-Digest              noarch  1.19-4.el9                 rhe\
127  l-9-for-x86_64-appstream-beta-rpms   28 k
128   perl-Digest-MD5          x86_64  2.58-4.el9                 rhe\
129  l-9-for-x86_64-appstream-beta-rpms   39 k
130   perl-DynaLoader          x86_64  1.47-479.el9               rhe\
131  l-9-for-x86_64-appstream-beta-rpms   35 k
```

```
 perl-Encode                x86_64   4:3.08-462.el9       rhe\
l-9-for-x86_64-appstream-beta-rpms   1.7 M
 perl-Errno                 x86_64   1.30-479.el9         rhe\
l-9-for-x86_64-appstream-beta-rpms    24 k
 perl-Error                 noarch   1:0.17029-7.el9      rhe\
l-9-for-x86_64-appstream-beta-rpms    46 k
 perl-Exporter              noarch   5.74-461.el9         rhe\
l-9-for-x86_64-appstream-beta-rpms    33 k
 perl-Fcntl                 x86_64   1.13-479.el9         rhe\
l-9-for-x86_64-appstream-beta-rpms    31 k
 perl-File-Basename         noarch   2.85-479.el9         rhe\
l-9-for-x86_64-appstream-beta-rpms    27 k
 perl-File-Find             noarch   1.37-479.el9         rhe\
l-9-for-x86_64-appstream-beta-rpms    35 k
 perl-File-Path             noarch   2.18-4.el9           rhe\
l-9-for-x86_64-appstream-beta-rpms    37 k
 perl-File-Temp             noarch   1:0.231.100-4.el9    rhe\
l-9-for-x86_64-appstream-beta-rpms    62 k
 perl-File-stat             noarch   1.09-479.el9         rhe\
l-9-for-x86_64-appstream-beta-rpms    27 k
 perl-FileHandle            noarch   2.03-479.el9         rhe\
l-9-for-x86_64-appstream-beta-rpms    25 k
 perl-Getopt-Long           noarch   1:2.52-4.el9         rhe\
l-9-for-x86_64-appstream-beta-rpms    63 k
 perl-Getopt-Std            noarch   1.12-479.el9         rhe\
l-9-for-x86_64-appstream-beta-rpms    25 k
 perl-Git                   noarch   2.31.1-2.el9.2       rhe\
l-9-for-x86_64-appstream-beta-rpms    44 k
 perl-HTTP-Tiny             noarch   0.076-460.el9        rhe\
l-9-for-x86_64-appstream-beta-rpms    57 k
 perl-IO                    x86_64   1.43-479.el9         rhe\
l-9-for-x86_64-appstream-beta-rpms   102 k
 perl-IPC-Open3             noarch   1.21-479.el9         rhe\
l-9-for-x86_64-appstream-beta-rpms    33 k
 perl-MIME-Base64           x86_64   3.16-4.el9           rhe\
```

```
 l-9-for-x86_64-appstream-beta-rpms    34 k
  perl-Net-SSLeay          x86_64   1.90-8.el9        rhe\
 l-9-for-x86_64-appstream-beta-rpms    377 k
  perl-POSIX               x86_64   1.94-479.el9      rhe\
 l-9-for-x86_64-appstream-beta-rpms    107 k
  perl-PathTools           x86_64   3.78-461.el9      rhe\
 l-9-for-x86_64-appstream-beta-rpms    92 k
  perl-Pod-Escapes         noarch   1:1.07-460.el9    rhe\
 l-9-for-x86_64-appstream-beta-rpms    21 k
  perl-Pod-Perldoc         noarch   3.28.01-461.el9   rhe\
 l-9-for-x86_64-appstream-beta-rpms    91 k
  perl-Pod-Simple          noarch   1:3.42-4.el9      rhe\
 l-9-for-x86_64-appstream-beta-rpms    228 k
  perl-Pod-Usage           noarch   4:2.01-4.el9      rhe\
 l-9-for-x86_64-appstream-beta-rpms    43 k
  perl-Scalar-List-Utils   x86_64   4:1.56-461.el9    rhe\
 l-9-for-x86_64-appstream-beta-rpms    76 k
  perl-SelectSaver         noarch   1.02-479.el9      rhe\
 l-9-for-x86_64-appstream-beta-rpms    21 k
  perl-Socket              x86_64   4:2.031-4.el9     rhe\
 l-9-for-x86_64-appstream-beta-rpms    58 k
  perl-Storable            x86_64   1:3.21-460.el9    rhe\
 l-9-for-x86_64-appstream-beta-rpms    97 k
  perl-Symbol              noarch   1.08-479.el9      rhe\
 l-9-for-x86_64-appstream-beta-rpms    24 k
  perl-Term-ANSIColor      noarch   5.01-461.el9      rhe\
 l-9-for-x86_64-appstream-beta-rpms    50 k
  perl-Term-Cap            noarch   1.17-460.el9      rhe\
 l-9-for-x86_64-appstream-beta-rpms    24 k
  perl-TermReadKey         x86_64   2.38-11.el9       rhe\
 l-9-for-x86_64-appstream-beta-rpms    40 k
  perl-Text-ParseWords     noarch   3.30-460.el9      rhe\
 l-9-for-x86_64-appstream-beta-rpms    18 k
  perl-Text-Tabs+Wrap      noarch   2013.0523-460.el9 rhe\
 l-9-for-x86_64-appstream-beta-rpms    25 k
```

```
 perl-Time-Local              noarch  2:1.300-7.el9        rhe\
l-9-for-x86_64-appstream-beta-rpms   36 k
 perl-URI                     noarch  5.09-3.el9           rhe\
l-9-for-x86_64-appstream-beta-rpms  125 k
 perl-base                    noarch  2.27-479.el9         rhe\
l-9-for-x86_64-appstream-beta-rpms   26 k
 perl-constant                noarch  1.33-461.el9         rhe\
l-9-for-x86_64-appstream-beta-rpms   25 k
 perl-if                      noarch  0.60.800-479.el9     rhe\
l-9-for-x86_64-appstream-beta-rpms   23 k
 perl-interpreter             x86_64  4:5.32.1-479.el9     rhe\
l-9-for-x86_64-appstream-beta-rpms   83 k
 perl-lib                     x86_64  0.65-479.el9         rhe\
l-9-for-x86_64-appstream-beta-rpms   24 k
 perl-libnet                  noarch  3.13-4.el9           rhe\
l-9-for-x86_64-appstream-beta-rpms  134 k
 perl-libs                    x86_64  4:5.32.1-479.el9     rhe\
l-9-for-x86_64-appstream-beta-rpms  2.2 M
 perl-mro                     x86_64  1.23-479.el9         rhe\
l-9-for-x86_64-appstream-beta-rpms   39 k
 perl-overload                noarch  1.31-479.el9         rhe\
l-9-for-x86_64-appstream-beta-rpms   55 k
 perl-overloading             noarch  0.02-479.el9         rhe\
l-9-for-x86_64-appstream-beta-rpms   23 k
 perl-parent                  noarch  1:0.238-460.el9      rhe\
l-9-for-x86_64-appstream-beta-rpms   15 k
 perl-podlators               noarch  1:4.14-460.el9       rhe\
l-9-for-x86_64-appstream-beta-rpms  118 k
 perl-subs                    noarch  1.03-479.el9         rhe\
l-9-for-x86_64-appstream-beta-rpms   21 k
 perl-vars                    noarch  1.05-479.el9         rhe\
l-9-for-x86_64-appstream-beta-rpms   22 k
 python3-babel                noarch  2.9.1-2.el9          rhe\
l-9-for-x86_64-appstream-beta-rpms  6.0 M
 python3-cffi                 x86_64  1.14.5-4.el9         rhe\
```

```
 1-9-for-x86_64-appstream-beta-rpms   257 k
  python3-cryptography     x86_64   3.4.7-5.el9              rhe\
 1-9-for-x86_64-appstream-beta-rpms   784 k
  python3-jinja2           noarch   2.11.3-4.el9            rhe\
 1-9-for-x86_64-appstream-beta-rpms   253 k
  python3-markupsafe       x86_64   1.1.1-12.el9            rhe\
 1-9-for-x86_64-appstream-beta-rpms    38 k
  python3-packaging        noarch   20.9-4.el9              rhe\
 1-9-for-x86_64-appstream-beta-rpms    81 k
  python3-ply              noarch   3.11-13.el9             rhe\
 1-9-for-x86_64-appstream-beta-rpms   110 k
  python3-pycparser        noarch   2.20-5.el9             rhe\
 1-9-for-x86_64-appstream-beta-rpms   139 k
  python3-pyparsing        noarch   2.4.7-7.1.el9          rhe\
 1-9-for-x86_64-baseos-beta-rpms      154 k
  python3-pytz             noarch   2021.1-4.el9            rhe\
 1-9-for-x86_64-appstream-beta-rpms    56 k
  python3-resolvelib       noarch   0.5.4-5.el9            rhe\
 1-9-for-x86_64-appstream-beta-rpms    38 k
  sshpass                  x86_64   1.09-4.el9             rhe\
 1-9-for-x86_64-appstream-beta-rpms    29 k
Installing weak dependencies:
  perl-IO-Socket-IP        noarch   0.41-5.el9             rhe\
 1-9-for-x86_64-appstream-beta-rpms    45 k
  perl-IO-Socket-SSL       noarch   2.070-6.el9            rhe\
 1-9-for-x86_64-appstream-beta-rpms   217 k
  perl-Mozilla-CA          noarch   20200520-6.el9         rhe\
 1-9-for-x86_64-appstream-beta-rpms    14 k
  perl-NDBM_File           x86_64   1.15-479.el9          rhe\
 1-9-for-x86_64-appstream-beta-rpms    33 k
Transaction Summary
================================================================\
=================================================
Install  79 Packages
Total download size: 24 M
```

```
Installed size: 101 M
Is this ok [y/N]: y
Downloading Packages:
(1/79): perl-IPC-Open3-1.21-479.el9.noarch.rpm                 \
            51 kB/s |  33 kB      00:00
(2/79): perl-libnet-3.13-4.el9.noarch.rpm                      \
           193 kB/s | 134 kB      00:00
(3/79): python3-pyparsing-2.4.7-7.1.el9.noarch.rpm            \
           221 kB/s | 154 kB      00:00
(4/79): perl-File-Basename-2.85-479.el9.noarch.rpm            \
           160 kB/s |  27 kB      00:00
(5/79): perl-Text-ParseWords-3.30-460.el9.noarch.rpm          \
           113 kB/s |  18 kB      00:00
(6/79): perl-Pod-Perldoc-3.28.01-461.el9.noarch.rpm           \
           516 kB/s |  91 kB      00:00
(7/79): python3-pytz-2021.1-4.el9.noarch.rpm                  \
           283 kB/s |  56 kB      00:00
(8/79): perl-Getopt-Long-2.52-4.el9.noarch.rpm                \
           368 kB/s |  63 kB      00:00
(9/79): perl-IO-Socket-SSL-2.070-6.el9.noarch.rpm             \
           918 kB/s | 217 kB      00:00
(10/79): perl-Class-Struct-0.66-479.el9.noarch.rpm            \
           173 kB/s |  32 kB      00:00
(11/79): perl-File-Find-1.37-479.el9.noarch.rpm               \
           214 kB/s |  35 kB      00:00
(12/79): perl-Digest-1.19-4.el9.noarch.rpm                    \
           137 kB/s |  28 kB      00:00
(13/79): perl-Mozilla-CA-20200520-6.el9.noarch.rpm            \
            77 kB/s |  14 kB      00:00
(14/79): perl-overload-1.31-479.el9.noarch.rpm                \
           309 kB/s |  55 kB      00:00
(15/79): perl-Term-Cap-1.17-460.el9.noarch.rpm                \
            80 kB/s |  24 kB      00:00
(16/79): perl-if-0.60.800-479.el9.noarch.rpm                  \
           101 kB/s |  23 kB      00:00
```

```
307  (17/79): perl-parent-0.238-460.el9.noarch.rpm                \
308            28 kB/s |  15 kB       00:00
309  (18/79): git-core-doc-2.31.1-2.el9.2.noarch.rpm             \
310            3.8 MB/s | 2.5 MB      00:00
311  (19/79): perl-File-stat-1.09-479.el9.noarch.rpm             \
312            145 kB/s |  27 kB      00:00
313  (20/79): perl-Term-ANSIColor-5.01-461.el9.noarch.rpm        \
314            294 kB/s |  50 kB      00:00
315  (21/79): perl-subs-1.03-479.el9.noarch.rpm                  \
316            117 kB/s |  21 kB      00:00
317  (22/79): perl-HTTP-Tiny-0.076-460.el9.noarch.rpm            \
318            327 kB/s |  57 kB      00:00
319  (23/79): perl-SelectSaver-1.02-479.el9.noarch.rpm           \
320            109 kB/s |  21 kB      00:00
321  (24/79): perl-Error-0.17029-7.el9.noarch.rpm                \
322            152 kB/s |  46 kB      00:00
323  (25/79): perl-Exporter-5.74-461.el9.noarch.rpm              \
324            168 kB/s |  33 kB      00:00
325  (26/79): perl-Symbol-1.08-479.el9.noarch.rpm                \
326            61 kB/s |  24 kB       00:00
327  (27/79): perl-overloading-0.02-479.el9.noarch.rpm           \
328            134 kB/s |  23 kB      00:00
329  (28/79): perl-vars-1.05-479.el9.noarch.rpm                  \
330            26 kB/s |  22 kB       00:00
331  (29/79): perl-Carp-1.50-460.el9.noarch.rpm                  \
332            38 kB/s |  31 kB       00:00
333  (30/79): perl-Fcntl-1.13-479.el9.x86_64.rpm                 \
334            181 kB/s |  31 kB      00:00
335  (31/79): perl-File-Temp-0.231.100-4.el9.noarch.rpm          \
336            348 kB/s |  62 kB      00:00
337  (32/79): perl-File-Path-2.18-4.el9.noarch.rpm               \
338            140 kB/s |  37 kB      00:00
339  (33/79): perl-AutoLoader-5.74-479.el9.noarch.rpm            \
340            109 kB/s |  31 kB      00:00
341  (34/79): perl-Pod-Simple-3.42-4.el9.noarch.rpm              \
```

```
342            774 kB/s |  228 kB        00:00
343  (35/79): perl-Git-2.31.1-2.el9.2.noarch.rpm                    \
344            164 kB/s |   44 kB        00:00
345  (36/79): perl-Pod-Escapes-1.07-460.el9.noarch.rpm             \
346             33 kB/s |   21 kB        00:00
347  (37/79): python3-ply-3.11-13.el9.noarch.rpm                   \
348            160 kB/s |  110 kB        00:00
349  (38/79): perl-IO-Socket-IP-0.41-5.el9.noarch.rpm              \
350            206 kB/s |   45 kB        00:00
351  (39/79): perl-FileHandle-2.03-479.el9.noarch.rpm              \
352            120 kB/s |   25 kB        00:00
353  (40/79): perl-Text-Tabs+Wrap-2013.0523-460.el9.noarch.rpm\
354            137 kB/s |   25 kB        00:00
355  (41/79): python3-pycparser-2.20-5.el9.noarch.rpm              \
356            778 kB/s |  139 kB        00:00
357  (42/79): perl-constant-1.33-461.el9.noarch.rpm                \
358            105 kB/s |   25 kB        00:00
359  (43/79): perl-URI-5.09-3.el9.noarch.rpm                       \
360            445 kB/s |  125 kB        00:00
361  (44/79): python3-jinja2-2.11.3-4.el9.noarch.rpm               \
362            990 kB/s |  253 kB        00:00
363  (45/79): perl-Time-Local-1.300-7.el9.noarch.rpm               \
364            204 kB/s |   36 kB        00:00
365  (46/79): perl-Pod-Usage-2.01-4.el9.noarch.rpm                 \
366            103 kB/s |   43 kB        00:00
367  (47/79): python3-resolvelib-0.5.4-5.el9.noarch.rpm            \
368             22 kB/s |   38 kB        00:01
369  (48/79): perl-base-2.27-479.el9.noarch.rpm                    \
370             41 kB/s |   26 kB        00:00
371  (49/79): perl-podlators-4.14-460.el9.noarch.rpm               \
372            407 kB/s |  118 kB        00:00
373  (50/79): perl-Getopt-Std-1.12-479.el9.noarch.rpm              \
374            142 kB/s |   25 kB        00:00
375  (51/79): perl-mro-1.23-479.el9.x86_64.rpm                     \
376            158 kB/s |   39 kB        00:00
```

```
(52/79): perl-Storable-3.21-460.el9.x86_64.rpm                   \
               525 kB/s |  97 kB        00:00
(53/79): python3-babel-2.9.1-2.el9.noarch.rpm                   \
               4.3 MB/s | 6.0 MB        00:01
(54/79): perl-IO-1.43-479.el9.x86_64.rpm                        \
               623 kB/s | 102 kB        00:00
(55/79): perl-Scalar-List-Utils-1.56-461.el9.x86_64.rpm         \
               423 kB/s |  76 kB        00:00
(56/79): perl-Net-SSLeay-1.90-8.el9.x86_64.rpm                  \
               1.7 MB/s | 377 kB        00:00
(57/79): perl-interpreter-5.32.1-479.el9.x86_64.rpm             \
               376 kB/s |  83 kB        00:00
(58/79): python3-markupsafe-1.1.1-12.el9.x86_64.rpm             \
               220 kB/s |  38 kB        00:00
(59/79): perl-Errno-1.30-479.el9.x86_64.rpm                     \
               129 kB/s |  24 kB        00:00
(60/79): perl-Digest-MD5-2.58-4.el9.x86_64.rpm                  \
               238 kB/s |  39 kB        00:00
(61/79): perl-lib-0.65-479.el9.x86_64.rpm                       \
                69 kB/s |  24 kB        00:00
(62/79): python3-packaging-20.9-4.el9.noarch.rpm                \
                46 kB/s |  81 kB        00:01
(63/79): perl-TermReadKey-2.38-11.el9.x86_64.rpm                \
               203 kB/s |  40 kB        00:00
(64/79): perl-Socket-2.031-4.el9.x86_64.rpm                     \
               312 kB/s |  58 kB        00:00
(65/79): perl-NDBM_File-1.15-479.el9.x86_64.rpm                 \
                81 kB/s |  33 kB        00:00
(66/79): perl-Encode-3.08-462.el9.x86_64.rpm                    \
               2.5 MB/s | 1.7 MB        00:00
(67/79): sshpass-1.09-4.el9.x86_64.rpm                          \
                19 kB/s |  29 kB        00:01
(68/79): perl-libs-5.32.1-479.el9.x86_64.rpm                    \
               3.0 MB/s | 2.2 MB        00:00
(69/79): perl-B-1.80-479.el9.x86_64.rpm                         \
```

```
               768 kB/s | 193 kB        00:00
(70/79): perl-PathTools-3.78-461.el9.x86_64.rpm              \
               504 kB/s |  92 kB        00:00
(71/79): perl-POSIX-1.94-479.el9.x86_64.rpm                 \
               158 kB/s | 107 kB        00:00
(72/79): perl-MIME-Base64-3.16-4.el9.x86_64.rpm             \
                90 kB/s |  34 kB        00:00
(73/79): perl-Data-Dumper-2.174-462.el9.x86_64.rpm          \
               222 kB/s |  58 kB        00:00
(74/79): git-core-2.31.1-2.el9.2.x86_64.rpm                 \
               3.3 MB/s | 3.6 MB        00:01
(75/79): git-2.31.1-2.el9.2.x86_64.rpm                      \
               656 kB/s | 128 kB        00:00
(76/79): perl-DynaLoader-1.47-479.el9.x86_64.rpm            \
               213 kB/s |  35 kB        00:00
(77/79): ansible-core-2.12.1-1.el9.x86_64.rpm               \
               3.7 MB/s | 2.4 MB        00:00
(78/79): python3-cffi-1.14.5-4.el9.x86_64.rpm               \
               127 kB/s | 257 kB        00:02
(79/79): python3-cryptography-3.4.7-5.el9.x86_64.rpm        \
               367 kB/s | 784 kB        00:02
-------------------------------------------------------------\
-------------------------------------------
Total                                                        \
               2.0 MB/s |  24 MB        00:12
Red Hat Enterprise Linux 9 for x86_64 - BaseOS Beta (RPMs\
)              1.3 MB/s | 1.6 kB        00:00
Importing GPG key 0xF21541EB:
 Userid     : "Red Hat, Inc. (beta key 2) <security@redha\
t.com>"
 Fingerprint: B08B 659E E86A F623 BC90 E8DB 938A 80CA F21\
5 41EB
 From       : /etc/pki/rpm-gpg/RPM-GPG-KEY-redhat-beta
Is this ok [y/N]: y
Key imported successfully
```

```
Red Hat Enterprise Linux 9 for x86_64 - BaseOS Beta (RPMs\
)              4.9 MB/s | 5.0 kB      00:00
Importing GPG key 0xFD431D51:
 Userid      : "Red Hat, Inc. (release key 2) <security@re\
dhat.com>"
 Fingerprint: 567E 347A D004 4ADE 55BA 8A5F 199E 2F91 FD4\
3 1D51
 From        : /etc/pki/rpm-gpg/RPM-GPG-KEY-redhat-release
Is this ok [y/N]: y
Key imported successfully
Importing GPG key 0xD4082792:
 Userid      : "Red Hat, Inc. (auxiliary key) <security@re\
dhat.com>"
 Fingerprint: 6A6A A7C9 7C88 90AE C6AE BFE2 F76F 66C3 D40\
8 2792
 From        : /etc/pki/rpm-gpg/RPM-GPG-KEY-redhat-release
Is this ok [y/N]: y
Key imported successfully
Running transaction check
Transaction check succeeded.
Running transaction test
Transaction test succeeded.
Running transaction
  Preparing        :                                      \
                                 1/1
  Installing       : git-core-2.31.1-2.el9.2.x86_64       \
                                 1/79
  Installing       : git-core-doc-2.31.1-2.el9.2.noarch   \
                                 2/79
  Installing       : perl-Digest-1.19-4.el9.noarch        \
                                 3/79
  Installing       : perl-FileHandle-2.03-479.el9.noarch  \
                                 4/79
  Installing       : perl-Digest-MD5-2.58-4.el9.x86_64    \
                                 5/79
```

```
  Installing      : perl-B-1.80-479.el9.x86_64            \
                                   6/79
  Installing      : perl-AutoLoader-5.74-479.el9.noarch \
                                   7/79
  Installing      : perl-Data-Dumper-2.174-462.el9.x86_6\
4                                  8/79
  Installing      : perl-libnet-3.13-4.el9.noarch        \
                                   9/79
  Installing      : perl-base-2.27-479.el9.noarch        \
                                  10/79
  Installing      : perl-Net-SSLeay-1.90-8.el9.x86_64    \
                                  11/79
  Installing      : perl-URI-5.09-3.el9.noarch           \
                                  12/79
  Installing      : perl-if-0.60.800-479.el9.noarch      \
                                  13/79
  Installing      : perl-Pod-Escapes-1:1.07-460.el9.noar\
ch                                14/79
  Installing      : perl-Text-Tabs+Wrap-2013.0523-460.el\
9.noarch                          15/79
  Installing      : perl-Time-Local-2:1.300-7.el9.noarch\
                                  16/79
  Installing      : perl-Mozilla-CA-20200520-6.el9.noarc\
h                                 17/79
  Installing      : perl-File-Path-2.18-4.el9.noarch    \
                                  18/79
  Installing      : perl-IO-Socket-IP-0.41-5.el9.noarch \
                                  19/79
  Installing      : perl-IO-Socket-SSL-2.070-6.el9.noarc\
h                                 20/79
  Installing      : perl-subs-1.03-479.el9.noarch        \
                                  21/79
  Installing      : perl-Class-Struct-0.66-479.el9.noarc\
h                                 22/79
  Installing      : perl-Term-ANSIColor-5.01-461.el9.noa\
```

```
517  rch                                      23/79
518     Installing     : perl-Term-Cap-1.17-460.el9.noarch    \
519                                            24/79
520     Installing     : perl-POSIX-1.94-479.el9.x86_64        \
521                                            25/79
522     Installing     : perl-Pod-Simple-1:3.42-4.el9.noarch \
523                                            26/79
524     Installing     : perl-IPC-Open3-1.21-479.el9.noarch   \
525                                            27/79
526     Installing     : perl-File-Temp-1:0.231.100-4.el9.noa\
527  rch                                      28/79
528     Installing     : perl-HTTP-Tiny-0.076-460.el9.noarch \
529                                            29/79
530     Installing     : perl-SelectSaver-1.02-479.el9.noarch\
531                                            30/79
532     Installing     : perl-Symbol-1.08-479.el9.noarch      \
533                                            31/79
534     Installing     : perl-File-stat-1.09-479.el9.noarch  \
535                                            32/79
536     Installing     : perl-Socket-4:2.031-4.el9.x86_64     \
537                                            33/79
538     Installing     : perl-podlators-1:4.14-460.el9.noarch\
539                                            34/79
540     Installing     : perl-Pod-Perldoc-3.28.01-461.el9.noa\
541  rch                                      35/79
542     Installing     : perl-Text-ParseWords-3.30-460.el9.no\
543  arch                                     36/79
544     Installing     : perl-overloading-0.02-479.el9.noarch\
545                                            37/79
546     Installing     : perl-Fcntl-1.13-479.el9.x86_64       \
547                                            38/79
548     Installing     : perl-mro-1.23-479.el9.x86_64         \
549                                            39/79
550     Installing     : perl-IO-1.43-479.el9.x86_64          \
551                                            40/79
```

```
    Installing       : perl-Pod-Usage-4:2.01-4.el9.noarch     \
                                       41/79
    Installing       : perl-parent-1:0.238-460.el9.noarch     \
                                       42/79
    Installing       : perl-File-Basename-2.85-479.el9.noar\
ch                                     43/79
    Installing       : perl-vars-1.05-479.el9.noarch         \
                                       44/79
    Installing       : perl-constant-1.33-461.el9.noarch     \
                                       45/79
    Installing       : perl-Getopt-Std-1.12-479.el9.noarch \
                                       46/79
    Installing       : perl-overload-1.31-479.el9.noarch     \
                                       47/79
    Installing       : perl-Scalar-List-Utils-4:1.56-461.el\
9.x86_64                               48/79
    Installing       : perl-Errno-1.30-479.el9.x86_64        \
                                       49/79
    Installing       : perl-Storable-1:3.21-460.el9.x86_64 \
                                       50/79
    Installing       : perl-MIME-Base64-3.16-4.el9.x86_64    \
                                       51/79
    Installing       : perl-Getopt-Long-1:2.52-4.el9.noarch\
                                       52/79
    Installing       : perl-Exporter-5.74-461.el9.noarch     \
                                       53/79
    Installing       : perl-Carp-1.50-460.el9.noarch         \
                                       54/79
    Installing       : perl-NDBM_File-1.15-479.el9.x86_64    \
                                       55/79
    Installing       : perl-PathTools-3.78-461.el9.x86_64    \
                                       56/79
    Installing       : perl-Encode-4:3.08-462.el9.x86_64     \
                                       57/79
    Installing       : perl-libs-4:5.32.1-479.el9.x86_64     \
```

```
                                              58/79
   Installing      : perl-interpreter-4:5.32.1-479.el9.x8\
6_64                                          59/79
   Installing      : perl-File-Find-1.37-479.el9.noarch  \
                                              60/79
   Installing      : perl-Error-1:0.17029-7.el9.noarch   \
                                              61/79
   Installing      : perl-lib-0.65-479.el9.x86_64         \
                                              62/79
   Installing      : perl-DynaLoader-1.47-479.el9.x86_64 \
                                              63/79
   Installing      : perl-TermReadKey-2.38-11.el9.x86_64 \
                                              64/79
   Installing      : perl-Git-2.31.1-2.el9.2.noarch       \
                                              65/79
   Installing      : git-2.31.1-2.el9.2.x86_64            \
                                              66/79
   Installing      : sshpass-1.09-4.el9.x86_64            \
                                              67/79
   Installing      : python3-markupsafe-1.1.1-12.el9.x86_\
64                                            68/79
   Installing      : python3-resolvelib-0.5.4-5.el9.noarc\
h                                             69/79
   Installing      : python3-ply-3.11-13.el9.noarch       \
                                              70/79
   Installing      : python3-pycparser-2.20-5.el9.noarch \
                                              71/79
   Installing      : python3-cffi-1.14.5-4.el9.x86_64     \
                                              72/79
   Installing      : python3-cryptography-3.4.7-5.el9.x86\
_64                                           73/79
   Installing      : python3-pytz-2021.1-4.el9.noarch     \
                                              74/79
   Installing      : python3-babel-2.9.1-2.el9.noarch     \
                                              75/79
```

```
  Installing       : python3-jinja2-2.11.3-4.el9.noarch   \
                                76/79
  Installing       : python3-pyparsing-2.4.7-7.1.el9.noar\
ch                              77/79
  Installing       : python3-packaging-20.9-4.el9.noarch \
                                78/79
  Installing       : ansible-core-2.12.1-1.el9.x86_64     \
                                79/79
  Running scriptlet: ansible-core-2.12.1-1.el9.x86_64     \
                                79/79
  Verifying        : python3-pyparsing-2.4.7-7.1.el9.noar\
ch                               1/79
  Verifying        : perl-libnet-3.13-4.el9.noarch        \
                                 2/79
  Verifying        : perl-IPC-Open3-1.21-479.el9.noarch  \
                                 3/79
  Verifying        : perl-File-Basename-2.85-479.el9.noar\
ch                               4/79
  Verifying        : perl-Text-ParseWords-3.30-460.el9.no\
arch                             5/79
  Verifying        : perl-Pod-Perldoc-3.28.01-461.el9.noa\
rch                              6/79
  Verifying        : python3-pytz-2021.1-4.el9.noarch     \
                                 7/79
  Verifying        : perl-IO-Socket-SSL-2.070-6.el9.noarc\
h                                8/79
  Verifying        : perl-Getopt-Long-1:2.52-4.el9.noarch\
                                 9/79
  Verifying        : perl-Class-Struct-0.66-479.el9.noarc\
h                               10/79
  Verifying        : perl-File-Find-1.37-479.el9.noarch  \
                                11/79
  Verifying        : perl-Digest-1.19-4.el9.noarch        \
                                12/79
  Verifying        : perl-Mozilla-CA-20200520-6.el9.noarc\
```

```
  h                                                 13/79
    Verifying        : perl-overload-1.31-479.el9.noarch      \
                                                   14/79
    Verifying        : git-core-doc-2.31.1-2.el9.2.noarch   \
                                                   15/79
    Verifying        : perl-Term-Cap-1.17-460.el9.noarch    \
                                                   16/79
    Verifying        : perl-parent-1:0.238-460.el9.noarch   \
                                                   17/79
    Verifying        : perl-if-0.60.800-479.el9.noarch      \
                                                   18/79
    Verifying        : perl-File-stat-1.09-479.el9.noarch   \
                                                   19/79
    Verifying        : perl-Term-ANSIColor-5.01-461.el9.noa\
  rch                                              20/79
    Verifying        : perl-subs-1.03-479.el9.noarch        \
                                                   21/79
    Verifying        : perl-Error-1:0.17029-7.el9.noarch    \
                                                   22/79
    Verifying        : perl-HTTP-Tiny-0.076-460.el9.noarch  \
                                                   23/79
    Verifying        : perl-SelectSaver-1.02-479.el9.noarch\
                                                   24/79
    Verifying        : perl-Exporter-5.74-461.el9.noarch    \
                                                   25/79
    Verifying        : perl-vars-1.05-479.el9.noarch        \
                                                   26/79
    Verifying        : perl-Carp-1.50-460.el9.noarch        \
                                                   27/79
    Verifying        : perl-Symbol-1.08-479.el9.noarch      \
                                                   28/79
    Verifying        : perl-overloading-0.02-479.el9.noarch\
                                                   29/79
    Verifying        : perl-Fcntl-1.13-479.el9.x86_64       \
                                                   30/79
```

```
  Verifying        : perl-AutoLoader-5.74-479.el9.noarch \
                              31/79
  Verifying        : perl-File-Temp-1:0.231.100-4.el9.noa\
rch                           32/79
  Verifying        : perl-File-Path-2.18-4.el9.noarch    \
                              33/79
  Verifying        : perl-Pod-Simple-1:3.42-4.el9.noarch \
                              34/79
  Verifying        : perl-Pod-Escapes-1:1.07-460.el9.noar\
ch                            35/79
  Verifying        : python3-ply-3.11-13.el9.noarch      \
                              36/79
  Verifying        : perl-Git-2.31.1-2.el9.2.noarch      \
                              37/79
  Verifying        : python3-resolvelib-0.5.4-5.el9.noarc\
h                             38/79
  Verifying        : perl-IO-Socket-IP-0.41-5.el9.noarch \
                              39/79
  Verifying        : perl-FileHandle-2.03-479.el9.noarch \
                              40/79
  Verifying        : perl-Text-Tabs+Wrap-2013.0523-460.el\
9.noarch                      41/79
  Verifying        : python3-pycparser-2.20-5.el9.noarch \
                              42/79
  Verifying        : perl-constant-1.33-461.el9.noarch   \
                              43/79
  Verifying        : perl-URI-5.09-3.el9.noarch          \
                              44/79
  Verifying        : python3-jinja2-2.11.3-4.el9.noarch  \
                              45/79
  Verifying        : perl-Pod-Usage-4:2.01-4.el9.noarch  \
                              46/79
  Verifying        : perl-Time-Local-2:1.300-7.el9.noarch\
                              47/79
  Verifying        : python3-babel-2.9.1-2.el9.noarch    \
```

```
                                                    48/79
  Verifying        : perl-base-2.27-479.el9.noarch          \
                                                    49/79
  Verifying        : perl-podlators-1:4.14-460.el9.noarch\
                                                    50/79
  Verifying        : perl-Getopt-Std-1.12-479.el9.noarch \
                                                    51/79
  Verifying        : python3-packaging-20.9-4.el9.noarch \
                                                    52/79
  Verifying        : perl-mro-1.23-479.el9.x86_64          \
                                                    53/79
  Verifying        : perl-Storable-1:3.21-460.el9.x86_64 \
                                                    54/79
  Verifying        : perl-IO-1.43-479.el9.x86_64           \
                                                    55/79
  Verifying        : perl-Scalar-List-Utils-4:1.56-461.el\
9.x86_64                                             56/79
  Verifying        : perl-Net-SSLeay-1.90-8.el9.x86_64   \
                                                    57/79
  Verifying        : perl-interpreter-4:5.32.1-479.el9.x8\
6_64                                                58/79
  Verifying        : python3-markupsafe-1.1.1-12.el9.x86_\
64                                                  59/79
  Verifying        : perl-Errno-1.30-479.el9.x86_64        \
                                                    60/79
  Verifying        : perl-Digest-MD5-2.58-4.el9.x86_64    \
                                                    61/79
  Verifying        : sshpass-1.09-4.el9.x86_64             \
                                                    62/79
  Verifying        : perl-lib-0.65-479.el9.x86_64          \
                                                    63/79
  Verifying        : perl-TermReadKey-2.38-11.el9.x86_64 \
                                                    64/79
  Verifying        : perl-Socket-4:2.031-4.el9.x86_64      \
                                                    65/79
```

```
    Verifying           : perl-NDBM_File-1.15-479.el9.x86_64    \
                                 66/79
    Verifying           : perl-Encode-4:3.08-462.el9.x86_64     \
                                 67/79
    Verifying           : perl-libs-4:5.32.1-479.el9.x86_64     \
                                 68/79
    Verifying           : perl-POSIX-1.94-479.el9.x86_64        \
                                 69/79
    Verifying           : perl-B-1.80-479.el9.x86_64            \
                                 70/79
    Verifying           : git-core-2.31.1-2.el9.2.x86_64        \
                                 71/79
    Verifying           : perl-PathTools-3.78-461.el9.x86_64    \
                                 72/79
    Verifying           : perl-MIME-Base64-3.16-4.el9.x86_64    \
                                 73/79
    Verifying           : python3-cffi-1.14.5-4.el9.x86_64      \
                                 74/79
    Verifying           : perl-Data-Dumper-2.174-462.el9.x86_6\
4                                75/79
    Verifying           : git-2.31.1-2.el9.2.x86_64             \
                                 76/79
    Verifying           : python3-cryptography-3.4.7-5.el9.x86\
_64                              77/79
    Verifying           : perl-DynaLoader-1.47-479.el9.x86_64 \
                                 78/79
    Verifying           : ansible-core-2.12.1-1.el9.x86_64      \
                                 79/79
Installed products updated.
Installed:
  ansible-core-2.12.1-1.el9.x86_64                       git-2.\
31.1-2.el9.2.x86_64
  git-core-2.31.1-2.el9.2.x86_64                         git-co\
re-doc-2.31.1-2.el9.2.noarch
  perl-AutoLoader-5.74-479.el9.noarch                    perl-B\
```

```
797   -1.80-479.el9.x86_64
798      perl-Carp-1.50-460.el9.noarch                          perl-C\
799   lass-Struct-0.66-479.el9.noarch
800      perl-Data-Dumper-2.174-462.el9.x86_64                  perl-D\
801   igest-1.19-4.el9.noarch
802      perl-Digest-MD5-2.58-4.el9.x86_64                      perl-D\
803   ynaLoader-1.47-479.el9.x86_64
804      perl-Encode-4:3.08-462.el9.x86_64                      perl-E\
805   rrno-1.30-479.el9.x86_64
806      perl-Error-1:0.17029-7.el9.noarch                      perl-E\
807   xporter-5.74-461.el9.noarch
808      perl-Fcntl-1.13-479.el9.x86_64                         perl-F\
809   ile-Basename-2.85-479.el9.noarch
810      perl-File-Find-1.37-479.el9.noarch                     perl-F\
811   ile-Path-2.18-4.el9.noarch
812      perl-File-Temp-1:0.231.100-4.el9.noarch                perl-F\
813   ile-stat-1.09-479.el9.noarch
814      perl-FileHandle-2.03-479.el9.noarch                    perl-G\
815   etopt-Long-1:2.52-4.el9.noarch
816      perl-Getopt-Std-1.12-479.el9.noarch                    perl-G\
817   it-2.31.1-2.el9.2.noarch
818      perl-HTTP-Tiny-0.076-460.el9.noarch                    perl-I\
819   0-1.43-479.el9.x86_64
820      perl-IO-Socket-IP-0.41-5.el9.noarch                    perl-I\
821   0-Socket-SSL-2.070-6.el9.noarch
822      perl-IPC-Open3-1.21-479.el9.noarch                     perl-M\
823   IME-Base64-3.16-4.el9.x86_64
824      perl-Mozilla-CA-20200520-6.el9.noarch                  perl-N\
825   DBM_File-1.15-479.el9.x86_64
826      perl-Net-SSLeay-1.90-8.el9.x86_64                      perl-P\
827   OSIX-1.94-479.el9.x86_64
828      perl-PathTools-3.78-461.el9.x86_64                     perl-P\
829   od-Escapes-1:1.07-460.el9.noarch
830      perl-Pod-Perldoc-3.28.01-461.el9.noarch                perl-P\
831   od-Simple-1:3.42-4.el9.noarch
```

```
832     perl-Pod-Usage-4:2.01-4.el9.noarch                    perl-S\
833  calar-List-Utils-4:1.56-461.el9.x86_64
834     perl-SelectSaver-1.02-479.el9.noarch                  perl-S\
835  ocket-4:2.031-4.el9.x86_64
836     perl-Storable-1:3.21-460.el9.x86_64                   perl-S\
837  ymbol-1.08-479.el9.noarch
838     perl-Term-ANSIColor-5.01-461.el9.noarch               perl-T\
839  erm-Cap-1.17-460.el9.noarch
840     perl-TermReadKey-2.38-11.el9.x86_64                   perl-T\
841  ext-ParseWords-3.30-460.el9.noarch
842     perl-Text-Tabs+Wrap-2013.0523-460.el9.noarch          perl-T\
843  ime-Local-2:1.300-7.el9.noarch
844     perl-URI-5.09-3.el9.noarch                            perl-b\
845  ase-2.27-479.el9.noarch
846     perl-constant-1.33-461.el9.noarch                     perl-i\
847  f-0.60.800-479.el9.noarch
848     perl-interpreter-4:5.32.1-479.el9.x86_64              perl-l\
849  ib-0.65-479.el9.x86_64
850     perl-libnet-3.13-4.el9.noarch                         perl-l\
851  ibs-4:5.32.1-479.el9.x86_64
852     perl-mro-1.23-479.el9.x86_64                          perl-o\
853  verload-1.31-479.el9.noarch
854     perl-overloading-0.02-479.el9.noarch                  perl-p\
855  arent-1:0.238-460.el9.noarch
856     perl-podlators-1:4.14-460.el9.noarch                  perl-s\
857  ubs-1.03-479.el9.noarch
858     perl-vars-1.05-479.el9.noarch                         python\
859  3-babel-2.9.1-2.el9.noarch
860     python3-cffi-1.14.5-4.el9.x86_64                      python\
861  3-cryptography-3.4.7-5.el9.x86_64
862     python3-jinja2-2.11.3-4.el9.noarch                    python\
863  3-markupsafe-1.1.1-12.el9.x86_64
864     python3-packaging-20.9-4.el9.noarch                   python\
865  3-ply-3.11-13.el9.noarch
866     python3-pycparser-2.20-5.el9.noarch                   python\
```

```
3-pyparsing-2.4.7-7.1.el9.noarch
   python3-pytz-2021.1-4.el9.noarch                          python\
3-resolvelib-0.5.4-5.el9.noarch
   sshpass-1.09-4.el9.x86_64
Complete!
[root@localhost devops]# ansible --version
ansible [core 2.12.1]
  config file = /etc/ansible/ansible.cfg
  configured module search path = ['/root/.ansible/plugin\
s/modules', '/usr/share/ansible/plugins/modules']
  ansible python module location = /usr/lib/python3.9/sit\
e-packages/ansible
  ansible collection location = /root/.ansible/collection\
s:/usr/share/ansible/collections
  executable location = /bin/ansible
  python version = 3.9.9 (main, Nov 22 2021, 00:00:00) [G\
CC 11.2.1 20211019 (Red Hat 11.2.1-6)]
  jinja version = 2.11.3
  libyaml = True
[root@localhost devops]# dnf info ansible-core
Updating Subscription Management repositories.
Last metadata expiration check: 1:42:32 ago on Fri 21 Jan\
 2022 04:15:49 PM CET.
Installed Packages
Name         : ansible-core
Version      : 2.12.1
Release      : 1.el9
Architecture : x86_64
Size         : 9.3 M
Source       : ansible-core-2.12.1-1.el9.src.rpm
Repository   : @System
From repo    : rhel-9-for-x86_64-appstream-beta-rpms
Summary      : SSH-based configuration management, deploy\
ment, and task execution system
URL          : http://ansible.com
```

```
902   License        : GPLv3+
903   Description    : Ansible is a radically simple model-driven\
904     configuration management,
905                  : multi-node deployment, and remote task exe\
906   cution system. Ansible works
907                  : over SSH and does not require any software\
908     or daemons to be installed
909                  : on remote nodes. Extension modules can be \
910   written in any language and
911                  : are transferred to managed machines automa\
912   tically.
913   [root@localhost devops]#
```

before execution

```
1    # dnf info ansible-core
2    Updating Subscription Management repositories.
3    Last metadata expiration check: 1:41:06 ago on Fri 21 Jan\
4     2022 04:15:49 PM CET.
5    Available Packages
6    Name          : ansible-core
7    Version       : 2.12.1
8    Release       : 1.el9
9    Architecture  : x86_64
10   Size          : 2.4 M
11   Source        : ansible-core-2.12.1-1.el9.src.rpm
12   Repository    : rhel-9-for-x86_64-appstream-beta-rpms
13   Summary       : SSH-based configuration management, deploy\
14   ment, and task execution system
15   URL           : http://ansible.com
16   License       : GPLv3+
17   Description   : Ansible is a radically simple model-driven\
18     configuration management,
19                 : multi-node deployment, and remote task exe\
20   cution system. Ansible works
21                 : over SSH and does not require any software\
```

```
22    or daemons to be installed
23                    : on remote nodes. Extension modules can be \
24    written in any language and
25                    : are transferred to managed machines automa\
26    tically.
27    [root@localhost devops]#
```

after execution

```
1   # dnf info ansible-core
2   Updating Subscription Management repositories.
3   Last metadata expiration check: 1:42:32 ago on Fri 21 Jan\
4    2022 04:15:49 PM CET.
5   Installed Packages
6   Name         : ansible-core
7   Version      : 2.12.1
8   Release      : 1.el9
9   Architecture : x86_64
10  Size         : 9.3 M
11  Source       : ansible-core-2.12.1-1.el9.src.rpm
12  Repository   : @System
13  From repo    : rhel-9-for-x86_64-appstream-beta-rpms
14  Summary      : SSH-based configuration management, deploy\
15  ment, and task execution system
16  URL          : http://ansible.com
17  License      : GPLv3+
18  Description  : Ansible is a radically simple model-driven\
19   configuration management,
20                : multi-node deployment, and remote task exe\
21  cution system. Ansible works
22                : over SSH and does not require any software\
23   or daemons to be installed
24                : on remote nodes. Extension modules can be \
25  written in any language and
26                : are transferred to managed machines automa\
27  tically.
```

```
28  [root@localhost devops]#
```

How to install Ansible in Amazon Linux 2 (AWS EC2)

How to install Ansible in Amazon Linux 2 using the Amazon Extras Library "amazon-linux-extras" and the EPEL (Extra Packages for Enterprise Linux) repositories.

The easier way to install and maintain Ansible inside Amazon Linux 2 are using the **Amazon Extras Library** and **EPEL** repositories.

How to install Ansible in Amazon Linux 2

- `ansible2` topic in Extras Library repository
- `ansible` in Extra Packages for Enterprise Linux (EPEL) additional packages for Enterprise Linux: Red Hat Enterprise Linux (RHEL), Rocky Linux and Scientific Linux (SL), Oracle Linux (OL), and Amazon Linux

The good news is that Ansible is included in the Extras Library included in Amazon Linux 2 repository using the "amazon-linux-extras" command.

Another option is to install and maintain Ansible inside Amazon Linux 2 is using the Extra Packages for Enterprise Linux (EPEL) additional repository.

This repository is maintained by the Fedora Special Interest Group and manages a high-quality set of additional packages for Enterprise Linux: Red Hat Enterprise Linux (RHEL), Rocky Linux and Scientific Linux (SL), Oracle Linux (OL), and Amazon Linux.

Links

- Amazon Linux 2[23]
- How do I enable the EPEL repository for my Amazon EC2 instance running CentOS, RHEL, or Amazon Linux?[24]
- Extras library (Amazon Linux 2)[25]
- Extra Packages for Enterprise Linux (EPEL)[26]

demo

How to install Ansible in Amazon Linux (EC2) 2 using the Amazon Extras Library and EPEL repositories.

Amazon Extras Library code

- Install-Ansible-Amazon Linux2-Amazon Extras Library.sh

```
1  #!/bin/bash
2  $ sudo yum update -y
3  $ sudo amazon-linux-extras install ansible2 -y
4  $ ansible --version
```

Amazon Extras Library execution

---

[23]https://aws.amazon.com/it/amazon-linux-2/

[24]https://aws.amazon.com/it/premiumsupport/knowledge-center/ec2-enable-epel/

[25]https://docs.aws.amazon.com/AWSEC2/latest/UserGuide/amazon-linux-ami-basics.html#extras-library

[26]https://docs.fedoraproject.org/en-US/epel/

```
$ ssh -i key.pem ec2-user@34.241.249.206


      __|  __|_  )
      _|  (     /   Amazon Linux 2 AMI
      ___|\___|___|

https://aws.amazon.com/amazon-linux-2/
-bash: warning: setlocale: LC_CTYPE: cannot change locale\
 (UTF-8): No such file or directory
[ec2-user@ip-172-31-36-49 ~]$ sudo su
[root@ip-172-31-36-49 ec2-user]# cat /etc/image-id
image_name="amzn2-ami-kernel-5.10-hvm"
image_version="2"
image_arch="x86_64"
image_file="amzn2-ami-kernel-5.10-hvm-2.0.20211201.0-x86_\
64.xfs.gpt"
image_stamp="7143-c998"
image_date="20211201182203"
recipe_name="amzn2 ami"
recipe_id="d46c60d3-613d-8f76-a3cd-4476-405e-a3e2-088c722\
9"
[root@ip-172-31-36-49 ec2-user]# cat /etc/os-release
NAME="Amazon Linux"
VERSION="2"
ID="amzn"
ID_LIKE="centos rhel fedora"
VERSION_ID="2"
PRETTY_NAME="Amazon Linux 2"
ANSI_COLOR="0;33"
CPE_NAME="cpe:2.3:o:amazon:amazon_linux:2"
HOME_URL="https://amazonlinux.com/"
[root@ip-172-31-36-49 ec2-user]# cat /etc/os-release
NAME="Amazon Linux"
VERSION="2"
ID="amzn"
```

```
36   ID_LIKE="centos rhel fedora"
37   VERSION_ID="2"
38   PRETTY_NAME="Amazon Linux 2"
39   ANSI_COLOR="0;33"
40   CPE_NAME="cpe:2.3:o:amazon:amazon_linux:2"
41   HOME_URL="https://amazonlinux.com/"
42   [root@ip-172-31-36-49 ec2-user]# yum update
43   Failed to set locale, defaulting to C
44   Loaded plugins: extras_suggestions, langpacks, priorities\
45   , update-motd
46   amzn2-core                                              \
47                      | 3.7 kB  00:00:00
48   amzn2extra-docker                                       \
49                      | 3.0 kB  00:00:00
50   amzn2extra-kernel-5.10                                  \
51                      | 3.0 kB  00:00:00
52   No packages marked for update
53   [root@ip-172-31-36-49 ec2-user]# amazon-linux-extras inst\
54   all ansible2
55   Installing ansible
56   Failed to set locale, defaulting to C
57   Loaded plugins: extras_suggestions, langpacks, priorities\
58   , update-motd
59   Cleaning repos: amzn2-core amzn2extra-ansible2 amzn2extra\
60   -docker amzn2extra-kernel-5.10
61   17 metadata files removed
62   6 sqlite files removed
63   0 metadata files removed
64   Failed to set locale, defaulting to C
65   Loaded plugins: extras_suggestions, langpacks, priorities\
66   , update-motd
67   amzn2-core                                              \
68                      | 3.7 kB  00:00:00
69   amzn2extra-ansible2                                     \
70                      | 3.0 kB  00:00:00
```

```
 71  amzn2extra-docker                                              \
 72                          | 3.0 kB   00:00:00
 73  amzn2extra-kernel-5.10                                         \
 74                          | 3.0 kB   00:00:00
 75  (1/9): amzn2-core/2/x86_64/group_gz                            \
 76                          | 2.5 kB   00:00:00
 77  (2/9): amzn2-core/2/x86_64/updateinfo                          \
 78                          | 424 kB   00:00:00
 79  (3/9): amzn2extra-docker/2/x86_64/primary_db                   \
 80                          |  86 kB   00:00:00
 81  (4/9): amzn2extra-kernel-5.10/2/x86_64/updateinfo              \
 82                          |   76 B   00:00:00
 83  (5/9): amzn2extra-kernel-5.10/2/x86_64/primary_db              \
 84                          | 5.3 MB   00:00:00
 85  (6/9): amzn2extra-ansible2/2/x86_64/primary_db                 \
 86                          |  39 kB   00:00:00
 87  (7/9): amzn2extra-docker/2/x86_64/updateinfo                   \
 88                          | 4.7 kB   00:00:00
 89  (8/9): amzn2extra-ansible2/2/x86_64/updateinfo                 \
 90                          |   76 B   00:00:00
 91  (9/9): amzn2-core/2/x86_64/primary_db                          \
 92                          |  58 MB   00:00:00
 93  Resolving Dependencies
 94  --> Running transaction check
 95  ---> Package ansible.noarch 0:2.9.23-1.amzn2 will be inst\
 96  alled
 97  --> Processing Dependency: sshpass for package: ansible-2\
 98  .9.23-1.amzn2.noarch
 99  --> Processing Dependency: python-paramiko for package: a\
100  nsible-2.9.23-1.amzn2.noarch
101  --> Processing Dependency: python-keyczar for package: an\
102  sible-2.9.23-1.amzn2.noarch
103  --> Processing Dependency: python-httplib2 for package: a\
104  nsible-2.9.23-1.amzn2.noarch
105  --> Processing Dependency: python-crypto for package: ans\
```

```
106  ible-2.9.23-1.amzn2.noarch
107  --> Running transaction check
108  ---> Package python-keyczar.noarch 0:0.71c-2.amzn2 will b\
109  e installed
110  ---> Package python2-crypto.x86_64 0:2.6.1-13.amzn2.0.3 w\
111  ill be installed
112  --> Processing Dependency: libtomcrypt.so.1()(64bit) for \
113  package: python2-crypto-2.6.1-13.amzn2.0.3.x86_64
114  ---> Package python2-httplib2.noarch 0:0.18.1-3.amzn2 wil\
115  l be installed
116  ---> Package python2-paramiko.noarch 0:1.16.1-3.amzn2.0.2\
117   will be installed
118  --> Processing Dependency: python2-ecdsa for package: pyt\
119  hon2-paramiko-1.16.1-3.amzn2.0.2.noarch
120  ---> Package sshpass.x86_64 0:1.06-1.amzn2.0.1 will be in\
121  stalled
122  --> Running transaction check
123  ---> Package libtomcrypt.x86_64 0:1.18.2-1.amzn2.0.1 will\
124   be installed
125  --> Processing Dependency: libtommath >= 1.0 for package:\
126   libtomcrypt-1.18.2-1.amzn2.0.1.x86_64
127  --> Processing Dependency: libtommath.so.1()(64bit) for p\
128  ackage: libtomcrypt-1.18.2-1.amzn2.0.1.x86_64
129  ---> Package python2-ecdsa.noarch 0:0.13.3-1.amzn2.0.1 wi\
130  ll be installed
131  --> Running transaction check
132  ---> Package libtommath.x86_64 0:1.0.1-4.amzn2.0.1 will b\
133  e installed
134  --> Finished Dependency Resolution
135  Dependencies Resolved
136  ==================================================================\
137  ===========================================
138   Package                 Arch            Version             \
139           Repository                 Size
140  ==================================================================\
```

```
141   ====================================================
142   Installing:
143    ansible                      noarch           2.9.23-1.amzn2      \
144           amzn2extra-ansible2         17 M
145   Installing for dependencies:
146    libtomcrypt                  x86_64           1.18.2-1.amzn2.0.1\
147           amzn2extra-ansible2         409 k
148    libtommath                   x86_64           1.0.1-4.amzn2.0.1 \
149           amzn2extra-ansible2         36 k
150    python-keyczar               noarch           0.71c-2.amzn2       \
151           amzn2extra-ansible2         218 k
152    python2-crypto               x86_64           2.6.1-13.amzn2.0.3\
153           amzn2extra-ansible2         476 k
154    python2-ecdsa                noarch           0.13.3-1.amzn2.0.1\
155           amzn2extra-ansible2         94 k
156    python2-httplib2             noarch           0.18.1-3.amzn2      \
157           amzn2extra-ansible2         125 k
158    python2-paramiko             noarch           1.16.1-3.amzn2.0.2\
159           amzn2extra-ansible2         259 k
160    sshpass                      x86_64           1.06-1.amzn2.0.1  \
161           amzn2extra-ansible2         22 k
162   Transaction Summary
163   ===============================================================\
164   ===============================================
165   Install  1 Package (+8 Dependent packages)
166   Total download size: 19 M
167   Installed size: 110 M
168   Is this ok [y/d/N]: y
169   Downloading packages:
170   (1/9): libtomcrypt-1.18.2-1.amzn2.0.1.x86_64.rpm             \
171                   | 409 kB  00:00:00
172   (2/9): libtommath-1.0.1-4.amzn2.0.1.x86_64.rpm               \
173                   |  36 kB  00:00:00
174   (3/9): python-keyczar-0.71c-2.amzn2.noarch.rpm              \
175                   | 218 kB  00:00:00
```

```
(4/9): python2-crypto-2.6.1-13.amzn2.0.3.x86_64.rpm        \
                     | 476 kB  00:00:00
(5/9): ansible-2.9.23-1.amzn2.noarch.rpm                   \
                     |  17 MB  00:00:00
(6/9): python2-ecdsa-0.13.3-1.amzn2.0.1.noarch.rpm         \
                     |  94 kB  00:00:00
(7/9): python2-httplib2-0.18.1-3.amzn2.noarch.rpm          \
                     | 125 kB  00:00:00
(8/9): sshpass-1.06-1.amzn2.0.1.x86_64.rpm                 \
                     |  22 kB  00:00:00
(9/9): python2-paramiko-1.16.1-3.amzn2.0.2.noarch.rpm      \
                     | 259 kB  00:00:00
----------------------------------------------------------------\
-------------------------------------------
Total                                                      \
            44 MB/s |  19 MB  00:00:00
Running transaction check
Running transaction test
Transaction test succeeded
Running transaction
  Installing : sshpass-1.06-1.amzn2.0.1.x86_64             \
                                    1/9
  Installing : python2-httplib2-0.18.1-3.amzn2.noarch      \
                                    2/9
  Installing : libtommath-1.0.1-4.amzn2.0.1.x86_64         \
                                    3/9
  Installing : libtomcrypt-1.18.2-1.amzn2.0.1.x86_64       \
                                    4/9
  Installing : python2-crypto-2.6.1-13.amzn2.0.3.x86_64    \
                                    5/9
  Installing : python-keyczar-0.71c-2.amzn2.noarch         \
                                    6/9
  Installing : python2-ecdsa-0.13.3-1.amzn2.0.1.noarch     \
                                    7/9
  Installing : python2-paramiko-1.16.1-3.amzn2.0.2.noarch\
```

```
211                                              8/9
212    Installing : ansible-2.9.23-1.amzn2.noarch          \
213                                              9/9
214   Verifying  : python2-ecdsa-0.13.3-1.amzn2.0.1.noarch  \
215                                              1/9
216   Verifying  : libtommath-1.0.1-4.amzn2.0.1.x86_64       \
217                                              2/9
218   Verifying  : python2-crypto-2.6.1-13.amzn2.0.3.x86_64  \
219                                              3/9
220   Verifying  : ansible-2.9.23-1.amzn2.noarch             \
221                                              4/9
222   Verifying  : python-keyczar-0.71c-2.amzn2.noarch       \
223                                              5/9
224   Verifying  : libtomcrypt-1.18.2-1.amzn2.0.1.x86_64     \
225                                              6/9
226   Verifying  : python2-paramiko-1.16.1-3.amzn2.0.2.noarch\
227                                              7/9
228   Verifying  : python2-httplib2-0.18.1-3.amzn2.noarch    \
229                                              8/9
230   Verifying  : sshpass-1.06-1.amzn2.0.1.x86_64           \
231                                              9/9
232 Installed:
233   ansible.noarch 0:2.9.23-1.amzn2
234 Dependency Installed:
235   libtomcrypt.x86_64 0:1.18.2-1.amzn2.0.1              libto\
236 mmath.x86_64 0:1.0.1-4.amzn2.0.1
237   python-keyczar.noarch 0:0.71c-2.amzn2               pytho\
238 n2-crypto.x86_64 0:2.6.1-13.amzn2.0.3
239   python2-ecdsa.noarch 0:0.13.3-1.amzn2.0.1           pytho\
240 n2-httplib2.noarch 0:0.18.1-3.amzn2
241   python2-paramiko.noarch 0:1.16.1-3.amzn2.0.2        sshpa\
242 ss.x86_64 0:1.06-1.amzn2.0.1
243 Complete!
244   0  ansible2=latest           enabled        \
245          [ =2.4.2  =2.4.6  =2.8  =stable ]
```

```
    2  httpd_modules              available    [ =1.0  =stabl\
e ]
    3  memcached1.5               available    \
        [ =1.5.1  =1.5.16  =1.5.17 ]
    5  postgresql9.6              available    \
        [ =9.6.6  =9.6.8  =stable ]
    6  postgresql10               available    [ =10  =stable\
 ]
    9  R3.4                       available    [ =3.4.3  =sta\
ble ]
   10  rust1                      available    \
        [ =1.22.1  =1.26.0  =1.26.1  =1.27.2  =1.31.0  =1\
.38.0
            =stable ]
   11  vim                        available    [ =8.0  =stabl\
e ]
   15  php7.2                     available    \
        [ =7.2.0  =7.2.4  =7.2.5  =7.2.8  =7.2.11  =7.2.1\
3  =7.2.14
            =7.2.16  =7.2.17  =7.2.19  =7.2.21  =7.2.22  =7\
.2.23
            =7.2.24  =7.2.26  =stable ]
   17  lamp-mariadb10.2-php7.2  available    \
        [ =10.2.10_7.2.0  =10.2.10_7.2.4  =10.2.10_7.2.5
            =10.2.10_7.2.8  =10.2.10_7.2.11  =10.2.10_7.2.13
            =10.2.10_7.2.14  =10.2.10_7.2.16  =10.2.10_7.2.\
17
            =10.2.10_7.2.19  =10.2.10_7.2.22  =10.2.10_7.2.\
23
            =10.2.10_7.2.24  =stable ]
   18  libreoffice                available    \
        [ =5.0.6.2_15  =5.3.6.1  =stable ]
   19  gimp                       available    [ =2.8.22 ]
   20  docker=latest              enabled      \
        [ =17.12.1  =18.03.1  =18.06.1  =18.09.9  =stable\
```

```
281     ]
282     21  mate-desktop1.x          available     \
283          [ =1.19.0  =1.20.0  =stable ]
284     22  GraphicsMagick1.3        available     \
285          [ =1.3.29  =1.3.32  =1.3.34  =stable ]
286     23  tomcat8.5                available     \
287          [ =8.5.31   =8.5.32   =8.5.38   =8.5.40   =8.5.42   =8\
288  .5.50
289             =stable ]
290     24  epel                     available     [ =7.11   =stab\
291  le ]
292     25  testing                  available     [ =1.0   =stabl\
293  e ]
294     26  ecs                      available     [ =stable ]
295     27  corretto8                available     \
296         [ =1.8.0_192  =1.8.0_202  =1.8.0_212  =1.8.0_222 \
297     =1.8.0_232
298            =1.8.0_242  =stable ]
299     28  firecracker              available     [ =0.11   =stab\
300  le ]
301     29  golang1.11               available     \
302          [ =1.11.3  =1.11.11  =1.11.13  =stable ]
303     30  squid4                   available     [ =4  =stable ]
304     31  php7.3                   available     \
305          [ =7.3.2  =7.3.3  =7.3.4  =7.3.6  =7.3.8  =7.3.9 \
306     =7.3.10
307            =7.3.11  =7.3.13  =stable ]
308     32  lustre2.10               available     \
309          [ =2.10.5  =2.10.8  =stable ]
310     33  java-openjdk11           available     [ =11  =stable\
311     ]
312     34  lynis                    available     [ =stable ]
313     35  kernel-ng                available     [ =stable ]
314     36  BCC                      available     [ =0.x  =stabl\
315  e ]
```

```
 37  mono                    available    [ =5.x  =stabl\
e ]
 38  nginx1                  available    [ =stable ]
 39  ruby2.6                 available    [ =2.6  =stabl\
e ]
 40  mock                    available    [ =stable ]
 41  postgresql11            available    [ =11  =stable\
 ]
 42  php7.4                  available    [ =stable ]
 43  livepatch               available    [ =stable ]
 44  python3.8               available    [ =stable ]
 45  haproxy2                available    [ =stable ]
 46  collectd                available    [ =stable ]
 47  aws-nitro-enclaves-cli  available    [ =stable ]
 48  R4                      available    [ =stable ]
  _  kernel-5.4              available    [ =stable ]
 50  selinux-ng              available    [ =stable ]
 51  php8.0                  available    [ =stable ]
 52  tomcat9                 available    [ =stable ]
 53  unbound1.13             available    [ =stable ]
 54  mariadb10.5             available    [ =stable ]
 55  kernel-5.10=latest      enabled      [ =stable ]
 56  redis6                  available    [ =stable ]
 57  ruby3.0                 available    [ =stable ]
 58  postgresql12            available    [ =stable ]
 59  postgresql13            available    [ =stable ]
 60  mock2                   available    [ =stable ]
 61  dnsmasq2.85             available    [ =stable ]
[root@ip-172-31-36-49 ec2-user]# ansible --version
ansible 2.9.23
  config file = /etc/ansible/ansible.cfg
  configured module search path = [u'/root/.ansible/plugi\
ns/modules', u'/usr/share/ansible/plugins/modules']
  ansible python module location = /usr/lib/python2.7/sit\
e-packages/ansible
```

```
351    executable location = /bin/ansible
352    python version = 2.7.18 (default, Jun 10 2021, 00:11:02\
353    ) [GCC 7.3.1 20180712 (Red Hat 7.3.1-13)]
354    [root@ip-172-31-36-49 ec2-user]# rpm -qa | grep ansible
355    ansible-2.9.23-1.amzn2.noarch
356    [root@ip-172-31-36-49 ec2-user]#
```

Amazon Extras Library after execution

```
1    # rpm -qa | grep ansible
2    ansible-2.9.23-1.amzn2.noarch
```

EPEL code

- Install-Ansible-Amazon Linux2-EPEL.sh

```
1    #!/bin/bash
2    $ sudo amazon-linux-extras install epel -y
3    $ sudo yum repolist
4    $ sudo yum-config-manager --enable epel
5    $ sudo amazon-linux-extras disable ansible2
6    $ sudo yum --enablerepo epel install ansible
7    $ ansible --version
```

EPEL execution

```
# yum remove ansible
Failed to set locale, defaulting to C
Loaded plugins: extras_suggestions, langpacks, priorities\
, update-motd
Resolving Dependencies
--> Running transaction check
---> Package ansible.noarch 0:2.9.23-1.amzn2 will be eras\
ed
--> Finished Dependency Resolution
Dependencies Resolved
====================================================================\
=========================================
 Package              Arch              Version               \
     Repository                  Size
====================================================================\
=========================================
Removing:
 ansible              noarch            2.9.23-1.amzn2        \
      @amzn2extra-ansible2        105 M
Transaction Summary
====================================================================\
=========================================
Remove  1 Package
Installed size: 105 M
Is this ok [y/N]: y
Downloading packages:
Running transaction check
Running transaction test
Transaction test succeeded
Running transaction
  Erasing    : ansible-2.9.23-1.amzn2.noarch                 \
                               1/1
  Verifying  : ansible-2.9.23-1.amzn2.noarch                 \
                               1/1
Removed:
```

```
36      ansible.noarch 0:2.9.23-1.amzn2
37   Complete!
38   [root@ip-172-31-36-49 ec2-user]# amazon-linux-extras inst\
39   all epel
40   Installing epel-release
41   Failed to set locale, defaulting to C
42   Loaded plugins: extras_suggestions, langpacks, priorities\
43   , update-motd
44   Cleaning repos: amzn2-core amzn2extra-ansible2 amzn2extra\
45   -docker amzn2extra-epel
46                   : amzn2extra-kernel-5.10
47   22 metadata files removed
48   8 sqlite files removed
49   0 metadata files removed
50   Failed to set locale, defaulting to C
51   Loaded plugins: extras_suggestions, langpacks, priorities\
52   , update-motd
53   amzn2-core                                              \
54                        | 3.7 kB  00:00:00
55   amzn2extra-ansible2                                     \
56                        | 3.0 kB  00:00:00
57   amzn2extra-docker                                       \
58                        | 3.0 kB  00:00:00
59   amzn2extra-epel                                         \
60                        | 3.0 kB  00:00:00
61   amzn2extra-kernel-5.10                                  \
62                        | 3.0 kB  00:00:00
63   (1/11): amzn2-core/2/x86_64/group_gz                    \
64                        | 2.5 kB  00:00:00
65   (2/11): amzn2-core/2/x86_64/updateinfo                  \
66                        | 424 kB  00:00:00
67   (3/11): amzn2extra-docker/2/x86_64/primary_db           \
68                        |  86 kB  00:00:00
69   (4/11): amzn2extra-epel/2/x86_64/updateinfo             \
70                        |  76 B  00:00:00
```

```
(5/11): amzn2extra-epel/2/x86_64/primary_db                        \
                        | 1.8 kB  00:00:00
(6/11): amzn2extra-kernel-5.10/2/x86_64/updateinfo                 \
                        |   76 B  00:00:00
(7/11): amzn2extra-kernel-5.10/2/x86_64/primary_db                 \
                        | 5.3 MB  00:00:00
(8/11): amzn2extra-ansible2/2/x86_64/updateinfo                    \
                        |   76 B  00:00:00
(9/11): amzn2extra-docker/2/x86_64/updateinfo                      \
                        | 4.7 kB  00:00:00
(10/11): amzn2extra-ansible2/2/x86_64/primary_db                   \
                        |  39 kB  00:00:00
(11/11): amzn2-core/2/x86_64/primary_db                            \
                        |  58 MB  00:00:00
Resolving Dependencies
--> Running transaction check
---> Package epel-release.noarch 0:7-11 will be installed
--> Finished Dependency Resolution
Dependencies Resolved

================================================================\

=================================================

 Package                    Arch             Version        \
         Repository                  Size

================================================================\

=================================================

Installing:
 epel-release               noarch           7-11           \
         amzn2extra-epel            15 k
Transaction Summary

================================================================\

=================================================

Install  1 Package
Total download size: 15 k
Installed size: 24 k
Is this ok [y/d/N]: y
```

```
106  Downloading packages:
107  epel-release-7-11.noarch.rpm                              \
108                      |  15 kB  00:00:00
109  Running transaction check
110  Running transaction test
111  Transaction test succeeded
112  Running transaction
113    Installing : epel-release-7-11.noarch                   \
114                                          1/1
115    Verifying  : epel-release-7-11.noarch                   \
116                                          1/1
117  Installed:
118    epel-release.noarch 0:7-11
119  Complete!
120   0  ansible2=latest          enabled       \
121        [ =2.4.2  =2.4.6  =2.8  =stable ]
122   2  httpd_modules            available   [ =1.0  =stabl\
123  e ]
124   3  memcached1.5             available     \
125        [ =1.5.1  =1.5.16  =1.5.17 ]
126   5  postgresql9.6            available     \
127        [ =9.6.6  =9.6.8  =stable ]
128   6  postgresql10             available   [ =10  =stable\
129  ]
130   9  R3.4                     available   [ =3.4.3  =sta\
131  ble ]
132  10  rust1                    available     \
133        [ =1.22.1  =1.26.0  =1.26.1  =1.27.2  =1.31.0  =1\
134  .38.0
135            =stable ]
136  11  vim                      available   [ =8.0  =stabl\
137  e ]
138  15  php7.2                   available     \
139        [ =7.2.0  =7.2.4  =7.2.5  =7.2.8  =7.2.11  =7.2.1\
140  3  =7.2.14
```

```
141              =7.2.16  =7.2.17  =7.2.19  =7.2.21  =7.2.22  =7\
142 .2.23
143              =7.2.24  =7.2.26  =stable ]
144   17  lamp-mariadb10.2-php7.2  available      \
145         [ =10.2.10_7.2.0  =10.2.10_7.2.4  =10.2.10_7.2.5
146           =10.2.10_7.2.8  =10.2.10_7.2.11  =10.2.10_7.2.13
147           =10.2.10_7.2.14  =10.2.10_7.2.16  =10.2.10_7.2.\
148 17
149           =10.2.10_7.2.19  =10.2.10_7.2.22  =10.2.10_7.2.\
150 23
151           =10.2.10_7.2.24  =stable ]
152   18  libreoffice              available    \
153         [ =5.0.6.2_15  =5.3.6.1  =stable ]
154   19  gimp                     available    [ =2.8.22 ]
155   20  docker=latest            enabled      \
156         [ =17.12.1  =18.03.1  =18.06.1  =18.09.9  =stable\
157 ]
158   21  mate-desktop1.x          available    \
159         [ =1.19.0  =1.20.0  =stable ]
160   22  GraphicsMagick1.3        available    \
161         [ =1.3.29  =1.3.32  =1.3.34  =stable ]
162   23  tomcat8.5                available    \
163         [ =8.5.31  =8.5.32  =8.5.38  =8.5.40  =8.5.42  =8\
164 .5.50
165           =stable ]
166   24  epel=latest              enabled      [ =7.11  =stab\
167 le ]
168   25  testing                  available    [ =1.0  =stabl\
169 e ]
170   26  ecs                      available    [ =stable ]
171   27  corretto8                available    \
172         [ =1.8.0_192  =1.8.0_202  =1.8.0_212  =1.8.0_222  \
173   =1.8.0_232
174           =1.8.0_242  =stable ]
175   28  firecracker              available    [ =0.11  =stab\
```

```
176  le ]
177   29  golang1.11              available    \
178        [ =1.11.3  =1.11.11  =1.11.13  =stable ]
179   30  squid4                  available   [ =4  =stable ]
180   31  php7.3                  available    \
181        [ =7.3.2  =7.3.3  =7.3.4  =7.3.6  =7.3.8  =7.3.9 \
182   =7.3.10
183          =7.3.11  =7.3.13  =stable ]
184   32  lustre2.10              available    \
185        [ =2.10.5  =2.10.8  =stable ]
186   33  java-openjdk11          available   [ =11  =stable\
187   ]
188   34  lynis                   available   [ =stable ]
189   35  kernel-ng               available   [ =stable ]
190   36  BCC                     available   [ =0.x  =stabl\
191   e ]
192   37  mono                    available   [ =5.x  =stabl\
193   e ]
194   38  nginx1                  available   [ =stable ]
195   39  ruby2.6                 available   [ =2.6  =stabl\
196   e ]
197   40  mock                    available   [ =stable ]
198   41  postgresql11            available   [ =11  =stable\
199   ]
200   42  php7.4                  available   [ =stable ]
201   43  livepatch               available   [ =stable ]
202   44  python3.8               available   [ =stable ]
203   45  haproxy2                available   [ =stable ]
204   46  collectd                available   [ =stable ]
205   47  aws-nitro-enclaves-cli  available   [ =stable ]
206   48  R4                      available   [ =stable ]
207   _   kernel-5.4              available   [ =stable ]
208   50  selinux-ng              available   [ =stable ]
209   51  php8.0                  available   [ =stable ]
210   52  tomcat9                 available   [ =stable ]
```

```
53  unbound1.13              available    [ =stable ]
54  mariadb10.5              available    [ =stable ]
55  kernel-5.10=latest       enabled      [ =stable ]
56  redis6                   available    [ =stable ]
57  ruby3.0                  available    [ =stable ]
58  postgresql12             available    [ =stable ]
59  postgresql13             available    [ =stable ]
60  mock2                    available    [ =stable ]
61  dnsmasq2.85              available    [ =stable ]
[root@ip-172-31-36-49 ec2-user]# yum repolist
Failed to set locale, defaulting to C
Loaded plugins: extras_suggestions, langpacks, priorities\
, update-motd
Existing lock /var/run/yum.pid: another copy is running a\
s pid 4695.
Another app is currently holding the yum lock; waiting fo\
r it to exit...
  The other application is: yum
    Memory : 110 M RSS (402 MB VSZ)
    Started: Sun Dec  5 10:04:44 2021 - 00:09 ago
    State  : Running, pid: 4695
Another app is currently holding the yum lock; waiting fo\
r it to exit...
  The other application is: yum
    Memory : 273 M RSS (565 MB VSZ)
    Started: Sun Dec  5 10:04:44 2021 - 00:11 ago
    State  : Running, pid: 4695
Another app is currently holding the yum lock; waiting fo\
r it to exit...
  The other application is: yum
    Memory : 318 M RSS (610 MB VSZ)
    Started: Sun Dec  5 10:04:44 2021 - 00:13 ago
    State  : Running, pid: 4695
Another app is currently holding the yum lock; waiting fo\
r it to exit...
```

```
    The other application is: yum
       Memory : 322 M RSS (614 MB VSZ)
       Started: Sun Dec  5 10:04:44 2021 - 00:15 ago
       State  : Running, pid: 4695
225 packages excluded due to repository priority protecti\
ons
repo id                                    repo name              \
                                    status
amzn2-core/2/x86_64                        Amazon Linux 2 core \
repository                                 26819
amzn2extra-ansible2/2/x86_64               Amazon Extras repo f\
or ansible2                                  63
amzn2extra-docker/2/x86_64                 Amazon Extras repo f\
or docker                                    55
amzn2extra-epel/2/x86_64                   Amazon Extras repo f\
or epel                                       1
amzn2extra-kernel-5.10/2/x86_64            Amazon Extras repo f\
or kernel-5.10                               86
epel/x86_64                                Extra Packages for E\
nterprise Linux 7 - x86_64          13464+225
repolist: 40488
[root@ip-172-31-36-49 ec2-user]# amazon-linux-extras disa\
ble ansible2
Beware that disabling topics is not supported after they \
are installed.
  0  ansible2                 available   \
      [ =2.4.2  =2.4.6  =2.8  =stable ]
  2  httpd_modules            available   [ =1.0  =stabl\
e ]
  3  memcached1.5             available   \
      [ =1.5.1  =1.5.16  =1.5.17 ]
  5  postgresql9.6            available   \
      [ =9.6.6  =9.6.8  =stable ]
  6  postgresql10             available   [ =10  =stable\
 ]
```

```
 9  R3.4                      available    [ =3.4.3  =sta\
ble ]
10  rust1                     available    \
     [ =1.22.1  =1.26.0  =1.26.1  =1.27.2  =1.31.0  =1\
.38.0
        =stable ]
11  vim                       available    [ =8.0  =stabl\
e ]
15  php7.2                    available    \
     [ =7.2.0  =7.2.4  =7.2.5  =7.2.8  =7.2.11  =7.2.1\
3  =7.2.14
        =7.2.16  =7.2.17  =7.2.19  =7.2.21  =7.2.22  =7\
.2.23
        =7.2.24  =7.2.26  =stable ]
17  lamp-mariadb10.2-php7.2  available    \
     [ =10.2.10_7.2.0  =10.2.10_7.2.4  =10.2.10_7.2.5
        =10.2.10_7.2.8  =10.2.10_7.2.11  =10.2.10_7.2.13
        =10.2.10_7.2.14  =10.2.10_7.2.16  =10.2.10_7.2.\
17
        =10.2.10_7.2.19  =10.2.10_7.2.22  =10.2.10_7.2.\
23
        =10.2.10_7.2.24  =stable ]
18  libreoffice               available    \
     [ =5.0.6.2_15  =5.3.6.1  =stable ]
19  gimp                      available    [ =2.8.22 ]
20  docker=latest             enabled      \
     [ =17.12.1  =18.03.1  =18.06.1  =18.09.9  =stable\
]
21  mate-desktop1.x           available    \
     [ =1.19.0  =1.20.0  =stable ]
22  GraphicsMagick1.3         available    \
     [ =1.3.29  =1.3.32  =1.3.34  =stable ]
23  tomcat8.5                 available    \
     [ =8.5.31  =8.5.32  =8.5.38  =8.5.40  =8.5.42  =8\
.5.50
```

```
316              =stable ]
317    24   epel=latest                enabled        [ =7.11   =stab\
318  le ]
319    25   testing                    available      [ =1.0   =stabl\
320  e ]
321    26   ecs                        available      [ =stable ]
322    27   corretto8                  available      \
323         [ =1.8.0_192  =1.8.0_202  =1.8.0_212  =1.8.0_222 \
324    =1.8.0_232
325             =1.8.0_242  =stable ]
326    28   firecracker                available      [ =0.11   =stab\
327  le ]
328    29   golang1.11                 available      \
329         [ =1.11.3  =1.11.11  =1.11.13  =stable ]
330    30   squid4                     available      [ =4  =stable ]
331    31   php7.3                     available      \
332         [ =7.3.2  =7.3.3  =7.3.4  =7.3.6  =7.3.8  =7.3.9 \
333    =7.3.10
334             =7.3.11  =7.3.13  =stable ]
335    32   lustre2.10                 available      \
336         [ =2.10.5  =2.10.8  =stable ]
337    33   java-openjdk11             available      [ =11  =stable\
338  ]
339    34   lynis                      available      [ =stable ]
340    35   kernel-ng                  available      [ =stable ]
341    36   BCC                        available      [ =0.x   =stabl\
342  e ]
343    37   mono                       available      [ =5.x   =stabl\
344  e ]
345    38   nginx1                     available      [ =stable ]
346    39   ruby2.6                    available      [ =2.6   =stabl\
347  e ]
348    40   mock                       available      [ =stable ]
349    41   postgresql11               available      [ =11   =stable\
350  ]
```

```
 42  php7.4                    available    [ =stable ]
 43  livepatch                 available    [ =stable ]
 44  python3.8                 available    [ =stable ]
 45  haproxy2                  available    [ =stable ]
 46  collectd                  available    [ =stable ]
 47  aws-nitro-enclaves-cli    available    [ =stable ]
 48  R4                        available    [ =stable ]
  _  kernel-5.4                available    [ =stable ]
 50  selinux-ng                available    [ =stable ]
 51  php8.0                    available    [ =stable ]
 52  tomcat9                   available    [ =stable ]
 53  unbound1.13               available    [ =stable ]
 54  mariadb10.5               available    [ =stable ]
 55  kernel-5.10=latest        enabled      [ =stable ]
 56  redis6                    available    [ =stable ]
 57  ruby3.0                   available    [ =stable ]
 58  postgresql12              available    [ =stable ]
 59  postgresql13              available    [ =stable ]
 60  mock2                     available    [ =stable ]
 61  dnsmasq2.85               available    [ =stable ]
[root@ip-172-31-36-49 ec2-user]# yum-config-manager --ena\
ble epel
Failed to set locale, defaulting to C
Loaded plugins: extras_suggestions, langpacks, priorities\
, update-motd
============================================== repo: epel ==\
==================================================
[epel]
async = True
bandwidth = 0
base_persistdir = /var/lib/yum/repos/x86_64/2
baseurl =
cache = 0
cachedir = /var/cache/yum/x86_64/2/epel
check_config_file_age = True
```

```
386    compare_providers_priority = 80
387    cost = 1000
388    deltarpm_metadata_percentage = 100
389    deltarpm_percentage =
390    enabled = True
391    enablegroups = True
392    exclude =
393    failovermethod = priority
394    ftp_disable_epsv = False
395    gpgcadir = /var/lib/yum/repos/x86_64/2/epel/gpgcadir
396    gpgcakey =
397    gpgcheck = True
398    gpgdir = /var/lib/yum/repos/x86_64/2/epel/gpgdir
399    gpgkey = file:///etc/pki/rpm-gpg/RPM-GPG-KEY-EPEL-7
400    hdrdir = /var/cache/yum/x86_64/2/epel/headers
401    http_caching = all
402    includepkgs =
403    ip_resolve =
404    keepalive = True
405    keepcache = False
406    mddownloadpolicy = sqlite
407    mdpolicy = group:small
408    mediaid =
409    metadata_expire = 21600
410    metadata_expire_filter = read-only:present
411    metalink = https://mirrors.fedoraproject.org/metalink?rep\
412    o=epel-7&arch=x86_64
413    minrate = 0
414    mirrorlist =
415    mirrorlist_expire = 86400
416    name = Extra Packages for Enterprise Linux 7 - x86_64
417    old_base_cache_dir =
418    password =
419    persistdir = /var/lib/yum/repos/x86_64/2/epel
420    pkgdir = /var/cache/yum/x86_64/2/epel/packages
```

```
421  priority = 99
422  proxy = False
423  proxy_dict =
424  proxy_password =
425  proxy_username =
426  repo_gpgcheck = False
427  report_instanceid = False
428  retries = 7
429  skip_if_unavailable = False
430  ssl_check_cert_permissions = True
431  sslcacert =
432  sslclientcert =
433  sslclientkey =
434  sslverify = True
435  throttle = 0
436  timeout = 5.0
437  ui_id = epel/x86_64
438  ui_repoid_vars = releasever,
439     basearch
440  username =
441  [root@ip-172-31-36-49 ec2-user]# yum --enablerepo epel in\
442  stall ansible
443  Failed to set locale, defaulting to C
444  Loaded plugins: extras_suggestions, langpacks, priorities\
445  , update-motd
446  amzn2-core                                                 \
447                       | 3.7 kB  00:00:00
448  amzn2extra-docker                                          \
449                       | 3.0 kB  00:00:00
450  amzn2extra-epel                                            \
451                       | 3.0 kB  00:00:00
452  amzn2extra-kernel-5.10                                     \
453                       | 3.0 kB  00:00:00
454  epel/x86_64/metalink                                       \
455                       |  21 kB  00:00:00
```

```
209 packages excluded due to repository priority protecti\
ons
Resolving Dependencies
--> Running transaction check
---> Package ansible.noarch 0:2.9.25-1.el7 will be instal\
led
--> Finished Dependency Resolution
Dependencies Resolved
==============================================================\
=============================================
 Package                Arch              Version         \
            Repository        Size
==============================================================\
=============================================
Installing:
 ansible                noarch            2.9.25-1.el7 \
                  epel              17 M
Transaction Summary
==============================================================\
=============================================
Install  1 Package
Total download size: 17 M
Installed size: 103 M
Is this ok [y/d/N]: y
Downloading packages:
warning: /var/cache/yum/x86_64/2/epel/packages/ansible-2.\
9.25-1.el7.noarch.rpm: Header V4 RSA/SHA256 Signature, ke\
y ID 352c64e5: NOKEY
Public key for ansible-2.9.25-1.el7.noarch.rpm is not ins\
talled
ansible-2.9.25-1.el7.noarch.rpm                           \
                 |  17 MB  00:00:03
Retrieving key from file:///etc/pki/rpm-gpg/RPM-GPG-KEY-E\
PEL-7
Importing GPG key 0x352C64E5:
```

```
Userid      : "Fedora EPEL (7) <epel@fedoraproject.org>"
Fingerprint: 91e9 7d7c 4a5e 96f1 7f3e 888f 6a2f aea2 352\
c 64e5
Package     : epel-release-7-11.noarch (@amzn2extra-epel)
From        : /etc/pki/rpm-gpg/RPM-GPG-KEY-EPEL-7
Is this ok [y/N]: y
Running transaction check
Running transaction test
Transaction test succeeded
Running transaction
  Installing : ansible-2.9.25-1.el7.noarch                   \
                                    1/1
  Verifying  : ansible-2.9.25-1.el7.noarch                   \
                                    1/1
Installed:
  ansible.noarch 0:2.9.25-1.el7
Complete!
[root@ip-172-31-36-49 ec2-user]# ansible --version
ansible 2.9.25
  config file = /etc/ansible/ansible.cfg
  configured module search path = [u'/root/.ansible/plugi\
ns/modules', u'/usr/share/ansible/plugins/modules']
  ansible python module location = /usr/lib/python2.7/sit\
e-packages/ansible
  executable location = /bin/ansible
  python version = 2.7.18 (default, Jun 10 2021, 00:11:02\
) [GCC 7.3.1 20180712 (Red Hat 7.3.1-13)]
[root@ip-172-31-36-49 ec2-user]# rpm -qa | grep ansible
ansible-2.9.25-1.el7.noarch
[root@ip-172-31-36-49 ec2-user]#
```

EPEL after execution

```
1   # rpm -qa | grep ansible
2   ansible-2.9.25-1.el7.noarch
```

Recap

Now you know how to install the latest version of Ansible in Amazon Linux using the Amazon Extras Library and EPEL repositories.

How to install Ansible in Debian 11

The easier way to install the latest version of Ansible and maintain up-to-date in Debian 11 using APT and the "main" default repository.

How to install Ansible in Debian

- Included in the "main" default repository

The good news is that Ansible is included in the default repository so you could install it simply with your usual package manager "apt".
You could expect the latest version of Ansible in the "main" repository.

demo

How to install Ansible in Debian using the apt package manager and the "main" default repository.

code

- install-ansible-debian.sh

```
1  #!/bin/bash
2  $ sudo apt-get update
3  $ sudo apt-get install ansible
4  $ sudo apt list –installed ansible
```

execution

```
1   ansible-pilot $ ssh devops@debian.example.com
2   Linux debian 5.10.0-9-amd64 #1 SMP Debian 5.10.70-1 (2021\
3   -09-30) x86_64
4   The programs included with the Debian GNU/Linux system ar\
5   e free software;
6   the exact distribution terms for each program are describ\
7   ed in the
8   individual files in /usr/share/doc/*/copyright.
9   Debian GNU/Linux comes with ABSOLUTELY NO WARRANTY, to th\
10  e extent
11  permitted by applicable law.
12  $ sudo su
13  root@debian:/home/devops# cat /etc/os-release
14  PRETTY_NAME="Debian GNU/Linux 11 (bullseye)"
15  NAME="Debian GNU/Linux"
16  VERSION_ID="11"
17  VERSION="11 (bullseye)"
18  VERSION_CODENAME=bullseye
19  ID=debian
20  HOME_URL="https://www.debian.org/"
21  SUPPORT_URL="https://www.debian.org/support"
22  BUG_REPORT_URL="https://bugs.debian.org/"
23  root@debian:/home/devops# cat /etc/deb
24  debconf.conf    debian_version
25  root@debian:/home/devops# cat /etc/debian_version
26  11.1
27  root@debian:/home/devops# apt-get update
28  Get:1 http://security.debian.org/debian-security bullseye\
29  -security InRelease [44.1 kB]
```

```
Hit:2 http://deb.debian.org/debian bullseye InRelease
Get:3 http://deb.debian.org/debian bullseye-updates InRel\
ease [39.4 kB]
Get:4 http://deb.debian.org/debian bullseye-backports InR\
elease [43.7 kB]
Get:5 http://deb.debian.org/debian bullseye-backports/mai\
n Sources.diff/Index [63.3 kB]
Get:6 http://deb.debian.org/debian bullseye-backports/mai\
n amd64 Packages.diff/Index [63.3 kB]
Get:7 http://deb.debian.org/debian bullseye-backports/mai\
n Sources T-2021-12-02-0202.04-F-2021-12-02-0202.04.pdiff\
 [29 B]
Get:7 http://deb.debian.org/debian bullseye-backports/mai\
n Sources T-2021-12-02-0202.04-F-2021-12-02-0202.04.pdiff\
 [29 B]
Get:8 http://deb.debian.org/debian bullseye-backports/mai\
n amd64 Packages T-2021-12-02-0202.04-F-2021-12-02-0202.0\
4.pdiff [257 B]
Get:8 http://deb.debian.org/debian bullseye-backports/mai\
n amd64 Packages T-2021-12-02-0202.04-F-2021-12-02-0202.0\
4.pdiff [257 B]
Fetched 254 kB in 1s (488 kB/s)
Reading package lists... Done
root@debian:/home/devops# apt-cache search ansible
ansible - Configuration management, deployment, and task \
execution system
ansible-lint - lint tool for Ansible playbooks
ansible-mitogen - Fast connection strategy for Ansible
shade-inventory - Ansible inventory script for OpenStack \
clouds
python3-reclass - hierarchical inventory backend for conf\
iguration management systems
reclass - hierarchical inventory backend for configuratio\
n management systems
reclass-doc - reclass documentation
```

```
65  vim-syntastic - Syntax checking hacks for vim
66  root@debian:/home/devops# apt-cache show ansible
67  Package: ansible
68  Version: 2.10.7+merged+base+2.10.8+dfsg-1
69  Installed-Size: 198790
70  Maintainer: Lee Garrett <debian@rocketjump.eu>
71  Architecture: all
72  Replaces: ansible-base (<= 2.10.5+dfsg-2)
73  Depends: python3-cryptography, python3-jinja2, python3-pa\
74  ckaging, python3-yaml, python3:any, openssh-client | pyth\
75  on3-paramiko (>= 2.6.0), python3-pycryptodome, python3-di\
76  stutils, python3-dnspython, python3-httplib2, python3-net\
77  addr
78  Recommends: python3-argcomplete, python3-jmespath, python\
79  3-kerberos, python3-libcloud, python3-selinux, python3-wi\
80  nrm, python3-xmltodict
81  Suggests: cowsay, sshpass
82  Breaks: ansible-base (<= 2.10.5+dfsg-2)
83  Description-en: Configuration management, deployment, and\
84   task execution system
85   Ansible is a radically simple model-driven configuration\
86   management,
87   multi-node deployment, and remote task execution system.\
88   Ansible works
89   over SSH and does not require any software or daemons to\
90   be installed
91   on remote nodes. Extension modules can be written in any\
92   language and
93   are transferred to managed machines automatically.
94   .
95   This package contains ansible-base 2.10.x and ansible-co\
96  llections 2.10.x merged
97   into one package.
98  Description-md5: de0a87781a6b6efa86ca20d1d1c64ce8
99  Homepage: https://www.ansible.com
```

```
100  Tag: admin::automation, admin::configuring, admin::file-d\
101  istribution,
102   admin::package-management, implemented-in::python,
103   interface::commandline, role::program, use::configuring,
104   works-with::software:running
105  Section: admin
106  Priority: optional
107  Filename: pool/main/a/ansible/ansible_2.10.7+merged+base+\
108  2.10.8+dfsg-1_all.deb
109  Size: 17685468
110  MD5sum: 159657e0be3d3f212fde43db1ac986cd
111  SHA256: 66474117b31f9b0bc816331c7b5f7424c77a496db5063da0d\
112  761cdbc814ef644
113  root@debian:/home/devops# apt-get install ansible
114  Reading package lists... Done
115  Building dependency tree... Done
116  Reading state information... Done
117  The following additional packages will be installed:
118    ieee-data libyaml-0-2 python3-argcomplete python3-cffi-\
119  backend python3-cryptography
120    python3-distutils python3-dnspython python3-jinja2 pyth\
121  on3-jmespath python3-kerberos
122    python3-lib2to3 python3-libcloud python3-lockfile pytho\
123  n3-markupsafe python3-netaddr
124    python3-ntlm-auth python3-packaging python3-pycryptodom\
125  e python3-pyparsing
126    python3-requests-kerberos python3-requests-ntlm python3\
127  -requests-toolbelt python3-selinux
128    python3-simplejson python3-winrm python3-xmltodict pyth\
129  on3-yaml
130  Suggested packages:
131    cowsay sshpass python-cryptography-doc python3-cryptogr\
132  aphy-vectors python3-sniffio
133    python3-trio python-jinja2-doc python-lockfile-doc ipyt\
134  hon3 python-netaddr-docs
```

```
135     python-pyparsing-doc
136 The following NEW packages will be installed:
137     ansible ieee-data libyaml-0-2 python3-argcomplete pytho\
138 n3-cffi-backend python3-cryptography
139     python3-distutils python3-dnspython python3-jinja2 pyth\
140 on3-jmespath python3-kerberos
141     python3-lib2to3 python3-libcloud python3-lockfile pytho\
142 n3-markupsafe python3-netaddr
143     python3-ntlm-auth python3-packaging python3-pycryptodom\
144 e python3-pyparsing
145     python3-requests-kerberos python3-requests-ntlm python3\
146 -requests-toolbelt python3-selinux
147     python3-simplejson python3-winrm python3-xmltodict pyth\
148 on3-yaml
149 0 upgraded, 28 newly installed, 0 to remove and 1 not upg\
150 raded.
151 Need to get 32.9 MB of archives.
152 After this operation, 280 MB of additional disk space wil\
153 l be used.
154 Do you want to continue? [Y/n] y
155 Get:1 http://deb.debian.org/debian bullseye/main amd64 py\
156 thon3-cffi-backend amd64 1.14.5-1 [85.8 kB]
157 Get:2 http://deb.debian.org/debian bullseye/main amd64 py\
158 thon3-cryptography amd64 3.3.2-1 [223 kB]
159 Get:3 http://deb.debian.org/debian bullseye/main amd64 py\
160 thon3-markupsafe amd64 1.1.1-1+b3 [15.2 kB]
161 Get:4 http://deb.debian.org/debian bullseye/main amd64 py\
162 thon3-jinja2 all 2.11.3-1 [114 kB]
163 Get:5 http://deb.debian.org/debian bullseye/main amd64 py\
164 thon3-pyparsing all 2.4.7-1 [109 kB]
165 Get:6 http://deb.debian.org/debian bullseye/main amd64 py\
166 thon3-packaging all 20.9-2 [33.5 kB]
167 Get:7 http://deb.debian.org/debian bullseye/main amd64 li\
168 byaml-0-2 amd64 0.2.2-1 [49.6 kB]
169 Get:8 http://deb.debian.org/debian bullseye/main amd64 py\
```

```
170   thon3-yaml amd64 5.3.1-5 [138 kB]
171   Get:9 http://deb.debian.org/debian bullseye/main amd64 py\
172   thon3-pycryptodome amd64 3.9.7+dfsg1-1+b2 [9910 kB]
173   Get:10 http://deb.debian.org/debian bullseye/main amd64 p\
174   ython3-lib2to3 all 3.9.2-1 [77.8 kB]
175   Get:11 http://deb.debian.org/debian bullseye/main amd64 p\
176   ython3-distutils all 3.9.2-1 [143 kB]
177   Get:12 http://deb.debian.org/debian bullseye/main amd64 p\
178   ython3-dnspython all 2.0.0-1 [103 kB]
179   Get:13 http://deb.debian.org/debian bullseye/main amd64 i\
180   eee-data all 20210605.1 [1889 kB]
181   Get:14 http://deb.debian.org/debian bullseye/main amd64 p\
182   ython3-netaddr all 0.7.19-5 [253 kB]
183   Get:15 http://deb.debian.org/debian bullseye/main amd64 a\
184   nsible all 2.10.7+merged+base+2.10.8+dfsg-1 [17.7 MB]
185   Get:16 http://deb.debian.org/debian bullseye/main amd64 p\
186   ython3-argcomplete all 1.8.1-1.5 [29.7 kB]
187   Get:17 http://deb.debian.org/debian bullseye/main amd64 p\
188   ython3-jmespath all 0.10.0-1 [21.7 kB]
189   Get:18 http://deb.debian.org/debian bullseye/main amd64 p\
190   ython3-kerberos amd64 1.1.14-3.1+b3 [24.1 kB]
191   Get:19 http://deb.debian.org/debian bullseye/main amd64 p\
192   ython3-lockfile all 1:0.12.2-2.2 [17.3 kB]
193   Get:20 http://deb.debian.org/debian bullseye/main amd64 p\
194   ython3-simplejson amd64 3.17.2-1 [61.7 kB]
195   Get:21 http://deb.debian.org/debian bullseye/main amd64 p\
196   ython3-libcloud all 3.2.0-2 [1615 kB]
197   Get:22 http://deb.debian.org/debian bullseye/main amd64 p\
198   ython3-ntlm-auth all 1.4.0-1 [21.6 kB]
199   Get:23 http://deb.debian.org/debian bullseye/main amd64 p\
200   ython3-requests-kerberos all 0.12.0-2 [13.0 kB]
201   Get:24 http://deb.debian.org/debian bullseye/main amd64 p\
202   ython3-requests-ntlm all 1.1.0-1.1 [6120 B]
203   Get:25 http://deb.debian.org/debian bullseye/main amd64 p\
204   ython3-requests-toolbelt all 0.9.1-1 [41.7 kB]
```

```
Get:26 http://deb.debian.org/debian bullseye/main amd64 p\
ython3-selinux amd64 3.1-3 [160 kB]
Get:27 http://deb.debian.org/debian bullseye/main amd64 p\
ython3-xmltodict all 0.12.0-2 [15.2 kB]
Get:28 http://deb.debian.org/debian bullseye/main amd64 p\
ython3-winrm all 0.3.0-2 [21.6 kB]
Fetched 32.9 MB in 6s (5494 kB/s)
perl: warning: Setting locale failed.
perl: warning: Please check that your locale settings:
 LANGUAGE = (unset),
 LC_ALL = (unset),
 LC_CTYPE = "UTF-8",
 LANG = "C.UTF-8"
    are supported and installed on your system.
perl: warning: Falling back to a fallback locale ("C.UTF-\
8").
locale: Cannot set LC_CTYPE to default locale: No such fi\
le or directory
locale: Cannot set LC_ALL to default locale: No such file\
 or directory
Selecting previously unselected package python3-cffi-back\
end:amd64.
(Reading database ... 25133 files and directories current\
ly installed.)
Preparing to unpack .../00-python3-cffi-backend_1.14.5-1_\
amd64.deb ...
Unpacking python3-cffi-backend:amd64 (1.14.5-1) ...
Selecting previously unselected package python3-cryptogra\
phy.
Preparing to unpack .../01-python3-cryptography_3.3.2-1_a\
md64.deb ...
Unpacking python3-cryptography (3.3.2-1) ...
Selecting previously unselected package python3-markupsaf\
e.
Preparing to unpack .../02-python3-markupsafe_1.1.1-1+b3_\
```

```
240  amd64.deb ...
241  Unpacking python3-markupsafe (1.1.1-1+b3) ...
242  Selecting previously unselected package python3-jinja2.
243  Preparing to unpack .../03-python3-jinja2_2.11.3-1_all.de\
244  b ...
245  Unpacking python3-jinja2 (2.11.3-1) ...
246  Selecting previously unselected package python3-pyparsing.
247  Preparing to unpack .../04-python3-pyparsing_2.4.7-1_all.\
248  deb ...
249  Unpacking python3-pyparsing (2.4.7-1) ...
250  Selecting previously unselected package python3-packaging.
251  Preparing to unpack .../05-python3-packaging_20.9-2_all.d\
252  eb ...
253  Unpacking python3-packaging (20.9-2) ...
254  Selecting previously unselected package libyaml-0-2:amd64.
255  Preparing to unpack .../06-libyaml-0-2_0.2.2-1_amd64.deb \
256  ...
257  Unpacking libyaml-0-2:amd64 (0.2.2-1) ...
258  Selecting previously unselected package python3-yaml.
259  Preparing to unpack .../07-python3-yaml_5.3.1-5_amd64.deb\
260  ...
261  Unpacking python3-yaml (5.3.1-5) ...
262  Selecting previously unselected package python3-pycryptod\
263  ome.
264  Preparing to unpack .../08-python3-pycryptodome_3.9.7+dfs\
265  g1-1+b2_amd64.deb ...
266  Unpacking python3-pycryptodome (3.9.7+dfsg1-1+b2) ...
267  Selecting previously unselected package python3-lib2to3.
268  Preparing to unpack .../09-python3-lib2to3_3.9.2-1_all.de\
269  b ...
270  Unpacking python3-lib2to3 (3.9.2-1) ...
271  Selecting previously unselected package python3-distutils.
272  Preparing to unpack .../10-python3-distutils_3.9.2-1_all.\
273  deb ...
274  Unpacking python3-distutils (3.9.2-1) ...
```

```
275  Selecting previously unselected package python3-dnspython.
276  Preparing to unpack .../11-python3-dnspython_2.0.0-1_all.\
277  deb ...
278  Unpacking python3-dnspython (2.0.0-1) ...
279  Selecting previously unselected package ieee-data.
280  Preparing to unpack .../12-ieee-data_20210605.1_all.deb .\
281  ..
282  Unpacking ieee-data (20210605.1) ...
283  Selecting previously unselected package python3-netaddr.
284  Preparing to unpack .../13-python3-netaddr_0.7.19-5_all.d\
285  eb ...
286  Unpacking python3-netaddr (0.7.19-5) ...
287  Selecting previously unselected package ansible.
288  Preparing to unpack .../14-ansible_2.10.7+merged+base+2.1\
289  0.8+dfsg-1_all.deb ...
290  Unpacking ansible (2.10.7+merged+base+2.10.8+dfsg-1) ...
291  Selecting previously unselected package python3-argcomple\
292  te.
293  Preparing to unpack .../15-python3-argcomplete_1.8.1-1.5_\
294  all.deb ...
295  Unpacking python3-argcomplete (1.8.1-1.5) ...
296  Selecting previously unselected package python3-jmespath.
297  Preparing to unpack .../16-python3-jmespath_0.10.0-1_all.\
298  deb ...
299  Unpacking python3-jmespath (0.10.0-1) ...
300  Selecting previously unselected package python3-kerberos.
301  Preparing to unpack .../17-python3-kerberos_1.1.14-3.1+b3\
302  _amd64.deb ...
303  Unpacking python3-kerberos (1.1.14-3.1+b3) ...
304  Selecting previously unselected package python3-lockfile.
305  Preparing to unpack .../18-python3-lockfile_1%3a0.12.2-2.\
306  2_all.deb ...
307  Unpacking python3-lockfile (1:0.12.2-2.2) ...
308  Selecting previously unselected package python3-simplejso\
309  n.
```

```
310  Preparing to unpack .../19-python3-simplejson_3.17.2-1_am\
311  d64.deb ...
312  Unpacking python3-simplejson (3.17.2-1) ...
313  Selecting previously unselected package python3-libcloud.
314  Preparing to unpack .../20-python3-libcloud_3.2.0-2_all.d\
315  eb ...
316  Unpacking python3-libcloud (3.2.0-2) ...
317  Selecting previously unselected package python3-ntlm-auth.
318  Preparing to unpack .../21-python3-ntlm-auth_1.4.0-1_all.\
319  deb ...
320  Unpacking python3-ntlm-auth (1.4.0-1) ...
321  Selecting previously unselected package python3-requests-\
322  kerberos.
323  Preparing to unpack .../22-python3-requests-kerberos_0.12\
324  .0-2_all.deb ...
325  Unpacking python3-requests-kerberos (0.12.0-2) ...
326  Selecting previously unselected package python3-requests-\
327  ntlm.
328  Preparing to unpack .../23-python3-requests-ntlm_1.1.0-1.\
329  1_all.deb ...
330  Unpacking python3-requests-ntlm (1.1.0-1.1) ...
331  Selecting previously unselected package python3-requests-\
332  toolbelt.
333  Preparing to unpack .../24-python3-requests-toolbelt_0.9.\
334  1-1_all.deb ...
335  Unpacking python3-requests-toolbelt (0.9.1-1) ...
336  Selecting previously unselected package python3-selinux.
337  Preparing to unpack .../25-python3-selinux_3.1-3_amd64.de\
338  b ...
339  Unpacking python3-selinux (3.1-3) ...
340  Selecting previously unselected package python3-xmltodict.
341  Preparing to unpack .../26-python3-xmltodict_0.12.0-2_all\
342  .deb ...
343  Unpacking python3-xmltodict (0.12.0-2) ...
344  Selecting previously unselected package python3-winrm.
```

```
Preparing to unpack .../27-python3-winrm_0.3.0-2_all.deb \
...
Unpacking python3-winrm (0.3.0-2) ...
Setting up python3-lockfile (1:0.12.2-2.2) ...
Setting up python3-requests-toolbelt (0.9.1-1) ...
Setting up libyaml-0-2:amd64 (0.2.2-1) ...
Setting up python3-ntlm-auth (1.4.0-1) ...
Setting up python3-pycryptodome (3.9.7+dfsg1-1+b2) ...
Setting up python3-kerberos (1.1.14-3.1+b3) ...
Setting up python3-yaml (5.3.1-5) ...
Setting up python3-markupsafe (1.1.1-1+b3) ...
Setting up python3-simplejson (3.17.2-1) ...
Setting up python3-xmltodict (0.12.0-2) ...
Setting up python3-jinja2 (2.11.3-1) ...
Setting up python3-pyparsing (2.4.7-1) ...
Setting up python3-jmespath (0.10.0-1) ...
Setting up ieee-data (20210605.1) ...
Setting up python3-dnspython (2.0.0-1) ...
Setting up python3-selinux (3.1-3) ...
Setting up python3-argcomplete (1.8.1-1.5) ...
Setting up python3-lib2to3 (3.9.2-1) ...
Setting up python3-cffi-backend:amd64 (1.14.5-1) ...
Setting up python3-distutils (3.9.2-1) ...
Setting up python3-packaging (20.9-2) ...
Setting up python3-cryptography (3.3.2-1) ...
Setting up python3-requests-kerberos (0.12.0-2) ...
Setting up python3-netaddr (0.7.19-5) ...
Setting up ansible (2.10.7+merged+base+2.10.8+dfsg-1) ...
Setting up python3-requests-ntlm (1.1.0-1.1) ...
Setting up python3-libcloud (3.2.0-2) ...
Setting up python3-winrm (0.3.0-2) ...
Processing triggers for man-db (2.9.4-2) ...
Processing triggers for libc-bin (2.31-13+deb11u2) ...
root@debian:/home/devops# ansible --version
ansible 2.10.8
```

```
380    config file = None
381    configured module search path = ['/root/.ansible/plugin\
382 s/modules', '/usr/share/ansible/plugins/modules']
383    ansible python module location = /usr/lib/python3/dist-\
384 packages/ansible
385    executable location = /usr/bin/ansible
386    python version = 3.9.2 (default, Feb 28 2021, 17:03:44)\
387    [GCC 10.2.1 20210110]
388 root@debian:/home/devops# apt list | grep ansible
389 WARNING: apt does not have a stable CLI interface. Use wi\
390 th caution in scripts.
391 ansible-lint/stable 4.3.7-1 all
392 ansible-mitogen/stable 0.3.0~rc1-4 all
393 ansible/stable,now 2.10.7+merged+base+2.10.8+dfsg-1 all [\
394 installed]
395 root@debian:/home/devops# dpkg -l | grep ansible
396 ii  ansible                        2.10.7+merged+base+2.10\
397 .8+dfsg-1 all            Configuration management, deployme\
398 nt, and task execution system
399 root@debian:/home/devops#
```

before execution

```
1  $ ssh devops@debian.example.com
2  Linux debian 5.10.0-9-amd64 #1 SMP Debian 5.10.70-1 (2021\
3  -09-30) x86_64
4  The programs included with the Debian GNU/Linux system ar\
5  e free software;
6  the exact distribution terms for each program are describ\
7  ed in the
8  individual files in /usr/share/doc/*/copyright.
9  Debian GNU/Linux comes with ABSOLUTELY NO WARRANTY, to th\
10 e extent
11 permitted by applicable law.
12 $ sudo su
13 root@debian:/home/devops# cat /etc/os-release
```

```
14  PRETTY_NAME="Debian GNU/Linux 11 (bullseye)"
15  NAME="Debian GNU/Linux"
16  VERSION_ID="11"
17  VERSION="11 (bullseye)"
18  VERSION_CODENAME=bullseye
19  ID=debian
20  HOME_URL="https://www.debian.org/"
21  SUPPORT_URL="https://www.debian.org/support"
22  BUG_REPORT_URL="https://bugs.debian.org/"
23  root@debian:/home/devops# cat /etc/deb
24  debconf.conf    debian_version
25  root@debian:/home/devops# cat /etc/debian_version
26  11.1
27  root@debian:/home/devops# apt list ansible --installed
28  Listing... Done
29  root@debian:/home/devops#
```

after execution

```
1  root@debian:/home/devops# apt list ansible --installed
2  Listing... Done
3  ansible/stable,now 2.10.7+merged+base+2.10.8+dfsg-1 all [\
4  installed]
5  root@debian:/home/devops# dpkg -l | grep ansible
6  ii  ansible                     2.10.7+merged+base+2.10\
7  .8+dfsg-1 all          Configuration management, deployme\
8  nt, and task execution system
9  root@debian:/home/devops#
```

Ansible For Linux

In this chapter you're going to discover the most common Ansible Modules to automate Linux System Administrator tasks.

Ansible terminology - ansible_hostname vs inventory_hostname vs ansible_fqdn

What is the difference between ansible_hostname vs inventory_-hostname vs ansible_fqdn in a practical example with Ansible Playbook?

These two ansible internal variables sometimes confuse one for another but they're fundamentally different.

ansible_hostname vs inventory_hostname vs ansible_fqdn

ansible_hostname and ansible_fqdn

Read from the target machine hostname from the facts:

- `ansible_hostname` read the hostname from the facts collected during the `gather_facts`
- Same as the `uname -n` or `hostname` command-line
- Need `gather_facts` enabled, otherwise the `ansible_facts` variable would be unavailable to use in your playbook
- Same as hostname of the target host
- As this is based on the `gather_facts` step. ansible_hostname not available in ad-hoc command

inventory_hostname

Read from Ansible inventory or hosts files:

- `inventory_hostname` read the hostname from the inventory configuration or the hosts file. Could be different from the hostname configuration of the remote system. It could be only a name on the controller machine
- `inventory_hostname` is always available to use in your play-book.
- Could be different from the hostname of the target host
- Available for both playbook and ad-hoc command

demo

Let me show you the difference between `ansible_hostname` vs `inventory_hostname` vs `ansible_fqdn` internal variables in a simple Ansible Playbook.

code

- hostnames.yml

```yaml
1  ---
2  - name: hostnames demo
3    hosts: all
4    gather_facts: true
5    tasks:
6      - name: print inventory_hostname
7        ansible.builtin.debug:
8          var: inventory_hostname
9      - name: print ansible_hostname
10       ansible.builtin.debug:
11         var: ansible_hostname
```

```
12        - name: print ansible_fqdn
13          ansible.builtin.debug:
14            var: ansible_fqdn
```

- inventory

```
1   foo.example.com ansible_host=192.168.0.190
2   [all:vars]
3   ansible_connection=ssh
4   ansible_user=devops
5   ansible_ssh_private_key_file=~/.ssh/id_rsa
```

execution

```
1    ansible-pilot $ ansible-playbook -i ansible\ statements/i\
2    nventory ansible\ statements/hostnames.yml
3    PLAY [hostnames demo] ***********************************\
4    ******************************************
5    TASK [Gathering Facts] **********************************\
6    ******************************************
7    ok: [foo.example.com]
8    TASK [print inventory_hostname] *************************\
9    ******************************************
10   ok: [foo.example.com] => {
11       "inventory_hostname": "foo.example.com"
12   }
13   TASK [print ansible_hostname] ***************************\
14   ******************************************
15   ok: [foo.example.com] => {
16       "ansible_hostname": "demo"
17   }
18   TASK [print ansible_fqdn] ******************************\
19   ******************************************
20   ok: [foo.example.com] => {
21       "ansible_fqdn": "demo.example.com"
```

```
22  }
23  PLAY RECAP ***********************************************\
24  *******************************************
25  foo.example.com              : ok=4    changed=0    unreach\
26  able=0    failed=0    skipped=0    rescued=0    ignored=0
27  ansible-pilot $
```

idempotency

```
1   ansible-pilot $ ansible-playbook -i ansible\ statements/i\
2   nventory ansible\ statements/hostnames.yml
3   PLAY [hostnames demo] ********************************\
4   *******************************************
5   TASK [Gathering Facts] ********************************\
6   *******************************************
7   ok: [foo.example.com]
8   TASK [print inventory_hostname] ***********************\
9   *******************************************
10  ok: [foo.example.com] => {
11      "inventory_hostname": "foo.example.com"
12  }
13  TASK [print ansible_hostname] *************************\
14  *******************************************
15  ok: [foo.example.com] => {
16      "ansible_hostname": "demo"
17  }
18  TASK [print ansible_fqdn] ****************************\
19  *******************************************
20  ok: [foo.example.com] => {
21      "ansible_fqdn": "demo.example.com"
22  }
23  PLAY RECAP ***********************************************\
24  *******************************************
25  foo.example.com              : ok=4    changed=0    unreach\
26  able=0    failed=0    skipped=0    rescued=0    ignored=0
27  ansible-pilot $
```

before execution

```
1   ansible-pilot $ ssh devops@192.168.0.190
2   [devops@demo ~]$ uname -a
3   Linux demo.example.com 4.18.0-348.e18.x86_64 #1 SMP Mon O\
4   ct 4 12:17:22 EDT 2021 x86_64 x86_64 x86_64 GNU/Linux
5   [devops@demo ~]$ uname -n
6   demo.example.com
7   [devops@demo ~]$ hostname
8   demo.example.com
9   [devops@demo ~]$
```

Recap

Now you know more about the Ansible internal variables `ansible_hostname`, `inventory_hostname` and `ansible_fqdn`.
You know how to use it based on your use case in your Ansible Playbook or Ansible Templates.

Three options to Safely Limit Ansible Playbooks Execution to a Single Machine

Three options to limit the execution of a potentially harmful Ansible Playbook to only one host.

Limit Ansible Playbook to only one HOSTNAME

- use `--limit` at runtime
- `hosts:` `HOSTNAME` Ansible Playbook

- `hosts: "{{ HOSTS }}"` Ansible Playbook

Let's deep dive into our use case to Limit Ansible Playbook to only one HOSTNAME.

I'm going to show three different ways to achieve this result:

using the `--limit` parameter at runtime, limit the HOSTNAME in the Playbook code and the most advanced way is to define a variable in the Ansible Playbook that you could populate on-demand.

Let's discuss the pros and cons of each option.

demo

In the following demo scenarios, I'd like to execute my harmful Ansible Playbook **ONLY** against demo.example.com host.

This is my demo inventory file:

```
1  [linux]
2  demo.example.com
3  demo2.example.com
4
5  [all:vars]
6  ansible_connection=ssh
7  ansible_user=devops
8  ansible_ssh_private_key_file=~/.ssh/id_rsa
```

Ansible command limit option

- `--limit`
- `ansible-playbook - limit HOSTNAME PLAYBOOK`

Using the `--limit` parameter of the `ansible-playbook` command is the easiest option to limit the execution of the code to only one

host.
The advantage is that you don't need to edit the Ansible Playbook code before executing to only one host.
The drawback is that you should remember every time you execute the command and sometimes humans are not so reliable.

code

- playbook.yml

```
1  ---
2  - name: harmful playbook
3    hosts: all
4    tasks:
5      - name: harmful task
6        ansible.builtin.debug:
7          msg: "harmful task"
```

execution

```
1  ansible-pilot $ ansible-playbook --limit demo.example.com\
2   -i limit/inventory limit/playbook.yml
3  PLAY [harmful playbook] ********************************\
4  *******************************************
5  TASK [Gathering Facts] ********************************\
6  *******************************************
7  ok: [demo.example.com]
8  TASK [harmful task] ********************************\
9  *******************************************
10 ok: [demo.example.com] => {
11     "msg": "harmful task"
12 }
13 PLAY RECAP ********************************\
14 *******************************************
15 demo.example.com           : ok=2    changed=0    unreach\
```

```
16  able=0      failed=0      skipped=0      rescued=0      ignored=0
17  ansible-pilot $
```

wrong execution

If we forgot the --limit option the result could be very harmful.

```
1   ansible-pilot $ ansible-playbook -i limit/inventory limit\
2   /playbook.yml
3   PLAY [harmful playbook] ********************************\
4   *******************************************
5   TASK [Gathering Facts] ********************************\
6   *******************************************
7   ok: [demo.example.com]
8   ok: [demo2.example.com]
9   TASK [harmful task] ***********************************\
10  *******************************************
11  ok: [demo.example.com] => {
12      "msg": "harmful task"
13  }
14  ok: [demo2.example.com] => {
15      "msg": "harmful task"
16  }
17  PLAY RECAP ********************************************\
18  *******************************************
19  demo.example.com            : ok=2     changed=0     unreach\
20  able=0     failed=0     skipped=0     rescued=0     ignored=0\
21
22  demo2.example.com           : ok=2     changed=0     unreach\
23  able=0     failed=0     skipped=0     rescued=0     ignored=0
24  ansible-pilot $
```

Ansible Playbook hosts

- hosts: HOSTNAME

- `ansible-playbook PLAYBOOK`

Using the `hosts` statement in the Ansible Playbook allows you to specify a host or a group of hosts for the execution.
The advantage is that is more reliable than manually specifying the hostname than using the `--limit` parameter from the command line.
The drawback is that you need to remember to edit the Ansible Playbook code every time. If you don't you're going to execute the code on the specified host, still a potential manual issue.

code

- playbook2.yml

```
1  ---
2  - name: harmful playbook
3    hosts: demo.example.com
4    tasks:
5      - name: harmful task
6        ansible.builtin.debug:
7          msg: "harmful task"
```

execution

```
ansible-pilot $ ansible-playbook -i limit/inventory limit\
/playbook2.yml
PLAY [harmful playbook] *********************************\
*********************************************
TASK [Gathering Facts] *********************************\
*********************************************
ok: [demo.example.com]
TASK [harmful task] ************************************\
*********************************************
ok: [demo.example.com] => {
    "msg": "harmful task"
}
PLAY RECAP *********************************************\
*********************************************
demo.example.com           : ok=2    changed=0    unreach\
able=0    failed=0    skipped=0    rescued=0    ignored=0
ansible-pilot $
```

Ansible Playbook hosts advanced

- hosts: "{{ HOSTS }}"
- ansible-playbook -e "HOSTS=demo.example.com" PLAYBOOK

Using the hosts statement in the Ansible Playbook allows you to specify also a variable that you could populate with a host or a group of host for the execution.

Basically, if you blindly execute the Ansible Playbook code on the command line is doing nothing. The only way is to process is to populate the host variable via an extra variable via the console line. The advantage is that is more reliable than manually specifying the hostname than using the --limit parameter from the command line.

This option combines the advantages of the previous option and my favorite as well.

code

- playbook3.yml

```
1    ---
2    - name: harmful playbook
3      hosts: "{{ HOSTS }}"
4      tasks:
5        - name: harmful task
6          ansible.builtin.debug:
7            msg: "harmful task"
```

execution

```
1    ansible-pilot $ ansible-playbook -i limit/inventory -e "H\
2    OSTS=demo.example.com" limit/playbook3.yml
3    PLAY [harmful playbook] *********************************\
4    *******************************************
5    TASK [Gathering Facts] *********************************\
6    *******************************************
7    ok: [demo.example.com]
8    TASK [harmful task] ************************************\
9    *******************************************
10   ok: [demo.example.com] => {
11       "msg": "harmful task"
12   }
13   PLAY RECAP ********************************************\
14   *******************************************
15   demo.example.com              : ok=2     changed=0     unreach\
16   able=0     failed=0     skipped=0     rescued=0     ignored=0
17   ansible-pilot $
```

wrong execution

```
 1  ansible-pilot $ ansible-playbook -i limit/inventory limit\
 2  /playbook3.yml
 3  [WARNING]: Could not match supplied host pattern, ignorin\
 4  g: HOSTS
 5  PLAY [harmful playbook] *********************************\
 6  ****************************************
 7  skipping: no hosts matched
 8  PLAY RECAP *********************************************\
 9  ****************************************
10  ansible-pilot $
```

Links

- Patterns: targeting hosts and groups[27]

Ansible modules - command vs shell

A comparison between command vs shell Ansible modules, when you really need to execute commands on Linux target hosts.
These two Ansible modules are confused one for another but they're fundamentally different.
Both modules allow you to execute command on a target host but in a slightly different way.

command vs shell

command

- execute commands against the target Unix-based hosts
- it bypasses the shell
- always set changed to True

---

[27]https://docs.ansible.com/ansible/latest/user_guide/intro_patterns.html

shell

- execute shell commands against the target Unix-based hosts
- redirections and shell's inbuilt functionality
- always set changed to True

The `command` and `shell` Ansible modules execute commands on the target node.

Generally speaking, is always better to use a specialized Ansible module to execute a task.

However, sometimes the only way is to execute a Linux `command` via command or `shell` module.

Let me reinforce again, you should avoid as much as possible the usage of command/shell instead of a better module.

Both modules execute commands on target nodes but in a sensible different way.

The `command` modules execute commands on the target machine without using the target shell, it simply executes the command. The target shell is for example the popular `bash`, `zsh`, or `sh`. As a side effect user environment, variable expansions, output redirections, stringing two commands together, and other shell features are not available. On the other side, every command executed using `shell` module has all shell features so it could be expanded in runtime. From the security point of view `command` module is more robust and has a more predictable outcome because it bypasses the `shell`.

Both modules returned **always** changed status because Ansible is not able to predict if the execution has or has not altered the target system.

command module

- Execute commands on targets

The "command" module is the default module in Ansible Ad-hoc mode. The command module is able to execute only the binaries on remote hosts. The command module won't be impacted by local shell variables because it bypasses the shell. At the same time, it may not be able to run "shell" built-in features and redirections.

shell module

- Execute shell commands on targets

The shell Ansible module is potentially more dangerous than the command module and should only be used when you actually really need the shell functionality. So if you're not stringing two commands together (using pipes or even just && or ;), you don't really need the shell module. Similarly, expanding shell variables or file global requires the shell module. If you're not using these features, don't use the shell module. Sometimes it's the only way, I know.

Links

- ansible.builtin.shell[28]
- ansible.builtin.command[29]

demo

The command vs shell Ansible modules in Ansible Playbook.
Let me show you the difference between command vs shell Ansible modules in an Ansible Playbook.

command code

---

[28]https://docs.ansible.com/ansible/latest/collections/ansible/builtin/shell_module.html
[29]https://docs.ansible.com/ansible/latest/collections/ansible/builtin/command_module.html

```
---
- name: command module demo
  hosts: all
  tasks:
    - name: check uptime
      ansible.builtin.command: uptime
      register: command_output
    - name: command output
      ansible.builtin.debug:
        var: command_output.stdout_lines
command execution
ansible-pilot $ ansible-playbook -i virtualmachines/demo/\
inventory commmand_shell/uptime.yml
PLAY [command module demo] *****************************\
**********************************************
TASK [Gathering Facts] ********************************\
**********************************************
ok: [demo.example.com]
TASK [check uptime] ***********************************\
**********************************************
changed: [demo.example.com]
TASK [command output] *********************************\
**********************************************
ok: [demo.example.com] => {
    "command_output.stdout_lines": [
        " 12:51:34 up 8 min,  1 user,  load average: 0.00\
, 0.05, 0.06"
    ]
}
PLAY RECAP ********************************************\
**********************************************
demo.example.com              : ok=3    changed=1    unreach\
able=0    failed=0    skipped=0    rescued=0    ignored=0
ansible-pilot $
shell code
```

```
36   ---
37   - name: shell module demo
38     hosts: all
39     tasks:
40       - name: list file(s) and folder(s)
41         ansible.builtin.shell: 'ls -l *'
42         register: command_output
43       - name: command output
44         ansible.builtin.debug:
45           var: command_output.stdout_lines
```

shell execution

```
1    ansible-pilot $ ansible-playbook -i virtualmachines/demo/\
2    inventory commmand_shell/list_files.yml
3    PLAY [shell module demo] ********************************\
4    ********************************************
5    TASK [Gathering Facts] *********************************\
6    ********************************************
7    ok: [demo.example.com]
8    TASK [list file(s) and folder(s)] *********************\
9    ********************************************
10   changed: [demo.example.com]
11   TASK [command output] **********************************\
12   ********************************************
13   ok: [demo.example.com] => {
14       "command_output.stdout_lines": [
15           "-rwxr-xr-x. 1 devops wheel 31 Mar 30 13:39 examp\
16   le.sh"
17       ]
18   }
19   PLAY RECAP *********************************************\
20   ********************************************
21   demo.example.com            : ok=3    changed=1    unreach\
22   able=0    failed=0    skipped=0    rescued=0    ignored=0
23   ansible-pilot $
```

wrong module code

```
1   ---
2   - name: shell module demo
3     hosts: all
4     tasks:
5       - name: list file(s) and folder(s)
6         ansible.builtin.command: 'ls -l *'
7         register: command_output
8       - name: command output
9         ansible.builtin.debug:
10            var: command_output.stdout_lines
```

wrong module execution

```
1   ansible-pilot $ ansible-playbook -i virtualmachines/demo/\
2   inventory commmand_shell/list_files_command.yaml
3   PLAY [shell module demo] *********************************\
4   *******************************************
5   TASK [Gathering Facts] **********************************\
6   *******************************************
7   ok: [demo.example.com]
8   TASK [list file(s) and folder(s)] **********************\
9   *******************************************
10  fatal: [demo.example.com]: FAILED! => {"changed": true, "\
11  cmd": ["ls", "-l", "*"], "delta": "0:00:00.003038", "end"\
12  : "2022-04-06 13:01:54.498403", "msg": "non-zero return c\
13  ode", "rc": 2, "start": "2022-04-06 13:01:54.495365", "st\
14  derr": "ls: cannot access '*': No such file or directory"\
15  , "stderr_lines": ["ls: cannot access '*': No such file o\
16  r directory"], "stdout": "", "stdout_lines": []}
17  PLAY RECAP *********************************************\
18  *******************************************
19  demo.example.com            : ok=1    changed=0    unreach\
20  able=0    failed=1    skipped=0    rescued=0    ignored=0
21  ansible-pilot $
```

Test host availability - Ansible module ping

Let's talk about Ansible module `ping`.
The full name is `ansible.builtin.ping`, which means that is part of the collection of modules "builtin" with ansible and shipped with it.
It's a module pretty stable and out for years.
It verify the ability of Ansible to login to the managed host and that there is a Python interpreter that is able to execute our code.
So it's pretty different for the ping in the network context.
It's the Linux corresponding to the Windows Ansible win_ping module.

Main parameters and return values

- data <u>string</u>

People usually don't specify any parameters or use the return value. For the parameter, it's possible to change the behavior from the default "pong" to the "crash" that raises an exception in case of failure.

- ping <u>string</u>

The return value default is the "pong" string, but you could customize it with the data parameter.

Demo

How to test host availability using the Ansible `ping` module.

```
1    ---
2    - name: ping module demo
3      hosts: all
4      become: false
5      tasks:
6        - name: test connection
7          ansible.builtin.ping:
```

How to print a text or a variable during the execution with Ansible

Let's talk about Ansible module debug.
It's part of the `ansible.builtin` collection so it's part of the collection of modules "builtin" with ansible and shipped with it.
It's a stable module and works with a variety of operating systems.
The purpose is to print statements during execution. This means not only text but also all the possible Ansible variables and facts.

 See also Ansible troubleshooting - undefined variable.

Parameters

- msg <u>string</u>
- var <u>string</u>
- verbosity <u>integer</u>

This module has three parameters. If you launch without any parameter the default "Hello world!" (with exclamation mark) is printed.
If we prefer to customize the message we need to specify the `msg`

parameter.

In the same way, the var parameter allows us to print a variable.

We could combine text and variables in the msg field. Please note that you need to use always the double brackets when we want the variable value.

The verbosity is for advanced users if you would like to hide our debug code in normal execution but keep it in the playbook if we need it in debug mode. The value could vary from 0 normal execution to 3.

Ansible debug module demo

In the following example we are going beyond the print of "Hello world!" text, printing a text, a variable, text and variable, and demonstrate to you how to use the verbosity level.

```
1   ---
2   - name: debug module demo
3     hosts: all
4     vars:
5       fruit: "apple"
6     tasks:
7       - name: debug message
8         ansible.builtin.debug:
9           msg: "our fruit is {{ fruit }}"
10          verbosity: 2
```

Edit single-line text - Ansible module lineinfile

Let's talk about the Ansible module lineinfile.

The full name is ansible.builtin.lineinfile, which means that is part of the collection of modules "builtin" with ansible and shipped with it.

It's a module pretty stable and out for years and it supports a large variety of operating systems.

You are able to insert, update and remove a single line of text in a file.

Parameters

- path <u>string</u> - file path
- line <u>string</u> - text
- insertafter/insertbefore <u>string</u> - EOF/regular expression
- validate <u>string</u> - validation command
- create <u>boolean</u> - create if not exist
- state <u>string</u> - present/absent
- owner/group/mode - permission
- setype/seuser/selevel - SELinux

The only required is "path", where you specify the filesystem path of the file you're going to edit. "line" is the line of text we would like to insert in the file, easy!

By default, the text is going to be inserted at the end of the file, but we could personalize it in a specific position with `insertafter` or `insertbefore`.

If there is any tool to validate the file we could specify it in the validate parameter, very useful for configuration files.

If the file does not exist we could also "create" it!

Usually, we would like to insert a text line but we could also remove using state in conjunction with parameter absent.

Let me also highlight that we could also specify some permissions or SELinux property.

demo

How to change a single line of parameter of the `/etc/ssh/sshd_config` OpenSSH configuration file in Linux using the `lineinfile` module and an Ansible Playbook.

- lineinfile.yml

```
1   ---
2   - name: lineinfile module demo
3     hosts: all
4     become: true
5     tasks:
6       - name: allow password authentication
7         ansible.builtin.lineinfile:
8           state: present
9           dest: /etc/ssh/sshd_config
10          regexp: "^PasswordAuthentication"
11          line: "PasswordAuthentication yes"
12          validate: 'sshd -t -f %s'
```

Edit multi-line text - Ansible module blockinfile

Let's talk about Ansible module `blockinfile`.

The full name is `ansible.builtin.blockinfile`, which means that is part of the collection of modules "builtin" with ansible and shipped with it.

It's a module pretty stable and out for years and it supports a large variety of operating systems.

You are able to insert, update and remove a block of multi-line text in a file. This block is going to be surrounded by customizable marker lines, just to identify that this edit was performed by Ansible.

See also Ansible troubleshooting - Indentation error.

Main Parameters

- path `string`
- block `string`
- insertafter/insertbefore `string`
- validate `string`
- create `boolean`
- state `string`
- marker_begin/marker_end `string`
- mode/owner/group
- setype/seuser/selevel

The only required is `path` parameter, where you specify the filesystem path of the file we're going to edit.

`block` parameter is the text we would like to insert in the file, easy!

By default, the text is going to be inserted at the end of the file, but we could personalize it in a specific position with `insertafter`/`insertbefore` parameter.

If there is any tool to validate the file we could specify in the validate parameter, very useful for configuration files.

If the file does not exist we could create it!

Usually, we would like to insert a text block but we could also remove using state in conjunction with parameter absent.

Our text is going to be surrounded by some markers, some comments, that show up that we did this edit with Ansible. We could customize the text as well.

Let me also highlight that we could also specify some permissions or SELinux property.

Demo

How to create a multiline text file in Linux with an Ansible
Playbook.

```
1    ---
2    - name: blockinfile module demo
3      hosts: all
4      become: true
5      tasks:
6    - name: Generate /etc/hosts file
7        ansible.builtin.blockinfile:
8          state: present
9          dest: /etc/hosts
10         content: |
11           192.168.0.200 demo demo.example.com
```

Pause execution - Ansible module pause

Let's talk about the Ansible module pause.
This module is also supported for Windows targets.
The full name is `ansible.builtin.pause`, which means that is part
of the collection of modules "builtin" with Ansible and shipped with
it.
The default behavior is to pause with a prompt.
It pauses Ansible playbook execution for a set amount of time, or
until a prompt is acknowledged.

Parameters

- minutes string - a positive number of minutes

- seconds string - a positive number of seconds
- prompt string - "Text message"

-echo boolean - yes/no

All parameters are optional.

The default behavior is to pause the execution with a prompt.

You could specify the amount of time using the parameters "minutes" and "seconds". Starting in Ansible 2.2, if you specify 0 or negative for minutes or seconds, it will wait for 1 second, previously it would wait indefinitely.

When minutes or seconds are specified, user input is not captured or echoed, regardless of the echo setting.

I'll cover the user input in another module.

demo

How to pause execution of an Ansible Playbook.

code

- pause.yml

```
1    ---
2    - name: pause module demo
3      hosts: all
4      vars:
5        wait_seconds: 10
6      tasks:
7        - name: pause for {{ wait_seconds | int }} second(s)
8          ansible.builtin.pause:
9            seconds: "{{ wait_seconds | int }}"
10   - name: message
11         ansible.builtin.debug:
12           msg: "The end"
```

output

```
1   $ ansible-playbook -i demo/inventory pause/pause.yml
2   PLAY [pause module demo] *******************************\
3   *****************************************
4   TASK [Gathering Facts] *********************************\
5   *****************************************
6   ok: [demo.example.com]
7   TASK [pause for 10 second(s)] **************************\
8   *****************************************
9   Pausing for 10 seconds
10  (ctrl+C then 'C' = continue early, ctrl+C then 'A' = abor\
11  t)
12  ok: [demo.example.com]
13  TASK [message] ****************************************\
14  *****************************************
15  ok: [demo.example.com] => {
16      "msg": "The end"
17  }
18  PLAY RECAP ********************************************\
19  *****************************************
20  demo.example.com              : ok=3    changed=0    unreach\
21  able=0    failed=0    skipped=0    rescued=0    ignored=0
```

output with manual continue (CTRL+C and "C")

```
1   $ ansible-playbook -i demo/inventory pause/pause.yml
2   PLAY [pause module demo] *******************************\
3   *****************************************
4   TASK [Gathering Facts] *********************************\
5   *****************************************
6   ok: [demo.example.com]
7   TASK [pause for 10 second(s)] **************************\
8   *****************************************
9   Pausing for 10 seconds
10  (ctrl+C then 'C' = continue early, ctrl+C then 'A' = abor\
```

```
11    t)
12    Press 'C' to continue the play or 'A' to abort
13    ok: [demo.example.com]
14    TASK [message] ****************************************\
15    ***************************************
16    ok: [demo.example.com] => {
17        "msg": "The end"
18    }
```

output with manual abort (CTRL+C and "A")

```
1     $ ansible-playbook -i demo/inventory pause/pause.yml
2     PLAY [pause module demo] ******************************\
3     ***************************************
4     TASK [Gathering Facts] ********************************\
5     ***************************************
6     ok: [demo.example.com]
7     TASK [pause for 10 second(s)] *************************\
8     ***************************************
9     Pausing for 10 seconds
10    (ctrl+C then 'C' = continue early, ctrl+C then 'A' = abor\
11    t)
12    Press 'C' to continue the play or 'A' to abort
13    fatal: [demo.example.com]: FAILED! => {"msg": "user reque\
14    sted abort!"}
15    NO MORE HOSTS LEFT ************************************\
16    ***************************************
17    PLAY RECAP ******************************************\
18    ***************************************
19    demo.example.com              : ok=1    changed=0    unreach\
20    able=0    failed=1    skipped=0    rescued=0    ignored=0
```

Execute command on the Ansible host - Ansible localhost

How to execute Ansible command(s) or task(s) on localhost using the connection plugin local and the right ansible internals variables. When Ansible becomes part of your daily workflow it is natural you would like to automate also task in your local machine.

Execute command on the Ansible host options

- `connection plugin`
- `delegate_to: localhost`
- `local_action`

There are three ways to execute modules and commands on the Ansible Controller host.

The first and my favorite is using the connection plugin `local` and applying it to the Ansible Play level of your Playbook. The tricky was is to adjust some ansible variables about the python interpreter. I consider it the best way nowadays.

The second way is using the `delegate_to` at the Task level. This has the advantage to delegate only one task to localhost but still needs only the implicit localhost scheme.

The third way is using the `local_action` statement. I personally don't like it but it's one alternative as well at Task level, so same as the previous.

Links

- Controlling where tasks run: delegation and local actions[30]

---

[30]https://docs.ansible.com/ansible/latest/user_guide/playbooks_delegation.html

- Implicit 'localhost'[31]

demo

How to Execute command on the Ansible host using connection: local method.

code

```
1   ---
2   - name: localhost demo
3     hosts: localhost
4     vars:
5       ansible_connection: local
6       ansible_python_interpreter: "{{ ansible_playbook_pyth\
7   on }}"
8     tasks:
9       - name: print hostname
10        ansible.builtin.debug:
11          msg: "{{ inventory_hostname }}"
```

execution

```
1   ansible-pilot $ ansible-playbook ansible\ statements/loca\
2   lhost.yml
3   [WARNING]: No inventory was parsed, only implicit localho\
4   st is available
5   [WARNING]: provided hosts list is empty, only localhost i\
6   s available. Note that the implicit
7   localhost does not match 'all'
8   PLAY [localhost demo] ********************************\
9   *****************************************
10  TASK [Gathering Facts] *******************************\
11  *****************************************
```

[31]https://docs.ansible.com/ansible/latest/inventory/implicit_localhost.html

```
12   ok: [localhost]
13   TASK [print hostname] ********************************\
14   ********************************************
15   ok: [localhost] => {
16       "msg": "localhost"
17   }
18   PLAY RECAP **************************************\
19   ********************************************
20   localhost                    : ok=2    changed=0    unreach\
21   able=0    failed=0    skipped=0    rescued=0    ignored=0
22   ansible-pilot $
```

idempotency

```
1    ansible-pilot $ ansible-playbook ansible\ statements/loca\
2    lhost.yml
3    [WARNING]: No inventory was parsed, only implicit localho\
4    st is available
5    [WARNING]: provided hosts list is empty, only localhost i\
6    s available. Note that the implicit
7    localhost does not match 'all'
8    PLAY [localhost demo] ********************************\
9    ********************************************
10   TASK [Gathering Facts] ********************************\
11   ********************************************
12   ok: [localhost]
13   TASK [print hostname] ********************************\
14   ********************************************
15   ok: [localhost] => {
16       "msg": "localhost"
17   }
18   PLAY RECAP **************************************\
19   ********************************************
20   localhost                    : ok=2    changed=0    unreach\
21   able=0    failed=0    skipped=0    rescued=0    ignored=0
22   ansible-pilot $
```

Read a file into a variable on host - Ansible lookup plugin file

How to automate the reading of example.txt file on Ansible host, assign to a variable and use in your Ansible Playbook code.

Ansible read a file into a variable

- `ansible.builtin.file`
- read file contents

Let's deep dive into the Ansible lookup plugin file.
Plugins are a way to expand the Ansible functionality. With lookup plugins specifically, you can load variables or templates with information from external sources.
The full name is `ansible.builtin.file`, it's part of `ansible-core` and is included in all Ansible installations.
The purpose of the `file` lookup plugin is to read file contents.

Parameters and Return Values

Parameters

- _terms string - path(s) of files to read

Return Values

- _raw list - content of file(s)

The parameters of the lookup plugin `file`.
The only required parameter is the default "_terms", with the path(s) of files to read.
The normal usage is to assign the lookup plugin to a variable name that you could use in your playbook.

demo

Read a file into a variable on the host with Ansible Playbook.

code

```
1  ---
2  - name: read file on host
3    hosts: all
4    vars:
5     contents: "{{ lookup('file','example.txt') }}"
6    tasks:
7     - name: print file
8       ansible.builtin.debug:
9        msg: "the content of file is {{ contents }}"
```

execution

```
ansible-pilot $ ansible-playbook -i virtualmachines/demo/\
inventory variables/read-file.yml
PLAY [read file on host] ********************************\
********************************************
TASK [Gathering Facts] *********************************\
********************************************
ok: [demo.example.com]
TASK [print file] **************************************\
********************************************
ok: [demo.example.com] => {
    "msg": "the content of file is example contents"
}
PLAY RECAP *********************************************\
********************************************
demo.example.com           : ok=2    changed=0    unreach\
able=0    failed=0    skipped=0    rescued=0    ignored=0
ansible-pilot $
```

idempotency

```
ansible-pilot $ ansible-playbook -i virtualmachines/demo/\
inventory variables/read-file.yml
PLAY [read file on host] ********************************\
***********************************************
TASK [Gathering Facts] *********************************\
***********************************************
ok: [demo.example.com]
TASK [print file] **************************************\
***********************************************
ok: [demo.example.com] => {
    "msg": "the content of file is example contents"
}
PLAY RECAP *********************************************\
***********************************************
demo.example.com           : ok=2    changed=0    unreach\
able=0    failed=0    skipped=0    rescued=0    ignored=0
ansible-pilot $
```

Reboot remote hosts - Ansible module reboot

Let's talk about the Ansible module reboot.

The full name is ansible.builtin.reboot which means is part of the collection of modules "builtin" with ansible and shipped with ansible-core.

This module is pretty stable and out for years and supports a large variety of operating systems.

The purpose is to reboot a remote machine, wait for it to go down, come back up, and respond to commands.

For Windows targets, use the ansible.windows.win_reboot module instead.

Parameters

- reboot_timeout _integer_ - 600
- msg _string_ - "Reboot initiated by Ansible"
- reboot_command _string_ - "[OS specific]"
- pre_reboot_delay _integer_ - 0
- post_reboot_delay _integer_ - 0
- test_command string - "whoami"
- boot_time_command string - "cat /proc/sys/kernel/random/-boot_id"

This module has not required parameters but some of them might are nice to know.

Let me summarize the most useful parameters.

The "reboot_timeout" defines how much time to expect before a machine returns up & running. The real timeout is double because of the process of reboot and test command success.

The first step in the reboot process is to print a message to all the logged users. You could keep the default "Reboot initiated by Ansible" or customize using the "msg" parameter.

Secondly is going to execute the reboot command, OS-specific. If you need a specific one, please customize the "reboot_command" parameter.

You could define also some extra delay time using the "pre_reboot_delay" or "post_reboot_delay" integer. Both default to zero.

Once rebooted the target host Ansible is going to verify the workstation fully working using a test command. The default is `whoami`, but you could customize using the "test_command" parameter.

This module could return also the amount of time indeed for bootstrap process reading throw kernel, specifically `/proc/sys/kernel/random/boot_id`.

demo

Let's jump into a real-life playbook on how to reboot remote hosts
with Ansible Playbook.

- reboot.yml

```
1    ---
2    - name: reboot module demo
3      hosts: all
4      become: true
5      tasks:
6        - name: reboot host(s)
7          ansible.builtin.reboot:
8            msg: "reboot by Ansible"
9            pre_reboot_delay: 5
10           post_reboot_delay: 10
11           test_command: "whoami"
```

Checkout git repository via HTTPS - Ansible module git

Let's talk about Ansible module git.
The full name is ansible.builtin.git which means is part of the
collection of modules "builtin" with ansible and shipped with it.
This module is pretty stable and out for years.
The purpose is to Deploy software (or files) from git checkouts in
our managed hosts.
If you would like to fetch via SSH please refer to: Checkout git
repository SSH - Ansible module git

Parameters and Return Values

The parameter list is pretty wide but I'll summarize the most useful.

- **repo** path
- **dest** string
- update boolean

The only required parameters are "repo" and "dest".

"repo" specifies the source repository URL.

"dest" specify the destination path.

The "update" retrieves new revisions from the already synched origin repository.

- after string

The most interesting return value is "after" which contains the last commit after the update process.

Demo

Let's jump in a real-life playbook to checkout a git repository with Ansible

```
1   ---
2   - name: git module demo
3     hosts: all
4     become: true
5     tasks:
6       - name: ensure git pkg installed
7         ansible.builtin.yum:
8           name: git
9           state: present
10
11      - name: checkout git repo
12        ansible.builtin.git:
13          repo: https://github.com/lucab85/ansible-pilot.git
14          dest: /home/devops/ansible-pilot
```

Checkout git repository via SSH - Ansible module git

Let's talk about Ansible module `git`.
The full name is `ansible.builtin.git` which means is part of the collection of modules "builtin" with ansible and shipped with it.
This module is pretty stable and out for years.
The purpose is to Deploy software (or files) from git checkouts in our managed hosts.
If you would like to fetch via SSH please refer to: Checkout git repository HTTPS - Ansible module git

Parameters and Return Values

The parameter list is pretty wide but I'll summarize the most useful.

- **repo** <u>path</u>

- **dest** string
- update boolean

- key_file path - SSH private key

The parameter list is pretty wide but I'll summarize the most useful.
The only required parameters are "repo" and "dest".
The "repo" parameter specifies the source repository URL, in our use case, in the SSH way.
The "dest" parameter specifies the destination path.
The "update" parameter retrieves new revisions from the already synched origin repository.
The "key_file" parameter specifies the path in the filesystem where to store the SSH private key.
Please note that the SSH private key is a path on the target host.
Please note also that the SSH public key needs to be already shared in your Git server.

- after string

The most interesting return value is "after" which contains the last commit after the update process.

Demo

Let's jump in a real-life playbook to checkout a git repository with Ansible

- git_ssh.yml

```yaml
1  ---
2  - name: git module demo
3    hosts: all
4    vars:
5      repo: "git@github.com:lucab85/ansible-pilot.git"
6      dest: "/home/devops/ansible-pilot"
7      sshkey: "~/.ssh/id_rsa"
8    tasks:
9      - name: ensure git pkg installed
10       ansible.builtin.yum:
11         name: git
12         state: present
13         update_cache: true
14       become: true
15
16     - name: checkout git repo
17       ansible.builtin.git:
18         repo: "{{ repo }}"
19         dest: "{{ dest }}"
20         key_file: "{{ sshkey }}"
```

Copy files to remote hosts - Local to Remote - Ansible module copy

Let's talk about the Ansible module `copy`.
The full name is `ansible.builtin.copy` which means is part of the
collection of modules "builtin" with ansible and shipped with it.
This module is pretty stable and out for years.
The purpose is to copy files to remote locations.
Please note that the opposite is done by Ansible fetch module.
For Windows target use Ansible win_copy module.

Parameters

- dest <u>path</u> - remote path
- src <u>string</u> - local path
- backup <u>boolean</u> - no / yes
- validate <u>string</u> - validation command
- checksum <u>string</u> 2.5+
- mode/owner/group
- setype/seuser/selevel

The only required parameter is dest which specifies the remote absolute path destination.

The src specifies the source file in the controller host. It could be a relative or absolute path. I recommend absolutely.

The backup boolean option allows you to create a backup if the utility overwrites any file.

If there is any tool to validate the file we could specify it in the validate parameter, very useful for configuration files.

Let me also highlight that we could also specify the permissions and SELinux properties.

Demo

How to to copy files to remote hosts in Linux with Ansible using the copy module.

code

- copy.yml

```
1    ---
2    - name: copy module demo
3      hosts: all
4      become: false
5      tasks:
6        - name: copy report.txt
7          ansible.builtin.copy:
8            src: report.txt
9            dest: /home/devops/report.txt
10           owner: devops
11           mode: '0644'
```

- report.txt

```
1    test report.txt
```

Copy files from remote hosts - Remote to Local - Ansible module fetch

Let's talk about the Ansible module `fetch`.
The full name is `ansible.builtin.fetch` which means is part of the collection of modules "builtin" with ansible and shipped with it.
This module is pretty stable and out for years.
The purpose is to copy files from remote locations. Please note that the opposite is done by Ansible copy module.

Parameters

- dest path
- src string

- fail_on_missing <u>boolean</u>
- validate_checksum <u>boolean</u>
- flat <u>boolean</u>

The parameter list is pretty wide but I'll summarize the most useful.

The only required parameter is "dest" which specifies a directory to save the file into and the "src" specifies the source files in the remote hosts. It
must be a file, not a directory.

The "fail_on_missing" boolean is set to true so the task is going to fail if the file doesn't exist.

The file is going to be transferred and validate in the source and the destination with a checksum. If we don't want this behavior we could override with
the "validate_checksum" option.

The "flat" option allows you to override the default behavior of appending hostname/path/to/file to the destination.

Demo

Let's jump in a real-life playbook to copy files from remote hosts with Ansible

- fetch.yml

```
1   ---
2   - name: fetch module demo
3     hosts: all
4     become: true
5     vars:
6       log_file: "/var/log/messages"
7       dump_dir: "logs"
8     tasks:
9       - name: fetch log
10        ansible.builtin.fetch:
11          src: "{{ log_file }}"
12          dest: "{{ dump_dir }}"
```

Start and enable services on boot on Linux remote hosts - Ansible module service_facts, service

How to enable services on boot on remote hosts with Ansible.

- ansible.builtin.service_facts
- Return service state information as fact data
- ansible.builtin.service
- Manage services

Let's talk about Ansible modules `service_facts` and `service`.
First, you need to acquire the information of the services on the target machine.
This task is performed by the Ansible module `service_facts`. You can't enable a service that doesn't exist, can you?
The effective actions are performed by the Ansible module service.
The full name is `ansible.builtin.service` which means that both these modules are part of the collection of modules "builtin" with

Ansible and shipped with it.

This module is pretty stable and out for years and its purpose is to manage services on remote hosts.

For Windows targets, use the `ansible.windows.win_service` module instead.

Parameters

- name path - name of the service
- state string - started / stopped / restarted / reloaded
- enabled boolean - no/yes
- arguments/args string - extra args

The parameter list is pretty wide but I'll summarize the most useful. The only required parameter is `name` that specifies the name of the service.

At least one between the `state` and `enabled` parameters is mandatory.

The `state` parameter defines the action that we are going to take. It has four alternative options:

- `started` and `stopped` options allow you to run or stop the service.
- `restarted` is a combination of stop and start - you could also customize the number of seconds between using the "sleep" parameter
- the `reloaded` option is useful if the service needs to reload the configuration file.

The `enable` parameter allows you to decide if the service should start on boot or not.

The `arguments` or `args` parameter allows you to specify some additional arguments provided on the command line.

demo

How to enable services on boot and start on remote hosts with Ansible Playbook.
Included code and demo with chronyd.service NTP server on a RedHat Enterprise Linux 8.

code

- service_enable_on_boot.yml

```
1   ---
2   - name: service module demo
3     hosts: all
4     become: true
5     vars:
6       services_on_boot:
7         - "chronyd.service"
8     tasks:
9       - name: populate service facts
10        ansible.builtin.service_facts:
11      - name: enable services on boot
12        ansible.builtin.service:
13          name: "{{ item }}"
14          enabled: true
15          state: started
16        when: "item in services"
17        with_items: '{{ services_on_boot }}'
```

execution

```
$ ansible-playbook -i virtualmachines/demo/inventory enab\
le\ services\ on\ boot/service.yml
PLAY [service module demo] ******************************\
**********************************************
TASK [Gathering Facts] **********************************\
**********************************************
ok: [demo.example.com]
TASK [populate service facts] ***************************\
**********************************************
ok: [demo.example.com]
TASK [enable services on boot] **************************\
**********************************************
changed: [demo.example.com] => (item=chronyd.service)
PLAY RECAP **********************************************\
**********************************************
demo.example.com             : ok=3    changed=1    unreach\
able=0    failed=0    skipped=0    rescued=0    ignored=0
```

before execution

```
$ ssh devops@demo.example.com
[devops@demo ~]$ sudo su
[root@demo devops]# cat /etc/redhat-release
Red Hat Enterprise Linux release 8.4 (Ootpa)
[root@demo devops]# rpm -qa | grep chrony
chrony-3.5-2.el8.x86_64
[root@demo devops]# systemctl status chronyd.service
  chronyd.service - NTP client/server
   Loaded: loaded (/usr/lib/systemd/system/chronyd.servic\
e; disabled; vendor preset: enabled)
   Active: inactive (dead)
     Docs: man:chronyd(8)
           man:chrony.conf(5)
[root@demo devops]#
```

after execution

```
$ ssh devops@demo.example.com
[devops@demo ~]$ sudo su
[root@demo devops]# systemctl status chronyd.service
 chronyd.service - NTP client/server
   Loaded: loaded (/usr/lib/systemd/system/chronyd.servic\
e; enabled; vendor preset: enabled)
   Active: active (running) since Mon 2021-11-29 11:29:53\
 UTC; 49s ago
     Docs: man:chronyd(8)
           man:chrony.conf(5)
  Process: 1729 ExecStartPost=/usr/libexec/chrony-helper \
update-daemon (code=exited, status=0/SUCC>
  Process: 1725 ExecStart=/usr/sbin/chronyd $OPTIONS (cod\
e=exited, status=0/SUCCESS)
 Main PID: 1727 (chronyd)
    Tasks: 1 (limit: 4943)
   Memory: 844.0K
   CGroup: /system.slice/chronyd.service
           └─1727 /usr/sbin/chronyd
Nov 29 11:29:53 demo.example.com systemd[1]: Starting NTP\
 client/server...
Nov 29 11:29:53 demo.example.com chronyd[1727]: chronyd v\
ersion 3.5 starting (+CMDMON +NTP +REFCLO>
Nov 29 11:29:53 demo.example.com chronyd[1727]: Frequency\
 -491.773 +/- 29.501 ppm read from /var/l>
Nov 29 11:29:53 demo.example.com chronyd[1727]: Using rig\
ht/UTC timezone to obtain leap second data
Nov 29 11:29:53 demo.example.com systemd[1]: Started NTP \
client/server.
Nov 29 11:29:59 demo.example.com chronyd[1727]: Selected \
source 81.25.28.124
Nov 29 11:29:59 demo.example.com chronyd[1727]: System cl\
ock TAI offset set to 37 seconds
Nov 29 11:29:59 demo.example.com chronyd[1727]: System cl\
```

```
ock wrong by 1.840437 seconds, adjustment>
Nov 29 11:30:00 demo.example.com chronyd[1727]: System cl\
ock was stepped by 1.840437 seconds
[root@demo devops]# reboot
Connection to demo.example.com closed by remote host.
Connection to demo.example.com closed.
ansible-pilot $ ssh devops@demo.example.com
[devops@demo ~]$ sudo su
[root@demo devops]# systemctl status chronyd.service
▢ chronyd.service - NTP client/server
   Loaded: loaded (/usr/lib/systemd/system/chronyd.servic\
e; enabled; vendor preset: enabled)
   Active: active (running) since Mon 2021-11-29 11:31:32\
 UTC; 28s ago
     Docs: man:chronyd(8)
           man:chrony.conf(5)
  Process: 825 ExecStartPost=/usr/libexec/chrony-helper u\
pdate-daemon (code=exited, status=0/SUCCE>
  Process: 811 ExecStart=/usr/sbin/chronyd $OPTIONS (code\
=exited, status=0/SUCCESS)
 Main PID: 820 (chronyd)
    Tasks: 1 (limit: 4943)
   Memory: 1.5M
   CGroup: /system.slice/chronyd.service
           └─820 /usr/sbin/chronyd
Nov 29 11:31:32 demo.example.com systemd[1]: Starting NTP\
 client/server...
Nov 29 11:31:32 demo.example.com chronyd[820]: chronyd ve\
rsion 3.5 starting (+CMDMON +NTP +REFCLOC>
Nov 29 11:31:32 demo.example.com chronyd[820]: Frequency \
-389.145 +/- 224.519 ppm read from /var/l>
Nov 29 11:31:32 demo.example.com chronyd[820]: Using righ\
t/UTC timezone to obtain leap second data
Nov 29 11:31:32 demo.example.com systemd[1]: Started NTP \
client/server.
```

```
70  Nov 29 11:31:39 demo.example.com chronyd[820]: Selected s\
71  ource 81.25.28.124
72  Nov 29 11:31:39 demo.example.com chronyd[820]: System clo\
73  ck TAI offset set to 37 seconds
74  Nov 29 11:31:39 demo.example.com chronyd[820]: System clo\
75  ck wrong by 2.026567 seconds, adjustment >
76  Nov 29 11:31:41 demo.example.com chronyd[820]: System clo\
77  ck was stepped by 2.026567 seconds
78  Nov 29 11:31:43 demo.example.com chronyd[820]: Selected s\
79  ource 89.221.210.188
80  [root@demo devops]#
```

Restart services on remote hosts - Ansible module service

Let's talk about the Ansible module `service`.

The full name is `ansible.builtin.service` which means is part of the collection of modules "builtin" with ansible and shipped with it.

This module is pretty stable and out for years.

The purpose is to controls services on remote hosts.

The Supported service systems include BSD, OpenRC, SysV, Solaris SMF, systemd, and upstart.

For Windows targets, use the `ansible.windows.win_service` module instead.

Parameters

- name <u>path</u> - name of the service
- state <u>string</u> - started / stopped / restarted / reloaded
- enabled <u>boolean</u> - no/yes
- sleep <u>integer</u> - seconds after the restart

- arguments/args <u>string</u> - extra args

The parameter list is pretty wide but I'll summarize the most useful. The only required parameter is "name" that specifies the name of the service.

At least one between the "state" and "enabled" parameters is mandatory.

The "state" parameter defines the action that we are going to take. It has four alternatives options: "started" and "stopped" options allow you to run or stop the service. "restarted" is a combination of stop and start - you could also customize the number of seconds between using the "sleep" parameter

The "reloaded" option is useful if the service needs to reload the configuration file.

The "enable" parameter allows you to decide if the service should start on boot or not.

The "arguments or args" parameter allows you to specify some additional arguments provided on the command line.

demo

Let's jump into a real-life playbook on how to controls services on remote hosts with Ansible Playbook.

- service.yml

```
1    ---
2    - name: service module demo
3      hosts: all
4      become: true
5      tasks:
6        - name: sshd restart
7          ansible.builtin.service:
8            name: sshd
9            state: restarted
10           enabled: true
```

Stop and disable services on boot on remote hosts - Ansible module service_facts, service

How to enable services on boot on remote hosts with Ansible.

- ansible.builtin.service_facts
- Return service state information as fact data
- ansible.builtin.service
- Manage services

Let's talk about Ansible modules `service_facts` and `service`.
First, you need to acquire the information of the services on the target machine.
This task is performed by the Ansible module `service_facts`. You can't enable a service that doesn't exist, can you?
The effective actions are performed by the Ansible module service.
The full name is `ansible.builtin.service` which means that both these modules are part of the collection of modules "builtin" with Ansible and shipped with it.
This module is pretty stable and out for years and its purpose is to

manage services on remote hosts.

For Windows targets, use the `ansible.windows.win_service` module instead.

Parameters

- name path - name of the service
- state string - started / stopped / restarted / reloaded
- enabled boolean - no/yes
- arguments/args string - extra args

The parameter list is pretty wide but I'll summarize the most useful. The only required parameter is "name" that specifies the name of the service.

At least one between the "state" and "enabled" parameters is mandatory.

The "state" parameter defines the action that we are going to take. It has four alternative options: "started" and "stopped" options allow you to run or stop the service. "restarted" is a combination of stop and start - you could also customize the number of seconds between using the "sleep" parameter

The "reloaded" option is useful if the service needs to reload the configuration file.

The "enable" parameter allows you to decide if the service should start on boot or not.

The "arguments or args" parameter allows you to specify some additional arguments provided on the command line.

demo

How to stop and disable services on boot on Linux remote hosts with Ansible Playbook.

The following code and demo use `chronyd.service` NTP server on a RedHat Enterprise Linux 8 machine.

code

- service_stop_disable_on_boot.yml

```yaml
1   ---
2   - name: service module demo
3     hosts: all
4     become: true
5     vars:
6       disable_services:
7         - "chronyd.service"
8     tasks:
9       - name: populate service facts
10        ansible.builtin.service_facts:
11
12      - name: disable services
13        ansible.builtin.service:
14          name: "{{ item }}"
15          enabled: false
16          state: stopped
17        when: "item in services"
18        with_items: '{{ disable_services }}'
```

execution

```
$ ansible-playbook -i virtualmachines/demo/inventory serv\
ices/service_stop_disable.yml
PLAY [service module demo] ***************************\
*******************************************
TASK [Gathering Facts] ******************************\
*******************************************
ok: [demo.example.com]
TASK [populate service facts] ***********************\
*******************************************
ok: [demo.example.com]
TASK [disable services] *****************************\
*******************************************
changed: [demo.example.com] => (item=chronyd.service)
PLAY RECAP ******************************************\
*******************************************
demo.example.com              : ok=3    changed=1    unreach\
able=0    failed=0    skipped=0    rescued=0    ignored=0
```

before execution

```
$ ssh devops@demo.example.com
[devops@demo ~]$ sudo su
[root@demo devops]# cat /etc/redhat-release
Red Hat Enterprise Linux release 8.4 (Ootpa)
[root@demo devops]# rpm -qa | grep chrony
chrony-3.5-2.el8.x86_64
[root@demo devops]# systemctl status chronyd.service
  chronyd.service - NTP client/server
   Loaded: loaded (/usr/lib/systemd/system/chronyd.servic\
e; enabled; vendor preset: enabled)
   Active: active (running) since Mon 2021-11-29 11:31:32\
 UTC; 1 day 21h ago
     Docs: man:chronyd(8)
           man:chrony.conf(5)
  Process: 825 ExecStartPost=/usr/libexec/chrony-helper u\
pdate-daemon (code-exited, status=0/SUCCE>
```

```
17     Process: 811 ExecStart=/usr/sbin/chronyd $OPTIONS (code\
18 =exited, status=0/SUCCESS)
19   Main PID: 820 (chronyd)
20      Tasks: 1 (limit: 4943)
21     Memory: 1.3M
22     CGroup: /system.slice/chronyd.service
23             └─820 /usr/sbin/chronyd
24 Nov 30 13:59:47 demo.example.com chronyd[820]: Can\'t syn\
25 chronise: no majority
26 Nov 30 14:20:47 demo.example.com chronyd[820]: Selected s\
27 ource 147.251.48.140
28 Nov 30 14:33:43 demo.example.com chronyd[820]: Selected s\
29 ource 89.221.218.101
30 Nov 30 14:39:26 demo.example.com chronyd[820]: Source 108\
31 .61.164.200 replaced with 5.79.75.37
32 Nov 30 15:01:14 demo.example.com chronyd[820]: Selected s\
33 ource 147.251.48.140
34 Dec 01 07:18:26 demo.example.com chronyd[820]: Forward ti\
35 me jump detected!
36 Dec 01 07:18:26 demo.example.com chronyd[820]: Can\'t syn\
37 chronise: no selectable sources
38 Dec 01 07:20:35 demo.example.com chronyd[820]: Selected s\
39 ource 147.251.48.140
40 Dec 01 07:23:49 demo.example.com chronyd[820]: Selected s\
41 ource 89.234.64.77
42 Dec 01 07:33:31 demo.example.com chronyd[820]: Selected s\
43 ource 89.221.218.101
44 [root@demo devops]#
```

after execution

```
$ ssh devops@demo.example.com
Last login: Wed Dec  1 08:39:40 2021 from 192.168.0.101
[devops@demo ~]$ sudo su
[root@demo devops]# systemctl status chronyd.service
 chronyd.service - NTP client/server
   Loaded: loaded (/usr/lib/systemd/system/chronyd.servic\
e; disabled; vendor preset: enabled)
   Active: inactive (dead)
     Docs: man:chronyd(8)
           man:chrony.conf(5)
Nov 30 15:01:14 demo.example.com chronyd[820]: Selected s\
ource 147.251.48.140
Dec 01 07:18:26 demo.example.com chronyd[820]: Forward ti\
me jump detected!
Dec 01 07:18:26 demo.example.com chronyd[820]: Can\'t syn\
chronise: no selectable sources
Dec 01 07:20:35 demo.example.com chronyd[820]: Selected s\
ource 147.251.48.140
Dec 01 07:23:49 demo.example.com chronyd[820]: Selected s\
ource 89.234.64.77
Dec 01 07:33:31 demo.example.com chronyd[820]: Selected s\
ource 89.221.218.101
Dec 01 08:39:23 demo.example.com systemd[1]: Stopping NTP\
 client/server...
Dec 01 08:39:23 demo.example.com chronyd[820]: chronyd ex\
iting
Dec 01 08:39:23 demo.example.com systemd[1]: chronyd.serv\
ice: Succeeded.
Dec 01 08:39:23 demo.example.com systemd[1]: Stopped NTP \
client/server.
[root@demo devops]# reboot
Connection to demo.example.com closed by remote host.
Connection to demo.example.com closed.
ansible-pilot $ ssh devops@demo.example.com
Last login: Wed Dec  1 08:40:41 2021 from 192.168.0.101
```

```
36  [devops@demo ~]$ sudo su
37  [root@demo devops]# uptime
38   08:41:08 up 0 min,  1 user,  load average: 0.28, 0.06, 0\
39  .02
40  [root@demo devops]# systemctl status chronyd.service
41  ▯ chronyd.service - NTP client/server
42     Loaded: loaded (/usr/lib/systemd/system/chronyd.servic\
43  e; disabled; vendor preset: enabled)
44     Active: inactive (dead)
45       Docs: man:chronyd(8)
46             man:chrony.conf(5)
47  [root@demo devops]#
```

Apply a file template - Ansible module template - HTML placeholder

How to apply a template file with Ansible.

- ansible.builtin.template
- Template a file out to a target host
- ansible_managed, template_host, template_uid, template_path, template_fullpath, template_destpath, and template_run_date

Today we're talking about Ansible module `template`.
The full name is `ansible.builtin.template`, it's part of `ansible-core` and is included in all Ansible installations.
It templates a file out to a target host. Templates are processed by the Jinja2 template language.
Also you could use also some special variables in your templates: `ansible_managed`, `template_host`, `template_uid`, `template_path`,

`template_fullpath`, `template_destpath`, and `template_run_date`.
It supports a large variety of Operating Systems.
For basic text formatting, use the Ansible `ansible.builtin.copy`
module or for empty file Ansible `ansible.builtin.file` module.
For Windows, use the `ansible.windows.win_template` module
instead.

Parameters

- src path - template ("templates/" dir)
- dest path - target location
- validate string - validation command before ("%s")
- backup boolean - no/yes
- mode/owner/group - permission
- setype/seuser/selevel - SELinux

Let me highlight the most useful parameters for template module.
The only required parameters are "src" and "dest".
The "src" parameter specifies the template file name. Templates
usually are stored under "templates" directories with ".j2" file
extension.
The "dest" parameter specifies the path where to render the template on the remote machine.
The "validate" parameters allow you to specify the validation
command to run before copying it into place. It's very useful with
configuration files for services.
Please note that the special escape sequence "%s" is going to be
expanded by Ansible with the destination path.
If the "backup" parameter is enabled Ansible creates a backup
file including the timestamp information before copying it to the
destination.
Let me also highlight that we could also specify the permissions
and SELinux properties.

demo

Apply a file template with Ansible Playbook

code

- template.yml

```yaml
---
- name: template module demo
  hosts: all
  become: true
  vars:
    page_title: "Placeholder"
    page_description: |
      This is my placeholder page example.
      Multiline is possible ;-)
  tasks:
    - name: install Nginx
      ansible.builtin.apt:
        name: nginx
        state: latest
- name: apply page template
    ansible.builtin.template:
      src: templates/placeholder.html.j2
      dest: /var/www/html/index.html
```

- templates/placeholder.html.j2

```
1   <html>
2   <head>
3     <title>{{ page_title }}</title>
4   </head>
5   <body>
6     <h1>{{ page_title }}</h1>
7     <p>{{ page_description }}</p>
8   </body>
9   </html>
```

execution

```
1   $ ansible-playbook -i virtualmachines/ubuntu/inventory ap\
2   ply\ template/template.yml
3
4   PLAY [template module demo] ****************************\
5   ****************************************
6
7   TASK [Gathering Facts] ********************************\
8   ****************************************
9   ok: [ubuntu.example.com]
10
11  TASK [install Nginx] **********************************\
12  ****************************************
13  changed: [ubuntu.example.com]
14
15  TASK [apply page template] ****************************\
16  ****************************************
17  changed: [ubuntu.example.com]
18
19  PLAY RECAP ********************************************\
20  ****************************************
21  ubuntu.example.com              : ok=3    changed=2    unreach\
22  able=0    failed=0    skipped=0    rescued=0    ignored=0
```

before execution

```
 1  $ ssh devops@ubuntu.example.com
 2  devops@ubuntu:~ $ sudo su
 3  root@ubuntu:/home/devops# lsb_release -a
 4  No LSB modules are available.
 5  Distributor ID: Ubuntu
 6  Description: Ubuntu 20.04.3 LTS
 7  Release: 20.04
 8  Codename: focal
 9  root@ubuntu:/home/devops# apt list installed nginx -a
10  Listing... Done
11  nginx/focal-updates,focal-updates,focal-security,focal-se\
12  curity 1.18.0-0ubuntu1.2 all
13  nginx/focal,focal 1.17.10-0ubuntu1 all
14
15  root@ubuntu:/home/devops# ls -al /var/
16  total 52
17  drwxr-xr-x 13 root root    4096 Oct 27 15:38 .
18  drwxr-xr-x 19 root root    4096 Oct 27 16:05 ..
19  drwxr-xr-x  2 root root    4096 Apr 15  2020 backups
20  drwxr-xr-x 12 root root    4096 Oct 27 15:43 cache
21  drwxrwxrwt  2 root root    4096 Oct 27 15:38 crash
22  drwxr-xr-x 41 root root    4096 Oct 27 15:49 lib
23  drwxrwsr-x  2 root staff   4096 Apr 15  2020 local
24  lrwxrwxrwx  1 root root       9 Oct 27 15:35 lock -> /run/\
25  lock
26  drwxrwxr-x 10 root syslog 4096 Nov 22 11:56 log
27  drwxrwsr-x  2 root mail   4096 Jul 31  2020 mail
28  drwxr-xr-x  2 root root   4096 Jul 31  2020 opt
29  lrwxrwxrwx  1 root root       4 Oct 27 15:35 run -> /run
30  drwxr-xr-x  2 root root   4096 Jul 10  2020 snap
31  drwxr-xr-x  4 root root   4096 Oct 27 15:35 spool
32  drwxrwxrwt  5 root root   4096 Nov 22 11:56 tmp
33  root@ubuntu:/home/devops# ls -al /var/www
34  ls: cannot access '/var/www': No such file or directory
```

after execution

```
$ ssh devops@ubuntu.example.com
devops@ubuntu:~ $ sudo su
root@ubuntu:/home/devops# apt list installed nginx -a
Listing... Done
nginx/focal-updates,focal-updates,focal-security,focal-se\
curity,now 1.18.0-0ubuntu1.2 all [installed]
nginx/focal,focal 1.17.10-0ubuntu1 all

root@ubuntu:/home/devops# ls -al /var/www/
total 12
drwxr-xr-x  3 root root 4096 Nov 22 12:06 .
drwxr-xr-x 14 root root 4096 Nov 22 12:06 ..
drwxr-xr-x  2 root root 4096 Nov 22 12:06 html
root@ubuntu:/home/devops# ls -al /var/www/html/
total 16
drwxr-xr-x 2 root root 4096 Nov 22 12:06 .
drwxr-xr-x 3 root root 4096 Nov 22 12:06 ..
-rw-r--r-- 1 root root  173 Nov 22 12:06 index.html
-rw-r--r-- 1 root root  612 Nov 22 12:06 index.nginx-debi\
an.html
root@ubuntu:/home/devops# less /var/www/html/index.html
root@ubuntu:/home/devops# cat /var/www/html/index.html
<html>
<head>
<title>Placeholder</title>
</head>
<body>
<h1>Placeholder</h1>
<p>This is my placeholder page example.
Multiline is possible ;-)
</p>
</body>
```

Loop in file template - Ansible module template - Generate hosts file

How to use a loop in a file template to the target host with Ansible? This is extremely useful for service configuration files, placeholder web pages, reports, and so much more use cases.

I'm going to show you a live demo with some simple Ansible code.

I'm Luca Berton and welcome to today's episode of Ansible Pilot.

Ansible loop in file template

- ansible.builtin.template
- Template a file out to a target host
- ansible_managed, template_host, template_uid, template_path, template_fullpath, template_destpath, and template_run_date

Today we're talking about the Ansible module `template`.

The full name is `ansible.builtin.template`, it's part of `ansible-core` and is included in all Ansible installations.

It templates a file out to a target host. Templates are processed by the Jinja2 template language.

Also you could use also some special variables in your templates: `ansible_managed`, `template_host`, `template_uid`, `template_path`, `template_fullpath`, `template_destpath`, and `template_run_date`.

It supports a large variety of Operating Systems.

For basic text formatting, use the Ansible `ansible.builtin.copy` module or for empty file Ansible `ansible.builtin.file` module.

For Windows, use the `ansible.windows.win_template` module instead.

Parameters

- src path - template ("templates/" dir)
- dest path - target location
- validate string - validation command before ("%s")
- backup boolean - no/yes
- mode/owner/group - permission
- setype/seuser/selevel - SELinux

Let me highlight the most useful parameters for the template module.

The only required parameters are "src" and "dest".

The "src" parameter specifies the template file name. Templates usually are stored under "templates" directories with ".j2" file extension.

The "dest" parameter specifies the path where to render the template to on the remote machine.

The "validate" parameters allow you to specify the validation command to run before copying it into place. It's very useful with configuration files for services.

Please note that the special escape sequence "%s" is going to be expanded by Ansible with the destination path.

If the "backup" parameter is enabled Ansible creates a backup file including the timestamp information before copying it to the destination.

Let me also highlight that we could also specify the permissions and SELinux properties.

demo

Loop in file template with Ansible Playbook.

You could find more information about Magic Variables: https://docs.ansible.com/ansible/latest/reference_appendices/special_variables.html

code

- generate_myhosts.yml

```yaml
1   ---
2   - name: template module demo
3     hosts: all
4     become: true
5     tasks:
6       - name: generate /etc/myhosts file
7         ansible.builtin.template:
8           src: templates/hosts.j2
9           dest: /etc/myhosts
10          owner: root
11          group: root
12          mode: '0644'
```

- hosts.j2

```jinja2
1   # {{ ansible_managed }}
2   127.0.0.1    localhost localhost.localdomain localhost4 lo\
3   calhost4.localdomain4
4   ::1          localhost localhost.localdomain localhost6 lo\
5   calhost6.localdomain6
6   {% for host in group['all'] %}
7   {{ hostvars[host]['ansible_host'] }} {{ hostvars[host]['i\
8   nventory_hostname'] }} {{ hostvars[host]['inventory_hostn\
9   ame_short'] }}
10  {% endfor %}
```

execution

```
1  $ ansible-playbook -i apply\ template/inventory apply\ te\
2  mplate/generate_myhosts.yml
3
4  PLAY [template module demo] ***************************\
5  *****************************************
6
7  TASK [Gathering Facts] *******************************\
8  ****************************************
9  ok: [demo.example.com]
10
11 TASK [generate /etc/myhosts file] ********************\
12 ****************************************
13 changed: [demo.example.com]
14
15 PLAY RECAP *******************************************\
16 ****************************************
17 demo.example.com           : ok=2    changed=1    unreach\
18 able=0    failed=0    skipped=0    rescued=0    ignored=0
```

before execution

```
1  $ ssh devops@demo.example.com
2  Last login: Tue Nov 23 17:10:30 2021 from 192.168.0.101
3  [devops@demo ~]$ sudo su
4  [root@demo devops]# ls -al /etc/myhosts
5  ls: cannot access '/etc/myhosts': No such file or directo\
6  ry
7  [root@demo devops]#
```

after execution

```
1   $ ssh devops@demo.example.com
2   Last login: Tue Nov 23 17:32:39 2021 from 192.168.0.101
3   [devops@demo ~]$ sudo su
4   [root@demo devops]# ls -al /etc/myhosts
5   -rw-r--r--. 1 root root 214 Nov 23 17:32 /etc/myhosts
6   [root@demo devops]# cat /etc/myhosts
7   # Ansible managed
8   127.0.0.1    localhost localhost.localdomain localhost4 lo\
9   calhost4.localdomain4
10  ::1              localhost localhost.localdomain localhost6 lo\
11  calhost6.localdomain6
12  192.168.0.190  demo.example.com demo
13  [devops@demo ~]$ exit
14  logout
15  Connection to demo.example.com closed.
16  ansible-pilot $ cat apply\ template/inventory
17  demo.example.com ansible_host=192.168.0.190
18
19  [all:vars]
20  ansible_connection=ssh
21  ansible_user=devops
```

Schedule a Cron Job task in Linux - Ansible module cron

How to automate the schedule of a Cron Job task in Linux with Ansible.

- ansible.builtin.cron
- Manage cron.d and crontab entries

Today we're talking about Ansible module cron.
The full name is ansible.builtin.cron, which means that is part of

the collection of modules "builtin" with ansible and shipped with it.

It's a module pretty stable and out for years and it works in a different variety of operating systems.

It manages cron.d and crontab entries.

For Windows targets, use the `ansible.windows.win_scheduled_task` module instead.

Parameters

- name string - crontab name
- state string - present/absent
- job string - command to execute
- user string - defaults to the current user
- minute, hour, day, month, weekday string - `'*'`, `'1-31'`, `'*/2'`
- special_time - annually/daily/hourly/monthly/reboot/weekly/yearly
- cron_file - NEVER use for /etc/crontab

The only required is `name`, where you specify the description of a crontab entry.

The parameter `state` sets whether the cron job is present or not in the target host.

The parameter `job` sets the command to execute or, if env is set, the value of the environment variable.

The parameter `user` sets the specific user for the crontab, when unset, this parameter defaults to the current user.

The most important part is the moment to run the crontab, specifically: `minute`, `hour`, `day`, `month`, `weekday`. In this field, you could use the star operator `"*"` to specify all the minutes, hours, weekdays, days, and months. You could be more specific with a single number, range, or intervals.

There are also some special times already defined in the parameter special_time. The options are: annually, daily, hourly, monthly, reboot, weekly, yearly.

Let me also highlight that we could also specify the "cron_file" if you want a specific name and not under the user.

Links

- cron_module[32]
- crontab.guru[33]

demo

How to schedule a Cron Job task in Linux with Ansible.

code

- cron.yml

```
1   ---
2   - name: cron module demo
3     hosts: all
4     tasks:
5     - name: "example cronjob"
6       ansible.builtin.cron:
7         name: "test"
8         state: present
9         minute: "*/2"
10        hour: "*"
11        day: "*"
12        month: "*"
13        weekday: "*"
14        job: 'logger "ansible-pilot"'
```

---

[32]https://docs.ansible.com/ansible/latest/collections/ansible/builtin/cron_module.html
[33]https://crontab.guru/

execution

```
$ ansible-playbook -i virtualmachines/demo/inventory sche\
dule\ cron\ job\ task/cron.yml
PLAY [cron module demo] *********************************\
*******************************************
TASK [Gathering Facts] *********************************\
*******************************************
ok: [demo.example.com]
TASK [example cronjob] *********************************\
*******************************************
changed: [demo.example.com]
PLAY RECAP *********************************************\
*******************************************
demo.example.com                : ok=2    changed=1    unreach\
able=0    failed=0    skipped=0    rescued=0    ignored=0
```

before execution

```
$ ssh devops@demo.example.com
Last login: Wed Dec  8 15:28:44 2021 from 192.168.0.101
[devops@demo ~]$ crontab -l
no crontab for devops
[devops@demo ~]$
```

after execution

```
$ ssh devops@demo.example.com
Last login: Wed Dec  8 15:30:58 2021 from 192.168.0.101
[devops@demo ~]$ crontab -l
#Ansible: test
*/2 * * * * logger "ansible-pilot"
[devops@demo ~]$ sudo tail -f /var/log/cron
Dec  8 15:26:47 rhel8 crond[905]: (CRON) INFO (Syslog wil\
l be used instead of sendmail.)
Dec  8 15:26:47 rhel8 crond[905]: (CRON) INFO (RANDOM_DEL\
AY will be scaled with factor 43% if used.)
Dec  8 15:26:47 rhel8 crond[905]: (CRON) INFO (running wi\
th inotify support)
Dec  8 15:26:47 rhel8 CROND[916]: (root) CMD (bash -c '/b\
in/updatedb ; rm --force /etc/cron.d/updatedb')
Dec  8 15:28:52 rhel8 crontab[5139]: (devops) LIST (devop\
s)
Dec  8 15:30:10 rhel8 crontab[5191]: (devops) LIST (devop\
s)
Dec  8 15:30:45 rhel8 crontab[5453]: (devops) LIST (devop\
s)
Dec  8 15:30:45 rhel8 crontab[5455]: (devops) REPLACE (de\
vops)
Dec  8 15:30:58 rhel8 crontab[5706]: (devops) LIST (devop\
s)
Dec  8 15:31:18 rhel8 crontab[5749]: (devops) LIST (devop\
s)
Dec  8 15:32:01 rhel8 CROND[5760]: (devops) CMD (logger "\
ansible-pilot")
Dec  8 15:34:01 rhel8 CROND[5766]: (devops) CMD (logger "\
ansible-pilot")
Dec  8 15:36:01 rhel8 CROND[5770]: (devops) CMD (logger "\
ansible-pilot")
Dec  8 15:38:01 rhel8 CROND[5775]: (devops) CMD (logger "\
ansible-pilot")
Dec  8 15:40:01 rhel8 CROND[5781]: (devops) CMD (logger "\
```

```
36  ansible-pilot")
37  Dec  8 15:42:01 rhel8 CROND[5787]: (devops) CMD (logger "\
38  ansible-pilot")
39  Dec  8 15:44:01 rhel8 CROND[5791]: (devops) CMD (logger "\
40  ansible-pilot")
41  Dec  8 15:46:01 rhel8 CROND[5796]: (devops) CMD (logger "\
42  ansible-pilot")
43  ^C
44  [devops@demo ~]$ sudo tail -f /var/log/messages
45  Dec  8 15:41:43 rhel8 systemd[1]: Started Cleanup of Temp\
46  orary Directories.
47  Dec  8 15:42:01 rhel8 systemd[1]: Started Session 18 of u\
48  ser devops.
49  Dec  8 15:42:01 rhel8 devops[5787]: ansible-pilot
50  Dec  8 15:42:01 rhel8 systemd[1]: session-18.scope: Succe\
51  eded.
52  Dec  8 15:44:01 rhel8 systemd[1]: Started Session 19 of u\
53  ser devops.
54  Dec  8 15:44:01 rhel8 devops[5791]: ansible-pilot
55  Dec  8 15:44:01 rhel8 systemd[1]: session-19.scope: Succe\
56  eded.
57  Dec  8 15:46:01 rhel8 systemd[1]: Started Session 20 of u\
58  ser devops.
59  Dec  8 15:46:01 rhel8 devops[5796]: ansible-pilot
60  Dec  8 15:46:01 rhel8 systemd[1]: session-20.scope: Succe\
61  eded.
62  Dec  8 15:48:01 rhel8 systemd[1]: Started Session 21 of u\
63  ser devops.
64  Dec  8 15:48:01 rhel8 devops[5807]: ansible-pilot
65  Dec  8 15:48:01 rhel8 systemd[1]: session-21.scope: Succe\
66  eded.
67  Dec  8 15:50:01 rhel8 systemd[1]: Starting system activit\
68  y accounting tool...
69  Dec  8 15:50:01 rhel8 systemd[1]: sysstat-collect.service\
70  : Succeeded.
```

```
71  Dec  8 15:50:01 rhel8 systemd[1]: Started system activity\
72   accounting tool.
73  Dec  8 15:50:01 rhel8 systemd[1]: Started Session 22 of u\
74  ser devops.
75  Dec  8 15:50:01 rhel8 devops[5814]: ansible-pilot
76  Dec  8 15:50:01 rhel8 systemd[1]: session-22.scope: Succe\
77  eded.
78  Dec  8 15:52:01 rhel8 systemd[1]: Started Session 23 of u\
79  ser devops.
80  Dec  8 15:52:01 rhel8 devops[5818]: ansible-pilot
81  Dec  8 15:52:01 rhel8 systemd[1]: session-23.scope: Succe\
82  eded.
83  Dec  8 15:54:01 rhel8 systemd[1]: Started Session 24 of u\
84  ser devops.
85  Dec  8 15:54:01 rhel8 devops[5823]: ansible-pilot
86  Dec  8 15:54:01 rhel8 systemd[1]: session-24.scope: Succe\
87  eded.
88  Dec  8 15:56:01 rhel8 systemd[1]: Started Session 25 of u\
89  ser devops.
90  Dec  8 15:56:01 rhel8 devops[5827]: ansible-pilot
91  Dec  8 15:56:01 rhel8 systemd[1]: session-25.scope: Succe\
92  eded.
```

How to Pass Variables to Ansible Playbook in command line? - Ansible extra variables

How to pass Pass Variables value to Ansible Playbook in command line?

- `--extra-vars "fruit=apple"`
- `--extra-vars '{"fruit":"apple"}'`
- `--extra-vars "@file.json"`

- `--extra-vars "@file.yml"`

Today we're talking about Ansible extra variables.

The easiest way to pass Pass Variables value to Ansible Playbook in the command line is using the extra variables parameter of the "ansible-playbook" command.

This is very useful to combine your Ansible Playbook with some pre-existent automation or script.

Let me clarify that this is specific for variables, there is another way to look for environment variables

The command line parameter is the `--extra-vars` `"variable=value"` and allows you to pass some value from the terminal to the playbook.

You could specify also the parameter in JSON format or include a JSON or a YAML file.

 See also How to print a text or a variable during the execution with Ansible

demo

How to pass extra Variables to Ansible Playbook in the command line.

code

```
1   ---
2   - name: extra variable demo
3     hosts: all
4     vars:
5       fruit: "banana"
6     task:
7       - name: print message
8         ansible.builtin.debug:
9           msg: "fruit is {{ fruit }}"
```

execution without extra variables

```
1   $ ansible-playbook --extra-vars="fruit=apple" -i virtualm\
2   achines/demo/inventory extra-variable/example.yml
3   PLAY [extra variable demo] ******************************\
4   *******************************************
5   TASK [Gathering Facts] ******************************\
6   *******************************************
7   ok: [demo.example.com]
8   TASK [message] ******************************************\
9   *******************************************
10  ok: [demo.example.com] => {
11      "msg": "fruit is apple"
12  }
13  PLAY RECAP ****************************************************\
14  *******************************************
15  demo.example.com            : ok=2     changed=0      unreach\
16  able=0     failed=0     skipped=0     rescued=0     ignored=0
17  ansible-pilot $
```

execution with a plain extra variable

```
$ ansible-playbook -i virtualmachines/demo/inventory --ex\
tra-vars="fruit=apple"  extra-variable/example.yml
PLAY [extra variable demo] *******************************\
*********************************************
TASK [Gathering Facts] ***********************************\
*********************************************
ok: [demo.example.com]
TASK [message] *******************************************\
*********************************************
ok: [demo.example.com] => {
    "msg": "fruit is apple"
}
PLAY RECAP ***********************************************\
*********************************************
demo.example.com              : ok=2    changed=0    unreach\
able=0    failed=0    skipped=0    rescued=0    ignored=0
ansible-pilot $
```

execution with a JSON extra variable

```
$ ansible-playbook -i virtualmachines/demo/inventory --ex\
tra-vars='{"fruit":"raspberry"}'  extra-variable/example.\
yml
PLAY [extra variable demo] *******************************\
*********************************************
TASK [Gathering Facts] ***********************************\
*********************************************
ok: [demo.example.com]
TASK [message] *******************************************\
*********************************************
ok: [demo.example.com] => {
    "msg": "fruit is raspberry"
}
PLAY RECAP ***********************************************\
*********************************************
demo.example.com              : ok=2    changed=0    unreach\
```

```
17   able=0      failed=0      skipped=0      rescued=0      ignored=0
18   ansible-pilot $
```

Break a string over multiple lines - Ansible Literal and Folded Block Scalar operators

How to Break a string over multiple lines with Ansible? And in general with YAML language.

- "|" - Literal Block Scalar operator
- ">" - Folded Block Scalar operator

Today we're talking about Ansible Break a string over multiple lines:
Basically, there are two different operators:

- the "|" - Literal Block Scalar"
- the ">" Folded Block Scalar"

It's easy for me to show you the behavior by example.

Examples

variable1 code

```
1  variable1: |
2   exactly as you see
3   will appear these three
4   lines of poetry
```

variable1 output

```
1   exactly as you see
2   will appear these three
3   lines of poetry\n
```

variable2 code

```
1  variable2: >
2   this is really a
3   single line of text
4   despite appearances
```

variable2 output

```
1  variable2: this is really a single line of text despite a\
2  ppearances\n
```

Welcome to the examples sections.

Let's assume we have two multi-line variables "variable1" and "variable2".

These are both multi-line variable but variable1 use the "|" - Literal Block Scalar" operator and variable 2 use the ">" Folded Block Scalar" operator.

The result of this is that variable1 remains multiline but variable2 has literally collapsed in a single line and substitutes newlines with spaces.

Please note that both variables have a newline at the end of the string.

Do you want to remove the newline at the end of the strings? Simply add a "-", a minus, after the "|" or ">" operator!

demo

Break a string over multiple lines with Ansible by examples.

code1

```
1  ---
2  - name: debug module demo
3    hosts: all
4    vars:
5     variable1: |
6       exactly as you see
7       will appear these three
8       lines of poetry
9     variable2: >
10      this is really a
11      single line of text
12      despite appearances
13   tasks:
14    - name: print variable1
15      ansible.builtin.debug:
16        var: variable1
17  - name: print variable2
18      ansible.builtin.debug:
19        var: variable2
```

execution1

```
$ ansible-playbook -i virtualmachines/demo/inventory prin\
t\ text\ variable\ during\ execution/multi-line.yml
PLAY [debug module demo] ********************************\
********************************************
TASK [Gathering Facts] *********************************\
********************************************
ok: [demo.example.com]
TASK [print variable1] *********************************\
********************************************
ok: [demo.example.com] => {
    "variable1": "exactly as you see\nwill appear these t\
hree\nlines of poetry\n"
}
TASK [print variable2] *********************************\
********************************************
ok: [demo.example.com] => {
    "variable2": "this is really a single line of text de\
spite appearances\n"
}
PLAY RECAP *********************************************\
********************************************
demo.example.com              : ok=3    changed=0    unreach\
able=0    failed=0    skipped=0    rescued=0    ignored=0
ansible-pilot $
```

code2

```yaml
---
- name: debug module demo
  hosts: all
  vars:
    variable1: |-
      exactly as you see
      will appear these three
      lines of poetry
    variable2: >-
      this is really a
      single line of text
      despite appearances
  tasks:
    - name: print variable1
      ansible.builtin.debug:
        var: variable1
- name: print variable2
      ansible.builtin.debug:
        var: variable2
```

execution2

```
$ ansible-playbook -i virtualmachines/demo/inventory prin\
t\ text\ variable\ during\ execution/multi-line.yml
PLAY [debug module demo] ********************************\
*******************************************
TASK [Gathering Facts] *********************************\
*******************************************
ok: [demo.example.com]
TASK [print variable1] *********************************\
*******************************************
ok: [demo.example.com] => {
    "variable1": "exactly as you see\nwill appear these t\
hree\nlines of poetry"
}
TASK [print variable2] *********************************\
```

```
15   ******************************************
16   ok: [demo.example.com] => {
17       "variable2": "this is really a single line of text de\
18   spite appearances"
19   }
20   PLAY RECAP ***********************************************\
21   ******************************************
22   demo.example.com            : ok=3    changed=0    unreach\
23   able=0    failed=0    skipped=0    rescued=0    ignored=0
24   ansible-pilot $
```

code3

```
1    ---
2    - name: debug module demo
3      hosts: all
4      vars:
5        variable1: |-
6          exactly as you see
7          will appear these three
8          lines of poetry
9        variable2: >-
10         this is really a
11         single line of text
12         despite appearances
13     tasks:
14       - name: print variable1
15         ansible.builtin.debug:
16           msg: "{{ variable1.split('\n') }}"
17   - name: print variable2
18         ansible.builtin.debug:
19           var: variable2
```

execution3

```
$ ansible-playbook -i virtualmachines/demo/inventory prin\
t\ text\ variable\ during\ execution/multi-line.yml
PLAY [debug module demo] *********************************\
*********************************************
TASK [Gathering Facts] **********************************\
*********************************************
ok: [demo.example.com]
TASK [print variable1] **********************************\
*********************************************
ok: [demo.example.com] => {
    "msg": [
        "exactly as you see",
        "will appear these three",
        "lines of poetry"
    ]
}
TASK [print variable2] **********************************\
*********************************************
ok: [demo.example.com] => {
    "variable2": "this is really a single line of text de\
spite appearances"
}
PLAY RECAP **********************************************\
*********************************************
demo.example.com              : ok=3    changed=0    unreach\
able=0    failed=0    skipped=0    rescued=0    ignored=0
ansible-pilot $
```

Read a file from remote hosts - Ansible module slurp

How to automate the read of /proc/cpuinfo file from Linux remote
host with Ansible. The file is copied as base 64 encoding and

decoded with an Ansible Filter.

- `ansible.builtin.slurp`
- Slurps a file from remote nodes
- Fetching a base64-encoded blob of the data in a remote file.

Today we're talking about the Ansible module `slurp`.
The full name is `ansible.builtin.slurp` which means is part of the collection of acmodules "builtin" with ansible and shipped with it. This module is pretty stable and out for years and supports Linux and Windows targets.
The purpose is to slurp a file from a remote location. Please note that the read operation is going to fetch a base64-encoded blob containing the data in a remote file.

Parameters

- src <u>string</u> - Remote file path

This module has only one parameter "src", which is also mandatory. The parameter "src" specifies the source files in the remote hosts. It must be a file, not a directory.

Links

- ansible.builtin.slurp[34]

demo

Read a file from remote hosts with Ansible Playbook.

code

---

[34] https://docs.ansible.com/ansible/latest/collections/ansible/builtin/slurp_module.html

```yaml
---
- name: slurp module demo
  hosts: all
  become: false
  vars:
    remotefile: "/proc/cpuinfo"
  tasks:
    - name: slurp remote file
      ansible.builtin.slurp:
        src: "{{ remotefile }}"
      register: slurpfile

    - name: print remote file
      ansible.builtin.debug:
        msg: "{{ slurpfile['content'] | b64decode }}"
```

execution

```
ansible-pilot $ ansible-playbook -i virtualmachines/demo/\
inventory read\ file\ from\ remote\ hosts/slurp.yml
PLAY [slurp module demo] *******************************\
********************************************
TASK [Gathering Facts] *********************************\
********************************************
ok: [demo.example.com]
TASK [slurp remote file] *******************************\
********************************************
ok: [demo.example.com]
TASK [print remote file] *******************************\
********************************************
ok: [demo.example.com] => {
    "msg": "processor\t: 0\nvendor_id\t: GenuineIntel\ncp\
u family\t: 6\nmodel\t\t: 158\nmodel name\t: Intel(R) Cor\
e(TM) i7-9750H CPU @ 2.60GHz\nstepping\t: 10\ncpu MHz\t\t\
: 2591.998\ncache size\t: 12288 KB\nphysical id\t: 0\nsib\
lings\t: 1\ncore id\t\t: 0\ncpu cores\t: 1\napicid\t\t: 0\
```

```
19   \ninitial apicid\t:  0\nfpu\t\t: yes\nfpu_exception\t: yes\
20   \ncpuid level\t:  22\nwp\t\t: yes\nflags\t\t:  fpu vme de p\
21   se tsc msr pae mce cx8 apic sep mtrr pge mca cmov pat pse\
22   36 clflush mmx fxsr sse sse2 ht syscall nx rdtscp lm cons\
23   tant_tsc rep_good nopl xtopology nonstop_tsc cpuid tsc_kn\
24   own_freq pni pclmulqdq monitor ssse3 cx16 pcid sse4_1 sse\
25   4_2 x2apic movbe popcnt aes xsave avx rdrand hypervisor l\
26   ahf_lm abm 3dnowprefetch invpcid_single pti fsgsbase avx2\
27    invpcid rdseed clflushopt md_clear flush_l1d\nbugs\t\t: \
28   cpu_meltdown spectre_v1 spectre_v2 spec_store_bypass l1tf\
29    mds swapgs itlb_multihit srbds\nbogomips\t: 5183.99\nclf\
30   lush size\t: 64\ncache_alignment\t: 64\naddress sizes\t: \
31   39 bits physical, 48 bits virtual\npower management:\n\n"
32   }
33   PLAY RECAP ********************************************\
34   *******************************************
35   demo.example.com              : ok=3    changed=0    unreach\
36   able=0    failed=0    skipped=0    rescued=0    ignored=0
37   ansible-pilot $
```

idempotency

```
1    ansible-pilot $ ansible-playbook -i virtualmachines/demo/\
2    inventory read\ file\ from\ remote\ hosts/slurp.yml
3    PLAY [slurp module demo] ********************************\
4    *****************************************
5    TASK [Gathering Facts] *********************************\
6    *****************************************
7    ok: [demo.example.com]
8    TASK [slurp remote file] ********************************\
9    *****************************************
10   ok: [demo.example.com]
11   TASK [print remote file] *******************************\
12   *****************************************
13   ok: [demo.example.com] => {
14       "msg". "processor\t. 0\nvendor_id\t: GenuineIntel\nap\
```

```
u family\t: 6\nmodel\t\t: 158\nmodel name\t: Intel(R) Cor\
e(TM) i7-9750H CPU @ 2.60GHz\nstepping\t: 10\ncpu MHz\t\t\
: 2591.998\ncache size\t: 12288 KB\nphysical id\t: 0\nsib\
lings\t: 1\ncore id\t\t: 0\ncpu cores\t: 1\napicid\t\t: 0\
\ninitial apicid\t: 0\nfpu\t\t: yes\nfpu_exception\t: yes\
\ncpuid level\t: 22\nwp\t\t: yes\nflags\t\t: fpu vme de p\
se tsc msr pae mce cx8 apic sep mtrr pge mca cmov pat pse\
36 clflush mmx fxsr sse sse2 ht syscall nx rdtscp lm cons\
tant_tsc rep_good nopl xtopology nonstop_tsc cpuid tsc_kn\
own_freq pni pclmulqdq monitor ssse3 cx16 pcid sse4_1 sse\
4_2 x2apic movbe popcnt aes xsave avx rdrand hypervisor l\
ahf_lm abm 3dnowprefetch invpcid_single pti fsgsbase avx2\
 invpcid rdseed clflushopt md_clear flush_l1d\nbugs\t\t: \
cpu_meltdown spectre_v1 spectre_v2 spec_store_bypass l1tf\
 mds swapgs itlb_multihit srbds\nbogomips\t: 5183.99\nclf\
lush size\t: 64\ncache_alignment\t: 64\naddress sizes\t: \
39 bits physical, 48 bits virtual\npower management:\n\n"
}
PLAY RECAP ****************************************\
*****************************************
demo.example.com           : ok=3    changed=0    unreach\
able=0    failed=0    skipped=0    rescued=0    ignored=0
ansible-pilot $
```

verification

```
ansible-pilot $ ssh devops@demo.example.com
Last login: Tue Jan 25 14:29:36 2022 from 192.168.0.102
[devops@demo ~]$ cat /proc/cpuinfo
processor : 0
vendor_id : GenuineIntel
cpu family : 6
model   : 158
model name : Intel(R) Core(TM) i7-9750H CPU @ 2.60GHz
stepping : 10
cpu MHz   : 2591.998
cache size : 12288 KB
physical id : 0
siblings : 1
core id   : 0
cpu cores : 1
apicid   : 0
initial apicid : 0
fpu   : yes
fpu_exception : yes
cpuid level : 22
wp   : yes
flags   : fpu vme de pse tsc msr pae mce cx8 apic sep mtrr\
 pge mca cmov pat pse36 clflush mmx fxsr sse sse2 ht sysc\
all nx rdtscp lm constant_tsc rep_good nopl xtopology non\
stop_tsc cpuid tsc_known_freq pni pclmulqdq monitor ssse3\
 cx16 pcid sse4_1 sse4_2 x2apic movbe popcnt aes xsave av\
x rdrand hypervisor lahf_lm abm 3dnowprefetch invpcid_sin\
gle pti fsgsbase avx2 invpcid rdseed clflushopt md_clear \
flush_l1d
bugs   : cpu_meltdown spectre_v1 spectre_v2 spec_store_byp\
ass l1tf mds swapgs itlb_multihit srbds
bogomips : 5183.99
clflush size : 64
cache_alignment : 64
address sizes : 39 bits physical, 48 bits virtual
```

```
36    power management:
37    [devops@demo ~]$
```

Read an environment variable - Ansible lookup plugin env"

How to automate the reading of HOME environmental variable and use it in your Ansible Playbook code with lookup plugin env.

Ansible read an environment variable

- ansible.builtin.env
- Read the value of environment variables

Let's deep dive into the Ansible lookup plugin env.
Plugins are a way to expand the Ansible functionality. With lookup plugins specifically, you can load variables or templates with information from external sources.
The full name is `ansible.builtin.env`, it's part of `ansible-core` and is included in all Ansible installations.
The purpose of the `env` lookup plugin is to read the value of environment variables.

Parameters and Return Value

Parameters

- _terms string - Environment variable

Return Values

- _raw list - Values from the environment variables

The parameters of plugin env.

The only required parameter is the default "_terms", with the name of the environment variable to read.
The normal usage is to assign the lookup plugin to a variable name but you could use it in your Ansible task directly.

demo

Read an environment variable with Ansible Playbook.

code

```
1   ---
2   - name: environment demo
3     hosts: all
4     tasks:
5       - name: display HOME
6         ansible.builtin.debug:
7           msg: "{{ lookup('env', 'HOME') }}"
```

execution

```
 1  ansible-pilot $ printenv | grep HOME
 2  HOME=/Users/lberton
 3  ansible-pilot $ ansible-playbook -i virtualmachines/demo/\
 4  inventory ansible\ statements/environment.yml
 5  PLAY [environment demo] *******************************\
 6  ******************************************
 7  TASK [Gathering Facts] ********************************\
 8  ******************************************
 9  ok: [demo.example.com]
10  TASK [display HOME] ***********************************\
11  ******************************************
12  ok: [demo.example.com] => {
13      "msg": "/Users/lberton"
14  }
15  PLAY RECAP ********************************************\
16  ******************************************
17  demo.example.com            : ok=2    changed=0    unreach\
18  able=0    failed=0    skipped=0    rescued=0    ignored=0
19  ansible-pilot $
```

idempotency

```
 1  ansible-pilot $ printenv | grep HOME
 2  HOME=/Users/lberton
 3  ansible-pilot $ ansible-playbook -i virtualmachines/demo/\
 4  inventory ansible\ statements/environment.yml
 5  PLAY [environment demo] *******************************\
 6  ******************************************
 7  TASK [Gathering Facts] ********************************\
 8  ******************************************
 9  ok: [demo.example.com]
10  TASK [display HOME] ***********************************\
11  ******************************************
12  ok: [demo.example.com] => {
13      "msg": "/Users/lberton"
14  }
```

```
15   PLAY RECAP *********************************************\
16   **********************************************
17   demo.example.com           : ok=2     changed=0     unreach\
18   able=0     failed=0     skipped=0     rescued=0     ignored=0
19   ansible-pilot $
```

Set remote environment per task or play - Ansible environment statement

How to set an EXAMPLE environmental variable at play and task Ansible Playbook code level and verify with echo Linux command.

Set remote environment per Ansible task or play

- `environment` statement

You could set the remote environment with the Ansible statement `environment`.

The `environment` statement could be applied at the task level or play level.

It's very useful to set for example proxy in a corporate environment. Please note the remote host environment is left untouched, it affect only Ansible Playbook life time.

Links

- Setting the remote environment[35]

---

[35]https://docs.ansible.com/ansible/latest/user_guide/playbooks_environment.html

demo

Set environment per Ansible Playbook task or play level.

code

```
1   ---
2   - name: remote environment demo
3     hosts: all
4     gather_facts: false
5     environment:
6       EXAMPLE: test1
7   tasks:
8       - name: diplay EXAMPLE
9         ansible.builtin.command: "echo $EXAMPLE"
10      - name: diplay EXAMPLE
11        ansible.builtin.command: "echo $EXAMPLE"
12        environment:
13          EXAMPLE: test2
```

execution

You need to run the playbook with the verbose option (-v) in order
to see the standard output on the console.

```
1   ansible-pilot $ ansible-playbook -i virtualmachines/demo/\
2   inventory ansible\ statements/environment-remote.yml
3   PLAY [remote environment demo] ************************\
4   ******************************************
5   TASK [diplay EXAMPLE] ********************************\
6   ******************************************
7   changed: [demo.example.com]
8   TASK [diplay EXAMPLE] ********************************\
9   ******************************************
10  changed: [demo.example.com]
```

```
11  PLAY RECAP ******************************************\
12  *********************************************
13  demo.example.com              : ok=2    changed=2    unreach\
14  able=0    failed=0    skipped=0    rescued=0    ignored=0
15  ansible-pilot $ ansible-playbook -i virtualmachines/demo/\
16  inventory ansible\ statements/environment-remote.yml -v
17  No config file found; using defaults
18  PLAY [remote environment demo] **************************\
19  *********************************************
20  TASK [diplay EXAMPLE] **********************************\
21  *********************************************
22  changed: [demo.example.com] => {"ansible_facts": {"discov\
23  ered_interpreter_python": "/usr/libexec/platform-python"}\
24  , "changed": true, "cmd": ["echo", "$EXAMPLE"], "delta": \
25  "0:00:00.002864", "end": "2022-02-21 09:05:33.059864", "m\
26  sg": "", "rc": 0, "start": "2022-02-21 09:05:33.057000", \
27  "stderr": "", "stderr_lines": [], "stdout": "test1", "std\
28  out_lines": ["test1"]}
29  TASK [diplay EXAMPLE] **********************************\
30  *********************************************
31  changed: [demo.example.com] => {"changed": true, "cmd": [\
32  "echo", "$EXAMPLE"], "delta": "0:00:00.002800", "end": "2\
33  022-02-21 09:05:33.416884", "msg": "", "rc": 0, "start": \
34  "2022-02-21 09:05:33.414084", "stderr": "", "stderr_lines\
35  ": [], "stdout": "test2", "stdout_lines": ["test2"]}
36  PLAY RECAP *********************************************\
37  *********************************************
38  demo.example.com              : ok=2    changed=2    unreach\
39  able=0    failed=0    skipped=0    rescued=0    ignored=0
40  ansible-pilot $
```

idempotency

```
ansible-pilot $ ansible-playbook -i virtualmachines/demo/\
inventory ansible\ statements/environment-remote.yml -v
No config file found; using defaults
PLAY [remote environment demo] **************************\
*******************************************
TASK [diplay EXAMPLE] **********************************\
*******************************************
changed: [demo.example.com] => {"ansible_facts": {"discov\
ered_interpreter_python": "/usr/libexec/platform-python"}\
, "changed": true, "cmd": ["echo", "$EXAMPLE"], "delta": \
"0:00:00.002864", "end": "2022-02-21 09:05:33.059864", "m\
sg": "", "rc": 0, "start": "2022-02-21 09:05:33.057000", \
"stderr": "", "stderr_lines": [], "stdout": "test1", "std\
out_lines": ["test1"]}
TASK [diplay EXAMPLE] **********************************\
*******************************************
changed: [demo.example.com] => {"changed": true, "cmd": [\
"echo", "$EXAMPLE"], "delta": "0:00:00.002800", "end": "2\
022-02-21 09:05:33.416884", "msg": "", "rc": 0, "start": \
"2022-02-21 09:05:33.414084", "stderr": "", "stderr_lines\
": [], "stdout": "test2", "stdout_lines": ["test2"]}
PLAY RECAP *********************************************\
*******************************************
demo.example.com               : ok=2    changed=2    unreach\
able=0    failed=0    skipped=0    rescued=0    ignored=0
ansible-pilot $
```

before execution

```
ansible-pilot $ ssh devops@demo.example.com
Last login: Fri Feb 18 16:07:48 2022 from 192.168.0.59
[devops@demo ~]$ echo $EXAMPLE
[devops@demo ~]$
```

after execution

```
1   ansible-pilot $ ssh devops@demo.example.com
2   Last login: Mon Feb 21 07:05:33 2022 from 192.168.251.111
3   [devops@demo ~]$ echo $EXAMPLE
```

Permanently Set Remote System Wide Environment Variables on Linux - /etc/environment - Ansible module lineinfile

How to automate the customization of System-Wide Environment Variables on Linux editing /etc/environment file using Ansible module lineinfile.

 See also: Ansible troubleshooting - Permission denied Errno 13

Permanently Set System-Wide Environment Variables on Remote Linux

- /etc/environment
- /etc/profile.d directory

There are principally two ways to configure System-Wide Environment Variables on Linux:

- /etc/environment is a system-wide configuration file, which means it is used by all users. It is owned by root so you need admin user privilege or sudo to modify it. Specifically, this file stores the system-wide locale and path settings.

- `/etc/profile` and `/etc/profile.d/*.sh` are the global initialization scripts. This file gets executed whenever a bash login shell is entered via console, terminal, ssh, or graphical user interface. The global scripts get executed before the user-specific scripts though, and the main `/etc/profile` executes all the `*.sh` scripts in `/etc/profile.d/` just before it exits.

Each user could customize their `~/.profile`, the user's personal shell initialization scripts. Every user has one and can edit their file without affecting others. This is the equivalent to `/etc/profile` for each user.

Links

- ansible.builtin.lineinfile[36]

demo

How to permanently set System-Wide Environment variables on Remote Linux with Ansible Playbook.

code

---

[36]https://docs.ansible.com/ansible/latest/collections/ansible/builtin/lineinfile_module.html

```
1   ---
2   - name: set environment demo
3     hosts: all
4     gather_facts: false
5     become: true
6     vars:
7       os_environment:
8         - key: EDITOR
9           value: vi
10        - key: MY_ENV_VARIABLE
11          value: ansiblepilot
12    tasks:
13      - name: customize /etc/environment
14        ansible.builtin.lineinfile:
15          dest: "/etc/environment"
16          state: present
17          regexp: "^{{ item.key }}="
18          line: "{{ item.key }}={{ item.value }}"
19        with_items: "{{ os_environment }}"
```

execution

```
1   ansible-pilot $ ansible-playbook -i virtualmachines/demo/\
2   inventory ansible\ statements/set-environment.yml
3   PLAY [set environment demo] ****************************\
4   ******************************************
5   TASK [customize /etc/environment] *********************\
6   ******************************************
7   changed: [demo.example.com] => (item={'key': 'EDITOR', 'v\
8   alue': 'vi'})
9   changed: [demo.example.com] => (item={'key': 'MY_ENV_VARI\
10  ABLE', 'value': 'ansiblepilot'})
11  PLAY RECAP ********************************************\
12  ******************************************
13  demo.example.com              : ok=1      changed=1      unreach\
14  able=0     failed=0     skipped=0     rescued=0     ignored=0
```

```
15   ansible-pilot $
```

idempotency

```
1    ansible-pilot $ ansible-playbook -i virtualmachines/demo/\
2    inventory ansible\ statements/set-environment.yml
3    PLAY [set environment demo] ****************************\
4    ******************************************
5    TASK [customize /etc/environment] ********************\
6    ******************************************
7    ok: [demo.example.com] => (item={'key': 'EDITOR', 'value'\
8    : 'vi'})
9    ok: [demo.example.com] => (item={'key': 'MY_ENV_VARIABLE'\
10   , 'value': 'ansiblepilot'})
11   PLAY RECAP *******************************************\
12   ******************************************
13   demo.example.com              : ok=1    changed=0    unreach\
14   able=0    failed=0    skipped=0    rescued=0    ignored=0
15   ansible-pilot $
```

before execution

```
1    ansible-pilot $ ssh devops@demo.example.com
2    Last login: Tue Feb 22 18:45:12 2022 from 192.168.131.111
3    [devops@demo ~]$ sudo su
4    [root@demo devops]# printenv | grep EDITOR
5    [root@demo devops]# printenv | grep MY_ENV_VARIABLE
6    [root@demo devops]# cat /etc/environment
7    [root@demo devops]#
```

after execution

```
1   ansible-pilot $ ssh devops@demo.example.com
2   Last login: Tue Feb 22 18:48:46 2022 from 192.168.131.111
3   [devops@demo ~]$ sudo su
4   [root@demo devops]# printenv | grep EDITOR
5   EDITOR=vi
6   [root@demo devops]# printenv | grep MY_ENV_VARIABLE
7   MY_ENV_VARIABLE=ansiblepilot
8   [root@demo devops]# cat /etc/environment
9   EDITOR=vi
10  MY_ENV_VARIABLE=ansiblepilot
11  [root@demo devops]#
```

Ansible Code reuse: Roles and Collections with Ansible Galaxy

In this chapter you're going to discover how to download and use Ansible Roles and Collection from Ansible Galaxy remote catalog.

Download and Use Ansible Galaxy Role - ansible-galaxy and requirements.yml

How to Download and use the Ansible Role lucab85.ansible_role_-log4shell to scan our Linux machine against Log4Shell Remote Code Execution Log4j (CVE-2021–44228) re-using Ansible artifacts (tasks, variables, defaults, handlers, modules, and plugins) published in Ansible Galaxy directory.

What is an Ansible Role?

- re-usable Ansible artifacts
- one role contains tasks, variables, defaults, handlers, modules, or other plugins
- easy to download and share via Ansible Galaxy

An Ansible **Role** is a set of re-usable Ansible artifacts.
It solves one problem and contains all the relevant tasks, variables, defaults, handlers, modules, or other plugins.

For Users, the Ansible Role is easy to download and share via Ansible Galaxy.

For Developers the Ansible Role is easy to upload and share via Ansible Galaxy. Plus an Ansible role has a defined standard directory structure and format.

What is Ansible Galaxy?

- Ansible Galaxy[37]
- lucab85/ansible_role_log4shell[38]

The website is available at the URL https://galaxy.ansible.com/.

The search engine, Tags, and Platform make it easy to find any content inside.

I recommend you carefully evaluate the quality of content before using it in your system.

Quality indicators are usually the quality assurance of code, the supported operating systems and platforms, the documentation, the release numbers, the presence of Changelog, the number of downloads, and the author or creator.

Please notice that the website contains Ansible Roles and Ansible Collections. Today we're focusing on Ansible Role content.

Links

- https://docs.ansible.com/ansible/latest/user_guide/play-books_reuse.html
- https://docs.ansible.com/ansible/latest/user_guide/play-books_reuse_roles.html#using-roles
- https://galaxy.ansible.com/
- https://galaxy.ansible.com/lucab85/ansible_role_log4shell

---

[37]https://galaxy.ansible.com/
[38]https://galaxy.ansible.com/lucab85/ansible_role_log4shell

demo

Let's jump into a real-life How to Download and Use the Ansible Galaxy Role `lucab85.ansible_role_log4shell`.

code

- role.yml

```
1    ---
2    - name: role demo
3      hosts: all
4      become: true
5      roles:
6        - role: lucab85.ansible_role_log4shell
7          detector_path: "/var/www"
```

- requirements.yml

```
1    ---
2    roles:
3      - name: lucab85.ansible_role_log4shell
```

execution before download

```
$ ansible-playbook -i virtualmachines/demo/inventory gala\
xy/role.yml
ERROR! the role 'lucab85.ansible_role_log4shell' was not \
found in /Users/lberton/prj/github/ansible-pilot/galaxy/r\
oles:/Users/lberton/.ansible/roles:/usr/share/ansible/rol\
es:/etc/ansible/roles:/Users/lberton/prj/github/ansible-p\
ilot/galaxy

The error appears to be in '/Users/lberton/prj/github/ans\
ible-pilot/galaxy/role.yml': line 5, column 8, but may
be elsewhere in the file depending on the exact syntax pr\
oblem.

The offending line appears to be:

  roles:
    - role: lucab85.ansible_role_log4shell
       ^ here
```

download execution

```
$ ansible-galaxy install -r galaxy/requirements.yml
Starting galaxy role install process
- downloading role 'ansible_role_log4shell', owned by luc\
ab85
- downloading role from https://github.com/lucab85/ansibl\
e-role-log4shell/archive/v0.4.1.tar.gz
- extracting lucab85.ansible_role_log4shell to /Users/lbe\
rton/.ansible/roles/lucab85.ansible_role_log4shell
- lucab85.ansible_role_log4shell (v0.4.1) was installed s\
uccessfully
```

execution after download

```
$ ansible-playbook -i virtualmachines/demo/inventory gala\
xy/role.yml

PLAY [role demo] ************************************\
***********************************

TASK [Gathering Facts] *********************************\
***********************************
ok: [demo.example.com]

TASK [lucab85.ansible_role_log4shell : dependency present\
s] ********************************
ok: [demo.example.com]

TASK [lucab85.ansible_role_log4shell : create detector di\
rectory] **************************
changed: [demo.example.com]

TASK [lucab85.ansible_role_log4shell : download detector \
file] ****************************
ok: [demo.example.com]

TASK [lucab85.ansible_role_log4shell : download detector \
signature] ***********************
ok: [demo.example.com]

TASK [lucab85.ansible_role_log4shell : gpg public key] **\
*****************************
changed: [demo.example.com]

TASK [lucab85.ansible_role_log4shell : gpg verify detecto\
r] *************************
changed: [demo.example.com]

TASK [lucab85.ansible_role_log4shell : remove any detecto\
```

```
r run directory] **************
ok: [demo.example.com]

TASK [lucab85.ansible_role_log4shell : create detector ru\
n directory] *****************
changed: [demo.example.com]

TASK [lucab85.ansible_role_log4shell : run detector/scann\
er] *************************
changed: [demo.example.com]

TASK [lucab85.ansible_role_log4shell : files in detector \
run directory] ***************
ok: [demo.example.com]

TASK [lucab85.ansible_role_log4shell : print vulnerable p\
ath(s) found] ****************
ok: [demo.example.com] => {
    "vulnerable": {
        "changed": false,
        "examined": 1,
        "failed": false,
        "files": [],
        "matched": 0,
        "msg": "All paths examined",
        "skipped_paths": {}
    }
}

TASK [ansible-role-log4shell : remove detector directory]\
    *********************
changed: [demo.example.com]

PLAY RECAP *********************************************\
*********************
```

```
71   instance                        : ok=14   changed=9    unreach\
72   able=0    failed=0   skipped=1    rescued=0    ignored=0
```

Download and Use Ansible Galaxy Collection - ansible-galaxy and requirements.yml

How to Download and use the Ansible Collection community.general re-using Ansible artifacts (tasks, variables, defaults, handlers, modules, and plugins) published in Ansible Galaxy directory.

What is an Ansible Collection?

- distribution format for Ansible content
- it contains the package and distributes playbooks, roles, modules, and plugins using collections
- easy to download and share via Ansible Galaxy

An Ansible **Collection** is a distribution format for Ansible content. It solves one problem and contains all the relevant contains the package and distributes playbooks, roles, modules, and plugins. For Users, the Ansible Collection is easy to download and share via Ansible Galaxy. For Developers the Ansible Collection is easy to upload and share via Ansible Galaxy. Plus an Ansible Collection has a defined standard directory structure and format.

What is Ansible Galaxy?

- Ansible Galaxy[39]

---

[39]https://galaxy.ansible.com/

The website is available at the URL https://galaxy.ansible.com/.

The search engine, Tags, and Platform make it easy to find any content inside.

I recommend you carefully evaluate the quality of content before using it in your system.

Quality indicators are usually the quality assurance of code, the supported operating systems and platforms, the documentation, the release numbers, the presence of Changelog, the number of downloads, and the author or creator.

Please notice that the website contains Ansible Roles and Ansible Collections. Today we're focusing on Ansible Role content.

Links

- Ansible Collections list[40]
- Ansible Collections Developer Guide[41]
- Ansible Collections migrating roles[42]
- community.general collection[43]

demo

Let's jump into a real-life How to Download and Use the Ansible Galaxy Collection `community.general` in a system with `ansible-core` installed.

code

- collection.yml

---

[40]https://github.com/ansible-collections
[41]https://docs.ansible.com/ansible/latest/dev_guide/developing_collections.html
[42]https://docs.ansible.com/ansible/latest/dev_guide/migrating_roles.html
[43]https://docs.ansible.com/ansible/latest/collections/community/general/

```
1   ---
2   - name: modprobe module demo
3     hosts: localhost
4     become: true
5     vars:
6       module_name: "dummy"
7       ansible_connection: local
8     tasks:
9       - name: load the module
10        community.general.modprobe:
11          name: "{{ module_name }}"
12          state: present
```

- requirements.yml

```
1   ---
2   collections:
3     - name: community.general
4       source: https://galaxy.ansible.com
```

execution without collection installed

```
1   $ ansible-playbook collection/collection.yml
2   [WARNING]: provided hosts list is empty, only localhost i\
3   s available. Note that the implicit
4   localhost does not match 'all'
5   ERROR! couldn't resolve module/action 'community.general.\
6   modprobe'. This often indicates a misspelling, missing co\
7   llection, or incorrect module path.
8
9   The error appears to be in '/home/devops/collection/colle\
10  ction.yml': line 10, column 7, but may
11  be elsewhere in the file depending on the exact syntax pr\
12  oblem.
13
```

```
14  The offending line appears to be:
15
16    tasks:
17      - name: load the module
18        ^ here
19  $
```

download execution

```
1   $ ansible-galaxy install -r collection/requirements.yml
2   Starting galaxy collection install process
3   Process install dependency map
4   Starting collection install process
5   Downloading https://galaxy.ansible.com/download/community\
6   -general-4.5.0.tar.gz to /home/devops/.ansible/tmp/ansibl\
7   e-local-24543cs6dck7/tmpaccd0umv/community-general-4.5.0-\
8   5msjuuoa
9   Installing 'community.general:4.5.0' to '/home/devops/.an\
10  sible/collections/ansible_collections/community/general'
11  community.general:4.5.0 was installed successfully
```

list installed collection

```
1   $ ansible-galaxy collection list
2
3   # /home/devops/.ansible/collections/ansible_collections
4   Collection          Version
5   ----------------- -------
6   community.general 4.5.0
7   $
```

execution with collection installed

```
$ ansible-playbook collection/collection.yml
[WARNING]: provided hosts list is empty, only localhost i\
s available. Note that the implicit
localhost does not match 'all'

PLAY [modprobe module demo] ****************************\
*******************************************

TASK [Gathering Facts] ********************************\
*******************************************
ok: [localhost]

TASK [load the module] ********************************\
*****************************************
changed: [localhost]

PLAY RECAP ********************************************\
*****************************************
localhost                  : ok=2    changed=1    unreach\
able=0    failed=0    skipped=0    rescued=0    ignored=0\


$
```

Ansible for Linux Filesystem

How to automate the interraction with Linux filesystem with Ansible. For example: file and directory creation, permission and delete.

Create an empty file - Ansible module file

How to create an empty ~/example.txt file or update the time of an already create file.

Ansible create an empty file

Let's talk about the Ansible module file.
The full name is ansible.builtin.file, which means that is part of the collection of modules "builtin" with ansible and shipped with it.
It's a module pretty stable and out for years.
It works in a different variety of operating systems.
It manages files and file properties.
For Windows targets, use the ansible.windows.win_file module instead.

Main Parameters

- path string (dest, name) - file path

- state string - file/absent/directory/hard/link/touch

This module has some parameters to perform any tasks.
The only required is "path", where you specify the file system path of the file you're going to edit.
The state defines the type of object we are modifying, the default is "file" but for our use case, we need the "touch" option.

demo

How to create an empty ~/example.txt file or update the time of an already create file with Ansible.

- file.yml

```yaml
1   ---
2   - name: file module demo
3     hosts: all
4     vars:
5       myfile: "~/example.txt"
6     tasks:
7       - name: Creating an empty file
8         ansible.builtin.file:
9           path: "{{ myfile }}"
10          state: touch
```

Create a text file - Ansible module copy

How to automate the creation of a text file with Ansible.

Let's talk about Ansible module copy.
The full name is ansible.builtin.copy which means is part of the

collection of modules "builtin" with ansible and shipped with it.
This module is pretty stable and out for years.
The purpose is to copy files to remote locations but it's also capable
to create some simple text files.
If you need a more complex configuration it's better to rely on the
template module.

Parameters

- dest path - destination file
- content string - text
- mode/owner/group - permission
- setype/seuser/selevel - SELinux

The only required parameter is dest which specifies the remote
absolute path destination.
The content parameter sets the contents of a file directly to the
specified value. It works only when dest is a file/
Please note that if you use a variable in the content parameter will
result in unpredictable output.
For advanced formatting or if the content contains a variable, use
the ansible.builtin.template module.
Let me also highlight that we could also specify the permissions
and SELinux properties.

demo

How to create an empty file ~/example.txt in Linux with Ansible.

code

- copy.yml

```yaml
1   ---
2   - name: copy module demo
3     hosts: all
4     vars:
5       myfile: "{{ ~/example.txt }}"
6     tasks:
7     - name: create a text file
8       ansible.builtin.copy:
9         dest: "{{ myfile }}"
10        content: |
11          line 1
12          line 2
```

Check if a file exists - Ansible module stat

How to check if a file exists in Ansible?

Let's talk about the Ansible module `stat`.
The full name is `ansible.builtin.stat`, which means that is part of the collection of modules "builtin" with ansible and shipped with it.
It's a module pretty stable and out for years.
It works in a different variety of operating systems.
It retrieves a file entry or a file system status.
For Windows target use the `ansible.windows.win_stat` module instead.

Mandatory Parameters

- path string

Main Return Values

- stat complex - exists

The only mandatory parameter is "path" which is the filesystem full path of the object to check.
The module returns a complex object, the property that is interesting for us is "exists". This attribute is "true" if the object exists.

demo

Let's jump in a real-life playbook to check if a file exists with Ansible.

code

- file_exist.yml

```yaml
---
- name: check if a file exist
  hosts: all
  become: false
  vars:
    myfile: /home/devops/test.txt
  tasks:
    - name: check if a file exists
      ansible.builtin.stat:
        path: "{{ myfile }}"
      register: file_data
- name: report file exists
      ansible.builtin.debug:
        msg: "The file {{ myfile }} exist"
      when: file_data.stat.exists
- name: report file not exists
```

```
17      ansible.builtin.debug:
18        msg: "The file {{ myfile }} doesn't exist"
19      when: not file_data.stat.exists
```

How to create a directory with Ansible?

How to automate the creation of "example" directory with Ansible.

- ansible.builtin.file
- Manage files and file properties

Today we're talking about the Ansible module file.
The full name is ansible.builtin.file, which means that is part of the collection of modules "builtin" with ansible and shipped with it.
It's a module pretty stable and out for years.
It works in a different variety of operating systems.
It manages files and file properties.
For Windows targets, use the `ansible.windows.win_file` module instead.

Parameters

- path string (dest, name) - file path
- state string - file/absent/directory/hard/link/touch
- mode/owner/group - permission
- setype/seuser/selevel - SELinux

This module has some parameters to perform any tasks.
The only required is "path", where you specify the filesystem path of the file you're going to edit.
The state defines the type of object we are modifying, the default is "file" but for our use case, we need the "directory" option.

Demo

How to create the "example" directory in the home of "devops" user in Linux with Ansible using the `file` module.

code

- create_directory.yml

```
1   ---
2   - name: file module demo
3     hosts: all
4     vars:
5       mydir: "~/example"
6     tasks:
7       - name: Creating a directory
8         ansible.builtin.file:
9           path: "{{ mydir }}"
10          state: directory
11          owner: devops
12          group: users
13          mode: '0644'
```

execution

```
1   $ ansible-playbook -i demo/inventory create\ directory/fi\
2   le.yml
3   PLAY [file module demo] *********************************\
4   **********************************
5   TASK [Gathering Facts] *********************************\
6   **********************************
7   ok: [demo.example.com]
8   TASK [Creating a directory] ****************************\
9   **********************************
10  changed: [demo.example.com]
11  PLAY RECAP *********************************************\
12  **********************************
13  demo.example.com              : ok=2    changed=1    unreach\
14  able=0    failed=0    skipped=0    rescued=0    ignored=0
```

before execution

```
1   $ ssh devops@demo.example.com
2   [devops@demo ~]$ ls -al
3   total 16
4   drwx------. 4 devops wheel  111 Nov 14 13:43 .
5   drwxr-xr-x. 5 root   root    50 Nov  8 17:07 ..
6   drwx------. 3 devops wheel   17 Sep  6 05:53 .ansible
7   -rw-------. 1 devops wheel 2849 Nov 14 13:43 .bash_history
8   -rw-r--r--. 1 devops wheel   18 Dec  4  2020 .bash_logout
9   -rw-r--r--. 1 devops wheel  141 Dec  4  2020 .bash_profile
10  -rw-r--r--. 1 devops wheel  376 Dec  4  2020 .bashrc
11  drwx------. 2 devops wheel   94 Sep 16 10:09 .ssh
12  [devops@demo ~]$
```

after execution

```
1   $ ssh devops@demo.example.com
2   [devops@demo ~]$ ls -al
3   total 16
4   drwx------. 5 devops wheel   126 Nov 14 13:45 .
5   drwxr-xr-x. 5 root    root     50 Nov  8 17:07 ..
6   drwx------. 3 devops wheel    17 Sep  6 05:53 .ansible
7   -rw-------. 1 devops wheel  2861 Nov 14 13:44 .bash_history
8   -rw-r--r--. 1 devops wheel    18 Dec  4  2020 .bash_logout
9   -rw-r--r--. 1 devops wheel   141 Dec  4  2020 .bash_profile
10  -rw-r--r--. 1 devops wheel   376 Dec  4  2020 .bashrc
11  drwx------. 2 devops wheel    94 Sep 16 10:09 .ssh
12  drw-r--r--. 2 devops users     6 Nov 14 13:45 example
```

How to check if a directory exists in Ansible?

How to verify if a directory exists with the Ansible module `stat`. The full name is `ansible.builtin.stat`, which means that is part of the collection of modules "builtin" with ansible and shipped with it.

It's a module pretty stable and out for years.

It works in a different variety of operating systems.

It retrieves a file entry or a file system status.

For Windows target use the `ansible.windows.win_stat` module instead.

Main parameters and return values

- path <u>string</u>

The only mandatory parameter is "path" which is the filesystem full path of the object to check.

- stat <u>complex</u>

The module returns a complex object, the property that is interesting for us is "isdir". This attribute is "true" if the object is a directory.

Demo

Let's jump in a real-life playbook to check if a directory exists with Ansible.

code

- directory_check_exists.yml

```yaml
---
- name: check if the directory exists
  hosts: all
  become: false
  vars:
    directory: "/tmp"
  tasks:
    - name: Check if the directory exists
      ansible.builtin.stat:
        path: "{{ directory }}"
      register: dir_to_check

    - name: Directory found
      ansible.builtin.debug:
        msg: "Directory {{ directory }} present"
      when: dir_to_check.stat.isdir is defined and dir_to\
_check.stat.isdir
```

How to rename a file or directory using an Ansible task on a remote system?

How to rename file/directory with Ansible.

First of all let me demystify that I'd like to propose a solution using only Ansible native modules, so no shell module to invoke the Unix utility mv.

Today we're talking about Ansible two modules copy and file

The full names are ansible.builtin.copy and ansible.builtin.file which means are part of the collection of modules "builtin" with ansible and shipped with it.

Both are these modules are pretty stable and out for years.

The purpose of the copy module is to copy files to remote locations. Once the file is successfully copied we could use the module file to delete the source file.

Parameters

Module copy

- dest path - destination
- src string - source
- remote_src boolean - no / yes

Module file

- path string (dest, name) - file path
- state string - file/absent/directory/hard/link/touch

The parameter list is pretty wide but I'll summarize the most useful. The only required parameter is "dest" which specifies the destination path.

The "src" specifies the source file presumed in the controller host. It could be a relative or absolute path.

From version 2.0, in the copy module, you can use the "remote_src" parameter.

If True it will search the file in the remote/target machine for the src.

From version 2.8 copy module remote_src supports recursive copying.

The only required is "path", where you specify the filesystem path of the file you're going to edit.

The state defines the type of object we are modifying, the default is "file" but we could also handle directories, hardlink, symlink, or only update the access time with the "touch" option.

For our use case, we are going to use the "absent" option.

Demo

Let's jump in a real-life playbook to rename files or directories with Ansible

code

- rename/file.yml

```yaml
1   ---
2   - name: rename file or directory
3     hosts: all
4     vars:
5       mysrc: "~/foo"
6       mydst: "~/bar"
7     tasks:
8       - name: Check if file exists
9         ansible.builtin.stat:
10          path: "{{ mysrc }}"
```

```
11          register: check_file_name
12   - name: print debug
13       ansible.builtin.debug:
14         var: check_file_name
15   - name: Copy file with new name
16       ansible.builtin.copy:
17         remote_src: true
18         src: "{{ mysrc }}"
19         dest: "{{ mydst }}"
20       when: check_file_name.stat.exists
21   - name: Remove old file
22       ansible.builtin.file:
23         path: "{{ mysrc }}"
24         state: absent
25       when: check_file_name.stat.exists
```

execution

- output file does not exist:

```
1   $ ansible-playbook -i demo/inventory rename/file.yml
2   PLAY [rename file or directory] ************************\
3   ****************************************************
4   TASK [Gathering Facts] ********************************\
5   ****************************************************
6   ok: [demo.example.com]
7   TASK [Check if file exists] ***************************\
8   ****************************************************
9   ok: [demo.example.com]
10  TASK [print debug] ************************************\
11  ****************************************************
12  ok: [demo.example.com] => {
13      "check_file_name": {
14          "changed": false,
15          "failed": false,
16          "stat": {
```

```
17                   "exists": false
18             }
19         }
20   }
21   TASK [Copy file with new name] *************************\
22   ******************************************************
23   skipping: [demo.example.com]
24   TASK [Remove old file] ********************************\
25   ******************************************************
26   skipping: [demo.example.com]
27   PLAY RECAP ********************************************\
28   ******************************************************
29   demo.example.com              : ok=3     changed=0    unreach\
30   able=0     failed=0     skipped=2    rescued=0    ignored=0
```

- output file exists:

```
1    $ ansible-playbook -i demo/inventory rename/file.yml
2    PLAY [rename file or directory] ***********************\
3    ******************************************************
4    TASK [Gathering Facts] ********************************\
5    ******************************************************
6    ok: [demo.example.com]
7    TASK [Check if file exists] ***************************\
8    ******************************************************
9    ok: [demo.example.com]
10   TASK [print debug] ************************************\
11   ******************************************************
12   ok: [demo.example.com] => {
13       "check_file_name": {
14           "changed": false,
15           "failed": false,
16           "stat": {
17               "atime": 1632319723.592112,
18               "attr_flags": "",
```

```
19                "attributes": [],
20                "block_size": 4096,
21                "blocks": 0,
22                "charset": "binary",
23                "checksum": "da39a3ee5e6b4b0d3255bfef95601890\
24   afd80709",
25                "ctime": 1632319723.592112,
26                "dev": 64768,
27                "device_type": 0,
28                "executable": false,
29                "exists": true,
30                "gid": 10,
31                "gr_name": "wheel",
32                "inode": 134764246,
33                "isblk": false,
34                "ischr": false,
35                "isdir": false,
36                "isfifo": false,
37                "isgid": false,
38                "islnk": false,
39                "isreg": true,
40                "issock": false,
41                "isuid": false,
42                "mimetype": "inode/x-empty",
43                "mode": "0644",
44                "mtime": 1632319723.592112,
45                "nlink": 1,
46                "path": "/home/devops/foo",
47                "pw_name": "devops",
48                "readable": true,
49                "rgrp": true,
50                "roth": true,
51                "rusr": true,
52                "size": 0,
53                "uid": 1001,
```

```
54              "version": "1745015340",
55              "wgrp": false,
56              "woth": false,
57              "writeable": true,
58              "wusr": true,
59              "xgrp": false,
60              "xoth": false,
61              "xusr": false
62          }
63       }
64   }
65   TASK [Copy file with new name] ************************\
66   ******************************************************
67   changed: [demo.example.com]
68   TASK [Remove old file] *******************************\
69   ******************************************************
70   changed: [demo.example.com]
71   PLAY RECAP *******************************************\
72   ******************************************************
73   demo.example.com           : ok=5    changed=2    unreach\
74   able=0    failed=0    skipped=0    rescued=0    ignored=0
```

- output directory exists:

```
1    $ ansible-playbook -i demo/inventory rename/file.yml
2    PLAY [rename file or directory] **********************\
3    ******************************************************
4    TASK [Gathering Facts] *******************************\
5    ******************************************************
6    ok: [demo.example.com]
7    TASK [Check if file exists] **************************\
8    ******************************************************
9    ok: [demo.example.com]
10   TASK [print debug] ***********************************\
11   ******************************************************
```

```
12   ok: [demo.example.com] => {
13       "check_file_name": {
14            "changed": false,
15            "failed": false,
16            "stat": {
17                 "atime": 1632319779.5021598,
18                 "attr_flags": "",
19                 "attributes": [],
20                 "block_size": 4096,
21                 "blocks": 0,
22                 "charset": "binary",
23                 "ctime": 1632319779.5021598,
24                 "dev": 64768,
25                 "device_type": 0,
26                 "executable": true,
27                 "exists": true,
28                 "gid": 10,
29                 "gr_name": "wheel",
30                 "inode": 898820,
31                 "isblk": false,
32                 "ischr": false,
33                 "isdir": true,
34                 "isfifo": false,
35                 "isgid": false,
36                 "islnk": false,
37                 "isreg": false,
38                 "issock": false,
39                 "isuid": false,
40                 "mimetype": "inode/directory",
41                 "mode": "0755",
42                 "mtime": 1632319779.5021598,
43                 "nlink": 2,
44                 "path": "/home/devops/foo",
45                 "pw_name": "devops",
46                 "readable": true,
```

```
47              "rgrp": true,
48              "roth": true,
49              "rusr": true,
50              "size": 6,
51              "uid": 1001,
52              "version": "1317302979",
53              "wgrp": false,
54              "woth": false,
55              "writeable": true,
56              "wusr": true,
57              "xgrp": true,
58              "xoth": true,
59              "xusr": true
60          }
61      }
62  }
63  TASK [Copy file with new name] ************************\
64  ****************************************************
65  ok: [demo.example.com]
66  TASK [Remove old file] *******************************\
67  ****************************************************
68  changed: [demo.example.com]
69  PLAY RECAP *******************************************\
70  ****************************************************
71  demo.example.com           : ok=5    changed=1    unreach\
72  able=0    failed=0    skipped=0    rescued=0    ignored=0
```

Change file permission - Ansible module file

How to change file or directory permission with Ansible?
I'm going to show you how to change chmod and group of a test.txt
file.

How to automate the change file/directory permission with Ansible.

Today we're talking about the Ansible module `file`.

The full name is `ansible.builtin.file`, which means that is part of the collection of modules "builtin" with ansible and shipped with it.

It's a module pretty stable and out for years.

It works in a different variety of operating systems.

It manages files and file properties.

For Windows targets, use the `ansible.windows.win_file` module instead.

Main Parameters

- path <u>string</u> (dest, name) - file path
- owner <u>string</u> - user
- group <u>string</u> - group
- mode <u>raw</u> - Ex: '0644' or 'u=rw,g=r,o=r'
- state <u>string</u> - file/absent/directory/hard/link/touch
- setype/seuser/selevel - SELinux

This module has some parameters to perform any tasks.

The only required is "path", where you specify the filesystem path of the file you're going to edit.

The parameter "owner" sets the user that should own the file/directory.

The parameter "group" sets the group that should own the file/directory.

The parameter "mode" sets the permissions in the UNIX way of the file/directory.

The state defines the type of object we are modifying, the default is "file" but we could handle also directories, hardlink, symlink, or only update the access time with the "touch" option.

Let me also highlight that we could also specify the SELinux properties.

demo

Let's jump in a real-life playbook to change file permission with Ansible.

code

- file.yml

```
 1   ---
 2   - name: file module demo
 3     hosts: all
 4     vars:
 5       myfile: "/home/devops/test.txt"
 6     become: false
 7     tasks:
 8       - name: check permission
 9         ansible.builtin.file:
10           path: "{{ myfile }}"
11           owner: "devops"
12           group: "users"
13           mode: '0777'
```

Add Execute Permission 755 Linux file - Ansible module file

How to automate the setting of execute permission 755 for example.sh Linux file with Ansible module file.
Assigning executive permission 755 in Linux is a very frequent need of a System Administrator that you could automate with Ansible.

Ansible Add Execute Permission

- `ansible.builtin.file`
- Manage files and file properties

Today we're talking about the Ansible module `file`.
The full name is ansible.builtin.file, which means that is part of the collection of modules "builtin" with ansible and shipped with it.
It's a module pretty stable and out for years.
It works in a different variety of operating systems.
It manages files and file properties.
For Windows targets, use the `ansible.windows.win_file` module instead.

Main Parameters

- path <u>string</u> (dest, name) - file path
- owner <u>string</u> - user
- group <u>string</u> - group
- mode <u>raw</u> - Ex: '0644' or 'u=rw,g=r,o=r'
- state <u>string</u> - file/absent/directory/hard/link/touch
- setype/seuser/selevel - SELinux

This module has some parameters to perform any tasks.
The only required is "path", where you specify the filesystem path of the file you're going to edit.
The parameter "owner" set the user that should own the file/directory.
The parameter "group" set the group that should own the file/directory.
The parameter "mode" set the permissions in the UNIX way of the file/directory.
The state defines the type of object we are modifying, the default is "file" but we could handle also directories, hard links, symlinks,

or only update the access time with the "touch" option.

Let me also highlight that we could also specify the SELinux properties.

Links

- ansible.builtin.file[44]

demo

How to Add Execute Permission 755 file on Linux with Ansible Playbook.

I'm going to show you how to set the `chmod +x` of an `example.sh` Linux file with Ansible.

code

- file_permission.yml

```
1  ---
2  - name: file module demo
3    hosts: all
4    vars:
5      myscript: "~/example.sh"
6    tasks:
7      - name: set execution permission
8        ansible.builtin.file:
9          dest: "{{ myscript }}"
10         mode: 'a+x'
```

- example.sh

---

[44]https://docs.ansible.com/ansible/latest/collections/ansible/builtin/file_module.html

```
1  #!/bin/bash
2  echo "Hello World"
```

execution

```
1   ansible-pilot $ ansible-playbook -i virtualmachines/demo/\
2   inventory file_management/file_permission.yml
3   PLAY [file module demo] *********************************\
4   *******************************************
5   TASK [Gathering Facts] *********************************\
6   *******************************************
7   ok: [demo.example.com]
8   TASK [set execution permission] ************************\
9   *******************************************
10  changed: [demo.example.com]
11  PLAY RECAP *********************************************\
12  *******************************************
13  demo.example.com              : ok=2     changed=1     unreach\
14  able=0     failed=0     skipped=0     rescued=0     ignored=0
15  ansible-pilot $
```

idempotency

```
1   ansible-pilot $ ansible-playbook -i virtualmachines/demo/\
2   inventory file_management/file_permission.yml
3   PLAY [file module demo] *********************************\
4   *******************************************
5   TASK [Gathering Facts] *********************************\
6   *******************************************
7   ok: [demo.example.com]
8   TASK [set execution permission] ************************\
9   *******************************************
10  ok: [demo.example.com]
11  PLAY RECAP *********************************************\
12  *******************************************
13  demo.example.com              : ok=2     changed=0     unreach\
```

```
14  able=0     failed=0     skipped=0     rescued=0     ignored=0
15  ansible-pilot $
```

before execution

```
1  ansible-pilot $ ssh devops@demo.example.com
2  Last login: Wed Mar 30 13:38:46 2022 from 192.168.0.59
3  [devops@demo ~]$ cat example.sh
4  #!/bin/bash
5  echo "Hello World"
6  [devops@demo ~]$[devops@demo ~]$ ls -al example.sh
7  -rw-r--r--. 1 devops wheel 31 Mar 30 13:39 example.sh
8  [devops@demo ~]$
```

after execution

```
1  ansible-pilot $ ssh devops@demo.example.com
2  Last login: Wed Mar 30 13:40:36 2022 from 192.168.0.59
3  [devops@demo ~]$ ls -al example.sh
4  -rwxr-xr-x. 1 devops wheel 31 Mar 30 13:39 example.sh
5  [devops@demo ~]$ ./example.sh
6  Hello World
7  [devops@demo ~]$ cat example.sh
8  #!/bin/bash
9  echo "Hello World"
```

Delete file or directory - Ansible module file

A real-life example about how the "deleteme" file or the "deleteme" directory with Ansible.

Let's talk about the Ansible module `file`.
The full name is `ansible.builtin.file`, which means that is part

of the collection of modules "builtin" with ansible and shipped with it.

It's a module pretty stable and out for years.

It works in a different variety of operating systems.

It manages files and file properties.

For Windows targets, use the `ansible.windows.win_file` module instead.

Main Parameters

- path <u>string</u> (dest, name) - file path
- owner <u>string</u> - user
- group <u>string</u> - group
- mode <u>raw</u> - Ex: '0644' or 'u=rw,g=r,o=r'
- state <u>string</u> - file/absent/directory/hard/link/touch
- setype/seuser/selevel - SELinux

The only required is "path", where you specify the file system path of the file you're going to edit.

The parameter "owner" sets the user that should own the file/directory.

The parameter "group" sets the group that should own the file/directory.

The parameter "mode" sets the permissions in the UNIX way of the file/directory.

The state defines the type of object we are modifying, the default is "file" but we could also handle directories, hard link, symlink, or only update the access time with the "touch" option.

For our use case, we are going to use the "absent" option.

Let me also highlight that we could also specify the SELinux properties.

demo

How to delete the "deleteme" file or the "deleteme" directory with Ansible.

- file.yml

```yaml
1    ---
2    - name: file module demo
3      hosts: all
4      vars:
5        mypath: "/home/devops/deleteme"
6      become: false
7      tasks:
8        - name: "{{ mypath }}" not present
9          ansible.builtin.file:
10           path: "{{ mypath }}"
11           state: "absent"
```

Download a file - Ansible module get_url

How to download a tarball from URL, verify the checksum, assign some permission with Ansible.

Let's talk about the Ansible module `get_url`.
The full name is `ansible.builtin.get_url`, which means that is part of the collection of modules "builtin" with ansible and shipped with it, part of `ansible-core`.
It's a module pretty stable and out for years.
It works in a different variety of operating systems.
It downloads files from HTTP, HTTPS, or FTP to node

For Windows targets, use the `ansible.windows.win_get_url` module instead.

See also Ansible troubleshooting - Destination does not exist

Parameters

- url string - URL
- dest string - path
- force string - no/yes
- checksum string - <algorithm>:<checksum|url>
- force_basic_auth/url_username/url_password/use_gssapi - HTTP basic auth/GSSAPI-Kerberos
- headers dictionary - custom HTTP headers
- http_agent string - "ansible-httpget"
- owner/group/mode string - permission
- setype/seuser/selevel - SELinux

The two required parameters are `url` and `dest`.
The `url` parameter specifies the URL of the resource you're going to download.
The `dest` parameter specifies the filesystem path where the resource is going to be saved on the target node.
Let's deep dive in the "force" parameter.
If "dest" is a file, Ansible is going to download every time the file.
If "dest" is a directory the default behavior is not to replace a file, until you toggle to `yes` the force parameter.
The parameter "checksum" is very useful to validate the consistency of the downloaded file.
You could specify the algorithm, usually sha1 or sha256, and directly the checksum or a URL for checksum.

You might need the third-party `hashlib` library for access to additional algorithms.

Another interesting parameter is "headers" which allow you to specify some custom HTTP headers.

Ansible presents himself as "ansible-httpget" in the web server logs, but you cust customize it in the "http_agent" parameter.

There are some additional parameters for authentication for example to handle HTTP basic authentication with username and password or for more complex GSSAPI-Kerberos scenarios using `httplib2` Python library.

Let me also highlight that we could also specify the permission and SELinux properties.

demo

How to download a `tar.gz` file from Internet and verify the SHA256 checksum with Ansible.

- get_url.yml

```yaml
---
- name: get_url module demo
  hosts: all
  become: false
  vars:
    myurl: "https://releases.ansible.com/ansible/ansible-\
2.9.25.tar.gz"
    mycrc: "sha256:https://releases.ansible.com/ansible/a\
nsible-2.9.25.tar.gz.sha"
    mydest: "/home/devops"
  tasks:
    - name: download file
      ansible.builtin.get_url:
        url: "{{ myurl }}"
```

```
15          dest: "{{ mydest }}"
16          checksum: "{{ mycrc }}"
17          mode: '0644'
18          owner: devops
19          group: wheel
```

Extract an archive - Ansible module unarchive

How to download a zip file and extract it in a user home directory.
The playbook is also taking care of the necessary softwre dependencies.

Let's talk about the Ansible module `unarchive`.
The full name is `ansible.builtin.unarchive`, which means that is part of the collection of modules "builtin" with ansible and shipped with it.
It's a module pretty stable and out for years.
It works in a different variety of operating systems.
It unpacks one archive after (optionally) copying it from the local machine
It can handle `.zip` files using `unzip` as well as `.tar`, `.tar.gz`, `.tar.bz2`, `.tar.xz`, and `.tar.zst` files using `gtar`. It requires `zipinfo`,`gtar` and `unzip` command on target host.
Please note that it requires a tarball (`.tar` archive) for the Unix file format.
For Windows targets, use the Ansible `community.windows.win_-unzip` module.

Parameters

- src <u>string</u> - path
- dest <u>string</u> - path

- remote_src <u>boolean</u> - no/yes
- validate_certs <u>boolean</u> - no/yes (https only)
- include/exclude <u>list</u> - directory and file entries
- extra_opts <u>string</u> - command-line options
- keep_newer <u>boolean</u> - no/yes
- mode/owner/group - permission
- setype/seuser/selevel - SELinux

The only mandatory parameters are `src` and `dst` which are the source and destination paths. The `src` is quite special because is supposed to be a local path on the Ansible controller.

We could switch to a remote path enabling the "remote_src" properties.

In the `src` parameter we could also enter a URL, so the archive is going to be downloaded before being expanded.

Other useful parameters are `include` and `exclude` that allows us to specify a subset of the archive to extract, specifically a list of inclusion or exclusion files or directories.

Just in case we need some extra command-line options we could specify in the `extra_opts` parameter.

If the files are already present on the target machine the default behavior is to not replace existing files that are newer than files from the archive, you could override enabling the `keep_newer` parameter.

Let me also highlight that we could also specify some permissions or SELinux properties.

demo

How to extract an archive in Ansible Playbook with Ansible.

- unarchive.yml

```yaml
---
- name: unarchive module demo
  hosts: all
  become: false
  vars:
    myurl: "https://github.com/lucab85/ansible-pilot/arch\
ive/refs/heads/master.zip"
  tasks:
    - name: extractor presents
      ansible.builtin.yum:
        name:
          - unzip
          - tar
        state: present
      become: true
- name: extract archive
      ansible.builtin.unarchive:
        src: "{{ myurl }}"
        dest: "/home/devops/"
        remote_src: true
        validate_certs: true
```

Create a symbolic link (also symlink or soft link) in Linux - Ansible module file

How to create an "example" symbolic/soft link to "/proc/cpuinfo" on Linux filesystem using Ansible.

Ansible create a symbolic link

- ansible.builtin.file

- Manage files and file properties

Let's talk about the Ansible module `file`.
The full name is `ansible.builtin.file`, which means that is part of the collection of modules "builtin" with ansible and shipped with it.
It's a module pretty stable and out for years.
It works in a different variety of operating systems.
It manages files and file properties.
For Windows targets, use the `ansible.windows.win_file` module instead.

 See also Create a hard link in Linux - Ansible module file

Parameters

- src string - symlink path
- dest string - destination file path
- state string - file/absent/symbolic link/hard/link/touch
- mode/owner/group - permission
- setype/seuser/selevel - SELinux

This module has some parameters to perform any tasks.
The two required fields are "src" and "dest" which specify the filesystem paths of the link and the target file.
The state defines the type of object we are modifying, the default is "file" but for our use case, we need the "link" option.
Let me highlight also the permission and SELinux parameters.

demo

How to create an "example" symbolic/soft link to "/proc/cpuinfo" on Linux filesystem using Ansible.

code

- create_symlink.yml

```yaml
1  ---
2  - name: file module demo
3    hosts: all
4    vars:
5      mylink: "~/example"
6      mysrc: "/proc/cpuinfo"
7    tasks:
8      - name: Creating a symlink
9        ansible.builtin.file:
10         src: "{{ mysrc }}"
11         dest: "{{ mylink }}"
12         state: link
```

execution

```
1   $ ansible-playbook -i demo/inventory create\ symlink/file\
2   .yml
3   PLAY [file module demo] ********************************\
4   **********************************
5   TASK [Gathering Facts] ********************************\
6   **********************************
7   ok: [demo.example.com]
8   TASK [Creating a symlink] ********************************\
9   **********************************
10  changed: [demo.example.com]
11  PLAY RECAP ********************************************\
12  **********************************
13  demo.example.com          : ok=2    changed=1    unreach\
14  able=0    failed=0    skipped=0    rescued=0    ignored=0
```

before execution

```
1    $ ssh devops@demo.example.com
2    [devops@demo ~]$ ls -al
3    total 16
4    drwx------. 4 devops wheel  111 Nov 14 14:26 .
5    drwxr-xr-x. 5 root   root    50 Nov  8 17:07 ..
6    drwx------. 3 devops wheel   17 Sep  6 05:53 .ansible
7    -rw-------. 1 devops wheel 3055 Nov 14 14:26 .bash_history
8    -rw-r--r--. 1 devops wheel   18 Dec  4  2020 .bash_logout
9    -rw-r--r--. 1 devops wheel  141 Dec  4  2020 .bash_profile
10   -rw-r--r--. 1 devops wheel  376 Dec  4  2020 .bashrc
11   drwx------. 2 devops wheel   94 Sep 16 10:09 .ssh
12   [devops@demo ~]$
```

after execution

```
1    $ ssh devops@demo.example.com
2    [devops@demo ~]$ ls -al
3    total 16
4    drwx------. 4 devops wheel  126 Nov 14 14:29 .
5    drwxr-xr-x. 5 root   root    50 Nov  8 17:07 ..
6    drwx------. 3 devops wheel   17 Sep  6 05:53 .ansible
7    -rw-------. 1 devops wheel 3067 Nov 14 14:28 .bash_history
8    -rw-r--r--. 1 devops wheel   18 Dec  4  2020 .bash_logout
9    -rw-r--r--. 1 devops wheel  141 Dec  4  2020 .bash_profile
10   -rw-r--r--. 1 devops wheel  376 Dec  4  2020 .bashrc
11   drwx------. 2 devops wheel   94 Sep 16 10:09 .ssh
12   lrwxrwxrwx. 1 devops wheel   13 Nov 14 14:29 example -> /\
13   proc/cpuinfo
14   [devops@demo ~]$ cat example | less
15   [devops@demo ~]$
```

Create a hard link in Linux - Ansible module file

How to create a "hard link" that references the "example.txt" text file in the Linux filesystem with Ansible.

Ansible creates a hard link

- `ansible.builtin.file`
- Manage files and file properties

Today we're talking about the Ansible module `file`.
The full name is `ansible.builtin.file`, which means that is part of the collection of modules "builtin" with ansible and shipped with it.
It's a module pretty stable and out for years.
It works in a different variety of operating systems.
It manages files and file properties.
For a symlink (or softlink) use see the following parameters of Ansible file module.
For Windows targets, use the `ansible.windows.win_file` module instead.

 See also Create a symbolic link (also symlink or soft link) in Linux - Ansible module file

Parameters

- src string - symlink path
- dest string - destination file path
- state string - file/absent/directory/link/hard/touch

- mode/owner/group - permission
- setype/seuser/selevel - SELinux

This module has some parameters to perform any tasks.
The two required fields are "src" and "dest" which specify the filesystem paths of the har link and the target file.
The state defines the type of object we are modifying, the default is "file" but for our use case, we need the "link" option.
Let me highlight also the permission and SELinux parameters.

demo

How to create a hard link that references the "example.txt" file with Ansible.

code

- create_hardlink.yml

```
 1   ---
 2   - name: file module demo
 3     hosts: all
 4     vars:
 5       mylink: "~/link"
 6       myfile: "~/example.txt"
 7     tasks:
 8       - name: Creating hardlink
 9         ansible.builtin.file:
10           src: "{{ myfile }}"
11           dest: "{{ mylink }}"
12           state: hard
```

execution

```
$ ansible-playbook -i virtualmachines/demo/inventory crea\
te\ link/hardlink.yml
PLAY [file module demo] ********************************\
*********************************************
TASK [Gathering Facts] *********************************\
*********************************************
ok: [demo.example.com]
TASK [Creating hardlink] *******************************\
*********************************************
changed: [demo.example.com]
PLAY RECAP *********************************************\
*********************************************
demo.example.com              : ok=2    changed=1    unreach\
able=0    failed=0    skipped=0    rescued=0    ignored=0
```

before execution

```
$ ssh devops@demo.example.com
[devops@demo ~]$ ls -al
total 16
drwx------. 4 devops wheel 111 Dec  1 15:07 .
drwxr-xr-x. 4 root   root   35 Nov 28 16:46 ..
drwx------. 3 devops wheel  17 Nov 28 16:46 .ansible
-rw-------. 1 devops wheel 224 Dec  1 15:07 .bash_history
-rw-r--r--. 1 devops wheel  18 Dec  4 2020 .bash_logout
-rw-r--r--. 1 devops wheel 141 Dec  4 2020 .bash_profile
-rw-r--r--. 1 devops wheel 376 Dec  4 2020 .bashrc
drwx------. 2 devops wheel  29 Nov 28 16:46 .ssh
[devops@demo ~]$ echo test > example.txt
[devops@demo ~]$ cat example.txt
test
[devops@demo ~]$
```

after execution

```
$ ssh devops@demo.example.com
[devops@demo ~]$ ls -al
total 24
drwx------. 4 devops wheel 142 Dec  1 15:09 .
drwxr-xr-x. 4 root   root    35 Nov 28 16:46 ..
drwx------. 3 devops wheel  17 Nov 28 16:46 .ansible
-rw-------. 1 devops wheel 276 Dec  1 15:08 .bash_history
-rw-r--r--. 1 devops wheel  18 Dec  4  2020 .bash_logout
-rw-r--r--. 1 devops wheel 141 Dec  4  2020 .bash_profile
-rw-r--r--. 1 devops wheel 376 Dec  4  2020 .bashrc
drwx------. 2 devops wheel  29 Nov 28 16:46 .ssh
-rw-r--r--. 2 devops wheel   5 Dec  1 15:08 example.txt
-rw-r--r--. 2 devops wheel   5 Dec  1 15:08 link
[devops@demo ~]$ cat link
test
[devops@demo ~]$ cat example.txt
test
[devops@demo ~]$ ls -al
total 24
drwx------. 4 devops wheel 142 Dec  1 15:09 .
drwxr-xr-x. 4 root   root    35 Nov 28 16:46 ..
drwx------. 3 devops wheel  17 Nov 28 16:46 .ansible
-rw-------. 1 devops wheel 276 Dec  1 15:08 .bash_history
-rw-r--r--. 1 devops wheel  18 Dec  4  2020 .bash_logout
-rw-r--r--. 1 devops wheel 141 Dec  4  2020 .bash_profile
-rw-r--r--. 1 devops wheel 376 Dec  4  2020 .bashrc
drwx------. 2 devops wheel  29 Nov 28 16:46 .ssh
-rw-r--r--. 2 devops wheel   5 Dec  1 15:08 example.txt
-rw-r--r--. 2 devops wheel   5 Dec  1 15:08 link
[devops@demo ~]$ chmod 777 link
[devops@demo ~]$ ls -al
total 24
drwx------. 4 devops wheel 142 Dec  1 15:09 .
drwxr-xr-x. 4 root   root    35 Nov 28 16:46 ..
drwx------. 3 devops wheel  17 Nov 28 16:46 .ansible
```

```
36  -rw-------. 1 devops wheel 276 Dec  1 15:08 .bash_history
37  -rw-r--r--. 1 devops wheel  18 Dec  4  2020 .bash_logout
38  -rw-r--r--. 1 devops wheel 141 Dec  4  2020 .bash_profile
39  -rw-r--r--. 1 devops wheel 376 Dec  4  2020 .bashrc
40  drwx------. 2 devops wheel  29 Nov 28 16:46 .ssh
41  -rwxrwxrwx. 2 devops wheel   5 Dec  1 15:08 example.txt
42  -rwxrwxrwx. 2 devops wheel   5 Dec  1 15:08 link
43  [devops@demo ~]$ touch link
44  [devops@demo ~]$ ls -al
45  total 24
46  drwx------. 4 devops wheel 142 Dec  1 15:09 .
47  drwxr-xr-x. 4 root   root   35 Nov 28 16:46 ..
48  drwx------. 3 devops wheel  17 Nov 28 16:46 .ansible
49  -rw-------. 1 devops wheel 276 Dec  1 15:08 .bash_history
50  -rw-r--r--. 1 devops wheel  18 Dec  4  2020 .bash_logout
51  -rw-r--r--. 1 devops wheel 141 Dec  4  2020 .bash_profile
52  -rw-r--r--. 1 devops wheel 376 Dec  4  2020 .bashrc
53  drwx------. 2 devops wheel  29 Nov 28 16:46 .ssh
54  -rwxrwxrwx. 2 devops wheel   5 Dec  1 15:10 example.txt
55  -rwxrwxrwx. 2 devops wheel   5 Dec  1 15:10 link
56  [devops@demo ~]$ touch link
57  [devops@demo ~]$ ls -al
58  total 24
59  drwx------. 4 devops wheel 142 Dec  1 15:09 .
60  drwxr-xr-x. 4 root   root   35 Nov 28 16:46 ..
61  drwx------. 3 devops wheel  17 Nov 28 16:46 .ansible
62  -rw-------. 1 devops wheel 359 Dec  1 15:11 .bash_history
63  -rw-r--r--. 1 devops wheel  18 Dec  4  2020 .bash_logout
64  -rw-r--r--. 1 devops wheel 141 Dec  4  2020 .bash_profile
65  -rw-r--r--. 1 devops wheel 376 Dec  4  2020 .bashrc
66  drwx------. 2 devops wheel  29 Nov 28 16:46 .ssh
67  -rwxrwxrwx. 2 devops wheel   5 Dec  1 15:19 example.txt
68  -rwxrwxrwx. 2 devops wheel   5 Dec  1 15:19 link
69  [devops@demo ~]$ ls -li *
70  134907033 -rwxrwxrwx. 2 devops wheel 5 Dec  1 15:19 examp\
```

```
71   le.txt
72   134907033 -rwxrwxrwx. 2 devops wheel 5 Dec  1 15:19 link
73   [devops@demo ~]$
```

Mount a Windows share in Linux SMB/CIFS - Ansible module mount

How to Mount a Windows share in Linux SMB/CIFS. The Ansible Playbook code is going to check the required packages, create the mount-point and setup the Windows network shared folder via SMB/CIFS protocol on the Linux target machine.

Ansible mount an SMB/CIFS filesystem

- ansible.posix.mount
- Control active and configured mount points

Today we're talking about the Ansible module mount.
The full name is `ansible.posix.mount`, which means that is part of the collection of modules "ansible.posix" to interact with POSIX platforms.
The purpose of the module is to Control active and configured mount points.
For Windows, use the `community.windows.win_mapped_drive` module instead.

Parameters

- path string - mount point (e.g. /mnt)
- state string - mounted / unmounted / present / absent / remounted

- src string - device or network volume
- fstype string - ext4, xfs, iso9660, nfs, cifs, etc.
- opts string - mount options

This module has many parameters to perform any task.

The only required are "path" and "state".

The parameter "path" specifies the path to the mount point (e.g. /mnt/).

The parameter "state" allows us to verify a specific state of the mount point. The options "mounted", "unmounted" and "remounted" change the device status. The "present" and "absent" options only change the `/etc/fstab` file.

The `src` parameter specifies the device or network volume for NFS or SMB/CIFS.

The `fstype` parameter specifies the filesystem type. For example: ext4, xfs, iso9660, nfs, cifs, etc.

The `opts` parameter allows us to specify some mount options, that vary for each filesystem type.

demo

Let's jump in a real-life Ansible Playbook to mount an SMB/CIFS filesystem.

code

- mount_cifs.yml

```yaml
1   ---
2   - name: mount module demo
3     hosts: all
4     become: true
5     vars:
6       uri: "//windows-pc/share"
7       username: "example@domain"
8       password: "password"
9       mountpoint: "/share"
10    tasks:
11      - name: utility present
12        ansible.builtin.package:
13          name: cifs-utils
14          state: present
15  - name: check mountpoint exist
16        ansible.builtin.file:
17          path: "{{ mountpoint }}"
18          state: directory
19          mode: '0755'
20          owner: root
21          group: root
22  - name: Mount network share
23        ansible.posix.mount:
24          src: "{{ uri }}"
25          path: "{{ mountpoint }}"
26          fstype: cifs
27          opts: 'username={{ username }},password={{ passwo\
28  rd }}'
29          state: mounted
```

execution

```
1   $ ansible-playbook -i demo/inventory mount\ drive/cifs.yml
2   PLAY [mount module demo] *********************************\
3   ****************************************************
4   TASK [Gathering Facts] **********************************\
5   ****************************************************
6   ok: [demo.example.com]
7   TASK [utility present] **********************************\
8   ****************************************************
9   changed: [demo.example.com]
10  TASK [check mountpoint exist] ***************************\
11  ****************************************************
12  changed: [demo.example.com]
13  TASK [Mount network share] ******************************\
14  ****************************************************
15  changed: [demo.example.com]
16  PLAY RECAP **********************************************\
17  ****************************************************
18  demo.example.com            : ok=4    changed=3    unreach\
19  able=0    failed=0    skipped=0    rescued=0    ignored=0
```

before execution

```
1   $ ssh devops@demo.example.com
2   [devops@demo ~]$ sudo su
3   [root@demo devops]# mount
4   sysfs on /sys type sysfs (rw,nosuid,nodev,noexec,relatime\
5   ,seclabel)
6   proc on /proc type proc (rw,nosuid,nodev,noexec,relatime)
7   devtmpfs on /dev type devtmpfs (rw,nosuid,seclabel,size=3\
8   95492k,nr_inodes=98873,mode=755)
9   securityfs on /sys/kernel/security type securityfs (rw,no\
10  suid,nodev,noexec,relatime)
11  tmpfs on /dev/shm type tmpfs (rw,nosuid,nodev,seclabel)
12  devpts on /dev/pts type devpts (rw,nosuid,noexec,relatime\
13  ,seclabel,gid=5,mode=620,ptmxmode=000)
14  tmpfs on /run type tmpfs (rw,nosuid,nodev,seclabel,mode=7\
```

```
15  55)
16  tmpfs on /sys/fs/cgroup type tmpfs (ro,nosuid,nodev,noexe\
17  c,seclabel,mode=755)
18  cgroup on /sys/fs/cgroup/systemd type cgroup (rw,nosuid,n\
19  odev,noexec,relatime,seclabel,xattr,release_agent=/usr/li\
20  b/systemd/systemd-cgroups-agent,name=systemd)
21  pstore on /sys/fs/pstore type pstore (rw,nosuid,nodev,noe\
22  xec,relatime,seclabel)
23  bpf on /sys/fs/bpf type bpf (rw,nosuid,nodev,noexec,relat\
24  ime,mode=700)
25  cgroup on /sys/fs/cgroup/rdma type cgroup (rw,nosuid,node\
26  v,noexec,relatime,seclabel,rdma)
27  cgroup on /sys/fs/cgroup/perf_event type cgroup (rw,nosui\
28  d,nodev,noexec,relatime,seclabel,perf_event)
29  cgroup on /sys/fs/cgroup/net_cls,net_prio type cgroup (rw\
30  ,nosuid,nodev,noexec,relatime,seclabel,net_cls,net_prio)
31  cgroup on /sys/fs/cgroup/freezer type cgroup (rw,nosuid,n\
32  odev,noexec,relatime,seclabel,freezer)
33  cgroup on /sys/fs/cgroup/cpuset type cgroup (rw,nosuid,no\
34  dev,noexec,relatime,seclabel,cpuset)
35  cgroup on /sys/fs/cgroup/pids type cgroup (rw,nosuid,node\
36  v,noexec,relatime,seclabel,pids)
37  cgroup on /sys/fs/cgroup/hugetlb type cgroup (rw,nosuid,n\
38  odev,noexec,relatime,seclabel,hugetlb)
39  cgroup on /sys/fs/cgroup/blkio type cgroup (rw,nosuid,nod\
40  ev,noexec,relatime,seclabel,blkio)
41  cgroup on /sys/fs/cgroup/memory type cgroup (rw,nosuid,no\
42  dev,noexec,relatime,seclabel,memory)
43  cgroup on /sys/fs/cgroup/devices type cgroup (rw,nosuid,n\
44  odev,noexec,relatime,seclabel,devices)
45  cgroup on /sys/fs/cgroup/cpu,cpuacct type cgroup (rw,nosu\
46  id,nodev,noexec,relatime,seclabel,cpu,cpuacct)
47  none on /sys/kernel/tracing type tracefs (rw,relatime,sec\
48  label)
49  configfs on /sys/kernel/config type configfs (rw,relatime)
```

```
/dev/mapper/rhel_rhel8-root on / type xfs (rw,relatime,se\
clabel,attr2,inode64,logbufs=8,logbsize=32k,noquota)
selinuxfs on /sys/fs/selinux type selinuxfs (rw,relatime)
systemd-1 on /proc/sys/fs/binfmt_misc type autofs (rw,rel\
atime,fd=31,pgrp=1,timeout=0,minproto=5,maxproto=5,direct\
,pipe_ino=18292)
debugfs on /sys/kernel/debug type debugfs (rw,relatime,se\
clabel)
mqueue on /dev/mqueue type mqueue (rw,relatime,seclabel)
hugetlbfs on /dev/hugepages type hugetlbfs (rw,relatime,s\
eclabel,pagesize=2M)
/dev/sda1 on /boot type xfs (rw,relatime,seclabel,attr2,i\
node64,logbufs=8,logbsize=32k,noquota)
tmpfs on /run/user/1001 type tmpfs (rw,nosuid,nodev,relat\
ime,seclabel,size=82872k,mode=700,uid=1001,gid=10)
[root@demo devops]# mount | grep share
[root@demo devops]# cat /etc/fstab
#
# /etc/fstab
# Created by anaconda on Wed Sep  1 00:06:23 2021
#
# Accessible filesystems, by reference, are maintained un\
der '/dev/disk/'.
# See man pages fstab(5), findfs(8), mount(8) and/or blki\
d(8) for more info.
#
# After editing this file, run 'systemctl daemon-reload' \
to update systemd
# units generated from this file.
#
/dev/mapper/rhel_rhel8-root /                       xfs  \
    defaults        0 0
UUID=ae6c1777-c1c9-42a1-8fcf-513077aac39b /boot            \
         xfs       defaults        0 0
/dev/mapper/rhel_rhel8-swap none                    swap \
```

```
85    defaults         0 0
86  [root@demo devops]#
```

after execution

```
1  $ ssh devops@demo.example.com
2  [devops@demo ~]$ sudo su
3  [root@demo devops]# mount
4  sysfs on /sys type sysfs (rw,nosuid,nodev,noexec,relatime\
5  ,seclabel)
6  proc on /proc type proc (rw,nosuid,nodev,noexec,relatime)
7  devtmpfs on /dev type devtmpfs (rw,nosuid,seclabel,size=3\
8  95492k,nr_inodes=98873,mode=755)
9  securityfs on /sys/kernel/security type securityfs (rw,no\
10 suid,nodev,noexec,relatime)
11 tmpfs on /dev/shm type tmpfs (rw,nosuid,nodev,seclabel)
12 devpts on /dev/pts type devpts (rw,nosuid,noexec,relatime\
13 ,seclabel,gid=5,mode=620,ptmxmode=000)
14 tmpfs on /run type tmpfs (rw,nosuid,nodev,seclabel,mode=7\
15 55)
16 tmpfs on /sys/fs/cgroup type tmpfs (ro,nosuid,nodev,noexe\
17 c,seclabel,mode=755)
18 cgroup on /sys/fs/cgroup/systemd type cgroup (rw,nosuid,n\
19 odev,noexec,relatime,seclabel,xattr,release_agent=/usr/li\
20 b/systemd/systemd-cgroups-agent,name=systemd)
21 pstore on /sys/fs/pstore type pstore (rw,nosuid,nodev,noe\
22 xec,relatime,seclabel)
23 bpf on /sys/fs/bpf type bpf (rw,nosuid,nodev,noexec,relat\
24 ime,mode=700)
25 cgroup on /sys/fs/cgroup/rdma type cgroup (rw,nosuid,node\
26 v,noexec,relatime,seclabel,rdma)
27 cgroup on /sys/fs/cgroup/perf_event type cgroup (rw,nosui\
28 d,nodev,noexec,relatime,seclabel,perf_event)
29 cgroup on /sys/fs/cgroup/net_cls,net_prio type cgroup (rw\
30 ,nosuid,nodev,noexec,relatime,seclabel,net_cls,net_prio)
31 cgroup on /sys/fs/cgroup/freezer type cgroup (rw,nosuid,n\
```

```
32  odev,noexec,relatime,seclabel,freezer)
33  cgroup on /sys/fs/cgroup/cpuset type cgroup (rw,nosuid,no\
34  dev,noexec,relatime,seclabel,cpuset)
35  cgroup on /sys/fs/cgroup/pids type cgroup (rw,nosuid,node\
36  v,noexec,relatime,seclabel,pids)
37  cgroup on /sys/fs/cgroup/hugetlb type cgroup (rw,nosuid,n\
38  odev,noexec,relatime,seclabel,hugetlb)
39  cgroup on /sys/fs/cgroup/blkio type cgroup (rw,nosuid,nod\
40  ev,noexec,relatime,seclabel,blkio)
41  cgroup on /sys/fs/cgroup/memory type cgroup (rw,nosuid,no\
42  dev,noexec,relatime,seclabel,memory)
43  cgroup on /sys/fs/cgroup/devices type cgroup (rw,nosuid,n\
44  odev,noexec,relatime,seclabel,devices)
45  cgroup on /sys/fs/cgroup/cpu,cpuacct type cgroup (rw,nosu\
46  id,nodev,noexec,relatime,seclabel,cpu,cpuacct)
47  none on /sys/kernel/tracing type tracefs (rw,relatime,sec\
48  label)
49  configfs on /sys/kernel/config type configfs (rw,relatime)
50  /dev/mapper/rhel_rhel8-root on / type xfs (rw,relatime,se\
51  clabel,attr2,inode64,logbufs=8,logbsize=32k,noquota)
52  selinuxfs on /sys/fs/selinux type selinuxfs (rw,relatime)
53  systemd-1 on /proc/sys/fs/binfmt_misc type autofs (rw,rel\
54  atime,fd=31,pgrp=1,timeout=0,minproto=5,maxproto=5,direct\
55  ,pipe_ino=18292)
56  debugfs on /sys/kernel/debug type debugfs (rw,relatime,se\
57  clabel)
58  mqueue on /dev/mqueue type mqueue (rw,relatime,seclabel)
59  hugetlbfs on /dev/hugepages type hugetlbfs (rw,relatime,s\
60  eclabel,pagesize=2M)
61  /dev/sda1 on /boot type xfs (rw,relatime,seclabel,attr2,i\
62  node64,logbufs=8,logbsize=32k,noquota)
63  tmpfs on /run/user/1001 type tmpfs (rw,nosuid,nodev,relat\
64  ime,seclabel,size=82872k,mode=700,uid=1001,gid=10)
65  //windows-pc/share on /share type cifs (rw,relatime,vers=\
66  default,cache=strict,username=username,uid=0,noforceuid,g\
```

```
67   id=0,noforcegid,addr=192.168.43.5,file_mode=0755,dir_mode\
68   =0755,soft,nounix,serverino,mapposix,rsize=4194304,wsize=\
69   4194304,bsize=1048576,echo_interval=60,actimeo=1)
70   [root@demo devops]# touch /share/test
71   [root@demo devops]# ls -al /share/test
72   -rwxr-xr-x. 1 root root 0 Nov 11 17:32 /share/test
73   [root@demo devops]# ls -al /share/
74   total 0
75   drwxr-xr-x.  2 root root   0 Nov 11 17:32 .
76   dr-xr-xr-x. 18 root root 237 Nov 11 17:31 ..
77   -rwxr-xr-x.  1 root root   0 Nov 11 17:32 test
78   [root@demo devops]# cat /etc/fstab
79   #
80   # /etc/fstab
81   # Created by anaconda on Wed Sep  1 00:06:23 2021
82   #
83   # Accessible filesystems, by reference, are maintained un\
84   der '/dev/disk/'.
85   # See man pages fstab(5), findfs(8), mount(8) and/or blki\
86   d(8) for more info.
87   #
88   # After editing this file, run 'systemctl daemon-reload' \
89   to update systemd
90   # units generated from this file.
91   #
92   /dev/mapper/rhel_rhel8-root /                       xfs   \
93      defaults        0 0
94   UUID=ae6c1777-c1c9-42a1-8fcf-513077aac39b /boot           \
95           xfs     defaults        0 0
96   /dev/mapper/rhel_rhel8-swap none                   swap \
97      defaults        0 0
98   #VAGRANT-BEGIN
99   # The contents below are automatically generated by Vagra\
100  nt. Do not modify.
101  #VAGRANT-END
```

```
102   //windows-pc/share /share cifs username=username,password\
103   =passowd 0 0
104   [root@demo devops]#
```

Mount an NFS share in Linux - Ansible module mount

How to mount an NFS share in Linux. The Ansible Playbook code is going to check the required packages, create the mount-point, and set up the NFS network shared folder using NFS4 protocol on the Linux target machine. Code for RedHat-like and Debian-like systems.

Ansible mounts an NFS Share in Linux

- ansible.posix.mount
- Control active and configured mount points

Today we're talking about the Ansible module mount.
The full name is `ansible.posix.mount`, which means that is part of the collection of modules "ansible.posix" to interact with POSIX platforms.
The purpose of the module is to control active and configured mount points.
For Windows, use the `community.windows.win_mapped_drive` module instead.

Parameters

- path string - mount point (e.g. /mnt)
- state string - mounted / unmounted / present / absent / remounted

- src string - device or network volume
- fstype string - ext4, xfs, iso9660, nfs, cifs, etc.
- opts string- mount options

This module has many parameters to perform any task.

The only required are "path" and "state".

The parameter "path" specifies the path to the mount point (e.g. /mnt/).

The parameter "state" allows us to verify a specific state of the mount point. The options "mounted", "unmounted" and "remounted" change the device status. The "present" and "absent" options only change the /etc/fstab file.

The src parameter specifies the device or network volume for NFS or SMB/CIFS.

The fstype parameter specifies the filesystem type. For example ext4, XFS, iso9660, NFS, CIFS, etc.

The opts parameter allows us to specify some mount options, that vary for each filesystem type.

demo

Let's jump in a real-life Ansible Playbook to mount an NFS share in Linux RedHat-like and Debian-like.

code

- mount_nfs.yml

```yaml
---
- name: mount module demo
  hosts: all
  become: true
  vars:
    mynfs: "192.168.0.200:/nfs/share"
    mountpoint: "/share"
    permission: '0777'
    myopts: 'rw,sync'
  tasks:
    - name: utility present redhat-like
      ansible.builtin.yum:
        name:
          - nfs-utils
          - nfs4-acl-tools
        state: present
      when: ansible_os_family == 'RedHat'

    - name: utility present debian-like
      ansible.builtin.apt:
        name:
          - nfs-common
          - nfs4-acl-tools
        state: present
      when: ansible_os_family == 'Debian'

    - name: check mountpoint exist
      ansible.builtin.file:
        path: "{{ mountpoint }}"
        state: directory
        mode: "{{ permission }}"
        owner: root
        group: root

    - name: mount network share
```

```
36        ansible.posix.mount:
37          src: "{{ mynfs }}"
38          path: "{{ mountpoint }}"
39          fstype: nfs
40          opts: "{{ myopts }}"
41          state: mounted
```

execution

```
1  $ ansible-playbook -i virtualmachines/demo/inventory moun\
2  t\ drive/nfs.yml
3  PLAY [mount module demo] *******************************\
4  *******************************************
5  TASK [Gathering Facts] ********************************\
6  *******************************************
7  ok: [demo.example.com]
8  TASK [utility present redhat-like] ********************\
9  *******************************************
10 changed: [demo.example.com]
11 TASK [utility present debian-like] ********************\
12 *******************************************
13 skipping: [demo.example.com]
14 TASK [check mountpoint exist] *************************\
15 *******************************************
16 changed: [demo.example.com]
17 TASK [mount network share] ****************************\
18 *******************************************
19 changed: [demo.example.com]
20 PLAY RECAP ********************************************\
21 *******************************************
22 demo.example.com           : ok=4    changed=3    unreach\
23 able=0    failed=0    skipped=1    rescued=0    ignored=0
```

before execution

```
$ ssh devops@demo.example.com
[devops@demo ~]$ sudo su
[root@demo devops]# cat /etc/redhat-release
Red Hat Enterprise Linux release 8.4 (Ootpa)
[root@demo devops]# yum list nfs-utils
Updating Subscription Management repositories.
Last metadata expiration check: 0:28:59 ago on Wed 24 Nov\
 2021 11:17:15 AM UTC.
Available Packages
nfs-utils.x86_64                      1:2.3.3-46.el8           \
                rhel-8-for-x86_64-baseos-rpms
[root@demo devops]# showmount --exports 192.168.0.200
bash: showmount: command not found
[root@demo devops]# ls -al /share
ls: cannot access '/share': No such file or directory
[root@demo devops]# cat /etc/fstab
#
# /etc/fstab
# Created by anaconda on Wed Sep  1 00:06:23 2021
#
# Accessible filesystems, by reference, are maintained un\
der '/dev/disk/'.
# See man pages fstab(5), findfs(8), mount(8) and/or blki\
d(8) for more info.
#
# After editing this file, run 'systemctl daemon-reload' \
to update systemd
# units generated from this file.
#
/dev/mapper/rhel_rhel8-root /                       xfs  \
   defaults        0 0
UUID=ae6c1777-c1c9-42a1-8fcf-513077aac39b /boot           \
          xfs     defaults        0 0
/dev/mapper/rhel_rhel8-swap none                    swap \
   defaults        0 0
```

```
36  [root@demo devops]# mount
37  sysfs on /sys type sysfs (rw,nosuid,nodev,noexec,relatime\
38  ,seclabel)
39  proc on /proc type proc (rw,nosuid,nodev,noexec,relatime)
40  devtmpfs on /dev type devtmpfs (rw,nosuid,seclabel,size=3\
41  95492k,nr_inodes=98873,mode=755)
42  securityfs on /sys/kernel/security type securityfs (rw,no\
43  suid,nodev,noexec,relatime)
44  tmpfs on /dev/shm type tmpfs (rw,nosuid,nodev,seclabel)
45  devpts on /dev/pts type devpts (rw,nosuid,noexec,relatime\
46  ,seclabel,gid=5,mode=620,ptmxmode=000)
47  tmpfs on /run type tmpfs (rw,nosuid,nodev,seclabel,mode=7\
48  55)
49  tmpfs on /sys/fs/cgroup type tmpfs (ro,nosuid,nodev,noexe\
50  c,seclabel,mode=755)
51  cgroup on /sys/fs/cgroup/systemd type cgroup (rw,nosuid,n\
52  odev,noexec,relatime,seclabel,xattr,release_agent=/usr/li\
53  b/systemd/systemd-cgroups-agent,name=systemd)
54  pstore on /sys/fs/pstore type pstore (rw,nosuid,nodev,noe\
55  xec,relatime,seclabel)
56  bpf on /sys/fs/bpf type bpf (rw,nosuid,nodev,noexec,relat\
57  ime,mode=700)
58  cgroup on /sys/fs/cgroup/cpuset type cgroup (rw,nosuid,no\
59  dev,noexec,relatime,seclabel,cpuset)
60  cgroup on /sys/fs/cgroup/rdma type cgroup (rw,nosuid,node\
61  v,noexec,relatime,seclabel,rdma)
62  cgroup on /sys/fs/cgroup/pids type cgroup (rw,nosuid,node\
63  v,noexec,relatime,seclabel,pids)
64  cgroup on /sys/fs/cgroup/hugetlb type cgroup (rw,nosuid,n\
65  odev,noexec,relatime,seclabel,hugetlb)
66  cgroup on /sys/fs/cgroup/cpu,cpuacct type cgroup (rw,nosu\
67  id,nodev,noexec,relatime,seclabel,cpu,cpuacct)
68  cgroup on /sys/fs/cgroup/freezer type cgroup (rw,nosuid,n\
69  odev,noexec,relatime,seclabel,freezer)
70  cgroup on /sys/fs/cgroup/blkio type cgroup (rw,nosuid,nod\
```

```
71   ev,noexec,relatime,seclabel,blkio)
72   cgroup on /sys/fs/cgroup/net_cls,net_prio type cgroup (rw\
73   ,nosuid,nodev,noexec,relatime,seclabel,net_cls,net_prio)
74   cgroup on /sys/fs/cgroup/perf_event type cgroup (rw,nosui\
75   d,nodev,noexec,relatime,seclabel,perf_event)
76   cgroup on /sys/fs/cgroup/memory type cgroup (rw,nosuid,no\
77   dev,noexec,relatime,seclabel,memory)
78   cgroup on /sys/fs/cgroup/devices type cgroup (rw,nosuid,n\
79   odev,noexec,relatime,seclabel,devices)
80   none on /sys/kernel/tracing type tracefs (rw,relatime,sec\
81   label)
82   configfs on /sys/kernel/config type configfs (rw,relatime)
83   /dev/mapper/rhel_rhel8-root on / type xfs (rw,relatime,se\
84   clabel,attr2,inode64,logbufs=8,logbsize=32k,noquota)
85   selinuxfs on /sys/fs/selinux type selinuxfs (rw,relatime)
86   mqueue on /dev/mqueue type mqueue (rw,relatime,seclabel)
87   hugetlbfs on /dev/hugepages type hugetlbfs (rw,relatime,s\
88   eclabel,pagesize=2M)
89   systemd-1 on /proc/sys/fs/binfmt_misc type autofs (rw,rel\
90   atime,fd=38,pgrp=1,timeout=0,minproto=5,maxproto=5,direct\
91   ,pipe_ino=18508)
92   debugfs on /sys/kernel/debug type debugfs (rw,relatime,se\
93   clabel)
94   /dev/sda1 on /boot type xfs (rw,relatime,seclabel,attr2,i\
95   node64,logbufs=8,logbsize=32k,noquota)
96   sunrpc on /var/lib/nfs/rpc_pipefs type rpc_pipefs (rw,rel\
97   atime)
98   tmpfs on /run/user/1001 type tmpfs (rw,nosuid,nodev,relat\
99   ime,seclabel,size=82872k,mode=700,uid=1001,gid=10)
100  [root@demo devops]#
```

after execution

```
 1  $ ssh devops@demo.example.com
 2  [devops@demo ~]$ sudo su
 3  [root@demo devops]# yum list nfs-utils
 4  Updating Subscription Management repositories.
 5  Last metadata expiration check: 0:31:28 ago on Wed 24 Nov\
 6   2021 11:17:15 AM UTC.
 7  Installed Packages
 8  nfs-utils.x86_64                    1:2.3.3-46.el8          \
 9              @rhel-8-for-x86_64-baseos-rpms
10  [root@demo devops]# showmount --exports 192.168.0.200
11  Export list for 192.168.0.200:
12  /nfs/share 192.168.0.200/24
13  [root@demo devops]# cat /etc/fstab
14  #
15  # /etc/fstab
16  # Created by anaconda on Wed Sep  1 00:06:23 2021
17  #
18  # Accessible filesystems, by reference, are maintained un\
19  der '/dev/disk/'.
20  # See man pages fstab(5), findfs(8), mount(8) and/or blki\
21  d(8) for more info.
22  #
23  # After editing this file, run 'systemctl daemon-reload' \
24  to update systemd
25  # units generated from this file.
26  #
27  /dev/mapper/rhel_rhel8-root /                       xfs  \
28     defaults         0 0
29  UUID=ae6c1777-c1c9-42a1-8fcf-513077aac39b /boot          \
30          xfs      defaults         0 0
31  /dev/mapper/rhel_rhel8-swap none                   swap \
32     defaults         0 0
33  192.168.0.200:/nfs/share /share nfs rw,sync 0 0
34  [root@demo devops]# mount
35  sysfs on /sys type sysfs (rw,nosuid,nodev,noexec,relatime\
```

```
36  ,seclabel)
37  proc on /proc type proc (rw,nosuid,nodev,noexec,relatime)
38  devtmpfs on /dev type devtmpfs (rw,nosuid,seclabel,size=3\
39  95492k,nr_inodes=98873,mode=755)
40  securityfs on /sys/kernel/security type securityfs (rw,no\
41  suid,nodev,noexec,relatime)
42  tmpfs on /dev/shm type tmpfs (rw,nosuid,nodev,seclabel)
43  devpts on /dev/pts type devpts (rw,nosuid,noexec,relatime\
44  ,seclabel,gid=5,mode=620,ptmxmode=000)
45  tmpfs on /run type tmpfs (rw,nosuid,nodev,seclabel,mode=7\
46  55)
47  tmpfs on /sys/fs/cgroup type tmpfs (ro,nosuid,nodev,noexe\
48  c,seclabel,mode=755)
49  cgroup on /sys/fs/cgroup/systemd type cgroup (rw,nosuid,n\
50  odev,noexec,relatime,seclabel,xattr,release_agent=/usr/li\
51  b/systemd/systemd-cgroups-agent,name=systemd)
52  pstore on /sys/fs/pstore type pstore (rw,nosuid,nodev,noe\
53  xec,relatime,seclabel)
54  bpf on /sys/fs/bpf type bpf (rw,nosuid,nodev,noexec,relat\
55  ime,mode=700)
56  cgroup on /sys/fs/cgroup/cpuset type cgroup (rw,nosuid,no\
57  dev,noexec,relatime,seclabel,cpuset)
58  cgroup on /sys/fs/cgroup/rdma type cgroup (rw,nosuid,node\
59  v,noexec,relatime,seclabel,rdma)
60  cgroup on /sys/fs/cgroup/pids type cgroup (rw,nosuid,node\
61  v,noexec,relatime,seclabel,pids)
62  cgroup on /sys/fs/cgroup/hugetlb type cgroup (rw,nosuid,n\
63  odev,noexec,relatime,seclabel,hugetlb)
64  cgroup on /sys/fs/cgroup/cpu,cpuacct type cgroup (rw,nosu\
65  id,nodev,noexec,relatime,seclabel,cpu,cpuacct)
66  cgroup on /sys/fs/cgroup/freezer type cgroup (rw,nosuid,n\
67  odev,noexec,relatime,seclabel,freezer)
68  cgroup on /sys/fs/cgroup/blkio type cgroup (rw,nosuid,nod\
69  ev,noexec,relatime,seclabel,blkio)
70  cgroup on /sys/fs/cgroup/net_cls,net_prio type cgroup (rw\
```

```
71  ,nosuid,nodev,noexec,relatime,seclabel,net_cls,net_prio)
72  cgroup on /sys/fs/cgroup/perf_event type cgroup (rw,nosui\
73  d,nodev,noexec,relatime,seclabel,perf_event)
74  cgroup on /sys/fs/cgroup/memory type cgroup (rw,nosuid,no\
75  dev,noexec,relatime,seclabel,memory)
76  cgroup on /sys/fs/cgroup/devices type cgroup (rw,nosuid,n\
77  odev,noexec,relatime,seclabel,devices)
78  none on /sys/kernel/tracing type tracefs (rw,relatime,sec\
79  label)
80  configfs on /sys/kernel/config type configfs (rw,relatime)
81  /dev/mapper/rhel_rhel8-root on / type xfs (rw,relatime,se\
82  clabel,attr2,inode64,logbufs=8,logbsize=32k,noquota)
83  selinuxfs on /sys/fs/selinux type selinuxfs (rw,relatime)
84  mqueue on /dev/mqueue type mqueue (rw,relatime,seclabel)
85  hugetlbfs on /dev/hugepages type hugetlbfs (rw,relatime,s\
86  eclabel,pagesize=2M)
87  systemd-1 on /proc/sys/fs/binfmt_misc type autofs (rw,rel\
88  atime,fd=38,pgrp=1,timeout=0,minproto=5,maxproto=5,direct\
89  ,pipe_ino=18508)
90  debugfs on /sys/kernel/debug type debugfs (rw,relatime,se\
91  clabel)
92  /dev/sda1 on /boot type xfs (rw,relatime,seclabel,attr2,i\
93  node64,logbufs=8,logbsize=32k,noquota)
94  sunrpc on /var/lib/nfs/rpc_pipefs type rpc_pipefs (rw,rel\
95  atime)
96  tmpfs on /run/user/1001 type tmpfs (rw,nosuid,nodev,relat\
97  ime,seclabel,size=82872k,mode=700,uid=1001,gid=10)
98  192.168.0.200:/nfs/share on /share type nfs4 (rw,relatime\
99  ,sync,vers=4.2,rsize=131072,wsize=131072,namlen=255,hard,\
100 proto=tcp,timeo=600,retrans=2,sec=sys,clientaddr=192.168.\
101 0.190,local_lock=none,addr=192.168.0.200)
102 [root@demo devops]# ls -al /share
103 total 0
104 drwxrwxrwx.  2 root    root      22 Nov 24 11:34 .
105 dr-xr-xr-x. 18 root    root     237 Nov 24 11:47 ..
```

```
106   -rw-r--r--.  1 nobody nobody    0 Nov 24 11:34 test.txt
107   [root@demo devops]# echo "test" > /share/test2.txt
108   [root@demo devops]# ls -al /share
109   total 4
110   drwxrwxrwx.  2 root   root    39 Nov 24 11:50 .
111   dr-xr-xr-x. 18 root   root   237 Nov 24 11:47 ..
112   -rw-r--r--.  1 nobody nobody    0 Nov 24 11:34 test.txt
113   -rw-r--r--.  1 nobody nobody    5 Nov 24 11:50 test2.txt
114   [root@demo devops]# cat /share/test2.txt
115   test
116   [root@demo devops]# df -h
117   Filesystem                  Size  Used Avail Use% Mounte\
118   d on
119   devtmpfs                    387M     0  387M   0% /dev
120   tmpfs                       405M     0  405M   0% /dev/s\
121   hm
122   tmpfs                       405M   11M  395M   3% /run
123   tmpfs                       405M     0  405M   0% /sys/f\
124   s/cgroup
125   /dev/mapper/rhel_rhel8-root  70G  3.2G   67G   5% /
126   /dev/sda1                   1014M  191M  824M  19% /boot
127   tmpfs                        81M     0   81M   0% /run/u\
128   ser/1001
129   192.168.0.200:/nfs/share     70G  2.5G   68G   4% /share
130   [root@demo devops]#
```

Concatenate multiple files in a specific order - Ansible module template and YAML

How to automate the concatenation of multiple files and format using a list in the YAML and Ansible module template with Jinja2 language. Included example with "a.txt", "b.txt" and "includes.yaml" files for Pandoc.

Ansible Concatenate multiple files in a specific order

- ansible.builtin.template
- Template a file out to a target host
- ansible_managed, template_host, template_uid, template_path, template_fullpath, template_destpath, and template_run_date

Let's talk about the Ansible module `template`.

The full name is `ansible.builtin.template`, it's part of `ansible-core` and is included in all Ansible installations.

It templates a file out to a target host. Templates are processed by the Jinja2 templating language.

Also you could use also some special variables in your templates: `ansible_managed`, `template_host`, `template_uid`, `template_path`, `template_fullpath`, `template_destpath`, and `template_run_date`.

It supports a large variety of Operating Systems.

For basic text formatting, use the Ansible `ansible.builtin.copy` module or for empty file Ansible `ansible.builtin.file` module.

For Windows, use the `ansible.windows.win_template` module instead.

Parameters

- src path - template ("templates/" dir)
- dest path - target location
- validate string - validation command before ("%s")
- backup boolean - no/yes
- mode/owner/group - permission
- setype/seuser/selevel - SELinux

Let me highlight the most useful parameters for the `template` module.

The only required parameters are "src" and "dest".

The "src" parameter specifies the template file name. Templates usually are stored under "templates" directories with the ".j2" file extension.

The "dest" parameter specifies the path where to render the template on the remote machine.

The "validate" parameters allow you to specify the validation command to run before copying it into place. It's very useful with configuration files for services.

Please note that the special escape sequence "%s" is going to be expanded by Ansible with the destination path.

If the "backup" parameter is enabled Ansible creates a backup file including the timestamp information before copying it to the destination.

Let me also highlight that we could also specify the permissions and SELinux properties.

demo

How to concatenate multiple files in a specific order with the Ansible module template and YAML.

code

- a.txt

```
1   A content
```

- b.txt

1   B content

- includes.yaml

```
1   input-files:
2     - concatenate/b.txt
3     - concatenate/a.txt
```

- concatenate.yml

```
1   ---
2   - name: concatenate demo
3     hosts: "{{ HOSTS }}"
4     become: false
5     gather_facts: true
6     vars:
7       myinput: "concatenate/includes.yaml"
8       myoutput: "concatenate/output.txt"
9     tasks:
10      - name: include file list
11        include_vars:
12          file: "{{ myinput }}"
13          name: files
14
15      - name: concatenate
16        ansible.builtin.template:
17          src: templates/concatenate.j2
18          dest: "{{ myoutput }}"
```

- concatenate.j2

```
{% for i in files["input-files"] %}
{{ lookup('file', i) }}
{% endfor %}
```

execution

```
ansible-pilot $ ansible-playbook -e "HOSTS=localhost" con\
catenate.yml
[WARNING]: No inventory was parsed, only implicit localho\
st is available
[WARNING]: provided hosts list is empty, only localhost i\
s available. Note that the implicit
localhost does not match 'all'
PLAY [concatenate demo] **********************************\
*******************************************
TASK [Gathering Facts] **********************************\
*******************************************
ok: [localhost]
TASK [include file list] *********************************\
******************************************
ok: [localhost]
TASK [concatenate] ***************************************\
******************************************
changed: [localhost]
PLAY RECAP **********************************************\
*******************************************
localhost                  : ok=3    changed=1    unreach\
able=0    failed=0    skipped=0    rescued=0    ignored=0
ansible-pilot $
```

idempotency

```
ansible-pilot $ ansible-playbook -e "HOSTS=localhost" con\
catenate.yml
[WARNING]: No inventory was parsed, only implicit localho\
st is available
[WARNING]: provided hosts list is empty, only localhost i\
s available. Note that the implicit
localhost does not match 'all'
PLAY [concatenate demo] ********************************\
*******************************************
TASK [Gathering Facts] *********************************\
*******************************************
ok: [localhost]
TASK [include file list] *******************************\
*******************************************
ok: [localhost]
TASK [concatenate] *************************************\
*******************************************
ok: [localhost]
PLAY RECAP *********************************************\
*******************************************
localhost                  : ok=3    changed=0    unreach\
able=0    failed=0    skipped=0    rescued=0    ignored=0
ansible-pilot $
```

before execution

```
1   ansible-pilot $ ls -al concatenate
2   total 24
3   drwxr-xr-x  5 lberton  staff  160 Feb  1 15:40 .
4   drwxr-xr-x  9 lberton  staff  288 Feb  1 15:08 ..
5   -rw-r--r--  1 lberton  staff    9 Feb  1 15:18 a.txt
6   -rw-r--r--  1 lberton  staff    9 Feb  1 15:18 b.txt
7   -rw-r--r--  1 lberton  staff   56 Feb  1 15:48 includes.y\
8   aml
9   ansible-pilot $ cat concatenate/a.txt
10  A content%
11  ansible-pilot $ cat concatenate/b.txt
12  B content%
13  ansible-pilot $ cat concatenate/includes.yaml
14  input-files:
15    - concatenate/b.txt
16    - concatenate/a.txt
17  ansible-pilot $
```

after execution

```
1   ansible-pilot $ ls -al concatenate
2   total 32
3   drwxr-xr-x  6 lberton  staff  192 Feb  1 15:50 .
4   drwxr-xr-x  9 lberton  staff  288 Feb  1 15:08 ..
5   -rw-r--r--  1 lberton  staff    9 Feb  1 15:18 a.txt
6   -rw-r--r--  1 lberton  staff    9 Feb  1 15:18 b.txt
7   -rw-r--r--  1 lberton  staff   56 Feb  1 15:48 includes.y\
8   aml
9   -rw-r--r--  1 lberton  staff   20 Feb  1 15:49 output.txt
10  ansible-pilot $ cat concatenate/output.txt
11  B content
12  A content
13  ansible-pilot $
```

Backup With Rsync - Local to Remote - Ansible module synchronize

How to automate the backup of an "examples" directory minimizing network usage on Linux using Ansible module synchronize and rsync utility.

Ansible backup with rsync

- `ansible.posix.synchronize`
- `synchronize` is a wrapper around rsync to make common tasks in your playbooks quick and easy.

Let's talk about the Ansible module `synchronize`.
The full name is `ansible.posix.synchronize`, which means that is part of the collection targeting POSIX platforms.
A wrapper around `rsync` to make common tasks in your playbooks quick and easy.
rsync is a utility for efficiently transferring and synchronizing files between a computer and a storage drive and across networked computers by comparing the modification times and sizes of files.
rsync must be installed on both the local and remote host.
Currently, there are only a few connection types that support synchronize (ssh, paramiko, local, and docker) because a sync strategy has been determined for those connection types.

Main Parameters

- src <u>string</u> - source path - absolute or relative
- dest <u>string</u> - destination path - absolute or relative
- archive <u>boolean</u> - mirrors the Rsync archive flag, enables recursive, links, perms, times, owner, group flags, and -D

- rsync_opts <u>string</u> - no/yes

The parameter list is pretty wide but these are the most important options of `synchronize` module.

The only mandatory parameters are "src" and "dest" parameters.

The "src" parameter is mandatory and specifies the path on the source host that will be synchronized to the destination. The path can be absolute or relative.

Same story for the `dest` parameter that specifies the path on the destination host that will be synchronized from the source.

Paths could be Local or Remote according to your needs.

The most useful parameter is "archive", which mirrors the Rsync archive flag, enables recursive, links, perms, times, owner, group flags, and -D. It's enabled by default so in the majority of use-cases you don't need to specify anything else. Please refer to the manual to enable/disable some specific settings.

It's possible to specify more Rsync parameters via the "rsync_opts" parameter.

Links

- rsync[45]
- ansible.posix.synchronize[46]

demo

How to backup with rsync with Ansible Playbook.

I'm going to show you how to replicate some directory tree in a Linux machine using the rsync utility via syncronize module.

code

---

[45]https://en.wikipedia.org/wiki/Rsync

[46]https://docs.ansible.com/ansible/latest/collections/ansible/posix/synchronize_module
html

```yaml
1  ---
2  - name: synchronize module demo
3    hosts: all
4    become: false
5    vars:
6      source: '~/prj/github/ansible-pilot/copy\ files\ to\ \
7  remote\ hosts/examples'
8      destination: 'example-backup'
9    tasks:
10     - name: rsync installed
11       ansible.builtin.package:
12         name: rsync
13         state: present
14       become: true
15 - name: data synchronization
16       ansible.posix.synchronize:
17         src: '{{ source }}'
18         dest: '{{ destination }}'
```

execution

```
1  ansible-pilot $ ansible-playbook -i virtualmachines/demo/\
2  inventory copy\ files\ to\ remote\ hosts/rsync.yml
3  PLAY [synchronize module demo] **************************\
4  *******************************************
5  TASK [Gathering Facts] *********************************\
6  *******************************************
7  ok: [demo.example.com]
8  TASK [rsync installed] *********************************\
9  *******************************************
10 ok: [demo.example.com]
11 TASK [data synchronization] ***************************\
12 *******************************************
13 changed: [demo.example.com]
14 PLAY RECAP ********************************************\
15 *******************************************
```

```
16   demo.example.com              : ok=3      changed=1     unreach\
17   able=0     failed=0     skipped=0     rescued=0     ignored=0
18   ansible-pilot $
19   idempotency
20   ansible-pilot $ ansible-playbook -i virtualmachines/demo/\
21   inventory copy\ files\ to\ remote\ hosts/rsync.yml
22   PLAY [synchronize module demo] *************************\
23   *******************************************
24   TASK [Gathering Facts] ********************************\
25   *******************************************
26   ok: [demo.example.com]
27   TASK [rsync installed] ********************************\
28   *******************************************
29   ok: [demo.example.com]
30   TASK [data synchronization] ***************************\
31   *******************************************
32   ok: [demo.example.com]
33   PLAY RECAP ********************************************\
34   *******************************************
35   demo.example.com              : ok=3      changed=0     unreach\
36   able=0     failed=0     skipped=0     rescued=0     ignored=0
37   ansible-pilot $
```

before execution

```
1    ansible-pilot $ ls -al copy\ files\ to\ remote\ hosts/exa\
2    mples
3    total 16
4    drwxr-xr-x  4 lberton  staff  128 Jan 17 11:54 .
5    drwxr-xr-x  9 lberton  staff  288 Mar 28 14:13 ..
6    -rw-r--r--  1 lberton  staff   16 Sep  4  2021 report.txt
7    -rw-r--r--  1 lberton  staff   16 Jan 17 11:52 report2.txt
8    ansible-pilot $ cat copy\ files\ to\ remote\ hosts/exampl\
9    es/report.txt
10   test report.txt
11   ansible-pilot $ cat copy\ files\ to\ remote\ hosts/exampl\
```

```
12   es/report2.txt
13   test report.txt
14   ansible-pilot $ ssh devops@demo.example.com
15   Last login: Mon Mar 28 12:22:14 2022 from 192.168.0.59
16   [devops@demo ~]$ ls -al
17   total 20
18   drwx------. 4 devops wheel   127 Mar 28 12:22 .
19   drwxr-xr-x. 4 root   root     35 Mar 24 17:44 ..
20   drwx------. 3 devops wheel    17 Mar 24 17:44 .ansible
21   -rw-------. 1 devops wheel   178 Mar 28 12:21 .bash_history
22   -rw-r--r--. 1 devops wheel    18 Jul 26  2021 .bash_logout
23   -rw-r--r--. 1 devops wheel   141 Jul 26  2021 .bash_profile
24   -rw-r--r--. 1 devops wheel   376 Jul 26  2021 .bashrc
25   drwx------. 2 devops wheel    29 Mar 24 17:44 .ssh
26   -rw-------. 1 devops wheel  1756 Mar 28 10:38 .viminfo
27   [devops@demo ~]$ rpm -qa | grep rsync
28   rsync-3.1.3-12.el8.x86_64
29   [devops@demo ~]$
```

after execution

```
1    ansible-pilot $ ssh devops@demo.example.com
2    Last login: Mon Mar 28 12:24:57 2022 from 192.168.0.59
3    [devops@demo ~]$ ls -al
4    total 20
5    drwx------. 5 devops wheel   149 Mar 28 12:24 .
6    drwxr-xr-x. 4 root   root     35 Mar 24 17:44 ..
7    drwx------. 3 devops wheel    17 Mar 24 17:44 .ansible
8    -rw-------. 1 devops wheel   211 Mar 28 12:24 .bash_history
9    -rw-r--r--. 1 devops wheel    18 Jul 26  2021 .bash_logout
10   -rw-r--r--. 1 devops wheel   141 Jul 26  2021 .bash_profile
11   -rw-r--r--. 1 devops wheel   376 Jul 26  2021 .bashrc
12   drwx------. 2 devops wheel    29 Mar 24 17:44 .ssh
13   -rw-------. 1 devops wheel  1756 Mar 28 10:38 .viminfo
14   drwxr-xr-x. 3 devops wheel    22 Mar 28 12:24 example-back\
15   up
```

```
16    [devops@demo ~]$ tree example-backup/
17    example-backup/
18    `-- examples
19        |-- report2.txt
20        `-- report.txt
21    1 directory, 2 files
22    [devops@demo ~]$ cat example-backup/examples/report.txt
23    test report.txt
24    [devops@demo ~]$ cat example-backup/examples/report2.txt
25    test report.txt
26    [devops@demo ~]$ ls -al example-backup/examples/
27    total 8
28    drwxr-xr-x. 2 devops wheel 43 Jan 17 10:54 .
29    drwxr-xr-x. 3 devops wheel 22 Mar 28 12:24 ..
30    -rw-r--r--. 1 devops wheel 16 Sep  4  2021 report.txt
31    -rw-r--r--. 1 devops wheel 16 Jan 17 10:52 report2.txt
32    [devops@demo ~]$
```

changes in the source directory

```
1    ansible-pilot $ touch copy\ files\ to\ remote\ hosts/exam\
2    ples/report3.txt
3    ansible-pilot $ ansible-playbook -i virtualmachines/demo/\
4    inventory copy\ files\ to\ remote\ hosts/rsync.yml
5    PLAY [synchronize module demo] ***************************\
6    *****************************************
7    TASK [Gathering Facts] **********************************\
8    *****************************************
9    ok: [demo.example.com]
10   TASK [rsync installed] **********************************\
11   *****************************************
12   ok: [demo.example.com]
13   TASK [data synchronization] *****************************\
14   *****************************************
15   changed: [demo.example.com]
16   PLAY RECAP **********************************************\
```

```
17   *******************************************
18   demo.example.com               : ok=3      changed=1      unreach\
19   able=0      failed=0      skipped=0      rescued=0      ignored=0
20   ansible-pilot $ ssh devops@demo.example.com                      \
21
22   Last login: Mon Mar 28 18:44:10 2022 from 192.168.0.59
23   [devops@demo ~]$ ls -al example-backup/
24   total 0
25   drwxr-xr-x. 3 devops wheel  22 Mar 28 12:24 .
26   drwx------. 5 devops wheel 149 Mar 28 12:24 ..
27   drwxr-xr-x. 2 devops wheel  62 Mar 28 12:44 examples
28   [devops@demo ~]$ ls -al example-backup/examples/
29   total 8
30   drwxr-xr-x. 2 devops wheel 62 Mar 28 12:44 .
31   drwxr-xr-x. 3 devops wheel 22 Mar 28 12:24 ..
32   -rw-r--r--. 1 devops wheel 16 Sep  4  2021 report.txt
33   -rw-r--r--. 1 devops wheel 16 Jan 17 10:52 report2.txt
34   -rw-r--r--. 1 devops wheel  0 Mar 28 18:44 report3.txt
35   [devops@demo ~]$
```

Ansible For Linux User Management

I'm going to show you how to Perform User Management Under Linux System: User Creation, Deletion, Change Attributes, Disable And Enable.

Ansible create a user account

How to create a user account with Ansible module `user`.
The full name is `ansible.builtin.user`, which means that is part of the collection of modules "builtin" with ansible and shipped with it.
It's a module pretty stable and out for years.
It manages user accounts.
It supports a huge variety of Linux distributions, SunOS and macOS, and FreeBSD.
This module uses Linux distributions `useradd` tool to create, on FreeBSD, this module uses `pw useradd`, On macOS, this module uses `dscl create`.
For Windows, use the `ansible.windows.win_user` module instead.

Parameters

- name <u>string</u> - username
- state <u>string</u> - present/absent
- password <u>string</u> – `{{ 'password' | password_hash('sha512', 'salt') }}`

- uid string comment string shell string expires string password_expire_min string password_expire_max string
- group/groups string - primary/membership group(s)
- create_home boolean - yes/no
- generate_ssh_key string ssh_key_bits string ssh_key_file string ssh_key_type string ssh_key_passphrase string

This module has some parameters to perform some tasks.

The only required is "name", which is the username.

The "state" parameter allows us to create or delete a user, in our use case the default it's already set to "present" to create a user. "password" is very often used in conjunction with the password_hash filter to generate a password. Please note that you could specify the encryption algorithm as well as the salt to make your password more robust.

We could specify all the usual Unix properties such as like uid, comment, shell, expires, password_expire_min, password_expire_max. Other important parameters are "group" and "groups". The first (without the "s" ending) indicate the primary group of the user, the second (with the "s" ending) set the other group members. So be very careful with the "s" ending, it could end up in a very different setup.

Usually, we would like to create a user home directory so the "create_home" parameter defaults to yes, but we could override if we don't need a home directory.

Let me also highlight that we could also generate an SSH key with a lot of options. The fingerprint and the public key are available in the long list of returned values.

code

How to create a user in Linux using an Ansible Playbook.

- user.yml

```yaml
1    ---
2    - name: user module demo
3      hosts: all
4      become: true
5      tasks:
6        - name: user example present
7          ansible.builtin.user:
8            name: example
9            password: "{{ 'password' | password_hash('sha512'\
10   , 'mysecretsalt') }}"
11           groups:
12             - wheel
13             - adm
14           state: "present"
15           shell: "/bin/bash"
16           system: false
17           create_home: true
18           home: "/home/example"
19           comment: "Ansible example"
20           generate_ssh_key: true
```

Ansible remove user account

Today we're talking about the Ansible module user.

The full name is ansible.builtin.user, which means that is part of the collection of modules "builtin" with ansible and shipped with it.

It's a module pretty stable and out for years, it manages user accounts.

It supports a huge variety of Linux distributions, SunOS and macOS, and FreeBSD.

This module uses Linux distributions userdel to delete, on FreeBSD, this module uses pw userdel, on macOS, this module uses dscl.

For Windows, use the ansible.windows.win_user module instead.

Parameters

- **name** <u>string</u> - username
- state <u>string</u> - present/absent
- remove <u>boolean</u> - **no**/yes

The only required is "name", which is the username. "state" allows us to create or delete a user, in the use case we need to specify "absent" to delete a user.

If we would like to try to remove the directories associated with the user, we need to set the parameter "remove".

The behavior is the same as `userdel --remove`.

Files in the user's home directory will be removed along with the home directory itself and the user's mail spool.

Files in other parts of the file system will have to be searched for and deleted manually.

code

Let's jump into a real-life Ansible Playbook to delete a user.

- <u>delete_user.yml</u>

```
1   ---
2   - name: user module demo
3     hosts: all
4     become: true
5     tasks:
6       - name: user example not present
7         ansible.builtin.user:
8           name: example
9           state: "absent"
10          remove: true
```

Ansible change user password

Today we're talking about the Ansible module user.
The full name is ansible.builtin.user, which means that is part of the collection of modules "builtin" with Ansible and shipped with it.
It's a module pretty stable and out for years, it manages user accounts.
It supports a huge variety of Linux distributions, SunOS and macOS, and FreeBSD.
For Windows, use the `ansible.windows.win_user` module instead.

Parameters

- name <u>string</u> - username
- state <u>string</u> - present/absent
- password <u>string</u> - Linux encrypted, macOS cleartext

The only required is `name`, which is the username.
In the parameter `state` we need to specify `present` options, obviously, we can't change a password of a non-existent account.
The most important parameter is `password` which allows you to specify the new password.
For macOS target, the password is in cleartext.
For the Linux target, the `password` must be encrypted before. We could use the `password_hash` filter to generate a password. Please note that you could specify the encryption algorithm as well as the salt to make your password more robust.

demo

How to change a user account password in Linux with Ansible.

code

- change_password.yml

```
1   ---
2   - name: user module demo
3     hosts: all
4     become: true
5     vars:
6       myuser: "example"
7       mypassword: "password"
8     tasks:
9       - name: change password
10        ansible.builtin.user:
11          name: "{{ myuser }}"
12          state: present
13          password: "{{ mypassword | password_hash('sha512'\
14  ) }}"
```

execution

```
1   $ ansible-playbook -i demo/inventory change\ user\ passwo\
2   rd/user.yaml
3   PLAY [user module demo] *********************************\
4   *******************************************
5   TASK [Gathering Facts] *********************************\
6   *******************************************
7   ok: [demo.example.com]
8   TASK [change password] *********************************\
9   *******************************************
10  changed: [demo.example.com]
11  PLAY RECAP *********************************************\
12  *******************************************
13  demo.example.com             : ok=2     changed=1     unreach\
14  able=0     failed=0     skipped=0     rescued=0     ignored=0
```

verification

```
1   $ sshpass -p 'password' example@demo.example.com
```

Please note: the `sshpass` must be installed on the system.

Ansible disable user account

How to disable a user account with Ansible using the Ansible module `user`.

Parameters

- name string - username
- state string - present/absent
- password_lock boolean - no/yes
- shell string - "/sbin/nologin"

The only required is "name", which is the username.

The parameter "state" allows us to create or delete a user.

The "password_lock" parameter specifies to lock the user password. This parameter uses the `passwd` tool on Linux systems to disables a password by changing it to a value that matches no possible encrypted value (it adds a '!' at the beginning of the password).

This parameter does not disable the user, only locks the password. This parameter does not always mean the user cannot log in using other methods.

The "shell" parameter specifies the user shell. A very special is the `nologin`. When a user with that shell logs in, they'll get a polite message saying 'This account is currently not available.' This message can be customized with the file /etc/nologin.txt.

demo

Let's jump into a real-life Ansible Playbook to disable a user.

code

- user_disable.yml

```
1   ---
2   - name: user module demo
3     hosts: all
4     become: true
5     vars:
6       myuser: "example"
7     tasks:
8       - name: disable user
9         ansible.builtin.user:
10          name: "{{ myuser }}"
11          state: present
12          password_lock: true
13          shell: "/sbin/nologin"
```

execution

```
1   $ ansible-playbook -i demo/inventory disable\ user\ accou\
2   nt/user.yml
3
4   PLAY [user module demo] ********************************\
5   *****************************************
6
7   TASK [Gathering Facts] ********************************\
8   *****************************************
9   ok: [demo.example.com]
10
11  TASK [disable user] ***********************************\
```

```
12   *******************************************
13   changed: [demo.example.com]
14
15   PLAY RECAP ***********************************************\
16   *******************************************
17   demo.example.com            : ok=2     changed=1     unreach\
18   able=0     failed=0     skipped=0     rescued=0     ignored=0
```

verification

```
1   $ ssh devops@demo.example.com
2   $ sudo su -
3   [root@demo ~]# getent passwd
4   example:x:1002:1002::/home/example:/sbin/nologin
5   [root@demo ~]# passwd -S example
6   example LK 2021-09-30 0 99999 7 -1 (Password locked.)
7   [root@demo ~]# grep example /etc/shadow
8   example:!!:18900:0:99999:7:::
```

Ansible enable user account

How to Enable a user account with Ansible using the Ansible module user.

See also Ansible troubleshooting - passwordless account.

Parameters

- name string - username
- state string - present/absent
- password_lock boolean - no/yes
- shell string - "/bin/bash"

The only required is "name", which is the username.

The parameter "state" allows us to create or delete a user.

The "password_lock" parameter specifies to unlock the user password if locked.

This parameter uses the `passwd` tool to change a password by changing it to a value that matches no possible encrypted value (it adds a '!' at the beginning of the password). To enable our user obviously we need to disable this parameter.

The "shell" parameter specifies the user shell. Two very special are the `nologin` and `false` shell. Apply the value of "/bin/bash" is going to restore user access.

demo

How to enable a user without password lock and with the appropriate shell in Linux with Ansible.

code

- user_enable.yml

```yaml
1   ---
2   - name: user module demo
3     hosts: all
4     become: true
5     vars:
6       myuser: "example"
7     tasks:
8       - name: enable user
9         ansible.builtin.user:
10          name: "{{ myuser }}"
11          state: present
12          password_lock: false
13          shell: "/bin/bash"
```

output

```
1  $ ansible-playbook -i demo/inventory enable\ user\ accoun\
2  t/user.yml
3  PLAY [user module demo] ********************************\
4  *********************************************
5  TASK [Gathering Facts] *********************************\
6  *********************************************
7  ok: [demo.example.com]
8  TASK [enable user] ************************************\
9  *********************************************
10 changed: [demo.example.com]
11 PLAY RECAP *******************************************\
12 *********************************************
13 demo.example.com          : ok=2    changed=1    unreach\
14 able=0    failed=0    skipped=0    rescued=0    ignored=0
```

verification

```
1  # getent passwd | grep example
2  example:x:1002:1002:Ansible example:/home/example:/bin/ba\
3  sh
4  # passwd -S example
5  example PS 2021-10-04 0 99999 7 -1 (Password set, SHA512 \
6  crypt.)
7  # grep example /etc/shadow
8  example:$6$mysecretsalt$MIJffjeQyfrKKrGkprGrDL/g2mCJa53ko\
9  LmYQuuLmY9y37pDvGKPXU1Ov3RbMi.tpQ9cWvxAzUVtBLe7KrZoU.:189\
10 04:0:99999:7:::
```

Ansible user password expiration

How to set user password expiration time on Linux with Ansible using the Ansible module user.

 See also Ansible troubleshooting - user module password_expiry_min bug and workaround.

Linux password aging policy

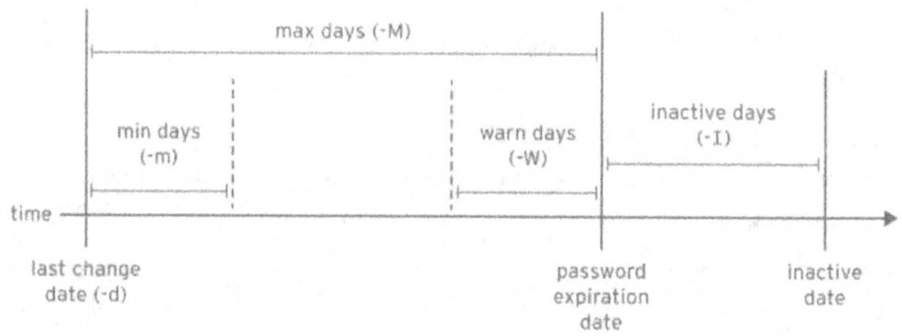

Linux password aging policy

This schema represents the Linux password aging policy.

Let me highlight that the Ansible native module user is able to set only the min days -m and max days -M parameter.

Max days set password policy for requesting password should be renewed, for example in every 90 days.

Min days set the minimum days should be waiting for changing the password again, for example after 7 days from the last change. To disable password aging specify the value of 99999.

For the other parameters, you need to rely on the chage command-line utility or via the Ansible shell module.

Parameters

- name string - username
- password_expire_min integer - Linux min days validity (-m)
- password_expire_max integer - Linux max days validity (-M)

This module has many parameters to perform any task.

The only required is "name", which is the username.

In the `password_expire_min` parameter you specify the value of the min days validity.

In the `password_expire_max` parameter you specify the value of the max days' validity.

Please note that these parameters are **Linux only**.

demo

Set user password expiration time with Ansible Playbook.

code

- user_password_expiration.yml

```
1   ---
2   - name: user module demo
3     hosts: all
4     become: true
5     vars:
6       myuser: "example"
7     tasks:
8       - name: password expiration
9         ansible.builtin.user:
10          name: "{{ myuser }}"
11          password_expire_min: 7
12          password_expire_max: 90
```

execution

```
1   $ ansible-playbook -i demo/inventory user\ expiration/use\
2   r.yml
3
4   PLAY [user module demo] ********************************\
5   ***************************************************
6
7   TASK [Gathering Facts] *********************************\
8   ***************************************************
9   ok: [demo.example.com]
10
11  TASK [password expiration] *****************************\
12  ***************************************************
13  changed: [demo.example.com]
14
15  PLAY RECAP ********************************************\
16  ***************************************************
17  demo.example.com               : ok=2    changed=1    unreach\
18  able=0    failed=0    skipped=0    rescued=0    ignored=0
```

before execution

```
1   $ ssh devops@demo.example.com
2   Last login: Mon Nov  8 17:07:10 2021 from 192.168.43.5
3   [devops@demo ~]$ sudo su
4   [root@demo devops]# chage --help
5   Usage: chage [options] LOGIN
6
7   Options:
8   -d, --lastday LAST_DAY        set date of last password c\
9   hange to LAST_DAY
10  -E, --expiredate EXPIRE_DATE  set account expiration date\
11   to EXPIRE_DATE
12  -h, --help                    display this help message a\
13  nd exit
14  -I, --inactive INACTIVE       set password inactive after\
15   expiration
```

```
16   to INACTIVE
17   -l, --list                          show account aging informat\
18   ion
19   -m, --mindays MIN_DAYS              set minimum number of days \
20   before password
21   change to MIN_DAYS
22   -M, --maxdays MAX_DAYS              set maximum number of days \
23   before password
24   change to MAX_DAYS
25   -R, --root CHROOT_DIR               directory to chroot into
26   -W, --warndays WARN_DAYS            set expiration warning days\
27    to WARN_DAYS
28
29   [root@demo devops]# chage -l example
30   Last password change       : Nov 08, 2021
31   Password expires      : never
32   Password inactive     : never
33   Account expires       : never
34   Minimum number of days between password change  : 0
35   Maximum number of days between password change  : 99999
36   Number of days of warning before password expires : 7
```

after execution

```
1    $ ssh devops@demo.example.com
2    Last login: Mon Nov  8 17:09:16 2021 from 192.168.43.5
3    [devops@demo ~]$ sudo su
4    [root@demo devops]# chage -l example
5    Last password change       : Nov 08, 2021
6    Password expires      : Feb 06, 2022
7    Password inactive     : never
8    Account expires       : never
9    Minimum number of days between password change  : 0
10   Maximum number of days between password change  : 90
11   Number of days of warning before password expires : 7
12   [root@demo devops]# passwd example
```

```
13  Changing password for user example.
14  New password:
15  BAD PASSWORD: The password is shorter than 8 characters
16  Retype new password:
17  passwd: all authentication tokens updated successfully.
18  [root@demo devops]# passwd example
19  Changing password for user example.
20  New password:
21  BAD PASSWORD: The password is shorter than 8 characters
22  Retype new password:
23  passwd: all authentication tokens updated successfully.
24  [root@demo devops]# su - example
25  [example@demo ~]$ passwd
26  Changing password for user example.
27  Current password:
28  New password:
29  BAD PASSWORD: The password is shorter than 8 characters
30  passwd: Authentication token manipulation error
```

Ansible creates a group

- ansible.builtin.group
- Add or remove groups

Let's talk about the Ansible module `group`.

The full name is `ansible.builtin.group`, which means that is part of the collection of modules "builtin" with ansible and shipped with it.

It's a module pretty stable and out for years.

It adds or removes groups.

It supports a huge variety of Linux distributions and macOS.

It relies on three Linux commands: `groupadd`, `groupdel` and `groupmod`.

For Windows, use the `ansible.windows.win_group` module instead.

Parameters

- name string - group name
- state string - present/absent
- system boolean - yes/no
- gid integer - GID to set for the group
- local string - "local" command alternatives

This module has some parameters to perform some tasks.
The only required is "name", which is the group name.
The "state" parameter allows us to create or delete a group, in our use case the default it's already set to "present" to create a group.
The "system" parameter allows for the creation of a system group, default it's not.
You could specify the "GID", the group identifier, in using the "gid" parameter.
The "local" parameter allows using the "local" command alternatives on platforms that implement it if you have a central authentication system.

demo

How to create a Linux group with Ansible.

code

- create_group.yml

```yaml
1  ---
2  - name: group module demo
3    hosts: all
4    become: true
5    vars:
6      mygroup: "example"
7    tasks:
8      - name: create group
9        ansible.builtin.group:
10         name: "{{ mygroup }}"
11         state: present
```

execution

```
1  $ ansible-playbook -i demo/inventory group/create.yml
2  PLAY [group module demo] *******************************\
3  *******************************************
4  TASK [Gathering Facts] *********************************\
5  *******************************************
6  ok: [demo.example.com]
7  TASK [create group] ***********************************\
8  *******************************************
9  changed: [demo.example.com]
10 PLAY RECAP ********************************************\
11 *******************************************
12 demo.example.com              : ok=2    changed=1    unreach\
13 able=0    failed=0    skipped=0    rescued=0    ignored=0
```

verification

```
1   $ ssh devops@demo.example.com
2   $ sudo su
3   # getent group | grep example
4
5   example:x:1001:
```

Ansible deletes a group account

How to delete a group in Linux with Ansible using the Ansible module group.

Parameters

- name string - group name
- state string - present/absent
- local string - "local" command alternatives

The only required is `name`, which is the group name.
The `state` parameter allows us to create or delete a group, in our use case set to "absent" to delete a group.
The `local` parameter allows using the "local" command alternatives on platforms that implement it if you have a central authentication system.

demo

How to delete a group in Linux with Ansible.

code

- group_delete.yml

```
1   ---
2   - name: group module demo
3     hosts: all
4     become: true
5     vars:
6       mygroup: "example"
7     tasks:
8       - name: delete group
9         ansible.builtin.group:
10          name: "{{ mygroup }}"
11          state: absent
```

execution

```
1   $ ansible-playbook -i demo/inventory group/delete.yml
2   PLAY [group module demo] ********************************\
3   ********************************************
4   TASK [Gathering Facts] *********************************\
5   ********************************************
6   ok: [demo.example.com]
7   TASK [delete group] ************************************\
8   ********************************************
9   changed: [demo.example.com]
10  PLAY RECAP *********************************************\
11  ********************************************
12  demo.example.com            : ok=2    changed=1    unreach\
13  able=0    failed=0    skipped=0    rescued=0    ignored=0
```

verification

```
$ ssh devops@demo.example.com
[devops@demo ~]$ sudo su
[root@demo devops]# getent group | grep example
[root@demo devops]# getent group
root:x:0:
bin:x:1:
daemon:x:2:
sys:x:3:
adm:x:4:
tty:x:5:
disk:x:6:
lp:x:7:
mem:x:8:
kmem:x:9:
wheel:x:10:
cdrom:x:11:
mail:x:12:
man:x:15:
dialout:x:18:
floppy:x:19:
games:x:20:
tape:x:33:
video:x:39:
ftp:x:50:
lock:x:54:
audio:x:63:
users:x:100:devops
nobody:x:65534:
dbus:x:81:
utmp:x:22:
utempter:x:35:
input:x:999:
kvm:x:36:
render:x:998:
systemd-journal:x:190:
```

```
36   systemd-coredump:x:997:
37   systemd-resolve:x:193:
38   tss:x:59:
39   polkitd:x:996:
40   ssh_keys:x:995:
41   unbound:x:994:
42   sssd:x:993:
43   chrony:x:992:
44   sshd:x:74:
45   vagrant:x:1000:
46   vboxsf:x:991:
47   slocate:x:21:
```

Ansible changes the User Primary Group on Linux

How to Change the User Primary Group on Linux with Ansible using the Ansible module `user`.

See also Ansible troubleshooting - chgrp failed.

Parameters

- name string - username
- group string - user's primary group (only one)
- groups list / elements=string - list of groups the user will be added to
- append boolean - no/yes - If yes, add the user to the groups specified in groups. If no, replace.

This module has many parameters, let me highlight the useful for our use case.

The only required is "name", which is the username.

The primary group is specified in the "group" parameter, every user need to be part of only one group.

The "groups" parameter specifies the list of additional groups that the user will be added to. This type of group sometimes is called also "secondary", "additional" or "supplementary".

The parameter "append" is very important. With the "yes" option, the user is going to be added to the specified groups.

With the "no" option, all group members are going to be overwritten with the specified groups.

So to recap is you specify the "no" option you are going to lose all the previous group associations, please be careful!

demo

How to change the User Primary Group on Linux with Ansible Playbook.

code

- user_group_changeprimary.yml

```yaml
---

- name: user module demo
  hosts: all
  become: true
  vars:
    myuser: "example"
    mygroup: "users"
  tasks:
    - name: change primary group
      ansible.builtin.user:
```

```
11          name: "{{ myuser }}"
12          group: "{{ mygroup }}"
```

execution

```
1  $ ansible-playbook -i virtualmachines/demo/inventory user\
2  s_and_groups/user_group_changeprimary.yml
3  PLAY [user module demo] *********************************\
4  *******************************************
5  TASK [Gathering Facts] *********************************\
6  *******************************************
7  ok: [demo.example.com]
8  TASK [change primare group] ****************************\
9  *******************************************
10 changed: [demo.example.com]
11 PLAY RECAP *********************************************\
12 *******************************************
13 demo.example.com          : ok=2    changed=1    unreach\
14 able=0    failed=0    skipped=0    rescued=0    ignored=0
15 ansible-pilot $
```

before execution

```
1  $ ssh devops@demo.example.com
2  Last login: Wed Dec 15 13:00:47 2021 from 192.168.0.101
3  [devops@demo ~]$ sudo su
4  [root@demo devops]# cat /etc/os-release
5  NAME="Red Hat Enterprise Linux"
6  VERSION="8.5 (Ootpa)"
7  ID="rhel"
8  ID_LIKE="fedora"
9  VERSION_ID="8.5"
10 PLATFORM_ID="platform:el8"
11 PRETTY_NAME="Red Hat Enterprise Linux 8.5 (Ootpa)"
12 ANSI_COLOR="0;31"
13 CPE_NAME="cpe:/o:redhat:enterprise_linux:8::baseos"
```

```
14   HOME_URL="https://www.redhat.com/"
15   DOCUMENTATION_URL="https://access.redhat.com/documentatio\
16   n/red_hat_enterprise_linux/8/"
17   BUG_REPORT_URL="https://bugzilla.redhat.com/"
18   REDHAT_BUGZILLA_PRODUCT="Red Hat Enterprise Linux 8"
19   REDHAT_BUGZILLA_PRODUCT_VERSION=8.5
20   REDHAT_SUPPORT_PRODUCT="Red Hat Enterprise Linux"
21   REDHAT_SUPPORT_PRODUCT_VERSION="8.5"
22   [root@demo devops]# getent passwd | grep example
23   example:x:1002:1002:Ansible example:/home/example:/bin/ba\
24   sh
25   [root@demo devops]# id example
26   uid=1002(example) gid=1002(example) groups=1002(example),\
27   10(wheel)
28   [root@demo devops]# groups example
29   example : example wheel
30   [root@demo devops]#
```

after execution

```
1    $ ssh devops@demo.example.com
2    [devops@demo ~]$ sudo su
3    [root@demo devops]# getent passwd | grep example
4    example:x:1002:100:Ansible example:/home/example:/bin/bash
5    [root@demo devops]# id example
6    uid=1002(example) gid=100(users) groups=100(users),10(whe\
7    el)
8    [root@demo devops]# groups example
9    example : users wheel
10   [root@demo devops]#
```

Ansible adds a user to a secondary group(s)

How to add a user to a second group on Linux with Ansible using the Ansible module user.

See also Ansible troubleshooting - chgrp failed.

Parameters

- name string - username
- group - user's primary group (only one)
- groups list / elements=string - list of groups user will be added to
- append boolean - no/yes - If yes, add the user to the groups specified in groups. If no, replace.

This module has many parameters, let me highlight the use for our use-case.
The only required is "name", which is the username.
The primary group is specified in the "group" parameter, every user needs to be part of only one group.
The "groups" parameter specifies the list of additional groups that the user will be added to. This type of group sometimes is called also "secondary", "additional" or "supplementary".
The parameter "append" is very important. With the "yes" option, the user is going to be added to the specified groups.
With the "no" option, all group members are going to be overwritten with the specified groups.
So to recap is you specify the "no" option you are going to lose all the previous group associations, please be careful!

demo

How to add a user to second a group in Linux with Ansible
Playbook.

code

- user_group_addsecondary.yml

```
1   ---
2   - name: user module demo
3     hosts: all
4     become: true
5     vars:
6       myuser: "example"
7       mygroups:
8         - adm
9         - sys
10    tasks:
11      - name: adding secondary group(s)
12        ansible.builtin.user:
13          name: "{{ myuser }}"
14          groups: "{{ mygroups }}"
15          append: true
```

execution

```
$ ansible-playbook -i virtualmachines/demo/inventory user\
s_and_groups/user_group_addsecondary.yml
PLAY [user module demo] ********************************\
************************************************
TASK [Gathering Facts] *********************************\
************************************************
ok: [demo.example.com]
TASK [adding secondary groups] *************************\
********************************************
changed: [demo.example.com]
PLAY RECAP ********************************************\
*******************************************
demo.example.com           : ok=2    changed=1    unreach\
able=0    failed=0    skipped=0    rescued=0    ignored=0
```

before execution

```
$ ssh devops@demo.example.com
[devops@demo ~]$ sudo su
[root@demo devops]# cat /etc/os-release
NAME="Red Hat Enterprise Linux"
VERSION="8.5 (Ootpa)"
ID="rhel"
ID_LIKE="fedora"
VERSION_ID="8.5"
PLATFORM_ID="platform:el8"
PRETTY_NAME="Red Hat Enterprise Linux 8.5 (Ootpa)"
ANSI_COLOR="0;31"
CPE_NAME="cpe:/o:redhat:enterprise_linux:8::baseos"
HOME_URL="https://www.redhat.com/"
DOCUMENTATION_URL="https://access.redhat.com/documentatio\
n/red_hat_enterprise_linux/8/"
BUG_REPORT_URL="https://bugzilla.redhat.com/"
REDHAT_BUGZILLA_PRODUCT="Red Hat Enterprise Linux 8"
REDHAT_BUGZILLA_PRODUCT_VERSION=8.5
REDHAT_SUPPORT_PRODUCT="Red Hat Enterprise Linux"
```

```
20   REDHAT_SUPPORT_PRODUCT_VERSION="8.5"
21   [root@demo devops]# getent passwd | grep example
22   example:x:1002:1002:Ansible example:/home/example:/bin/ba\
23   sh
24   [root@demo devops]# id example
25   uid=1002(example) gid=1002(example) groups=1002(example),\
26   10(wheel)
27   [root@demo devops]# groups example
28   example : example wheel
29   [root@demo devops]# grep example /etc/group
30   wheel:x:10:example
31   example:x:1002:
32   [root@demo devops]#
```

after execution

```
1    $ ssh devops@demo.example.com
2    [devops@demo ~]$ sudo su
3    [root@demo devops]# id example
4    uid=1002(example) gid=1002(example) groups=1002(example),\
5    3(sys),4(adm),10(wheel)
6    [root@demo devops]# groups example
7    example : example sys adm wheel
8    [root@demo devops]# getent passwd | grep example
9    example:x:1002:1002:Ansible example:/home/example:/bin/ba\
10   sh
11   [root@demo devops]# grep example /etc/group
12   sys:x:3:example
13   adm:x:4:example
14   wheel:x:10:example
15   example:x:1002:
16   [root@demo devops]#
```

Ansible Playbook Code interact with Web Services API

Ansible modules to automate interaction with Web Services API.

Submit a GET request to a REST API endpoint - Interact with web services - Ansible module uri

How to retrieve a JSON list of users via a GET request to a REST API web service HTTPS endpoint from a remote Linux host in a few lines of Ansible code.

See also Ansible troubleshooting - urlopen error.

Ansible submits a GET request to a REST API endpoint

- ansible.builtin.uri
- Interacts with web services supports Digest, Basic, and WSSE HTTP authentication mechanisms

Today we're talking about Ansible module `uri`.
The full name is `ansible.builtin.uri`, which means that is part of the collection of modules "builtin" with ansible and shipped with it.

It's a module pretty stable and out for years and it works in a different variety of POSIX operating systems.

It interacts with web services and supports Digest, Basic, and WSSE HTTP authentication mechanisms.

If you need to download content, use the ["Download a file - Ansible module get url.md" >}}).

For Windows targets, use the `ansible.windows.win_uri` module instead.

Parameters

- url string - (http|https)://host.domain[:port]/path
- method string - "GET", "POST", "PUT", "PATCH", "DELETE"
- user (url_username), password (url_password) string - username, password credentials
- force_basic_auth boolean - no,yes - Basic authentication header
- status_code list/integer - [200, 202]
- headers dictionary - custom HTTP headers, Content-Type
- body_format string - raw, json, `form-urlencoded`, `form-multipart`
- body raw - request body
- return_content boolean - no/yes - return the body of the response
- timeout integer - 30 seconds

This module has some parameters to perform any tasks.

The only required is "`url`", where you specify the API URL.

The parameter "method" specifies the HTTP method of the request: "GET", "POST", "PUT", "PATCH", "DELETE".

The parameters "user" and "password" specify the credentials to access the API. Several authentications methods are supported, for the simplest is the Basic HTTP authentication remember to enable the "force_basic_auth" boolean.

The parameter "status_code" sets the expected single or list of expected HTTP status codes. The most commons are okay is 200, not fount is 404, and so on... If Please note that Ansible is going to return an error if the status code is different.

The parameter "headers" set the custom HTTP headers and HTTP Content-Type.

The parameter "body_format" sets the serialization format of the body content. Default is raw, but you could customize it to send an image for example. There are some restrictions with Content-Type and some serializations.

The parameter "return_content" is very important to return the body of the response as a "content" key in the dictionary result.

The default timeout is set to 30 seconds, but you could customize it with the "timeout" parameter.

Links

- ReqRes API[47]
- API list of users[48]
- Ansible uri module[49]

demo

Let's jump into a real-life playbook on how to submit a GET request to a REST API endpoint with Ansible.

code

- get_list_users.yml

---

[47]https://reqres.in/
[48]https://reqres.in/api/users?page=2
[49]https://docs.ansible.com/ansible/latest/collections/ansible/builtin/uri_module.html

```
1   ---
2   - name: uri module demo
3     hosts: all
4     become: false
5     vars:
6       server: "https://reqres.in"
7       endpoint: "/api/users?page=2"
8     tasks:
9       - name: list users
10        ansible.builtin.uri:
11          url: "{{ server }}{{ endpoint }}"
12          method: GET
13          status_code: 200
14          timeout: 30
15        register: result
16
17      - name: debug
18        ansible.builtin.debug:
19          var: result.json.data
```

API

browser result (https://reqres.in/api/users?page=2):

```
1   {"page":2,"per_page":6,"total":12,"total_pages":2,"data":\
2   [{"id":7,"email":"michael.lawson@reqres.in","first_name":\
3   "Michael","last_name":"Lawson","avatar":"https://reqres.i\
4   n/img/faces/7-image.jpg"},{"id":8,"email":"lindsay.fergus\
5   on@reqres.in","first_name":"Lindsay","last_name":"Ferguso\
6   n","avatar":"https://reqres.in/img/faces/8-image.jpg"},{"\
7   id":9,"email":"tobias.funke@reqres.in","first_name":"Tobi\
8   as","last_name":"Funke","avatar":"https://reqres.in/img/f\
9   aces/9-image.jpg"},{"id":10,"email":"byron.fields@reqres.\
10  in","first_name":"Byron","last_name":"Fields","avatar":"h\
11  ttps://reqres.in/img/faces/10-image.jpg"},{"id":11,"email\
12  ":"george.edwards@reqres.in","first_name":"George","last_\
```

```
13  name":"Edwards","avatar":"https://reqres.in/img/faces/11-\
14  image.jpg"},{"id":12,"email":"rachel.howell@reqres.in","f\
15  irst_name":"Rachel","last_name":"Howell","avatar":"https:\
16  //reqres.in/img/faces/12-image.jpg"}],"support":{"url":"h\
17  ttps://reqres.in/#support-heading","text":"To keep ReqRes\
18   free, contributions towards server costs are appreciated\
19  !"}}
```

execution

```
1   $ ansible-playbook -i virtualmachines/demo/inventory inte\
2   rract\ webservices/list_users.yml
3   PLAY [uri module demo] ********************************\
4   *******************************************
5   TASK [Gathering Facts] *******************************\
6   *******************************************
7   ok: [demo.example.com]
8   TASK [list users] ************************************\
9   *******************************************
10  ok: [demo.example.com]
11  TASK [debug] *****************************************\
12  *******************************************
13  ok: [demo.example.com] => {
14      "result.json.data": [
15          {
16              "avatar": "https://reqres.in/img/faces/7-imag\
17  e.jpg",
18              "email": "michael.lawson@reqres.in",
19              "first_name": "Michael",
20              "id": 7,
21              "last_name": "Lawson"
22          },
23          {
24              "avatar": "https://reqres.in/img/faces/8-imag\
25  e.jpg",
26              "email": "lindsay.ferguson@reqres.in",
```

```
27              "first_name": "Lindsay",
28              "id": 8,
29              "last_name": "Ferguson"
30          },
31          {
32              "avatar": "https://reqres.in/img/faces/9-imag\
33  e.jpg",
34              "email": "tobias.funke@reqres.in",
35              "first_name": "Tobias",
36              "id": 9,
37              "last_name": "Funke"
38          },
39          {
40              "avatar": "https://reqres.in/img/faces/10-ima\
41  ge.jpg",
42              "email": "byron.fields@reqres.in",
43              "first_name": "Byron",
44              "id": 10,
45              "last_name": "Fields"
46          },
47          {
48              "avatar": "https://reqres.in/img/faces/11-ima\
49  ge.jpg",
50              "email": "george.edwards@reqres.in",
51              "first_name": "George",
52              "id": 11,
53              "last_name": "Edwards"
54          },
55          {
56              "avatar": "https://reqres.in/img/faces/12-ima\
57  ge.jpg",
58              "email": "rachel.howell@reqres.in",
59              "first_name": "Rachel",
60              "id": 12,
61              "last_name": "Howell"
```

```
62                }
63            ]
64    }
```

Token-Based Authentication in REST API - Interact with web-service - Ansible module uri - Authentication request using the REST API token

How to retrieve a JSON token via a POST authentication request using a JSON body formed by email and password to a REST API web service HTTPS endpoint from a remote Linux host in a few lines of Ansible code.

See also Ansible troubleshooting - urlopen error.

Ansible Token Based Authentication in REST API

- ansible.builtin.uri
- Interacts with web services supports Digest, Basic, and WSSE HTTP authentication mechanisms

Today we're talking about the Ansible module uri.
The full name is `ansible.builtin.uri`, which means that is part of the collection of modules "builtin" with ansible and shipped with it.
It's a module pretty stable and out for years and it works in a different variety of POSIX operating systems.
It interacts with web services and supports Digest, Basic, and WSSE HTTP authentication mechanisms.
If you need to download content, use the ["Download a file -

Ansible module get url.md" >}}).

For Windows targets, use the `ansible.windows.win_uri` module instead.

Parameters

- url string - (http|https)://host.domain[:port]/path
- method string - "GET", "POST", "PUT", "PATCH", "DELETE"
- user (url_username), password (url_password) string - username, password
- force_basic_auth boolean - no,yes - Basic authentication header
- status_code list/integer - [200, 202]
- headers dictionary - custom HTTP headers, Content-Type
- body_format string - raw, json, form-urlencoded, form-multipart
- body raw
- return_content boolean - no/yes - return the body of the response
- timeout integer - 30

This module has some parameters to perform any tasks.

The only required is "url", where you specify the API URL.

The parameter "method" specifies the HTTP method of the request: "GET", "POST", "PUT", "PATCH", "DELETE".

The parameters "user" and "password" specify the credentials to access the API. Several authentications methods are supported, for the simplest is the Basic HTTP authentication remember to enable the "force_basic_auth" boolean.

The parameter "status_code" sets the expected single or list of expected HTTP status codes. The most commons are okay is 200, not fount is 404, and so on... If Please note that Ansible is going to return an error if the status code is different.

The parameter "headers" set the custom HTTP headers and HTTP

Content-Type.

The parameter "body_format" sets the serialization format of the body content. Default is raw, but you could customize it to send an image for example. There are some restrictions with Content-Type and some serializations.

The parameter "return_content" is very important to return the body of the response as a "content" key in the dictionary result.

The default timeout is set to 30 seconds, but you could customize it with the "timeout" parameter.

Links

- Ansible uri module[50]
- ReqRes API[51]

demo

Let's jump into a real-life playbook on how to Token Based Authentication in REST API with Ansible.

code successful login

- post_login_correct.yml

---

[50]https://docs.ansible.com/ansible/latest/collections/ansible/builtin/uri_module.html
[51]https://reqres.in/

```yaml
1   ---
2   - name: uri module demo
3     hosts: all
4     become: false
5     vars:
6       server: "https://reqres.in"
7       endpoint: "/api/login"
8     tasks:
9       - name: login
10        ansible.builtin.uri:
11          url: "{{ server }}{{ endpoint }}"
12          method: POST
13          body_format: json
14          body: '{
15            "email": "eve.holt@reqres.in",
16            "password": "cityslicka"
17          }'
18          status_code: 200
19          timeout: 30
20        register: result
21      - name: token
22        ansible.builtin.debug:
23          var: result.json.token
```

execution successful login

```
$ ansible-playbook -i virtualmachines/demo/inventory inte\
rract\ webservices/post_login.yml
PLAY [uri module demo] ********************************\
********************************************
TASK [Gathering Facts] ********************************\
********************************************
ok: [demo.example.com]
TASK [login] *****************************************\
********************************************
ok: [demo.example.com]
TASK [token] *****************************************\
********************************************
ok: [demo.example.com] => {
    "result.json.token": "QpwL5tke4Pnpja7X4"
}
PLAY RECAP *******************************************\
********************************************
demo.example.com           : ok=3    changed=0    unreach\
able=0    failed=0    skipped=0    rescued=0    ignored=0
```

code unsuccessful login

- post_login_incorrect.yml

```
---
- name: uri module demo
  hosts: all
  become: false
  vars:
    server: "https://reqres.in"
    endpoint: "/api/login"
  tasks:
    - name: login
      ansible.builtin.uri:
        url: "{{ server }}{{ endpoint }}"
```

```
12          method: POST
13          body_format: json
14          body: '{
15            "email": "wronguser",
16            "password": "cityslicka"
17          }'
18          status_code: 200
19          timeout: 30
20        register: result
21      - name: token
22        ansible.builtin.debug:
23          var: result.json.token
```

execution unsuccessful login

```
1  $ ansible-playbook -i virtualmachines/demo/inventory inte\
2  rract\ webservices/post_login_incorrect.yml
3  PLAY [uri module demo] ***********************************\
4  ******************************************
5  TASK [Gathering Facts] ***********************************\
6  ******************************************
7  ok: [demo.example.com]
8  TASK [login] *********************************************\
9  ******************************************
10 fatal: [demo.example.com]: FAILED! => {"access_control_al\
11 low_origin": "*", "alt_svc": "h3=\":443\"; ma=86400, h3-2\
12 9=\":443\"; ma=86400, h3-28=\":443\"; ma=86400, h3-27=\":\
13 443\"; ma=86400", "cf_cache_status": "DYNAMIC", "cf_ray":\
14  "6bcf380f2d97694b-FRA", "changed": false, "connection": \
15 "close", "content_length": "26", "content_type": "applica\
16 tion/json; charset=utf-8", "date": "Mon, 13 Dec 2021 12:3\
17 3:06 GMT", "elapsed": 0, "etag": "W/\"1a-EGIcyP6BIiCX15Gb\
18 1aph5CGf4VQ\"", "expect_ct": "max-age=604800, report-uri=\
19 \"https://report-uri.cloudflare.com/cdn-cgi/beacon/expect\
20 -ct\"", "json": {"error": "user not found"}, "msg": "Stat\
21 us code was 400 and not [200]: HTTP Error 400: Bad Reques\
```

```
22  t", "nel": "{\"success_fraction\":0,\"report_to\":\"cf-ne\
23  l\",\"max_age\":604800}", "redirected": false, "report_to\
24  ": "{\"endpoints\":[{\"url\":\"https:\\/\\/a.nel.cloudfla\
25  re.com\\/report\\/v3?s=E27%2Fk34cldTXza600IDyqOnqo3kO6HrR\
26  mrXN7DDi8bI%2F6Rrhytd%2F2mvOFfQ1tk7lOiv2KY5fBpdnUzz2tl7l9\
27  XVxIAwp8nW0VLVSGRJFILki0iTP7LymmUfVSEQ%3D\"}],\"group\":\\
28  "cf-nel\",\"max_age\":604800}", "server": "cloudflare", "\
29  status": 400, "url": "https://reqres.in/api/login", "via"\
30  : "1.1 vegur", "x_powered_by": "Express"}
31  PLAY RECAP *********************************************\
32  *******************************************
33  demo.example.com           : ok=1    changed=0    unreach\
34  able=0    failed=1    skipped=0    rescued=0    ignored=0
```

Ansible For Containers

The Ansible Modules to Automate Containers Tasks.

Let's start installing the Docker Engine.

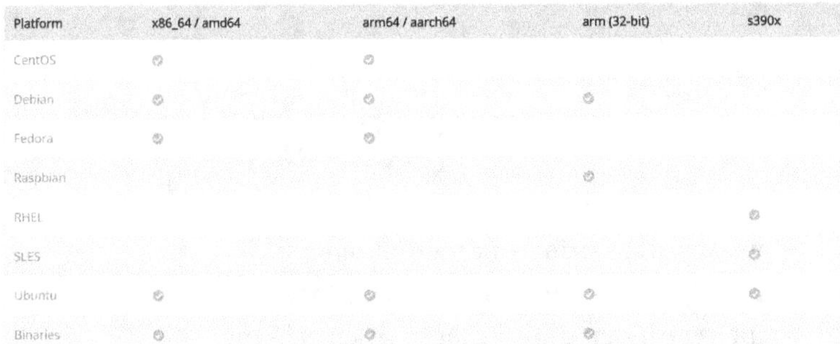

Platform	x86_64 / amd64	arm64 / aarch64	arm (32-bit)	s390x
CentOS	✓	✓		
Debian	✓	✓	✓	
Fedora	✓	✓		
Raspbian			✓	
RHEL				✓
SLES				✓
Ubuntu	✓	✓	✓	✓
Binaries	✓	✓	✓	

Docker Engine Supported platforms

Ansible install Docker in Debian-like systems

- Add Docker key ⇒ ansible.builtin.apt_key
- Add Docker repository ⇒ ansible.builtin.apt_repository
- Update apt cache and install Docker ⇒ ansible.builtin.apt

In order to install Docker on a Debian-like system we need to perform three main steps.

The first step is to download the GPG signature key for the repository. You are going to use the `ansible.builtin.apt_key` Ansible module.

This encrypted key verifies the genuinity of the packages and the repository and guarantees that the software is the same as Docker releases.

The second step is to add the add Docker repository to the distribution. It's an extra website were `apt`, your distribution package manager looks like for software.

You are going to use the `ansible.builtin.apt_repository` Ansible module.

The third step is to update the apt cache for the available packages and install Docker (`docker-ce`) using the `ansible.builtin.apt` Ansible module.

Parameters

- apt-key url string - URL
- apt-key state string - present/absent
- apt_repository repo string - repository
- apt_repository state string - present/absent
- apt name string - name or package specific
- apt state string - latest/present/absent
- apt update_cache boolean - no/yes

For the `ansible.builtin.apt_key` Ansible module I'm going to use two parameters: "URL" and "state".

The "url" parameter specifies the URL of the repository GPG signature key and the "state" verify that is present in our system after the execution.

For the `ansible.builtin.apt_repository` Ansible module I'm going to use two parameters: "repo" and "state".

The "repo" parameter specifies the repository parameters and the "state" verify that is present in our system after the execution.

For the `ansible.builtin.apt` Ansible module I'm going to use three parameters: "name", "state", and "update_cache".

The "name" parameter specifies the package name (Docker in our use-case) and the "state" verify that is present in our system after the execution.

Before installing the package the "update_cache" performs an update of the apt-cache to ensure that the latest version of the package is going to be downloaded.

Links

- Install Docker Engine[52]

demo

Install Docker in Debian-like systems with Ansible Playbook

updated

Package docker-ce changed name to docker.

```
1  ---
2  - name: install Docker
3    hosts: all
4    become: true
5    tasks:
6      - name: Install apt-transport-https
7        ansible.builtin.apt:
8          name:
9            - apt-transport-https
10           - ca-certificates
11           - lsb-release
12           - gnupg
13         state: latest
14         update_cache: true
15
16     - name: Add signing key
17       ansible.builtin.apt_key:
```

---

[52]https://docs.docker.com/engine/install/

```
18          url: "https://download.docker.com/linux/{{ ansibl\
19 e_distribution | lower }}/gpg"
20          state: present
21
22      - name: Add repository into sources list
23        ansible.builtin.apt_repository:
24          repo: "deb [arch={{ ansible_architecture }}] http\
25 s://download.docker.com/linux/{{ ansible_distribution | l\
26 ower }} {{ ansible_distribution_release }} stable"
27          state: present
28          filename: docker
29
30      - name: Install Docker
31        ansible.builtin.apt:
32          name:
33            - docker
34            - docker.io
35            - docker-compose
36            - docker-registry
37          state: latest
38          update_cache: true
```

code

```
1  ---
2  - name: install Docker
3    hosts: all
4    become: true
5    tasks:
6      - name: Install apt-transport-https
7        ansible.builtin.apt:
8          name:
9            - apt-transport-https
10           - ca-certificates
11           - lsb-release
12           - gnupg
```

```
13        state: latest
14        update_cache: true
15
16    - name: Add signing key
17      ansible.builtin.apt_key:
18        url: "https://download.docker.com/linux/{{ ansibl\
19 e_distribution | lower }}/gpg"
20        state: present
21
22    - name: Add repository into sources list
23      ansible.builtin.apt_repository:
24        repo: "deb [arch={{ ansible_architecture }}] http\
25 s://download.docker.com/linux/{{ ansible_distribution | l\
26 ower }} {{ ansible_distribution_release }} stable"
27        state: present
28        filename: docker
29
30    - name: Install Docker
31      ansible.builtin.apt:
32        name:
33          - docker-ce
34          - docker-ce-cli
35          - containerd.io
36        state: latest
37        update_cache: true
```

execution

```
ansible-pilot $ ansible-playbook -i virtualmachines/ubunt\
u/inventory install\ Docker/debian.yml
PLAY [install Docker] ******************************\
**********************************************
TASK [Gathering Facts] *****************************\
**********************************************
ok: [ubuntu.example.com]
TASK [Install apt-transport-https] *****************\
**********************************************
changed: [ubuntu.example.com]
TASK [Add signing key] *****************************\
**********************************************
changed: [ubuntu.example.com]
TASK [Add repository into sources list] ************\
**********************************************
changed: [ubuntu.example.com]
TASK [Install docker-ce] ***************************\
**********************************************
changed: [ubuntu.example.com]
PLAY RECAP *****************************************\
**********************************************
ubuntu.example.com          : ok=5    changed=4    unreach\
able=0    failed=0    skipped=0    rescued=0    ignored=0
ansible-pilot $
```

idempotency

```
ansible-pilot $ ansible-playbook -i virtualmachines/ubunt\
u/inventory install\ Docker/debian.yml
PLAY [install Docker] ********************************\
*******************************************
TASK [Gathering Facts] ******************************\
*******************************************
ok: [ubuntu.example.com]
TASK [Install apt-transport-https] ******************\
*******************************************
ok: [ubuntu.example.com]
TASK [Add signing key] ******************************\
*******************************************
ok: [ubuntu.example.com]
TASK [Add repository into sources list] *************\
*******************************************
ok: [ubuntu.example.com]
TASK [Install docker-ce] ****************************\
*******************************************
ok: [ubuntu.example.com]
PLAY RECAP ******************************************\
*******************************************
ubuntu.example.com        : ok=5    changed=0    unreach\
able=0    failed=0    skipped=0    rescued=0    ignored=0
ansible-pilot $
```

before execution

```
 1  $ ssh devops@ubuntu.example.com
 2  Last login: Mon Nov 22 12:06:47 2021 from 192.168.0.102
 3  $ lsb_release -a
 4  No LSB modules are available.
 5  Distributor ID: Ubuntu
 6  Description: Ubuntu 20.04.3 LTS
 7  Release: 20.04
 8  Codename: focal
 9  $ docker --version
10  -sh: 2: docker: not found
11  $ apt list installed docker-ce -a
12  Listing... Done
13  $
```

after execution

```
 1  $ ssh devops@ubuntu.example.com
 2  Last login: Mon Jan 24 08:53:26 2022 from 192.168.0.102
 3  $ sudo su
 4  root@ubuntu:/home/devops# cat /etc/apt/sources.list.d/doc\
 5  ker.list
 6  deb [arch=amd64] https://download.docker.com/linux/ubuntu\
 7   focal stable
 8  root@ubuntu:/home/devops# docker --version
 9  Docker version 20.10.12, build e91ed57
10  root@ubuntu:/home/devops# apt list installed docker-ce -a
11  Listing... Done
12  docker-ce/focal,now 5:20.10.12~3-0~ubuntu-focal amd64 [in\
13  stalled]
14  docker-ce/focal 5:20.10.11~3-0~ubuntu-focal amd64
15  docker-ce/focal 5:20.10.10~3-0~ubuntu-focal amd64
16  docker-ce/focal 5:20.10.9~3-0~ubuntu-focal amd64
17  docker-ce/focal 5:20.10.8~3-0~ubuntu-focal amd64
18  docker-ce/focal 5:20.10.7~3-0~ubuntu-focal amd64
19  docker-ce/focal 5:20.10.6~3-0~ubuntu-focal amd64
20  docker-ce/focal 5:20.10.5~3-0~ubuntu-focal amd64
```

```
21    docker-ce/focal 5:20.10.4~3-0~ubuntu-focal amd64
22    docker-ce/focal 5:20.10.3~3-0~ubuntu-focal amd64
23    docker-ce/focal 5:20.10.2~3-0~ubuntu-focal amd64
24    docker-ce/focal 5:20.10.1~3-0~ubuntu-focal amd64
25    docker-ce/focal 5:20.10.0~3-0~ubuntu-focal amd64
26    docker-ce/focal 5:19.03.15~3-0~ubuntu-focal amd64
27    docker-ce/focal 5:19.03.14~3-0~ubuntu-focal amd64
28    docker-ce/focal 5:19.03.13~3-0~ubuntu-focal amd64
29    docker-ce/focal 5:19.03.12~3-0~ubuntu-focal amd64
30    docker-ce/focal 5:19.03.11~3-0~ubuntu-focal amd64
31    docker-ce/focal 5:19.03.10~3-0~ubuntu-focal amd64
32    docker-ce/focal 5:19.03.9~3-0~ubuntu-focal amd64
33    root@ubuntu:/home/devops# docker run hello-world
34    Unable to find image 'hello-world:latest' locally
35    latest: Pulling from library/hello-world
36    2db29710123e: Pull complete
37    Digest: sha256:975f4b14f326b05db86e16de00144f9c12257553bb\
38    a9484fed41f9b6f2257800
39    Status: Downloaded newer image for hello-world:latest
40    Hello from Docker!
41    This message shows that your installation appears to be w\
42    orking correctly.
43    To generate this message, Docker took the following steps:
44     1. The Docker client contacted the Docker daemon.
45     2. The Docker daemon pulled the "hello-world" image from\
46     the Docker Hub.
47        (amd64)
48     3. The Docker daemon created a new container from that i\
49    mage which runs the
50        executable that produces the output you are currently\
51     reading.
52     4. The Docker daemon streamed that output to the Docker \
53    client, which sent it
54        to your terminal.
55    To try something more ambitious, you can run an Ubuntu co\
```

```
56  ntainer with:
57   $ docker run -it ubuntu bash
58  Share images, automate workflows, and more with a free Do\
59  cker ID:
60   https://hub.docker.com/
61  For more examples and ideas, visit:
62   https://docs.docker.com/get-started/
63  root@ubuntu:/home/devops#
```

Ansible install Docker in RedHat-like systems

- Add Docker key ⇒ ansible.builtin.rpm_key
- Add Docker repository ⇒ ansible.builtin.yum_repository
- Update yum cache and install Docker ⇒ ansible.builtin.yum

In order to install Docker on a RedHat-like system we need to perform three main steps.

The first step is to download the GPG signature key for the repository. You are going to use the `ansible.builtin.rpm_key` Ansible module.

This encrypted key verifies the genuinity of the packages and the repository and guarantees that the software is the same as Docker releases.

The second step is to add the add Docker repository to the distribution. It's an extra website where `yum/DNF`, your distribution package manager looks like for software.

You are going to use the `ansible.builtin.yum_repository` Ansible module.

The third step is to update the yum cache for the available packages and install Docker using the `ansible.builtin.yum` Ansible module.

Parameters

- rpm_key key string - URL
- rpm_key state string - present/absent
- yum_repository name string - repository
- yum_repository baseurl string - URL
- yum_repository gpgcheck boolean gpgkey string - GPG check and key URL
- yum name string - name or package specific
- yum state string - latest/present/absent
- yum update_cache boolean - no/yes

For the `ansible.builtin.rpm_key` Ansible module I'm going to use two parameters: "key" and "state".

The "key" parameter specifies the URL or the key ID of the repository GPG signature key and the "state" verify that is present in our system after the execution.

For the `ansible.builtin.yum_repository` Ansible module I'm going to use four parameters: "name", "baseurl", "gpgcheck" and "gpgkey".

The "name" parameter specifies the repository parameters and the "baseurl" URL of it.

The "gpgcheck" parameter enables the GPG verification with the URL specified in "gpgkey" parameter.

For the `ansible.builtin.yum` Ansible module I'm going to use three parameters: "name", "state", and "update_cache".

The "name" parameter specifies the package name (Docker in our use-case) and the "state" verify that is present in our system after the execution.

Before installing the package the "update_cache" performs an update of the yum cache to ensure that the latest version of the package is going to be downloaded.

Links

- https://docs.docker.com/engine/install/
- https://github.com/docker/docker.github.io/issues/13463

demo

Install Docker in RedHat-like systems with Ansible Playbook.

code

```yaml
---
- name: install Docker
  hosts: all
  become: true
  tasks:
    - name: set mydistribution
      ansible.builtin.set_fact:
        mydistribution: "{{ 'rhel' if (ansible_distributi\
on == 'Red Hat Enterprise Linux') else (ansible_distribut\
ion | lower) }}"

    - name: Add signing key
      ansible.builtin.rpm_key:
        key: "https://download.docker.com/linux/{{ mydist\
ribution }}/gpg"
        state: present

    - name: Add repository into repo.d list
      ansible.builtin.yum_repository:
        name: docker
        description: docker repository
        baseurl: "https://download.docker.com/linux/{{ my\
distribution }}/$releasever/$basearch/stable"
        enabled: true
```

```
25           gpgcheck: true
26           gpgkey: "https://download.docker.com/linux/{{ myd\
27    istribution }}/gpg"
28
29       - name: Install Docker
30         ansible.builtin.yum:
31           name:
32             - docker-ce
33             - docker-ce-cli
34             - containerd.io
35           state: latest
36           update_cache: true
37
38       - name: Start Docker
39         ansible.builtin.service:
40           name: "docker"
41           enabled: true
42           state: started
```

execution

```
1    ansible-pilot $ ansible-playbook -i virtualmachines/fedor\
2    a35/inventory install\ Docker/redhat.yml
3    PLAY [install Docker] ************************************\
4    *******************************************
5    TASK [Gathering Facts] **********************************\
6    *******************************************
7    ok: [fedora.example.com]
8    TASK [set mydistribution] *******************************\
9    *******************************************
10   ok: [fedora.example.com]
11   TASK [Add signing key] **********************************\
12   *******************************************
13   changed: [fedora.example.com]
14   TASK [Add repository into repo.d list] *****************\
15   *******************************************
```

```
16   changed: [fedora.example.com]
17   TASK [Install Docker] ********************************\
18   *******************************************
19   changed: [fedora.example.com]
20   TASK [Start Docker] *********************************\
21   *******************************************
22   changed: [fedora.example.com]
23   PLAY RECAP *************************************************\
24   *******************************************
25   fedora.example.com          : ok=6    changed=4    unreach\
26   able=0     failed=0    skipped=0    rescued=0    ignored=0
27   ansible-pilot $
```

idempotency

```
1    ansible-pilot $ ansible-playbook -i virtualmachines/fedor\
2    a35/inventory install\ Docker/redhat.yml
3    PLAY [install Docker] *******************************\
4    *******************************************
5    TASK [Gathering Facts] ********************************\
6    *******************************************
7    ok: [fedora.example.com]
8    TASK [set mydistribution] *****************************\
9    *******************************************
10   ok: [fedora.example.com]
11   TASK [Add signing key] ********************************\
12   *******************************************
13   ok: [fedora.example.com]
14   TASK [Add repository into repo.d list] *****************\
15   *******************************************
16   ok: [fedora.example.com]
17   TASK [Install Docker] *********************************\
18   *******************************************
19   ok: [fedora.example.com]
20   TASK [Start Docker] *********************************\
21   *******************************************
```

```
22  ok: [fedora.example.com]
23  PLAY RECAP *****************************************\
24  ******************************************
25  fedora.example.com          : ok=6    changed=0    unreach\
26  able=0    failed=0    skipped=0    rescued=0    ignored=0
27  ansible-pilot $
```

before execution

```
1   ansible-pilot $ ssh devops@fedora.example.com
2   The authenticity of host 'fedora.example.com (192.168.0.2\
3   02)' can't be established.
4   ECDSA key fingerprint is SHA256:0p22EqPJKxL+ytcLbPjHTXu/b\
5   jWp2pNkPbfr+EKYxtQ.
6   Are you sure you want to continue connecting (yes/no/[fin\
7   gerprint])? yes
8   Warning: Permanently added 'fedora.example.com,192.168.0.\
9   202' (ECDSA) to the list of known hosts.
10  [devops@fedora ~]$ sudo su
11  [root@fedora devops]# cat /etc/os-release
12  NAME="Fedora Linux"
13  VERSION="35 (Cloud Edition)"
14  ID=fedora
15  VERSION_ID=35
16  VERSION_CODENAME=""
17  PLATFORM_ID="platform:f35"
18  PRETTY_NAME="Fedora Linux 35 (Cloud Edition)"
19  ANSI_COLOR="0;38;2;60;110;180"
20  LOGO=fedora-logo-icon
21  CPE_NAME="cpe:/o:fedoraproject:fedora:35"
22  HOME_URL="https://fedoraproject.org/"
23  DOCUMENTATION_URL="https://docs.fedoraproject.org/en-US/f\
24  edora/f35/system-administrators-guide/"
25  SUPPORT_URL="https://ask.fedoraproject.org/"
26  BUG_REPORT_URL="https://bugzilla.redhat.com/"
27  REDHAT_BUGZILLA_PRODUCT="Fedora"
```

```
28   REDHAT_BUGZILLA_PRODUCT_VERSION=35
29   REDHAT_SUPPORT_PRODUCT="Fedora"
30   REDHAT_SUPPORT_PRODUCT_VERSION=35
31   PRIVACY_POLICY_URL="https://fedoraproject.org/wiki/Legal:\
32   PrivacyPolicy"
33   VARIANT="Cloud Edition"
34   VARIANT_ID=cloud
35   [root@fedora devops]# ls -al /etc/yum.repos.d/
36   total 28
37   drwxr-xr-x. 1 root root  328 Oct 26 05:41 .
38   drwxr-xr-x. 1 root root 2638 Jan 24 17:57 ..
39   -rw-r--r--. 1 root root  728 Oct 11 17:29 fedora-cisco-op\
40   enh264.repo
41   -rw-r--r--. 1 root root 1302 Oct 11 17:29 fedora-modular.\
42   repo
43   -rw-r--r--. 1 root root 1239 Oct 11 17:29 fedora.repo
44   -rw-r--r--. 1 root root 1349 Oct 11 17:29 fedora-updates-\
45   modular.repo
46   -rw-r--r--. 1 root root 1286 Oct 11 17:29 fedora-updates.\
47   repo
48   -rw-r--r--. 1 root root 1391 Oct 11 17:29 fedora-updates-\
49   testing-modular.repo
50   -rw-r--r--. 1 root root 1344 Oct 11 17:29 fedora-updates-\
51   testing.repo
52   [root@fedora devops]# docker --version
53   bash: docker: command not found
54   [root@fedora devops]# rpm -qa | grep docker
55   [root@fedora devops]# yum list installed docker-ce
56   Error: No matching Packages to list
57   [root@fedora devops]#
```

after execution

```
ansible-pilot $ ssh devops@fedora.example.com
Last login: Mon Jan 24 18:02:56 2022 from 192.168.0.102
[devops@fedora ~]$ sudo su
[root@fedora devops]# ls -al /etc/yum.repos.d/
total 32
drwxr-xr-x. 1 root root  350 Jan 24 18:00 .
drwxr-xr-x. 1 root root 2670 Jan 24 18:02 ..
-rw-r--r--. 1 root root  204 Jan 24 18:00 docker.repo
-rw-r--r--. 1 root root  728 Oct 11 17:29 fedora-cisco-op\
enh264.repo
-rw-r--r--. 1 root root 1302 Oct 11 17:29 fedora-modular.\
repo
-rw-r--r--. 1 root root 1239 Oct 11 17:29 fedora.repo
-rw-r--r--. 1 root root 1349 Oct 11 17:29 fedora-updates-\
modular.repo
-rw-r--r--. 1 root root 1286 Oct 11 17:29 fedora-updates.\
repo
-rw-r--r--. 1 root root 1391 Oct 11 17:29 fedora-updates-\
testing-modular.repo
-rw-r--r--. 1 root root 1344 Oct 11 17:29 fedora-updates-\
testing.repo
[root@fedora devops]# cat /etc/yum.repos.d/docker.repo
[docker]
async = 1
baseurl = https://download.docker.com/linux/fedora/$relea\
sever/$basearch/stable
enabled = 1
gpgcheck = 1
gpgkey = https://download.docker.com/linux/fedora/gpg
name = docker repository
[root@fedora devops]# rpm -qa | grep docker
docker-scan-plugin-0.12.0-3.fc35.x86_64
docker-ce-cli-20.10.12-3.fc35.x86_64
docker-ce-rootless-extras-20.10.12-3.fc35.x86_64
docker-ce-20.10.12-3.fc35.x86_64
```

```
[root@fedora devops]# yum list installed docker-ce
Installed Packages
docker-ce.x86_64                            3:20.10.12-3\
.fc35                              @docker
[root@fedora devops]# docker --version
Docker version 20.10.12, build e91ed57
[root@fedora devops]# docker run hello-world
Unable to find image 'hello-world:latest' locally
latest: Pulling from library/hello-world
2db29710123e: Pull complete
Digest: sha256:975f4b14f326b05db86e16de00144f9c12257553bb\
a9484fed41f9b6f2257800
Status: Downloaded newer image for hello-world:latest
Hello from Docker!
This message shows that your installation appears to be w\
orking correctly.
To generate this message, Docker took the following steps:
 1. The Docker client contacted the Docker daemon.
 2. The Docker daemon pulled the "hello-world" image from\
 the Docker Hub.
    (amd64)
 3. The Docker daemon created a new container from that i\
mage which runs the
    executable that produces the output you are currently\
 reading.
 4. The Docker daemon streamed that output to the Docker \
client, which sent it
    to your terminal.
To try something more ambitious, you can run an Ubuntu co\
ntainer with:
 $ docker run -it ubuntu bash
Share images, automate workflows, and more with a free Do\
cker ID:
 https://hub.docker.com/
For more examples and ideas, visit:
```

```
71    https://docs.docker.com/get-started/
72    [root@fedora devops]#
```

Install Red Hat CodeReady Containers to run OpenShift 4 in macOS

How to install Red Hat CodeReady Containers to run a full Open-Shift 4 cluster in your Mac running macOS Big Sur and use the command line and the web interface.

What is Red Hat CodeReady Containers

- an OpenShift 4 cluster for local development
- minimum 4 vCPU, 8 GB RAM, 35 GB storage

CodeReady Containers is designed for local development and testing on an OpenShift 4 cluster.
The CodeReady Containers requires at least:

- 4 virtual CPUs (vCPUs)
- 8 GB of RAM memory
- 35 GB of storage space

demo

How to Install Red Hat CodeReady Containers in MacOS and simple usage.

- Red Hat OpenShift 4 on your laptop: Introducing Red Hat CodeReady Containers[53]

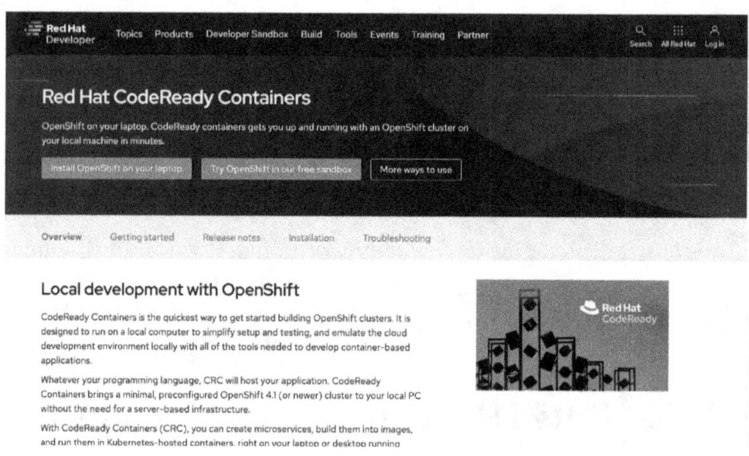

Red Hat CodeReady Containers website

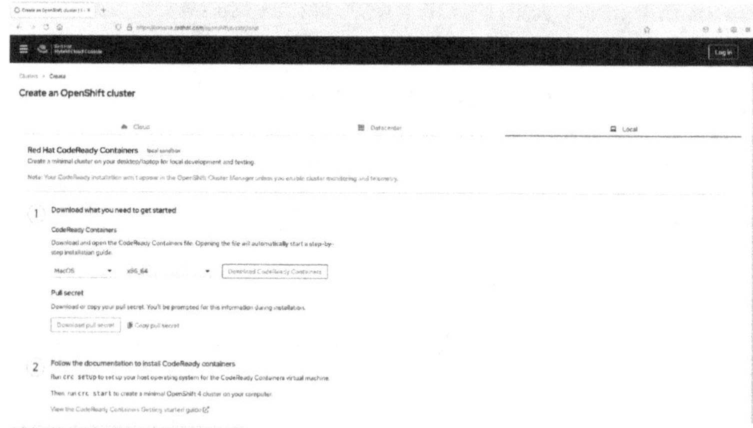

Red Hat CodeReady Containers download

---

[53]https://developers.redhat.com/blog/2019/09/05/red-hat-openshift-4-on-your-laptop-introducing-red-hat-codeready-containers

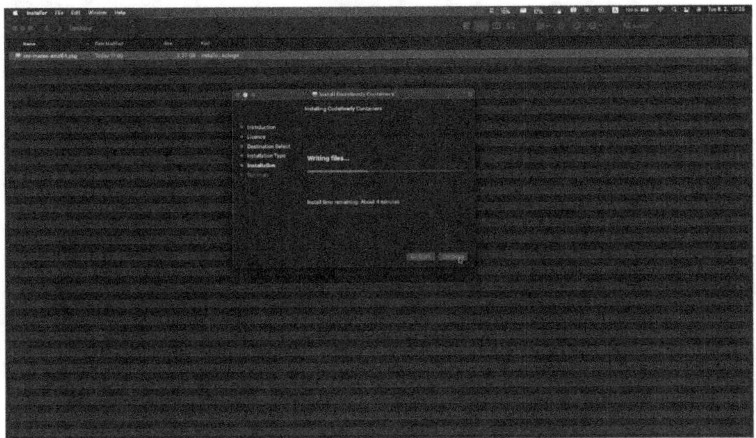

Red Hat CodeReady Containers macOS installer

cluster setup

```
1  ansible-pilot $ crc status
2  Machine does not exist. Use 'crc start' to create it
3  ansible-pilot $ crc setup
4  CodeReady Containers is constantly improving and we would\
5   like to know more about usage (more details at https://d\
6  evelopers.redhat.com/article/tool-data-collection)
7  Your preference can be changed manually if desired using \
8  'crc config set consent-telemetry <yes/no>'
9  Would you like to contribute anonymous usage statistics? \
10 [y/N]: y
11 Thanks for helping us! You can disable telemetry with the\
12  command 'crc config set consent-telemetry no'.
13 INFO Checking if running as non-root
14 INFO Checking if crc-admin-helper executable is cached
15 INFO Checking for obsolete admin-helper executable
16 INFO Checking if running on a supported CPU architecture
17 INFO Checking minimum RAM requirements
18 INFO Checking if running emulated on a M1 CPU
19 INFO Checking if HyperKit is installed
```

```
20  INFO Checking if qcow-tool is installed
21  INFO Checking if crc-driver-hyperkit is installed
22  INFO Checking if CodeReady Containers daemon is running
23  INFO Checking if launchd configuration for tray exists
24  INFO Creating launchd configuration for tray
25  INFO Check if CodeReady Containers tray is running
26  INFO Checking if CRC bundle is extracted in '$HOME/.crc'
27  INFO Checking if /Applications/CodeReady Containers.app/C\
28  ontents/Resources/crc_hyperkit_4.9.15.crcbundle exists
29  INFO Extracting bundle from the CRC executable
30  INFO Ensuring directory /Applications/CodeReady Container\
31  s.app/Contents/Resources exists
32  INFO Uncompressing crc_hyperkit_4.9.15.crcbundle
33  crc.qcow2: 11.70 GiB / 11.70 GiB [----------------------\
34  --------------------------------] 100.00%
35  Your system is correctly setup for using CodeReady Contai\
36  ners, you can now run 'crc start' to start the OpenShift \
37  cluster
```

cluster start

```
1   ansible-pilot $ crc start
2   INFO Checking if running as non-root
3   INFO Checking if crc-admin-helper executable is cached
4   INFO Checking for obsolete admin-helper executable
5   INFO Checking if running on a supported CPU architecture
6   INFO Checking minimum RAM requirements
7   INFO Checking if running emulated on a M1 CPU
8   INFO Checking if HyperKit is installed
9   INFO Checking if qcow-tool is installed
10  INFO Checking if crc-driver-hyperkit is installed
11  CodeReady Containers requires a pull secret to download c\
12  ontent from Red Hat.
13  You can copy it from the Pull Secret section of https://c\
14  loud.redhat.com/openshift/create/local.
15  ? Please enter the pull secret *************************\
```

```
*********************************************************\
*********************************************************\
*********************************************************\
*********************************************************\
*********************************************************\
*******************************************************
INFO Loading bundle: crc_hyperkit_4.9.15...
INFO Creating CodeReady Containers VM for OpenShift 4.9.1\
5...
INFO Generating new SSH Key pair...
INFO Generating new password for the kubeadmin user
INFO Starting CodeReady Containers VM for OpenShift 4.9.1\
5...
INFO CodeReady Containers instance is running with IP 127\
.0.0.1
INFO CodeReady Containers VM is running
INFO Updating authorized keys...
INFO Check internal and public DNS query...
INFO Check DNS query from host...
INFO Verifying validity of the kubelet certificates...
INFO Starting OpenShift kubelet service
INFO Waiting for kube-apiserver availability... [takes ar\
ound 2min]
INFO Adding user\'s pull secret to the cluster...
INFO Updating SSH key to machine config resource...
INFO Waiting for user\'s pull secret part of instance dis\
k...
INFO Changing the password for the kubeadmin user
INFO Updating cluster ID...
INFO Updating root CA cert to admin-kubeconfig-client-ca \
configmap...
INFO Starting OpenShift cluster... [waiting for the clust\
er to stabilize]
INFO All operators are available. Ensuring stability...
INFO Operators are stable (2/3)...
```

```
51  INFO Operators are stable (3/3)...
52  INFO Adding crc-admin and crc-developer contexts to kubec\
53  onfig...
54  Started the OpenShift cluster.
55  The server is accessible via web console at:
56    https://console-openshift-console.apps-crc.testing
57  Log in as administrator:
58    Username: kubeadmin
59    Password: YSW9N-SmFPP-jiu2f-nNmfc
60  Log in as user:
61    Username: developer
62    Password: developer
63  Use the 'oc' command line interface:
64    $ eval $(crc oc-env)
65    $ oc login -u developer https://api.crc.testing:6443
66  ansible-pilot $
```

cluster status

```
1   ansible-pilot $ oc status
2   In project example on server https://api.crc.testing:6443
3   You have no services, deployment configs, or build config\
4   s.
5   Run 'oc new-app' to create an application.
6   ansible-pilot $ crc status
7   CRC VM:          Running
8   OpenShift:       Running (v4.9.15)
9   Disk Usage:      13.36GB of 32.74GB (Inside the CRC VM)
10  Cache Usage:     12.79GB
11  Cache Directory: /Users/lberton/.crc/cache
12  ansible-pilot $
13  cluster example project
14  Started the OpenShift cluster.
15  The server is accessible via web console at:
16    https://console-openshift-console.apps-crc.testing
17  Log in as administrator:
```

```
18     Username: kubeadmin
19     Password: WhDvM-c8WiV-zJ8iH-UKhKV
20 Log in as user:
21     Username: developer
22     Password: developer
23 Use the 'oc' command line interface:
24     $ eval $(crc oc-env)
25     $ oc login -u developer https://api.crc.testing:6443
26 ansible-pilot $ eval $(crc oc-env)
27 ansible-pilot $ oc login -u developer https://api.crc.tes\
28 ting:6443
29 Logged into "https://api.crc.testing:6443" as "developer"\
30  using existing credentials.
31 You don't have any projects. You can try to create a new \
32 project, by running
33 oc new-project <projectname>
34 ansible-pilot $ oc new-project example
35 Now using project "example" on server "https://api.crc.te\
36 sting:6443".
37 You can add applications to this project with the 'new-ap\
38 p' command. For example, try:
39 oc new-app rails-postgresql-example
40 to build a new example application in Ruby. Or use kubect\
41 l to deploy a simple Kubernetes application:
42 kubectl create deployment hello-node --image=k8s.gcr.io/s\
43 erve_hostname
44 ansible-pilot $
```

cluster webui

The server is accessible via web console at:
https://console-openshift-console.apps-crc.testing

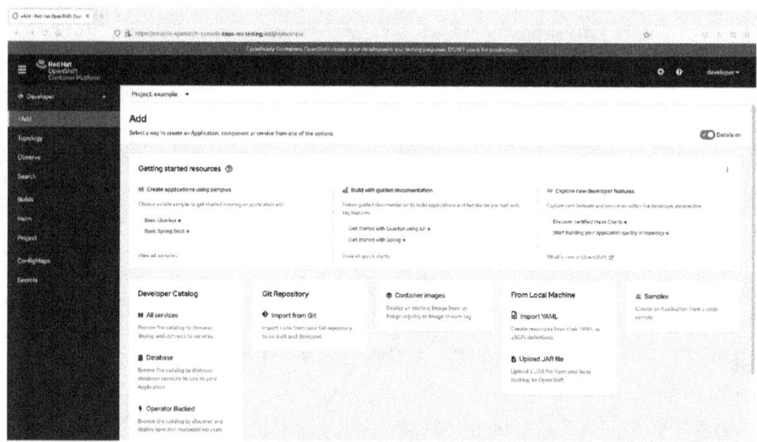

Red Hat CodeReady Containers webui

cluster stop

```
1   ansible-pilot $ crc stop
2   INFO Stopping kubelet and all containers...
3   INFO Stopping the OpenShift cluster, this may take a few \
4   minutes...
5   Stopped the OpenShift cluster
6   ansible-pilot $ crc status
7   CRC VM:          Stopped
8   OpenShift:       Stopped (v4.9.15)
9   Disk Usage:      0B of 0B (Inside the CRC VM)
10  Cache Usage:     12.79GB
11  Cache Directory: /Users/lberton/.crc/cache
12  ansible-pilot $
```

cluster restart

```
ansible-pilot $ crc stop
INFO Stopping kubelet and all containers...
INFO Stopping the OpenShift cluster, this may take a few \
minutes...
Stopped the OpenShift cluster
ansible-pilot $ crc status
CRC VM:              Stopped
OpenShift:          Stopped (v4.9.15)
Disk Usage:         0B of 0B (Inside the CRC VM)
Cache Usage:        12.79GB
Cache Directory: /Users/lberton/.crc/cache
ansible-pilot $ crc start
INFO Checking if running as non-root
INFO Checking if crc-admin-helper executable is cached
INFO Checking for obsolete admin-helper executable
INFO Checking if running on a supported CPU architecture
INFO Checking minimum RAM requirements
INFO Checking if running emulated on a M1 CPU
INFO Checking if HyperKit is installed
INFO Checking if qcow-tool is installed
INFO Checking if crc-driver-hyperkit is installed
INFO Starting CodeReady Containers VM for OpenShift 4.9.1\
5...
INFO CodeReady Containers instance is running with IP 127\
.0.0.1
INFO CodeReady Containers VM is running
INFO Check internal and public DNS query...
INFO Check DNS query from host...
INFO Verifying validity of the kubelet certificates...
INFO Starting OpenShift kubelet service
INFO Waiting for kube-apiserver availability... [takes ar\
ound 2min]
INFO Waiting for user\'s pull secret part of instance dis\
k...
INFO Starting OpenShift cluster... [waiting for the clust\
```

```
36  er to stabilize]
37  INFO All operators are available. Ensuring stability...
38  INFO Operators are stable (2/3)...
39  INFO Operators are stable (3/3)...
40  INFO Adding crc-admin and crc-developer contexts to kubec\
41  onfig...
42  Started the OpenShift cluster.
43  The server is accessible via web console at:
44    https://console-openshift-console.apps-crc.testing
45  Log in as administrator:
46    Username: kubeadmin
47    Password: WhDvM-c8WiV-zJ8iH-UKhKV
48  Log in as user:
49    Username: developer
50    Password: developer
51  Use the 'oc' command line interface:
52    $ eval $(crc oc-env)
53    $ oc login -u developer https://api.crc.testing:6443
54  ansible-pilot $
```

Recap

Now you know how to install Red Hat CodeReady Containers in MacOS and how to manage the OpenShifft 4 cluster, start, stop, restart, status.

Create Kubernetes K8s or OpenShift OCP namespace project - Ansible module k8s

How to automate the "myapp" namespace project created using the Ansible module k8s for Kubernetes K8s or OpenShift OCP.

Ansible creates Kubernetes or OpenShift namespace project

- `kubernetes.core.k8s`
- Manage Kubernetes (K8s) objects

Let's talk about the Ansible module `k8s`.
The full name is `kubernetes.core.k8s`, which means that is part of the collection of modules of Ansible to interact with Kubernetes and Red Hat OpenShift clusters.
It manages Kubernetes (K8s) objects.

Parameters

- name <u>string</u> /namespace <u>string</u> - object name / namespace
- api_version <u>string</u> - "v1"
- kind <u>string</u> - object model
- state <u>string</u> - present/absent/patched
- definition <u>string</u> - YAML definition
- src <u>path</u> - path for YAML definition
- template <u>raw</u> - YAML template definition
- validate <u>dictionary</u> - validate resource definition

There is a long list of parameters of the `k8s` module. Let me summarize the most used.
Most of the parameters are very generic and allow you to combine them for many use-cases.
The `name` and `namespace` specify object name and/or the object namespace. They are useful to create, delete, or discover an object without providing a full resource definition.
The `api_version` parameter specifies the Kubernetes API version, the default is "v1" for version 1.
The `kind` parameter specifies an object model.
The state like for other modules determines if an object should

be created - `present` option, patched - `patched` option, or deleted - `absent` option.

The `definition` parameter allows you to provide a valid YAML definition (string, list, or dictionary) for an object when creating or updating.

If you prefer to specify a file for the YAML definition, the `src` parameter provides a path to a file containing a valid YAML definition of an object or objects to be created or updated.

You could also specify a YAML definition template with the `template` parameter.

You might find useful also the `validate` parameter in order to define how to validate the resource definition against the Kubernetes schema. Please note that requires the `kubernetes-validate` python module.

Links

- kubernetes.core.k8s - Manage Kubernetes (K8s) objects - Ansible Documentation[54]

demo

How to create Kubernetes namespace project with Ansible Playbook.

This demo uses Red Hat CodeReady Containers OpenShift 4 Cluster.

See also: Install Red Hat CodeReady Containers to run OpenShift 4 in macOS

code

---

[54]https://docs.ansible.com/ansible/latest/collections/kubernetes/core/k8s_module.html

```yaml
1  ---
2  - name: k8s demo
3    hosts: localhost
4    gather_facts: false
5    connection: local
6    vars:
7      project_name: "myapp"
8    tasks:
9      - name: create {{ project_name }} namespace
10       kubernetes.core.k8s:
11         api_version: v1
12         kind: Namespace
13         name: "{{ project_name }}"
14         state: present
```

execution

```
1  ansible-pilot $ crc status
2  CRC VM:          Running
3  OpenShift:       Running (v4.9.15)
4  Disk Usage:      15.71GB of 32.74GB (Inside the CRC VM)
5  Cache Usage:     12.79GB
6  Cache Directory: /Users/lberton/.crc/cache
7  ansible-pilot $ crc start
8  INFO A CodeReady Containers VM for OpenShift 4.9.15 is al\
9  ready running
10 Started the OpenShift cluster.
11 The server is accessible via web console at:
12   https://console-openshift-console.apps-crc.testing
13 Log in as administrator:
14   Username: kubeadmin
15   Password: WhDvM-c8WiV-zJ8iH-UKhKV
16 Log in as user:
17   Username: developer
18   Password: developer
19 Use the 'oc' command line interface:
```

```
20     $ eval $(crc oc-env)
21     $ oc login -u developer https://api.crc.testing:6443
22 ansible-pilot $ eval $(crc oc-env)
23 ansible-pilot $ oc login -u kubeadmin https://api.crc.tes\
24 ting:6443
25 Logged into "https://api.crc.testing:6443" as "kubeadmin"\
26  using existing credentials.
27 You have access to 65 projects, the list has been suppres\
28 sed. You can list all projects with 'oc projects'
29 Using project "example".
30 ansible-pilot $ ansible-playbook kubernetes/namespace.yml
31 [WARNING]: No inventory was parsed, only implicit localho\
32 st is available
33 [WARNING]: provided hosts list is empty, only localhost i\
34 s available. Note that the implicit
35 localhost does not match 'all'
36 PLAY [k8s demo] ****************************************\
37 ********************************************
38 TASK [create myapp namespace] *************************\
39 ********************************************
40 changed: [localhost]
41 PLAY RECAP ********************************************\
42 ********************************************
43 localhost                  : ok=1    changed=1    unreach\
44 able=0    failed=0    skipped=0    rescued=0    ignored=0
45 ansible-pilot $
```

idempotency

```
ansible-pilot $ ansible-playbook kubernetes/namespace.yml
[WARNING]: No inventory was parsed, only implicit localho\
st is available
[WARNING]: provided hosts list is empty, only localhost i\
s available. Note that the implicit
localhost does not match 'all'
PLAY [k8s demo] ***************************************\
*********************************************
TASK [create myapp namespace] ************************\
*****************************************
ok: [localhost]
PLAY RECAP *******************************************\
*********************************************
localhost                  : ok=1    changed=0    unreach\
able=0    failed=0    skipped=0    rescued=0    ignored=0
ansible-pilot $
```

before execution

```
ansible-pilot $ oc projects | grep myapp
ansible-pilot $ oc projects
You have access to the following projects and can switch \
between them with ' project <projectname>':
default
  * example
    kube-node-lease
    kube-public
    kube-system
    openshift
    openshift-apiserver
    openshift-apiserver-operator
    openshift-authentication
    openshift-authentication-operator
    openshift-cloud-controller-manager
    openshift-cloud-controller-manager-operator
    openshift-cloud-credential-operator
```

```
18      openshift-cluster-csi-drivers
19      openshift-cluster-machine-approver
20      openshift-cluster-node-tuning-operator
21      openshift-cluster-samples-operator
22      openshift-cluster-storage-operator
23      openshift-cluster-version
24      openshift-config
25      openshift-config-managed
26      openshift-config-operator
27      openshift-console
28      openshift-console-operator
29      openshift-console-user-settings
30      openshift-controller-manager
31      openshift-controller-manager-operator
32      openshift-dns
33      openshift-dns-operator
34      openshift-etcd
35      openshift-etcd-operator
36      openshift-host-network
37      openshift-image-registry
38      openshift-infra
39      openshift-ingress
40      openshift-ingress-canary
41      openshift-ingress-operator
42      openshift-insights
43      openshift-kni-infra
44      openshift-kube-apiserver
45      openshift-kube-apiserver-operator
46      openshift-kube-controller-manager
47      openshift-kube-controller-manager-operator
48      openshift-kube-scheduler
49      openshift-kube-scheduler-operator
50      openshift-kube-storage-version-migrator-operator
51      openshift-kubevirt-infra
52      openshift-machine-api
```

```
53      openshift-machine-config-operator
54      openshift-marketplace
55      openshift-monitoring
56      openshift-multus
57      openshift-network-diagnostics
58      openshift-network-operator
59      openshift-node
60      openshift-oauth-apiserver
61      openshift-openstack-infra
62      openshift-operator-lifecycle-manager
63      openshift-operators
64      openshift-ovirt-infra
65      openshift-sdn
66      openshift-service-ca
67      openshift-service-ca-operator
68      openshift-user-workload-monitoring
69      openshift-vsphere-infra
70  Using project "example" on server "https://api.crc.testin\
71  g:6443".
72  ansible-pilot $
```

after execution

```
1   ansible-pilot $ oc projects | grep myapp
2       myapp
3   ansible-pilot $ oc projects
4   You have access to the following projects and can switch \
5   between them with ' project <projectname>':
6   default
7     * example
8       kube-node-lease
9       kube-public
10      kube-system
11      myapp
12      openshift
13      openshift-apiserver
```

```
14        openshift-apiserver-operator
15        openshift-authentication
16        openshift-authentication-operator
17        openshift-cloud-controller-manager
18        openshift-cloud-controller-manager-operator
19        openshift-cloud-credential-operator
20        openshift-cluster-csi-drivers
21        openshift-cluster-machine-approver
22        openshift-cluster-node-tuning-operator
23        openshift-cluster-samples-operator
24        openshift-cluster-storage-operator
25        openshift-cluster-version
26        openshift-config
27        openshift-config-managed
28        openshift-config-operator
29        openshift-console
30        openshift-console-operator
31        openshift-console-user-settings
32        openshift-controller-manager
33        openshift-controller-manager-operator
34        openshift-dns
35        openshift-dns-operator
36        openshift-etcd
37        openshift-etcd-operator
38        openshift-host-network
39        openshift-image-registry
40        openshift-infra
41        openshift-ingress
42        openshift-ingress-canary
43        openshift-ingress-operator
44        openshift-insights
45        openshift-kni-infra
46        openshift-kube-apiserver
47        openshift-kube-apiserver-operator
48        openshift-kube-controller-manager
```

```
49      openshift-kube-controller-manager-operator
50      openshift-kube-scheduler
51      openshift-kube-scheduler-operator
52      openshift-kube-storage-version-migrator-operator
53      openshift-kubevirt-infra
54      openshift-machine-api
55      openshift-machine-config-operator
56      openshift-marketplace
57      openshift-monitoring
58      openshift-multus
59      openshift-network-diagnostics
60      openshift-network-operator
61      openshift-node
62      openshift-oauth-apiserver
63      openshift-openstack-infra
64      openshift-operator-lifecycle-manager
65      openshift-operators
66      openshift-ovirt-infra
67      openshift-sdn
68      openshift-service-ca
69      openshift-service-ca-operator
70      openshift-user-workload-monitoring
71      openshift-vsphere-infra
72  Using project "example" on server "https://api.crc.testin\
73  g:6443".
74  ansible-pilot $
```

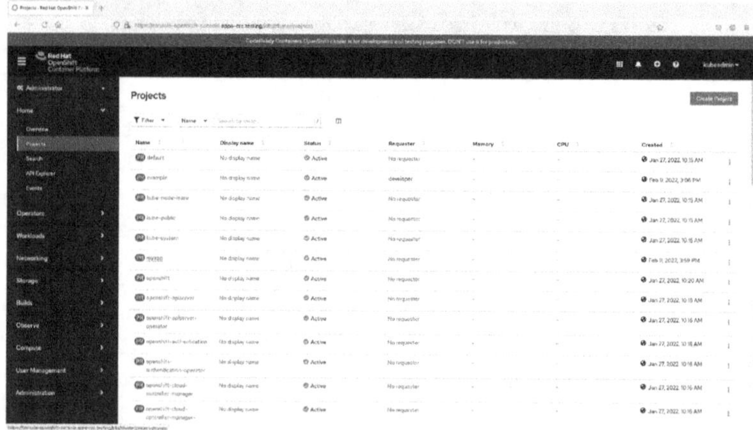

Red Hat CodeReady Containers web UI

Install Zoom flatpak in Debian-like systems - Ansible module flatpak

How to automate the installation of Zoom flatpak system-wide in Debian-like systems using Ansible module flatpak.

Ansible install Zoom flatpak in Debian-like systems

- `community.general.flatpak`
- Manage flatpaks

Let's talk about the Ansible module `flatpak`.

The full name is `community.general.flatpak`, it's part of `community.general` modules maintained by the Ansible Community.

The purpose of the `flatpak` module is to Manage flatpaks in the target system.

Parameters

- name <u>string</u> - flatpak name
- state <u>string</u> - present/absent
- method <u>string</u> - system/user
- remote <u>string</u> - flathub
- no_dependencies <u>string</u> - no/yes
- executable <u>string</u> - flatpak

Let me summarize the parameters of `flatpak` module.

The only required is "name", where you specify the flatpak name to install or remove.

The parameter "state" specifies if you would like to perform the install action ("present" option) or the remove action ("absent" option).

The parameter "method" specifies if you would like to install the flatpak system-wide (default) or only for the current user.

The following parameters are more for advanced users.

For example specify a different source with `remote` parameter other than the default "flathub"; not install the dependency "no_dependencies" parameter or if the `executable` is different than the usual `flatpak`.

Links

- Flatpak technology[55]
- Zoom flatpak[56]

demo

How to install Zoom flatpak in Debian-like systems with Ansible Playbook.

---

[55]https://flatpak.org/
[56]https://flathub.org/apps/details/us.zoom.Zoom

code

```
1    ---
2    - name: flatpak module demo
3      hosts: all
4      become: true
5      gather_facts: false
6      tasks:
7        - name: flatpak present
8          ansible.builtin.apt:
9            name: flatpak
10           state: present
11       - name: flathub flatpak repo
12         community.general.flatpak_remote:
13           name: flathub
14           state: present
15           flatpakrepo_url: https://dl.flathub.org/repo/flat\
16   hub.flatpakrepo
17           method: system
18       - name: install Zoom via flatpak
19         community.general.flatpak:
20           name: us.zoom.Zoom
21           state: present
22           method: system
```

execution

```
ansible-pilot $ ansible-playbook -i virtualmachines/ubunt\
u2110desktop/inventory container/flatpak_debian.yml
PLAY [flatpak module demo] ****************************\
*******************************************
TASK [flatpak present] *******************************\
*******************************************
changed: [ubuntu2110.example.com]
TASK [flathub flatpak repo] **************************\
*******************************************
changed: [ubuntu2110.example.com]
TASK [install Zoom via flatpak] **********************\
*******************************************
changed: [ubuntu2110.example.com]
PLAY RECAP *******************************************\
*******************************************
ubuntu2110.example.com     : ok=3     changed=3     unreach\
able=0    failed=0    skipped=0    rescued=0    ignored=0
ansible-pilot $
```

idempotency

```
ansible-pilot $ ansible-playbook -i virtualmachines/ubunt\
u2110desktop/inventory container/flatpak_debian.yml
PLAY [flatpak module demo] ****************************\
*******************************************
TASK [flatpak present] *******************************\
*******************************************
ok: [ubuntu2110.example.com]
TASK [flathub flatpak repo] **************************\
*******************************************
ok: [ubuntu2110.example.com]
TASK [install Zoom via flatpak] **********************\
*******************************************
ok: [ubuntu2110.example.com]
PLAY RECAP *******************************************\
*******************************************
```

```
16  ubuntu2110.example.com      : ok=3    changed=0     unreach\
17  able=0    failed=0    skipped=0    rescued=0    ignored=0
18  ansible-pilot $
```

before execution

```
1   ansible-pilot $ ssh devops@ubuntu2110.example.com
2   Welcome to Ubuntu 21.10 (GNU/Linux 5.13.0-30-generic x86_\
3   64)
4   * Documentation:  https://help.ubuntu.com
5    * Management:        https://landscape.canonical.com
6    * Support:           https://ubuntu.com/advantage
7   0 updates can be applied immediately.
8   The programs included with the Ubuntu system are free sof\
9   tware;
10  the exact distribution terms for each program are describ\
11  ed in the
12  individual files in /usr/share/doc/*/copyright.
13  Ubuntu comes with ABSOLUTELY NO WARRANTY, to the extent p\
14  ermitted by
15  applicable law.
16  $ flatpak list
17  -sh: 1: flatpak: not found
18  $ flatpak remotes
19  -sh: 2: flatpak: not found
20  $ cat /etc/os-release
21  PRETTY_NAME="Ubuntu 21.10"
22  NAME="Ubuntu"
23  VERSION_ID="21.10"
24  VERSION="21.10 (Impish Indri)"
25  VERSION_CODENAME=impish
26  ID=ubuntu
27  ID_LIKE=debian
28  HOME_URL="https://www.ubuntu.com/"
29  SUPPORT_URL="https://help.ubuntu.com/"
30  BUG_REPORT_URL="https://bugs.launchpad.net/ubuntu/"
```

```
31  PRIVACY_POLICY_URL="https://www.ubuntu.com/legal/terms-an\
32  d-policies/privacy-policy"
33  UBUNTU_CODENAME=impish
34  $ exit
35  Connection to ubuntu2110.example.com closed.
36  ansible-pilot $
```

after execution

```
 1  ansible-pilot $ ssh devops@ubuntu2110.example.com
 2  Welcome to Ubuntu 21.10 (GNU/Linux 5.13.0-30-generic x86_\
 3  64)
 4  * Documentation:  https://help.ubuntu.com
 5   * Management:      https://landscape.canonical.com
 6   * Support:         https://ubuntu.com/advantage
 7  0 updates can be applied immediately.
 8  Last login: Wed Mar  2 06:33:23 2022 from 192.168.0.59
 9  $ flatpak list
10  Name                    Application ID                      \
11      Version      Branch    Installation
12  Freedesktop Platform    org.freedesktop.Platform           \
13      21.08.10    21.08    system
14  Mesa                    org.freedesktop.Platform.GL.defaul\
15  t   21.3.5      21.08    system
16  openh264                org.freedesktop.Platform.openh264 \
17      2.1.0       2.0      system
18  Zoom                    us.zoom.Zoom                       \
19      5.9.6.2225  stable   system
20  $ flatpak remotes
21  Name      Options
22  flathub system
23  $
```

Install Zoom flatpak in RedHat-like systems - Ansible module flatpak

How to automate the installation of Zoom flatpak system-wide in RedHat-like systems using Ansible module flatpak.

Ansible install Zoom flatpak in RedHat-like systems

- `community.general.flatpak`
- Manage flatpaks

Let's explore the the Ansible module `flatpak`.
The full name is `community.general.flatpak`, it's part of `community.general` modules maintained by the Ansible Community.
The purpose of the `flatpak` module is to Manage flatpaks in the target system.

Parameters

- name <u>string</u> - flatpak name
- state <u>string</u> - present/absent
- method <u>string</u> - system/user
- remote <u>string</u> - flathub
- no_dependencies <u>string</u> - no/yes
- executable <u>string</u> - flatpak

Let me summarize the parameters of `flatpak` module.
The only required is "name", where you specify the flatpak name to install or remove.
The parameter "state" specifies if you would like to perform the

install action ("present" option) or the remove action ("absent" option).

The parameter "method" specifies if you would like to install the flatpak system-wide (default) or only for the current user.

The following parameters are more for advanced users.

For example specify a different source with `remote` parameter other than the default "flathub"; not install the dependency "no_dependencies" parameter or if the `executable` is different than the usual `flatpak`.

Links

- Flatpak technology[57]
- Zoom flatpak[58]

demo

How to install Zoom flatpak in RedHat-like systems with Ansible Playbook.

code

```
1   ---
2   - name: flatpak module demo
3     hosts: all
4     become: true
5     gather_facts: false
6     tasks:
7       - name: flatpak present
8         ansible.builtin.yum:
9           name: flatpak
10          state: present
```

---

[57]https://flatpak.org/
[58]https://flathub.org/apps/details/us.zoom.Zoom

```
11      - name: flathub flatpak repo
12        community.general.flatpak_remote:
13          name: flathub
14          state: present
15          flatpakrepo_url: https://dl.flathub.org/repo/flat\
16 hub.flatpakrepo
17          method: system
18      - name: install Zoom via flatpak
19        community.general.flatpak:
20          name: us.zoom.Zoom
21          state: present
22          method: system
```

execution

```
1  ansible-pilot $ ansible-playbook -i virtualmachines/fedor\
2  a35/inventory container/flatpak_redhat.yml
3  PLAY [flatpak module demo] *****************************\
4  *******************************************
5  TASK [flatpak present] ********************************\
6  *******************************************
7  changed: [fedora.example.com]
8  TASK [flathub flatpak repo] ***************************\
9  *******************************************
10 changed: [fedora.example.com]
11 TASK [install Zoom via flatpak] ***********************\
12 *******************************************
13 changed: [fedora.example.com]
14 PLAY RECAP ********************************************\
15 *******************************************
16 fedora.example.com           : ok=3    changed=3    unreach\
17 able=0    failed=0    skipped=0    rescued=0    ignored=0
18 ansible-pilot $
```

idempotency

```
ansible-pilot $ ansible-playbook -i virtualmachines/fedor\
a35/inventory container/flatpak_redhat.yml
PLAY [flatpak module demo] ******************************\
*******************************************
TASK [flatpak present] **********************************\
*******************************************
ok: [fedora.example.com]
TASK [flathub flatpak repo] *****************************\
*******************************************
ok: [fedora.example.com]
TASK [install Zoom via flatpak] *************************\
*******************************************
ok: [fedora.example.com]
PLAY RECAP **********************************************\
*******************************************
fedora.example.com          : ok=3    changed=0    unreach\
able=0    failed=0    skipped=0    rescued=0    ignored=0
ansible-pilot $
```

before execution

```
ansible-pilot $ ssh devops@fedora.example.com
[devops@fedora ~]$ cat /etc/os-release
NAME="Fedora Linux"
VERSION="35 (Cloud Edition)"
ID=fedora
VERSION_ID=35
VERSION_CODENAME=""
PLATFORM_ID="platform:f35"
PRETTY_NAME="Fedora Linux 35 (Cloud Edition)"
ANSI_COLOR="0;38;2;60;110;180"
LOGO=fedora-logo-icon
CPE_NAME="cpe:/o:fedoraproject:fedora:35"
HOME_URL="https://fedoraproject.org/"
DOCUMENTATION_URL="https://docs.fedoraproject.org/en-US/f\
edora/f35/system-administrators-guide/"
```

```
16  SUPPORT_URL="https://ask.fedoraproject.org/"
17  BUG_REPORT_URL="https://bugzilla.redhat.com/"
18  REDHAT_BUGZILLA_PRODUCT="Fedora"
19  REDHAT_BUGZILLA_PRODUCT_VERSION=35
20  REDHAT_SUPPORT_PRODUCT="Fedora"
21  REDHAT_SUPPORT_PRODUCT_VERSION=35
22  PRIVACY_POLICY_URL="https://fedoraproject.org/wiki/Legal:\
23  PrivacyPolicy"
24  VARIANT="Cloud Edition"
25  VARIANT_ID=cloud
26  [devops@fedora ~]$ flatpak list
27  -bash: flatpak: command not found
28  [devops@fedora ~]$ flatpak remotes
29  -bash: flatpak: command not found
30  [devops@fedora ~]$ rpm -qa | grep flatpak
```

after execution

```
1   ansible-pilot $ ssh devops@fedora.example.com
2   [devops@fedora ~]$ flatpak list
3   Name                      Application ID                      \
4       Version      Branch    Installation
5   Freedesktop Platform    org.freedesktop.Platform              \
6       21.08.11     21.08     system
7   Mesa                      org.freedesktop.Platform.GL.defaul\
8   t   21.3.6       21.08     system
9   openh264                  org.freedesktop.Platform.openh264 \
10      2.1.0        2.0       system
11  Zoom                      us.zoom.Zoom                        \
12      5.9.6.2225   stable    system
13  [devops@fedora ~]$ flatpak remotes
14  Name    Options
15  flathub system
16  [devops@fedora ~]$
```

Update Zoom flatpak(s) in Linux systems - Ansible module command

How to automate the update of the Zoom flatpak from version 5.9.1.1380 to 5.9.6.2225 in Linux using Ansible module command.

Ansible update Zoom flatpak in Linux systems

- `ansible.builtin.command`
- Execute commands on targets

Let's talk about the Ansible module `command`.
The full name is `ansible.builtin.command`, it's part of `ansible.builtin` modules maintained by the Ansible Core.
The purpose of the `command` module is to Execute commands on a target system.

demo

How to Update Zoom flatpak in Linux systems with Ansible Playbook.

code

```yaml
1  ---
2  - name: flatpak update demo
3    hosts: all
4    become: true
5    gather_facts: false
6    tasks:
7      - name: update flatpak(s)
8        ansible.builtin.command: "flatpak update --noninter\
9  active"
```

execution

```
1  ansible-pilot $ ansible-playbook -i virtualmachines/ubunt\
2  u2110desktop/inventory container/flatpak_update.yml
3  PLAY [flatpak update demo] *******************************\
4  *******************************************
5  TASK [update flatpak(s)] *********************************\
6  *******************************************
7  changed: [ubuntu2110.example.com]
8  PLAY RECAP ***********************************************\
9  *******************************************
10 ubuntu2110.example.com      : ok=1    changed=1    unreach\
11 able=0    failed=0    skipped=0    rescued=0    ignored=0
12 ansible-pilot $
```

before execution

```
ansible-pilot $ ssh devops@ubuntu2110.example.com
Welcome to Ubuntu 21.10 (GNU/Linux 5.13.0-30-generic x86_\
64)
* Documentation:  https://help.ubuntu.com
 * Management:     https://landscape.canonical.com
 * Support:        https://ubuntu.com/advantage
0 updates can be applied immediately.
Last login: Thu Mar  3 06:39:45 2022 from 192.168.0.59
$ flapak list
-sh: 1: flapak: not found
$ flatpak list
Name                     Application ID                    \
    Version      Branch   Installation
Freedesktop Platform    org.freedesktop.Platform          \
    21.08.11     21.08    system
Mesa                     org.freedesktop.Platform.GL.defaul\
t   21.3.6      21.08    system
openh264                 org.freedesktop.Platform.openh264 \
    2.1.0        2.0     system
Zoom                     us.zoom.Zoom                      \
    5.9.1.1380   stable   system
$
```

after execution

```
ansible-pilot $ ssh devops@ubuntu2110.example.com
Welcome to Ubuntu 21.10 (GNU/Linux 5.13.0-30-generic x86_\
64)
* Documentation:  https://help.ubuntu.com
 * Management:     https://landscape.canonical.com
 * Support:        https://ubuntu.com/advantage
0 updates can be applied immediately.
Last login: Thu Mar  3 07:05:53 2022 from 192.168.0.59
$ flatpak list
Name                     Application ID                    \
    Version      Branch   Installation
```

```
12   Freedesktop Platform    org.freedesktop.Platform          \
13       21.08.11       21.08    system
14   Mesa                    org.freedesktop.Platform.GL.defaul\
15   t   21.3.6         21.08    system
16   openh264                org.freedesktop.Platform.openh264 \
17       2.1.0          2.0      system
18   Zoom                    us.zoom.Zoom                      \
19       5.9.6.2225     stable   system
20   $
```

Install Spotify snap in Debian-like systems - Ansible module snap

How to automate the installation of Spotify snap system-wide in Debian-like systems using Ansible module snap.

Ansible installs Spotify snap on Debian-like systems

- `community.general.snap`
- Manages snaps

Let's talk about the Ansible module `snap`.
The full name is `community.general.snap`, it's part of `community.general` modules maintained by the Ansible Community.
The purpose of the `snap` module is to Manage snaps in the target system.

Parameters

- name <u>string</u> - snap name

- state <u>string</u> - present/absent
- channel <u>string</u> - "stable"
- classic <u>boolean</u> - no/yes

Let me summarize the parameters of `snap` module.

The only required is "name", where you specify the snap name to install or remove.

The parameter "state" specifies if you would like to perform the install action ("present" option) or the remove action ("absent" option).

The parameter "channel" specifies which channel to use, default the "stable" channel.

The parameter "classic" allows the confinement allows a snap to have the same level of access to the system as "classic" packages.

Links

- community.general.snap[59]
- spotify snap[60]

demo

code

---

[59]https://docs.ansible.com/ansible/latest/collections/community/general/snap_module.html

[60]https://snapcraft.io/spotify

```
1   ---
2   - name: snap module demo
3     hosts: all
4     become: true
5     gather_facts: false
6     tasks:
7       - name: snapd present
8         ansible.builtin.apt:
9           name: snapd
10          state: present
11      - name: install Spotify via snap
12        community.general.snap:
13          name: spotify
14          state: present
```

execution

```
1   ansible-pilot $ ansible-playbook -i virtualmachines/ubunt\
2   u2110desktop/inventory container/snap_debian.yml
3   PLAY [snap module demo] *********************************\
4   *****************************************
5   TASK [snapd present] ***********************************\
6   *****************************************
7   ok: [ubuntu2110.example.com]
8   TASK [install Spotify via snap] ************************\
9   *****************************************
10  changed: [ubuntu2110.example.com]
11  PLAY RECAP *********************************************\
12  *****************************************
13  ubuntu2110.example.com     : ok=2     changed=1     unreach\
14  able=0     failed=0     skipped=0     rescued=0     ignored=0
15  ansible-pilot $
```

idempotency

```
ansible-pilot $ ansible-playbook -i virtualmachines/ubunt\
u2110desktop/inventory container/snap_debian.yml
PLAY [snap module demo] ********************************\
*******************************************
TASK [snapd present] **********************************\
*******************************************
ok: [ubuntu2110.example.com]
TASK [install Spotify via snap] ***********************\
*******************************************
ok: [ubuntu2110.example.com]
PLAY RECAP ********************************************\
*******************************************
ubuntu2110.example.com       : ok=2    changed=0    unreach\
able=0    failed=0    skipped=0    rescued=0    ignored=0
ansible-pilot $
```

before execution

```
ansible-pilot $ ssh devops@ubuntu2110.example.com
Welcome to Ubuntu 21.10 (GNU/Linux 5.13.0-30-generic x86_\
64)
* Documentation:  https://help.ubuntu.com
 * Management:     https://landscape.canonical.com
 * Support:        https://ubuntu.com/advantage
0 updates can be applied immediately.
Last login: Thu Mar  3 07:06:34 2022 from 192.168.0.59
$ snap --version
snap    2.54.3.2
snapd   2.54.3.2
series  16
ubuntu  21.10
kernel  5.13.0-30-generic
$ snap list
Name            Version          Rev     Tracking    \
      Publisher   Notes
bare            1.0              5       latest/sta\
```

```
19  le      canonical✓  base
20  core                 16-2.54.3              12725    latest/stab\
21  le      canonical✓  core
22  core20               20220215               1361     latest/stab\
23  le      canonical✓  base
24  firefox              97.0.1-1               1025     latest/stab\
25  le/…  mozilla✓     -
26  gnome-3-38-2004      0+git.1f9014a          99       latest/stab\
27  le/…  canonical✓   -
28  gtk-common-themes  0.1-59-g7bca6ae          1519     latest/stab\
29  le/…  canonical✓   -
30  snap-store           3.38.0-66-gbd5b8f7  558       latest/stab\
31  le/…  canonical✓   -
32  $
```

after execution

```
1   ansible-pilot $ ssh devops@ubuntu2110.example.com
2   Welcome to Ubuntu 21.10 (GNU/Linux 5.13.0-30-generic x86_\
3   64)
4   * Documentation:  https://help.ubuntu.com
5    * Management:      https://landscape.canonical.com
6    * Support:         https://ubuntu.com/advantage
7   0 updates can be applied immediately.
8   Last login: Thu Mar  3 08:36:22 2022 from 192.168.0.59
9   $ snap list
10  Name                 Version                      Rev    Tra\
11  cking           Publisher    Notes
12  bare                 1.0                          5      lat\
13  est/stable    canonical✓  base
14  core                 16-2.54.3                    12725  lat\
15  est/stable    canonical✓  core
16  core18               20211215                     2284   lat\
17  est/stable    canonical✓  base
18  core20               20220215                     1361   lat\
19  est/stable    canonical✓  base
```

```
20   firefox               97.0.1-1                          1025   lat\
21   est/stable/…  mozilla✓     -
22   gnome-3-28-1804    3.28.0-19-g98f9e67.98f9e67  161    lat\
23   est/stable    canonical✓  -
24   gnome-3-38-2004    0+git.1f9014a               99     lat\
25   est/stable/…  canonical✓  -
26   gtk-common-themes  0.1-59-g7bca6ae             1519   lat\
27   est/stable/…  canonical✓  -
28   snap-store         3.38.0-66-gbd5b8f7          558    lat\
29   est/stable/…  canonical✓  -
30   spotify            1.1.77.643.g3c4c6fc6         57     lat\
31   est/stable    spotify✓    -
32   $
```

Install Spotify snap in RedHat-like systems - Ansible module snap

How to automate the installation of Spotify snap system-wide in RedHat-like systems using Ansible module snap.

Ansible installs Spotify snap on RedHat-like systems

- `community.general.snap`
- Manages snaps

Let's talk about the Ansible module `snap`.

The full name is `community.general.snap`, it's part of `community.general` modules maintained by the Ansible Community.

The purpose of the `snap` module is to Manage snaps in the target system.

Parameters

- name <u>string</u> - snap name
- state <u>string</u> - present/absent
- channel <u>string</u> - "stable"
- classic <u>boolean</u> - no/yes

Let me summarize the parameters of snap module.

The only required is "name", where you specify the snap name to install or remove.

The parameter "state" specifies if you would like to perform the install action ("present" option) or the remove action ("absent" option).

The parameter "channel" specifies which channel to use, default the "stable" channel.

The parameter "classic" allows the confinement allows a snap to have the same level of access to the system as "classic" packages.

Links

- community.general.snap[61]
- spotify snap[62]
- Installing snap on Fedora[63]

demo

code

---

[61]https://docs.ansible.com/ansible/latest/collections/community/general/snap_module.html

[62]https://snapcraft.io/spotify

[63]https://snapcraft.io/docs/installing-snap-on-fedora

```yaml
---
- name: snap module demo
  hosts: all
  become: true
  gather_facts: false
  tasks:
    - name: snapd present
      ansible.builtin.yum:
        name:
          - snapd
          - fuse
          - squashfs-tools
          - squashfuse
          - kernel-modules
        state: present
    - name: symlink /snap
      ansible.builtin.file:
        src: "/var/lib/snapd/snap"
        dest: "/snap"
        state: link
    - name: load squashfs module
      community.general.modprobe:
        name: "squashfs"
        state: present
    - name: install Spotify via snap
      community.general.snap:
        name: spotify
        state: present
```

execution

```
1  ansible-pilot $ ansible-playbook -i virtualmachines/fedor\
2  a35/inventory container/snap_redhat.yml
3  PLAY [snap module demo] ********************************\
4  *********************************************
5  TASK [snapd present] **********************************\
6  *********************************************
7  changed: [fedora.example.com]
8  TASK [symlink /snap] **********************************\
9  *********************************************
10 ok: [fedora.example.com]
11 TASK [load squashfs module] ***************************\
12 *********************************************
13 changed: [fedora.example.com]
14 TASK [install Spotify via snap] ***********************\
15 *********************************************
16 changed: [fedora.example.com]
17 PLAY RECAP ********************************************\
18 *********************************************
19 fedora.example.com         : ok=4    changed=3    unreach\
20 able=0    failed=0    skipped=0    rescued=0    ignored=0
21 ansible-pilot $
```

idempotency

```
1  ansible-pilot $ ansible-playbook -i virtualmachines/fedor\
2  a35/inventory container/snap_redhat.yml
3  PLAY [snap module demo] ********************************\
4  *********************************************
5  TASK [snapd present] **********************************\
6  *********************************************
7  ok: [fedora.example.com]
8  TASK [symlink /snap] **********************************\
9  *********************************************
10 ok: [fedora.example.com]
11 TASK [load squashfs module] ***************************\
12 *********************************************
```

```
13  ok: [fedora.example.com]
14  TASK [install Spotify via snap] ************************\
15  *************************************
16  ok: [fedora.example.com]
17  PLAY RECAP ***********************************************\
18  *************************************
19  fedora.example.com          : ok=4    changed=0    unreach\
20  able=0    failed=0    skipped=0    rescued=0    ignored=0
21  ansible-pilot $
```

before execution

```
1   ansible-pilot $ ssh devops@fedora.example.com
2   [devops@fedora ~]$ cat /etc/os-release
3   NAME="Fedora Linux"
4   VERSION="35 (Cloud Edition)"
5   ID=fedora
6   VERSION_ID=35
7   VERSION_CODENAME=""
8   PLATFORM_ID="platform:f35"
9   PRETTY_NAME="Fedora Linux 35 (Cloud Edition)"
10  ANSI_COLOR="0;38;2;60;110;180"
11  LOGO=fedora-logo-icon
12  CPE_NAME="cpe:/o:fedoraproject:fedora:35"
13  HOME_URL="https://fedoraproject.org/"
14  DOCUMENTATION_URL="https://docs.fedoraproject.org/en-US/f\
15  edora/f35/system-administrators-guide/"
16  SUPPORT_URL="https://ask.fedoraproject.org/"
17  BUG_REPORT_URL="https://bugzilla.redhat.com/"
18  REDHAT_BUGZILLA_PRODUCT="Fedora"
19  REDHAT_BUGZILLA_PRODUCT_VERSION=35
20  REDHAT_SUPPORT_PRODUCT="Fedora"
21  REDHAT_SUPPORT_PRODUCT_VERSION=35
22  PRIVACY_POLICY_URL="https://fedoraproject.org/wiki/Legal:\
20  PrivacyPolicy"
24  VARIANT="Cloud Edition"
```

```
25   VARIANT_ID=cloud
26   [devops@fedora ~]$ snap list
27   -bash: snap: command not found
28   [devops@fedora ~]$ dnf list snapd
29   Last metadata expiration check: 0:22:10 ago on Fri 04 Mar\
30    2022 05:16:58 AM UTC.
31   Available Packages
32   snapd.x86_64                                     2.54.3-1.fc3\
33   5                                  updates
34   [devops@fedora ~]$ exit
35   logout
36   Connection to fedora.example.com closed.
37   ansible-pilot $
```

after execution

```
1    ansible-pilot $ ssh devops@fedora.example.com
2    [devops@fedora ~]$ dnf list snapd
3    Last metadata expiration check: 0:27:34 ago on Fri 04 Mar\
4     2022 05:16:58 AM UTC.
5    Installed Packages
6    snapd.x86_64                                     2.54.3-1.fc3\
7    5                                 @updates
8    [devops@fedora ~]$ lsmod | grep squashfs
9    squashfs              69632  6
10   [devops@fedora ~]$ ls -al /snap/
11   total 4
12   drwxr-xr-x. 1 root root 126 Mar  4 10:43 .
13   drwxr-xr-x. 1 root root 234 Mar  4 10:43 ..
14   drwxr-xr-x. 1 root root  16 Mar  4 10:41 bare
15   drwxr-xr-x. 1 root root  14 Mar  4 10:42 bin
16   drwxr-xr-x. 1 root root  22 Mar  4 10:41 core18
17   drwxr-xr-x. 1 root root  20 Mar  4 10:43 gnome-3-28-1804
18   drwxr-xr-x. 1 root root  22 Mar  4 10:42 gtk-common-themes
19   -r--r--r--. 1 root root 590 Mar  4 10:40 README
20   drwxr-xr-x. 1 root root  24 Mar  4 10:40 snapd
```

```
21   drwxr-xr-x. 1 root root  18 Mar  4 10:42 spotify
22   [devops@fedora ~]$ snap list
23   Name                    Version                     Rev     Tra\
24   cking        Publisher    Notes
25   bare                    1.0                          5       lat\
26   est/stable   canonical✓   base
27   core18                  20211215                    2284     lat\
28   est/stable   canonical✓   base
29   gnome-3-28-1804    3.28.0-19-g98f9e67.98f9e67  161     lat\
30   est/stable   canonical✓   -
31   gtk-common-themes  0.1-59-g7bca6ae             1519     lat\
32   est/stable   canonical✓   -
33   snapd                   2.54.3                     14978    lat\
34   est/stable   canonical✓   snapd
35   spotify                 1.1.80.699.gc3dac750        58      lat\
36   est/stable   spotify✓     -
37   [devops@fedora ~]$
```

Deploy Apache Web Server in a Docker Container for Debian-like systems - Ansible modules docker_image and docker_container

How to automate the setup of a detached Apache httpd Web Server tag:latest in a Docker Container pass-throw of port 8080 to 80 with a custom webroot for Debian-like systems.

Setup Apache Web Server in a Docker Container for Debian-like systems

- install packages ⇒ ansible.builtin.apt

- docker py module ⇒ `ansible.builtin.pip`
- pull image ⇒ `community.docker.docker_image`
- document root ⇒ `ansible.builtin.file`
- custom index.html ⇒ `ansible.builtin.copy`
- run container ⇒ `community.docker.docker_container`

Let's talk about how to deploy a web server apache httpd in a Docker Container for Debian-like Linux systems.

The full process requires six steps that you could automate with different Ansible modules.

Firstly you need to install some python packages and dependencies using the `ansible.builtin.apt` Ansible module.

Secondly, you need to install the Docker Module for Python using the `ansible.builtin.pip` Ansible module.

Thirdly, you need to pull the image for the docker hub registry using the `community.docker.docker_image` Ansible module.

Fourthly, you need to create the document root with the right permission with the `ansible.builtin.file` module.

Fifty, you need to create the custom index.html with `ansible.builtin.copy` Ansible module. You could upgrade this step using the `template` module.

Finally, you could run the `webserver` container setting the right port and volume settings using the `community.docker.docker_container` Ansible module.

Links

- httpd image on docker hub[64]
- community.docker.docker_image[65]
- community.docker.docker_container[66]

---

[64]https://hub.docker.com/_/httpd

[65]https://docs.ansible.com/ansible/latest/collections/community/docker/docker_image_module.html

[66]https://docs.ansible.com/ansible/latest/collections/community/docker/docker_container_module.html

demo

How to setup Apache Web Server in a Docker Container for Debian-like systems with Ansible Playbook.

code

```
1   ---
2   - name: deploy httpd on container
3     hosts: all
4     become: true
5     gather_facts: false
6     vars:
7       webroot: "/webroot/"
8     tasks:
9       - name: system packages present
10        ansible.builtin.apt:
11          name:
12            - python3-pip
13            - virtualenv
14            - python3-setuptools
15          state: latest
16          update_cache: true
17      - name: Docker Module for Python
18        ansible.builtin.pip:
19          name: docker
20      - name: pull image
21        community.docker.docker_image:
22          name: httpd
23          source: pull
24          tag: latest
25      - name: webroot present
26        ansible.builtin.file:
27          path: "{{ webroot }}"
28          state: directory
29      - name: custom index.html
```

```
30            ansible.builtin.copy:
31              dest: "{{ webroot}}index.html"
32              content: |
33                Custom Web Page
34        - name: run httpd container
35          community.docker.docker_container:
36            name: webserver
37            image: httpd
38            state: started
39            detach: true
40            exposed_ports:
41              - 80
42            ports:
43              - 8080:80
44            volumes: "{{ webroot }}:/usr/local/apache2/htdocs\
45  /"
```

execution

```
1  ansible-pilot $ ansible-playbook -i virtualmachines/ubunt\
2  u/inventory container/docker_httpd_debian.yml
3  PLAY [deploy httpd on container] ***********************\
4  ******************************************
5  TASK [system packages present] ************************\
6  ******************************************
7  changed: [ubuntu.example.com]
8  TASK [Docker Module for Python] ***********************\
9  ******************************************
10 ok: [ubuntu.example.com]
11 TASK [pull image] *************************************\
12 ******************************************
13 changed: [ubuntu.example.com]
14 TASK [webroot present] ********************************\
15 ******************************************
16 changed: [ubuntu.example.com]
17 TASK [custom index.html] ******************************\
```

```
18  *****************************************
19  changed: [ubuntu.example.com]
20  TASK [run httpd container] *****************************\
21  *****************************************
22  changed: [ubuntu.example.com]
23  PLAY RECAP *********************************************\
24  *****************************************
25  ubuntu.example.com        : ok=6    changed=5    unreach\
26  able=0    failed=0    skipped=0    rescued=0    ignored=0
27  ansible-pilot $
```

before execution

```
1   $ docker --version
2   Docker version 20.10.7, build 20.10.7-0ubuntu5~20.04.2
3   $ sudo docker images ls
4   REPOSITORY   TAG        IMAGE ID   CREATED   SIZE
5   $ sudo docker containers ls
6   docker: 'containers' is not a docker command.
7   See 'docker --help'
8   $ sudo docker container ls
9   CONTAINER ID   IMAGE      COMMAND   CREATED   STATUS    PO\
10  RTS       NAMES
11  $
```

after execution

```
1   ansible-pilot $ ssh devops@ubuntu.example.com
2   $ sudo docker images ls
3   REPOSITORY    TAG         IMAGE ID    CREATED    SIZE
4   $ sudo docker container ls
5   CONTAINER ID    IMAGE       COMMAND              CREATED     \
6        STATUS            PORTS                NAMES
7   c477f001191f    httpd      "httpd-foreground"   50 seconds \
8   ago    Up 49 seconds   0.0.0.0:8080->80/tcp    webserver
9   $
```

Custom Web Page

Apache Web Server in a Docker Container for Debian-like systems

Deploy Apache Web Server in a Podman Container for RedHat-like systems - Ansible modules podman_image and podman_container

How to automate the setup of a detached Apache httpd Web Server tag:latest in a Podman Container pass-throw of port 8080 to 80 for RedHat-like systems.

Setup Apache Web Server in a Podman Container for RedHat-like systems

- install packages ⇒ `ansible.builtin.yum`
- custom index.html ⇒ `ansible.builtin.copy`
- pull image ⇒ `containers.podman.podman_image`
- run container ⇒ `containers.podman.podman_container`

Today we're talking about how to Deploy a web server apache httpd in a Podman Container for RedHat-like Linux systems.

The full process requires four steps that you could automate with different Ansible modules.

Firstly you need to verify that `podman` and it dependency is successfully installed on the target system using the `ansible.builtin.yum` Ansible module.

Secondly, you need to create the custom index.html with `ansible.builtin.copy` Ansible module. You could upgrade this step using the `template` module.

Thirdly, you need to pull the image for the container hub registry using the `containers.podman.podman_image` Ansible module.

Finally, you could run the webserver container setting the right port and settings using the `containers.podman.podman_container` Ansible module.

Links

- containers.podman.podman_image[67]
- containers.podman.podman_container[68]
- httpd image[69]

demo

How to Setup Apache Web Server in a Podman Container for RedHat-like systems with Ansible Playbook.

code

```
1   ---
2   - name: deploy httpd container
3     hosts: all
4     become: true
5     gather_facts: false
6     vars:
7       webroot: "/webroot"
8     tasks:
9       - name: podman installed
10        ansible.builtin.yum:
11          name: podman
12          state: latest
13
```

[67]https://docs.ansible.com/ansible/latest/collections/containers/podman/podman_image_module.html
[68]https://docs.ansible.com/ansible/latest/collections/containers/podman/podman_container_module.html
[69]https://hub.docker.com/_/httpd

```yaml
14      - name: pull image
15        containers.podman.podman_image:
16          name: httpd
17          pull: true
18          tag: latest
19
20      - name: webroot present
21        ansible.builtin.file:
22          path: "{{ webroot }}"
23          state: directory
24          owner: "root"
25          group: "root"
26          mode: '0777'
27          setype: "container_share_t"
28
29      - name: custom index.html
30        ansible.builtin.copy:
31          dest: "{{ webroot }}/index.html"
32          content: |
33            Custom Web Page
34          setype: "container_share_t"
35
36      - name: run httpd container
37        containers.podman.podman_container:
38          name: webserver
39          image: httpd
40          state: started
41          detach: true
42          expose:
43            - 80
44          ports:
45            - 8080:80
46          volume:
47            - "{{ webroot }}:/usr/local/apache2/htdocs/:exe\
48        o"
```

execution

```
ansible-pilot $ ansible-playbook -i virtualmachines/demo/\
inventory container/podman_httpd_redhat2.yml

PLAY [deploy httpd on container] ***********************\
*********************************************

TASK [podman installed] ********************************\
*****************************************
changed: [demo.example.com]

TASK [pull image] **************************************\
*****************************************
changed: [demo.example.com]

TASK [webroot present] *********************************\
*****************************************
changed: [demo.example.com]

TASK [custom index.html] *******************************\
*****************************************
changed: [demo.example.com]

TASK [run httpd container] *****************************\
*****************************************
changed: [demo.example.com]

PLAY RECAP *********************************************\
*****************************************
demo.example.com            : ok=5    changed=5    unreach\
able=0    failed=0    skipped=0    rescued=0    ignored=0\


ansible-pilot $
```

idempotency

```
ansible-pilot $ ansible-playbook -i virtualmachines/demo/\
inventory container/podman_httpd_redhat2.yml

PLAY [deploy httpd on container] ***********************\
**********************************************

TASK [podman installed] *******************************\
**********************************************
ok: [demo.example.com]

TASK [pull image] *************************************\
**********************************************
ok: [demo.example.com]

TASK [webroot present] ********************************\
**********************************************
changed: [demo.example.com]

TASK [custom index.html] ******************************\
**********************************************
ok: [demo.example.com]

TASK [run httpd container] ****************************\
**********************************************
changed: [demo.example.com]

PLAY RECAP ********************************************\
**********************************************
demo.example.com           : ok=5    changed=2    unreach\
able=0    failed=0    skipped=0    rescued=0    ignored=0\


ansible-pilot $
```

before execution

```
ansible-pilot $ ssh devops@demo.example.com
Last login: Thu Mar 10 13:26:52 2022 from 192.168.0.59
[devops@demo ~]$ cat /etc/os-release
NAME="Red Hat Enterprise Linux"
VERSION="8.5 (Ootpa)"
ID="rhel"
ID_LIKE="fedora"
VERSION_ID="8.5"
PLATFORM_ID="platform:el8"
PRETTY_NAME="Red Hat Enterprise Linux 8.5 (Ootpa)"
ANSI_COLOR="0;31"
CPE_NAME="cpe:/o:redhat:enterprise_linux:8::baseos"
HOME_URL="https://www.redhat.com/"
DOCUMENTATION_URL="https://access.redhat.com/documentatio\
n/red_hat_enterprise_linux/8/"
BUG_REPORT_URL="https://bugzilla.redhat.com/"
REDHAT_BUGZILLA_PRODUCT="Red Hat Enterprise Linux 8"
REDHAT_BUGZILLA_PRODUCT_VERSION=8.5
REDHAT_SUPPORT_PRODUCT="Red Hat Enterprise Linux"
REDHAT_SUPPORT_PRODUCT_VERSION="8.5"
[devops@demo ~]$ podman images
-bash: podman: command not found
[devops@demo ~]$ podman ps -a
-bash: podman: command not found
[devops@demo ~]$ dnf info podman
Not root, Subscription Management repositories not updated
This system is not registered with an entitlement server.\
 You can use subscription-manager to register.
Extra Packages for Enterprise Linux 8 - x86_64              \
          4.0 MB/s |  11 MB      00:02
Extra Packages for Enterprise Linux Modular 8 - x86_64     \
          1.1 MB/s | 979 kB      00:00
Red Hat Enterprise Linux 8 for x86_64 - AppStream (RPMs) \
          5.2 MB/s |  39 MB      00:07
```

```
Red Hat Enterprise Linux 8 for x86_64 - BaseOS (RPMs)      \
            5.1 MB/s |   43 MB      00:08
Last metadata expiration check: 0:00:01 ago on Thu 10 Mar\
 2022 01:49:01 PM UTC.
Available Packages
Name          : podman
Epoch         : 1
Version       : 3.4.2
Release       : 9.module+el8.5.0+13852+150547f7
Architecture  : x86_64
Size          : 12 M
Source        : podman-3.4.2-9.module+el8.5.0+13852+150547\
f7.src.rpm
Repository    : rhel-8-for-x86_64-appstream-rpms
Summary       : Manage Pods, Containers and Container Imag\
es
URL           : https://podman.io/
License       : ASL 2.0 and GPLv3+
Description   : podman (Pod Manager) is a fully featured c\
ontainer engine that is a simple
              : daemonless tool.  podman provides a Docker\
-CLI comparable command line that
              : eases the transition from other container \
engines and allows the management of
              : pods, containers and images.  Simply put: \
alias docker=podman.
              : Most podman commands can be run as a regul\
ar user, without requiring
              : additional privileges.
              :
              : podman uses Buildah(1) internally to creat\
e container images.
              : Both tools share image (not container) sto\
rage, hence each can use or
              ; manipulate images (but not containers) cre\
```

```
70  ated by the other.
71                      :
72                      : Manage Pods, Containers and Container Imag\
73  es
74                      : podman Simple management tool for pods, co\
75  ntainers and images
76  [devops@demo ~]$
```

after execution

```
 1  ansible-pilot $ ssh devops@demo.example.com
 2  Last login: Thu Mar 24 17:39:48 2022 from 192.168.0.59
 3  [devops@demo ~]$ sudo su
 4  [root@demo devops]# cat /etc/os-release
 5  NAME="Red Hat Enterprise Linux"
 6  VERSION="8.5 (Ootpa)"
 7  ID="rhel"
 8  ID_LIKE="fedora"
 9  VERSION_ID="8.5"
10  PLATFORM_ID="platform:el8"
11  PRETTY_NAME="Red Hat Enterprise Linux 8.5 (Ootpa)"
12  ANSI_COLOR="0;31"
13  CPE_NAME="cpe:/o:redhat:enterprise_linux:8::baseos"
14  HOME_URL="https://www.redhat.com/"
15  DOCUMENTATION_URL="https://access.redhat.com/documentatio\
16  n/red_hat_enterprise_linux/8/"
17  BUG_REPORT_URL="https://bugzilla.redhat.com/"
18
19  REDHAT_BUGZILLA_PRODUCT="Red Hat Enterprise Linux 8"
20  REDHAT_BUGZILLA_PRODUCT_VERSION=8.5
21  REDHAT_SUPPORT_PRODUCT="Red Hat Enterprise Linux"
22  REDHAT_SUPPORT_PRODUCT_VERSION="8.5"
23  [root@demo devops]# podman images
24  REPOSITORY                    TAG          IMAGE ID        CREATE\
25  D       SIZE
26  docker.io/library/httpd   latest       b9bd7e513e0f   7 days\
```

```
ago  148 MB
[root@demo devops]# podman ps -a
CONTAINER ID  IMAGE                             COMMAND    \
      CREATED        STATUS         PORTS           \
      NAMES
804debe95694  docker.io/library/httpd:latest  httpd-foreg\
round  58 seconds ago  Up 58 seconds ago  0.0.0.0:8080->8\
0/tcp  webserver
[root@demo devops]# dnf info podman
Updating Subscription Management repositories.
Last metadata expiration check: 0:12:45 ago on Thu 24 Mar\
 2022 05:28:22 PM UTC.
Installed Packages
Name         : podman
Epoch        : 1
Version      : 3.4.2
Release      : 9.module+el8.5.0+13852+150547f7
Architecture : x86_64
Size         : 48 M
Source       : podman-3.4.2-9.module+el8.5.0+13852+150547\
f7.src.rpm
Repository   : @System
From repo    : rhel-8-for-x86_64-appstream-rpms
Summary      : Manage Pods, Containers and Container Imag\
es
URL          : https://podman.io/
License      : ASL 2.0 and GPLv3+
Description  : podman (Pod Manager) is a fully featured c\
ontainer engine that is a simple
             : daemonless tool. podman provides a Docker\
-CLI comparable command line that
             : eases the transition from other container \
engines and allows the management of
             : pods, containers and images. Simply put: \
alias docker=podman.
```

```
            : Most podman commands can be run as a regul\
ar user, without requiring
                : additional privileges.
                :
                : podman uses Buildah(1) internally to creat\
e container images.
                : Both tools share image (not container) sto\
rage, hence each can use or
                : manipulate images (but not containers) cre\
ated by the other.
                :
                : Manage Pods, Containers and Container Imag\
es
                : podman Simple management tool for pods, co\
ntainers and images

[root@demo devops]# podman inspect webserver
[
    {
        "Id": "804debe95694391a50b4e597cda2cbe7d5e88bc89d\
a9efaf2325c871fc3c1688",
        "Created": "2022-03-24T17:39:49.78841153Z",
        "Path": "httpd-foreground",
        "Args": [
            "httpd-foreground"
        ],
[...]
```

Custom Web Page

Apache Web Server in a Docker Container for RedHat-like systems

Ansible For Linux Security

In this chapter you're going to discover how to Automate the most common Linux Security tasks.

Set sysctl kernel parameters - Ansible module sysctl

How to automate the setting or verification of the Linux sysctl kernel parameter `vm.swappiness` to "5" with Ansible.

Ansible set sysctl kernel parameters

- ansible.posix.sysctl
- Manage entries in sysctl.conf

Today we're talking about the Ansible module sysctl.
The full name is `ansible.posix.sysctl`, which means that is part of the collection of modules "ansible.posix" to interact with POSIX platforms.
The purpose of the module is to manage entries in the `sysctl.conf` file.

Parameters

- name string (key) - Parameter name
- value string - Parameter value

- reload boolean - yes/no
- state string - present/absent
- sysctl_file string - "/etc/sysctl.conf"
- sysctl_set string - no/yes - sysctl -w
- ignoreerrors boolean - no/yes

Let me summarize the parameters of `sysctl` module.

The only required is `name`, where you specify the parameter name to access or edit.

The parameter `value` sets the value of the sysctl parameter.

The parameter `reload`, default to yes, reload the configuration file if any changes occur.

The parameter `state` sets the presence or absence of the parameter in the sysctl file.

The parameter `sysctl_file` allows specifying the configuration file for sysctl, default to "/etc/sysctl.conf".

The parameter `sysctl_set` allows you to configure a parameter permanently, that survives after reboot.

The parameter `ignoreerrors` allow you to ignore errors about unknown keys, default to "no".

Links

- sysctl_module[70]

demo

How to set sysctl kernel parameters in Linux with Ansible.

code

---

[70]https://docs.ansible.com/ansible/latest/collections/ansible/posix/sysctl_module.html

```
 1  ---
 2  - name: sysctl module demo
 3    hosts: all
 4    become: true
 5    vars:
 6      sysctl_name: "vm.swappiness"
 7      sysctl_value: "5"
 8    tasks:
 9      - name: set sysctl
10        ansible.posix.sysctl:
11          name: "{{ sysctl_name }}"
12          value: "{{ sysctl_value }}"
13          state: present
14          sysctl_set: true
15          reload: true
```

execution

```
 1  $ ansible-playbook -i virtualmachines/demo/inventory sysc\
 2  tl/sysctl.yml
 3  PLAY [sysctl module demo] *******************************\
 4  ******************************************
 5  TASK [Gathering Facts] *********************************\
 6  ******************************************
 7  ok: [demo.example.com]
 8  TASK [ansible.posix.sysctl] ****************************\
 9  ******************************************
10  changed: [demo.example.com]
11  PLAY RECAP *********************************************\
12  ******************************************
13  demo.example.com              : ok=2    changed=1    unreach\
14  able=0    failed=0    skipped=0    rescued=0    ignored=0
```

idempotency

```
$ ansible-playbook -i virtualmachines/demo/inventory sysc\
tl/sysctl.yml
PLAY [sysctl module demo] ********************************\
*********************************************
TASK [Gathering Facts] **********************************\
*********************************************
ok: [demo.example.com]
TASK [ansible.posix.sysctl] *****************************\
*********************************************
ok: [demo.example.com]
PLAY RECAP **********************************************\
*********************************************
demo.example.com              : ok=2     changed=0     unreach\
able=0     failed=0     skipped=0     rescued=0     ignored=0
```

before execution

```
$ ssh devops@demo.example.com
Last login: Fri Jan  7 07:26:29 2022 from 192.168.0.102
[devops@demo ~]$ sudo su
[root@demo devops]# sysctl -a | less
[root@demo devops]# sysctl vm.swappiness
vm.swappiness = 30
[root@demo devops]# cat /etc/sysctl.conf
# sysctl settings are defined through files in
# /usr/lib/sysctl.d/, /run/sysctl.d/, and /etc/sysctl.d/.
#
# Vendors settings live in /usr/lib/sysctl.d/.
# To override a whole file, create a new file with the sa\
me in
# /etc/sysctl.d/ and put new settings there. To override
# only specific settings, add a file with a lexically lat\
er
# name in /etc/sysctl.d/ and put new settings there.
#
# For more information, see sysctl.conf(5) and sysctl.d(5\
```

```
20   ).
21   net.ipv6.conf.all.disable_ipv6=1
22   [root@demo devops]#
```

after execution

```
1    $ ssh devops@demo.example.com
2    Last login: Tue Jan 11 17:41:18 2022 from 192.168.0.102
3    [devops@demo ~]$ sudo su
4    [root@demo devops]# sysctl vm.swappiness
5    vm.swappiness = 5
6    [root@demo devops]# reboot
7    Connection to demo.example.com closed by remote host.
8    Connection to demo.example.com closed.
9    ansible-pilot $ ssh devops@demo.example.com
10   Last login: Tue Jan 11 17:41:44 2022 from 192.168.0.102
11   [devops@demo ~]$ sudo su
12   [root@demo devops]# sysctl vm.swappiness
13   vm.swappiness = 5
14   [root@demo devops]# cat /etc/sysctl.conf
15   # sysctl settings are defined through files in
16   # /usr/lib/sysctl.d/, /run/sysctl.d/, and /etc/sysctl.d/.
17   #
18   # Vendors settings live in /usr/lib/sysctl.d/.
19   # To override a whole file, create a new file with the sa\
20   me in
21   # /etc/sysctl.d/ and put new settings there. To override
22   # only specific settings, add a file with a lexically lat\
23   er
24   # name in /etc/sysctl.d/ and put new settings there.
25   #
26   # For more information, see sysctl.conf(5) and sysctl.d(5\
27   ).
28   net.ipv6.conf.all.disable_ipv6=1
29   vm.swappiness=5
30   [root@demo devops]# uname -a
```

```
31  Linux demo.example.com 4.18.0-348.e18.x86_64 #1 SMP Mon O\
32  ct 4 12:17:22 EDT 2021 x86_64 x86_64 x86_64 GNU/Linux
33  [root@demo devops]#
```

Load and Unload Kernel Modules in Linux - Ansible module modprobe

How to automate the Linux Kernel module loading of the "dummy" module with parameters on an example machine with Ansible.

Ansible Load and Unload Kernel Modules in Linux

- community.general.modprobe
- Load or unload kernel modules

Today we're talking about the Ansible module modprobe.
The full name is community.general.modprobe, which means that is part of the collection of modules "community.general" maintained by the Ansible Community.
The purpose of the module is to Load or unload kernel modules.

Parameters

- name string - Name of kernel module
- params string - Modules parameters
- state string - present/absent - Load / Unload

The parameters of the module modprobe[71].
The only required parameter is "name", with the full Linux kernel

---

[71]https://docs.ansible.com/ansible/latest/collections/community/general/modprobe module.html

module name.

The parameter "params" allows you to specify some module parameters. Default is an empty string.

The parameter "state" specifies the status of the Linux Kernel module. The option "present" means that the module must be loaded.
The option "absent" means that the module must be unloaded.

demo

Load and Unload Kernel Modules in Linux with Ansible Playbook.

code

```
1   ---
2   - name: modprobe module demo
3     hosts: all
4     become: true
5     vars:
6       module_name: "dummy"
7       module_params: "numdummies=2"
8     tasks:
9       - name: load the module
10        community.general.modprobe:
11          name: "{{ module_name }}"
12          state: present
13          params: "{{ module_params }}"
```

execution

```
$ ansible-playbook -i virtualmachines/demo/inventory modp\
robe/modprobe.yml
PLAY [modprobe module demo] ****************************\
*******************************************
TASK [Gathering Facts] ********************************\
*******************************************
ok: [demo.example.com]
TASK [Add the dummy module] ***************************\
*******************************************
changed: [demo.example.com]
PLAY RECAP ********************************************\
*******************************************
demo.example.com                : ok=2    changed=1    unreach\
able=0    failed=0    skipped=0    rescued=0    ignored=0
idempotency
$ ansible-playbook -i virtualmachines/demo/inventory modp\
robe/modprobe.yml
PLAY [modprobe module demo] ****************************\
*******************************************
TASK [Gathering Facts] ********************************\
*******************************************
ok: [demo.example.com]
TASK [Add the dummy module] ***************************\
*******************************************
ok: [demo.example.com]
PLAY RECAP ********************************************\
*******************************************
demo.example.com                : ok=2    changed=0    unreach\
able=0    failed=0    skipped=0    rescued=0    ignored=0
```

before execution

```
$ ssh devops@demo.example.com
Last login: Tue Jan 11 21:12:15 2022 from 192.168.0.102
[devops@demo ~]$ sudo su
[root@demo devops]# lsmod
Module                      Size  Used by
nft_fib_inet               16384  1
nft_fib_ipv4               16384  1 nft_fib_inet
nft_fib_ipv6               16384  1 nft_fib_inet
nft_fib                    16384  3 nft_fib_ipv6,nft_fib_ipv4\
,nft_fib_inet
nft_reject_inet            16384  4
nf_reject_ipv4            16384  1 nft_reject_inet
nf_reject_ipv6            16384  1 nft_reject_inet
nft_reject                16384  1 nft_reject_inet
nft_ct                    20480  9
nf_tables_set             49152  12
nft_chain_nat             16384  12
nf_nat                    45056  1 nft_chain_nat
nf_conntrack             172032  2 nf_nat,nft_ct
nf_defrag_ipv6            20480  1 nf_conntrack
nf_defrag_ipv4            16384  1 nf_conntrack
ip_set                    49152  0
nf_tables                172032  259 nft_ct,nft_reject_inet,\
nft_fib_ipv6,nft_fib_ipv4,nft_chain_nat,nf_tables_set,nft\
_reject,nft_fib,nft_fib_inet
nfnetlink                 16384  3 nf_tables,ip_set
intel_rapl_msr            16384  0
intel_rapl_common         24576  1 intel_rapl_msr
intel_pmc_core_pltdrv     16384  0
intel_pmc_core            45056  0
intel_powerclamp          16384  0
crct10dif_pclmul          16384  1
crc32_pclmul              16384  0
ghash_clmulni_intel       16384  0
rapl                      20480  0
```

```
pcspkr                    16384  0
joydev                    24576  0
video                     49152  0
i2c_piix4                 24576  0
xfs                     1544192  2
libcrc32c                 16384  4 nf_conntrack,nf_nat,nf_ta\
bles,xfs
sd_mod                    53248  3
t10_pi                    16384  1 sd_mod
sg                        40960  0
ata_generic               16384  0
vboxvideo                 45056  1
drm_ttm_helper            16384  1 vboxvideo
ttm                       77824  2 vboxvideo,drm_ttm_helper
drm_kms_helper           253952  1 vboxvideo
drm                      573440  5 drm_kms_helper,vboxvideo,\
drm_ttm_helper,ttm
ata_piix                  36864  2
libata                   270336  2 ata_piix,ata_generic
crc32c_intel              24576  1
serio_raw                 16384  0
e1000                    151552  0
syscopyarea               16384  1 drm_kms_helper
sysfillrect               16384  1 drm_kms_helper
sysimgblt                 16384  1 drm_kms_helper
vboxguest                385024  1
fb_sys_fops               16384  1 drm_kms_helper
dm_mirror                 28672  0
dm_region_hash            20480  1 dm_mirror
dm_log                    20480  2 dm_region_hash,dm_mirror
dm_mod                   151552  9 dm_log,dm_mirror
[root@demo devops]# lsmod | grep dummy
[root@demo devops]# uname -a
Linux demo.example.com 4.18.0-348.el8.x86_64 #1 SMP Mon O\
ct 4 12:17:22 EDT 2021 x86_64 x86_64 x86_64 GNU/Linux
```

71 [root@demo devops]#

after execution

```
1   $ ssh devops@demo.example.com
2   Last login: Wed Jan 12 07:35:19 2022 from 192.168.0.101
3   [devops@demo ~]$ sudo su
4   [root@demo devops]# lsmod | grep dummy
5   dummy                  16384  0
6   [root@demo devops]# less /var/log/messages
7   [root@demo devops]# tail /var/log/messages
8   Jan 12 07:35:04 demo systemd-udevd[4297]: Using default i\
9   nterface naming scheme
10  'rhel-8.0'.
11  Jan 12 07:35:04 demo systemd-udevd[4297]: link_config: au\
12  tonegotiation is unset
13  or enabled, the speed and duplex are not writable.
14  Jan 12 07:35:04 demo systemd-udevd[4297]: Could not gener\
15  ate persistent MAC addr
16  ess for dummy1: No such file or directory
17  Jan 12 07:35:18 demo ansible-ansible.legacy.setup[4440]: \
18  Invoked with gather_sub
19  set=['all'] gather_timeout=10 filter=[] fact_path=/etc/an\
20  sible/facts.d
21  Jan 12 07:35:19 demo ansible-community.general.modprobe[4\
22  593]: Invoked with name
23  =dummy state=present params=numdummies=2
24  Jan 12 07:35:19 demo chronyd[826]: Selected source 94.124\
25  .107.190 (2.rhel.pool.n
26  tp.org)
27  Jan 12 07:35:19 demo chronyd[826]: Selected source 213.19\
28  2.54.227 (2.rhel.pool.n
29  tp.org)
30  [root@demo devops]# modinfo dummy
31  filename:       /lib/modules/4.18.0-348.el8.x86_64/kernel\
32  /drivers/net/dummy.ko.xz
```

```
33  version:         1.0
34  alias:           rtnl-link-dummy
35  license:         GPL
36  rhelversion:     8.5
37  srcversion:      FF01F2D4C53E7F939842380
38  depends:
39  intree:          Y
40  name:            dummy
41  vermagic:        4.18.0-348.el8.x86_64 SMP mod_unload modv\
42  ersions
43  sig_id:          PKCS#7
44  signer:          Red Hat Enterprise Linux kernel signing k\
45  ey
46  sig_key:         77:A4:0E:A4:5E:89:11:3E:DC:EE:6E:4B:55:AA\
47  :F2:1A:6C:4A:91:21
48  sig_hashalgo:    sha256
49  signature:       25:AD:03:5D:FD:85:A6:3D:E4:8F:3F:70:52:0F\
50  :97:20:C9:6A:C3:32:
51    F9:15:C3:AE:E6:03:FB:7B:04:3E:0E:B3:50:0C:49:1A:D1:31:9\
52  6:C3:
53    6D:02:C4:32:C1:2A:D4:28:41:5B:CD:D9:C1:B2:D0:68:9C:24:D\
54  4:0E:
55    EA:B6:8C:41:4A:76:49:64:02:D8:6E:9A:3F:92:91:C6:DF:3C:1\
56  4:88:
57    05:BE:62:CE:E9:19:F0:84:28:19:38:3A:D4:F8:28:C2:51:0F:4\
58  6:6D:
59    7A:9D:D5:8B:D5:A2:3C:93:08:4E:37:39:EA:98:7D:DE:15:9A:A\
60  3:54:
61    D3:25:42:28:EF:72:A9:74:BA:8E:0B:3D:E3:84:38:BA:4D:4B:4\
62  3:F2:
63    DD:8D:BC:FF:6B:C0:41:31:8B:2B:88:C4:77:1E:8E:A0:4D:40:2\
64  3:6E:
65    BF:00:E1:2A:E2:04:49:F9:7F:8E:6C:1C:92:3D:68:D2:38:26:7\
66  B:75:
67    2C:E5:56:73:A8:6A:7D:2E:15:06:34:87:2B:8F:6B:36:BC:08:4\
```

```
68    8:9E:
69      55:9E:D7:16:F7:5A:94:7F:BA:06:F8:85:3F:D1:91:7A:CB:33:E\
70    8:73:
71      A9:2E:C8:B9:1F:F9:10:BB:D1:9A:FF:9B:CA:38:26:C2:A4:02:0\
72    6:07:
73      35:20:91:75:FA:D7:8A:AA:A7:44:76:97:2D:A5:73:6C:1E:F5:D\
74    6:BD:
75      26:03:48:CA:96:34:48:5A:34:A0:7C:F1:C1:A8:73:D3:89:2B:E\
76    C:F3:
77      73:9B:FC:A1:C3:32:84:1A:05:2B:D2:6B:E4:3C:AD:FE:22:AC:2\
78    0:D7:
79      2F:5B:38:52:B9:F8:EB:93:FE:95:2B:A5:E2:CB:A3:24:C1:4E:2\
80    9:EE:
81      6F:DD:49:45:31:DF:21:9B:09:D4:10:06:0D:AA:99:38:78:2E:7\
82    2:3C:
83      8D:F0:80:C8:A8:B7:E1:72:11:E1:08:0A:A4:20:0F:D2:98:4A:3\
84    2:30:
85      2C:7D:14:68:F6:A8:21:3F:DD:B5:42:A3:35:7A:BC:7A:52:2B:0\
86    E:CC:
87      92:23:4D:7E
88    parm:             numdummies:Number of dummy pseudo devices\
89     (int)
90    [root@demo devops]#
```

Recap

Now you know how to Load and Unload Kernel Modules in Linux with Ansible.

Set the SELinux Policy States and Modes on Linux - Ansible module selinux

How to automate the setting and verification of the "enforcing" SELinux mode and state with "targeted" policy and relabel the filesystem if necessary on Linux target with Ansible.

SELinux Modes and States

- `enforcing` - enabled, load security policy "targeted" and active
- `permissive` - enabled, load security policy, log, don't deny
- `disabled` - disabled, not load security policy

What is SELinux?

Security-Enhanced Linux (SELinux) is a Linux kernel security module that provides a mechanism for supporting access control security policies, including mandatory access controls (MAC).

Let's quickly recap the three SELinux Modes: enforcing, permissive and disabled.

The "enforce" mode is recommended, SELinux is enabled and fully operates. It applies the security policy to the entire system.

Please note that in this mode SELinux is expected to deny some actions that don't complain about the security policy. You could choose the name of the security policy, most distributions use the "targeted" security policy out-of-the-box. It's the recommended option for production systems.

The "permissive" mode is someway in the middle, SELinux is enabled and load the security policy. It labels objects and emits access denial entries in the logs, but it does not actually deny any operations. This mode is useful in the development and debugging. The "disabled" mode completely disables the SELinux system. This option is discouraged.

More advanced user ser set the system running in enforcing mode but individual domain as permissive.

Ansible set the SELinux Policy States and Modes on Linux

- `ansible.posix.selinux`
- Change policy and the state of SELinux

Today we're talking about Ansible module `selinux`.

The full name is `ansible.posix.selinux`, which means that is part of the collection of modules to interact with POSIX systems.

It's a module pretty stable and out for years, it manages SELinux policy.

It supports a huge variety of Linux distributions and POSIX systems.

It requires `libselinux-python` or `libselinux-python3` library installed on the target system.

Parameters

- state string - enforcing/permissive/disabled - SELinux mode
- policy - "targeted"
- configfile string - "/etc/selinux/config"

Let's see the parameter of the `selinux` Ansible module.

The only required is `state`, which is the SELinux mode.

For this parameter the three options are available: `enforcing`, `permissive`, and `disabled`.

When the system is in `enforcing` and `permissive` modes you need to specify also the policy to enable it.

The parameter `policy` is designed for this purpose. For example `targeted` policy.

By default, all these values apply to the SELinux configuration file saved in the "/etc/selinux/config". You could customize using the `configfile` parameter.

Links

- selinux_module[72]
- Fedora Changing SELinux states and modes[73]
- selinux_permissive_module[74]

demo

How to set the SELinux Policy States and Modes on Linux with Ansible Playbook.

code

```
1    ---
2    - name: selinux module demo
3      hosts: all
4      become: true
5      vars:
6        selinux_state: "enforcing"
7        selinux_policy: "targeted"
8      tasks:
9        - name: SELinux policy and state
10           ansible.posix.selinux:
```

---

[72]https://docs.ansible.com/ansible/latest/collections/ansible/posix/selinux_module.html
[73]https://docs.fedoraproject.org/en-US/quick-docs/changing-selinux-states-and-modes/
[74]https://docs.ansible.com/ansible/latest/collections/community/general/selinux_permissive_module.html

```
11          state: "{{ selinux_state }}"
12          policy: "{{ selinux_policy }}"
13        notify: relabel and reboot
14    handlers:
15      - name: relabel files on next boot
16        ansible.builtin.file:
17          path: "/.autorelabel"
18          state: touch
19        when:
20          - selinux_state != 'disabled'
21        listen: "relabel and reboot"
22      - name: reboot host
23        ansible.builtin.reboot:
24        listen: "relabel and reboot"execution
```

execution

```
1  $ ansible-playbook -i virtualmachines/demo/inventory seli\
2  nux/policy_modes.yml
3  PLAY [selinux module demo] *******************************\
4  *******************************************
5  TASK [Gathering Facts] **********************************\
6  *******************************************
7  ok: [demo.example.com]
8  TASK [SELinux policy and state] *************************\
9  *******************************************
10 changed: [demo.example.com]
11 RUNNING HANDLER [relabel files on next boot] ***********\
12 *******************************************
13 changed: [demo.example.com]
14 RUNNING HANDLER [reboot host] **************************\
15 *******************************************
16 changed: [demo.example.com]
17 PLAY RECAP *********************************************\
18 *******************************************
19 demo.example.com            : ok=4    changed=3    unreach\
```

```
20  able=0      failed=0     skipped=0     rescued=0     ignored=0
```

idempotency

```
1   $ ansible-playbook -i virtualmachines/demo/inventory seli\
2   nux/policy_modes.yml
3   PLAY [selinux module demo] *****************************\
4   *****************************************
5   TASK [Gathering Facts] ********************************\
6   *****************************************
7   ok: [demo.example.com]
8   TASK [SELinux policy and state] ***********************\
9   *****************************************
10  ok: [demo.example.com]
11  PLAY RECAP ********************************************\
12  *****************************************
13  demo.example.com              : ok=2     changed=0     unreach\
14  able=0      failed=0     skipped=0     rescued=0     ignored=0
```

before execution

```
1   $ ssh devops@demo.example.com
2   [devops@demo ~]$ sudo su
3   [root@demo devops]# getenforce
4   Permissive
5   [root@demo devops]# sestatus
6   SELinux status:                enabled
7   SELinuxfs mount:               /sys/fs/selinux
8   SELinux root directory:        /etc/selinux
9   Loaded policy name:            targeted
10  Current mode:                  permissive
11  Mode from config file:         enforcing
12  Policy MLS status:             enabled
13  Policy deny_unknown status:    allowed
14  Memory protection checking:    actual (secure)
```

```
15   Max kernel policy version:        33
16   [root@demo devops]#
```

after execution

```
1    $ ssh devops@demo.example.com
2    [devops@demo ~]$ sudo su
3    [root@demo devops]# getenforce
4    Enforcing
5    [root@demo devops]# sestatus
6    SELinux status:                 enabled
7    SELinuxfs mount:                /sys/fs/selinux
8    SELinux root directory:         /etc/selinux
9    Loaded policy name:             targeted
10   Current mode:                   enforcing
11   Mode from config file:          enforcing
12   Policy MLS status:              enabled
13   Policy deny_unknown status:     allowed
14   Memory protection checking:     actual (secure)
15   Max kernel policy version:      33
```

Configure Kernel Parameters in RedHat-like Linux systems - Ansible system role

How to automate the configuration of Kernel Parameters (sysctl, sysfs, and hugepages) in RedHat-like Linux systems using Linux System Role "linux-system-role.kernel_settings" from Ansible Galaxy.

Ansible Configure Kernel Parameters in RedHat-like systems

- `linux-system-roles` Fedora, Enterprise Linux & CentOS
- `rhel-system-roles` package Red Hat Enterprise Linux

Today we're talking about `linux-system-role`.

This is a swiss army that you need to absolutely add to your IT knowledge.

Currently, there are 21 roles to configure a lot of system properties. The roles are developed and tested for RedHat-like systems but the project might expand in the future.

It's available as a package named `linux-system-role` for Fedora, Enterprise Linux, and CentOS.

In Red Hat Enterprise Linux is named `rhel-system-roles` and is available since RHEL 8.

If you would like to know more about the available roles and jump immediately to the Ansible Galaxy page or the official website.

Links

- https://galaxy.ansible.com/linux-system-roles
- https://linux-system-roles.github.io/

demo

Configure Kernel Parameters in RedHat-like Linux systems with Ansible System Role.

code

```yaml
1   ---
2   - name: kernel_settings demo
3     hosts: all
4     become: true
5     vars:
6       kernel_settings_sysctrl:
7         - name: fs.file-max
8           value: 400000
9         - name: kernel.threads-max
10          value: 65536
11      kernel_settings_sysfs:
12        - name: /sys/class/net/lo/mtu
13          value: 65000
14      kernel_settings_transparent_hugepages: madvise
15  roles:
16      - linux-system-roles.kernel_settings
```

execution

```
1   $ ansible-playbook -i inventory kernel_settings.yml
2   PLAY [kernel_settings demo] ****************************\
3   *****************************************
4   TASK [Gathering Facts] ********************************\
5   *****************************************
6   [DEPRECATION WARNING]: Distribution fedora 35 on host fed\
7   ora.example.com should use
8   /usr/bin/python3, but is using /usr/bin/python for backwa\
9   rd compatibility with prior Ansible
10  releases. A future Ansible release will default to using \
11  the discovered platform python for this
12  host. See https://docs.ansible.com/ansible/2.9/reference_\
13  appendices/interpreter_discovery.html for
14  more information. This feature will be removed in version\
15   2.12. Deprecation warnings can be
16  disabled by setting deprecation_warnings=False in ansible\
17   .cfg.
```

```
18  ok: [fedora.example.com]
19  TASK [linux-system-roles.kernel_settings : Set version sp\
20  ecific variables] ************************
21  ok: [fedora.example.com]
22  TASK [linux-system-roles.kernel_settings : Ensure require\
23  d packages are installed] ****************
24  ok: [fedora.example.com]
25  TASK [linux-system-roles.kernel_settings : Ensure require\
26  d services are enabled and started] ******
27  ok: [fedora.example.com] => (item=tuned)
28  TASK [linux-system-roles.kernel_settings : Ensure kernel \
29  settings profile directory exists] *******
30  ok: [fedora.example.com]
31  TASK [linux-system-roles.kernel_settings : Generate a con\
32  figuration for kernel settings] **********
33  ok: [fedora.example.com]
34  TASK [linux-system-roles.kernel_settings : Apply kernel s\
35  ettings] *********************************
36  changed: [fedora.example.com]
37  TASK [linux-system-roles.kernel_settings : tuned apply se\
38  ttings] **********************************
39  changed: [fedora.example.com]
40  TASK [linux-system-roles.kernel_settings : verify setting\
41  s] ***************************************
42  included: /usr/share/linux-system-roles/kernel_settings/t\
43  asks/verify_settings.yml for fedora.example.com
44  TASK [linux-system-roles.kernel_settings : check that set\
45  tings are applied correctly] ************
46  ok: [fedora.example.com]
47  TASK [linux-system-roles.kernel_settings : get last verif\
48  y results from log] *********************
49  skipping: [fedora.example.com]
50  TASK [linux-system-roles.kernel_settings : report errors \
51  that are not bootloader errors] **********
52  skipping: [fedora.example.com]
```

```
53  TASK [linux-system-roles.kernel_settings : notify user th\
54  at reboot is needed to apply changes] ****
55  skipping: [fedora.example.com]
56  TASK [linux-system-roles.kernel_settings : set the flag t\
57  hat reboot is needed to apply changes] ***
58  skipping: [fedora.example.com]
59  RUNNING HANDLER [linux-system-roles.kernel_settings : reb\
60  oot the managed host to apply kernel_settings changes] **\
61  *
62  skipping: [fedora.example.com]
63  RUNNING HANDLER [linux-system-roles.kernel_settings : cle\
64  ar the kernel_settings_reboot_required flag] ***
65  skipping: [fedora.example.com]
66  PLAY RECAP *********************************************\
67  *******************************************
68  fedora.example.com          : ok=10   changed=2   unreach\
69  able=0    failed=0    skipped=6    rescued=0    ignored=0
70  [devops@fedora ~]$
```

idempotency

```
1   $ ansible-playbook -i inventory kernel_settings.yml
2   PLAY [kernel_settings demo] *****************************\
3   *******************************************
4   TASK [Gathering Facts] *********************************\
5   *******************************************
6   [DEPRECATION WARNING]: Distribution fedora 35 on host fed\
7   ora.example.com should use
8   /usr/bin/python3, but is using /usr/bin/python for backwa\
9   rd compatibility with prior Ansible
10  releases. A future Ansible release will default to using \
11  the discovered platform python for this
12  host. See https://docs.ansible.com/ansible/2.9/reference_\
13  appendices/interpreter_discovery.html for
14  more information. This feature will be removed in version\
15   2.12. Deprecation warnings can be
```

```
disabled by setting deprecation_warnings=False in ansible\
.cfg.
ok: [fedora.example.com]
TASK [linux-system-roles.kernel_settings : Set version sp\
ecific variables] ************************
ok: [fedora.example.com]
TASK [linux-system-roles.kernel_settings : Ensure require\
d packages are installed] ****************
ok: [fedora.example.com]
TASK [linux-system-roles.kernel_settings : Ensure require\
d services are enabled and started] ******
ok: [fedora.example.com] => (item=tuned)
TASK [linux-system-roles.kernel_settings : Ensure kernel \
settings profile directory exists] *******
ok: [fedora.example.com]
TASK [linux-system-roles.kernel_settings : Generate a con\
figuration for kernel settings] **********
ok: [fedora.example.com]
TASK [linux-system-roles.kernel_settings : Apply kernel s\
ettings] *********************************
ok: [fedora.example.com]
TASK [linux-system-roles.kernel_settings : tuned apply se\
ttings] **********************************
skipping: [fedora.example.com]
TASK [linux-system-roles.kernel_settings : verify setting\
s] ***************************************
skipping: [fedora.example.com]
TASK [linux-system-roles.kernel_settings : notify user th\
at reboot is needed to apply changes] ****
skipping: [fedora.example.com]
TASK [linux-system-roles.kernel_settings : set the flag t\
hat reboot is needed to apply changes] ***
skipping: [fedora.example.com]
PLAY RECAP ***********************************************\
*****************************************
```

```
51  fedora.example.com              : ok=7      changed=0     unreach\
52  able=0      failed=0      skipped=4     rescued=0      ignored=0
53  [devops@fedora ~]$
```

Verification

```
1  [devops@fedora ~]$ sysctl kernel.threads-max
2  kernel.threads-max = 7414
3  [devops@fedora ~]$ cat /sys/class/net/lo/mtu
4  65001
5  [devops@fedora ~]$ cat /sys/kernel/mm/transparent_hugepag\
6  e/enabled
7  always [madvise] never
8  [devops@fedora ~]$
```

Enable or Disable SELinux Boolean on Linux - Ansible module seboolean

How to automate the enabling of the "httpd_use_nfs" SELinux boolean and make it persistent after a reboot on Linux with Ansible.

Ansible Enable or Disable SELinux Boolean on Linux

- ansible.posix.seboolean
- Toggles SELinux booleans

Today we're talking about Ansible module `seboolean`.
The full name is `ansible.posix.seboolean`, which means that is part of the collection of modules to interact with POSIX systems.
It's a module pretty stable and out for years, it toggles SELinux booleans.

It supports a huge variety of Linux distributions and POSIX systems.

It requires the `python3-libsemanage` or `libsemanage-python` package installed on the target system.

Parameters

- name string - The name of the boolean
- state boolean - no/yes
- persistent boolean - no/yes
- ignore_selinux_state boolean - no/yes

Let's see the parameter of the `seboolean` Ansible module.

The only mandatory parameters are "name" and "state".

The parameter "name" specifies the name of the SELinux boolean that we would like to modify.

The parameter "state" allows you to enable or disable the SELinux boolean immediately in the running system.

The parameter "persistent" allows you to specify if the state change is going to be applied to the next boot.

The special parameter "ignore_selinux_state" is useful for scenarios (chrooted environment) where you can't get the current SELinux state.

Links

- apache_selinux man page[75]
- SELinux Booleans CentOS[76]
- SELinux Booleans Gentoo[77]

---

[75]https://linux.die.net/man/8/apache_selinux
[76]https://wiki.centos.org/TipsAndTricks/SelinuxBooleans
[77]https://wiki.gentoo.org/wiki/SELinux/Tutorials/Using_SELinux_booleans

- RHEL8 - Adjusting the policy for sharing NFS and CIFS volumes using SELinux booleans[78]

demo

How to enable or disable SELinux Boolean on Linux with Ansible Playbook.

code

```
1   ---
2   - name: seboolean module demo
3     hosts: all
4     become: true
5     vars:
6       selinux_boolean: "httpd_use_nfs"
7       selinux_value: true
8     tasks:
9       - name: package present
10         ansible.builtin.package:
11           name: "python3-libsemanage"
12           state: present
13       - name: set SELinux boolean
14         ansible.posix.seboolean:
15           name: "{{ selinux_boolean }}"
16           state: "{{ selinux_value }}"
17           persistent: true
```

execution

---

[78]https://access.redhat.com/documentation/en-us/red_hat_enterprise_linux/8/html-single/using_selinux/index#adjusting-the-policy-for-sharing-nfs-and-cifs-volumes-using-selinux-booleans_configuring-selinux-for-applications-and-services-with-non-standard-configurations

```
$ ansible-playbook -i virtualmachines/demo/inventory seli\
nux/selinux_boolean.yml
PLAY [seboolean module demo] ****************************\
***********************************************
TASK [Gathering Facts] *********************************\
***********************************************
ok: [demo.example.com]
TASK [package present] *********************************\
***********************************************
changed: [demo.example.com]
TASK [set SELinux boolean] *****************************\
***********************************************
changed: [demo.example.com]
PLAY RECAP *********************************************\
***********************************************
demo.example.com             : ok=3    changed=2    unreach\
able=0    failed=0    skipped=0    rescued=0    ignored=0
ansible-pilot $
```

idempotency

```
$ ansible-playbook -i virtualmachines/demo/inventory seli\
nux/selinux_boolean.yml
PLAY [seboolean module demo] ****************************\
***********************************************
TASK [Gathering Facts] *********************************\
***********************************************
ok: [demo.example.com]
TASK [package present] *********************************\
***********************************************
ok: [demo.example.com]
TASK [set SELinux boolean] *****************************\
***********************************************
ok: [demo.example.com]
PLAY RECAP *********************************************\
***********************************************
```

```
16   demo.example.com                   : ok=3     changed=0     unreach\
17   able=0     failed=0     skipped=0     rescued=0     ignored=0
18   ansible-pilot $
```

before execution

```
1    $ ssh devops@demo.example.com
2    [devops@demo ~]$ sudo su
3    [root@demo devops]# sestatus
4    SELinux status:                 enabled
5    SELinuxfs mount:                /sys/fs/selinux
6    SELinux root directory:         /etc/selinux
7    Loaded policy name:             targeted
8    Current mode:                   enforcing
9    Mode from config file:          enforcing
10   Policy MLS status:              enabled
11   Policy deny_unknown status:     allowed
12   Memory protection checking:     actual (secure)
13   Max kernel policy version:      33
14   [root@demo devops]# getsebool httpd_use_nfs
15   httpd_use_nfs --> off
16   [root@demo devops]#
```

after execution

```
1    $ ssh devops@demo.example.com
2    [devops@demo ~]$ sudo su
3    [root@demo devops]# getsebool httpd_use_nfs
4    httpd_use_nfs --> on
5    [root@demo devops]# reboot
6    Connection to demo.example.com closed by remote host.
7    Connection to demo.example.com closed.
8    ansible-pilot $ ssh devops@demo.example.com
9    [devops@demo ~]$ sudo su
10   [root@demo devops]# getsebool httpd_use_nfs
```

```
11   httpd_use_nfs --> on
12   [root@demo devops]#
```

Enable or Disable Permissive Domain in SELinux policy on Linux - Ansible module selinux_permissive

How to automate the enabling or disabling of SELinux Permissive policy per single process or domain keeping the whole system under enforcing policy and make it persistent after a reboot on Linux with Ansible.

SELinux Permissive Domain

What is SELinux?
Security-Enhanced Linux (SELinux) is a Linux kernel security module that provides a mechanism for supporting access control security policies, including mandatory access controls (MAC).

What is SELinux Permissive Domain?

SELinux Permissive Domains allow an administrator to configure a single process (domain) to run permissive, rather than making the whole system permissive.

Ansible Enable or Disable Permissive Domain in SELinux policy

- `community.general.selinux_permissive`
- Change permissive domain in SELinux policy

Today we're talking about Ansible module `selinux_permissive`. The full name is `community.general.selinux_permissive`, which means that is part of the collection of modules to community-supported for Ansible.

It supports a huge variety of Linux distributions and it changes the permissive domain in SELinux policy.

It requires the `policycoreutils-python` package installed on the target system for `semanage` utility.

Parameters

- **domain** (name) string - the name of the domain
- **permissive** boolean - no/yes
- no_reload boolean - **no**/yes

Let's see the parameter of the `selinux_permissive` Ansible module. The only mandatory parameters are `domain` and `permissive`.

The parameter `domain` or alias `name` specifies the name of the SELinux domain that we would add to the list of permissive domains.

The parameter `permissive` allows you to enable or disable the SELinux permissive domain immediately in the running system.

The parameter `no_reload` disables the policy reloading after a change of the setting. Default is "no", which causes the reloading of the policy.

Links

- Ansible selinux_permissive_module module[79]
- PermissiveDomainRecipe[80]
- semanage[81]

---

[79]https://docs.ansible.com/ansible/latest/collections/community/general/selinux_permissive_module.html

[80]https://selinuxproject.org/page/PermissiveDomainRecipe

[81]https://www.redhat.com/sysadmin/semanage-keep-selinux-enforcing

demo

How to enable or disable **permissive domain** in SELinux policy on Linux with Ansible Playbook.

code

```
1   ---
2   - name: selinux_permissive module demo
3     hosts: all
4     become: true
5     tasks:
6       - name: semanage present
7         ansible.builtin.package:
8           name: "policycoreutils-python-utils"
9           state: present
10      - name: Change the httpd_t domain to permissive
11        community.general.selinux_permissive:
12          name: httpd_t
13          permissive: true
```

execution

```
1   $ ansible-playbook -i virtualmachines/demo/inventory seli\
2   nux/selinux_permissivedomain.yml
3   PLAY [selinux_permissive module demo] ******************\
4   *******************************************
5   TASK [Gathering Facts] ********************************\
6   *******************************************
7   ok: [demo.example.com]
8   TASK [semanage present] *******************************\
9   *******************************************
10  changed: [demo.example.com]
11  TASK [Change the httpd_t domain to permissive] ********\
12  *******************************************
13  changed: [demo.example.com]
```

```
14  PLAY RECAP ***********************************************\
15  *******************************************
16  demo.example.com              : ok=3     changed=2     unreach\
17  able=0     failed=0     skipped=0     rescued=0     ignored=0
18  ansible-pilot $
```

idempotency

```
1   $ ansible-playbook -i virtualmachines/demo/inventory seli\
2   nux/selinux_permissivedomain.yml
3   PLAY [selinux_permissive module demo] *******************\
4   *******************************************
5   TASK [Gathering Facts] *********************************\
6   *******************************************
7   ok: [demo.example.com]
8   TASK [semanage present] ********************************\
9   *******************************************
10  ok: [demo.example.com]
11  TASK [Change the httpd_t domain to permissive] *********\
12  *******************************************
13  ok: [demo.example.com]
14  PLAY RECAP ***********************************************\
15  *******************************************
16  demo.example.com              : ok=3     changed=0     unreach\
17  able=0     failed=0     skipped=0     rescued=0     ignored=0
18  ansible-pilot $
```

before execution

```
1   $ ssh devops@demo.example.com
2   [devops@demo ~]$ sudo su
3   [root@demo devops]# sestatus
4   SELinux status:                 enabled
5   SELinuxfs mount:                /sys/fs/selinux
6   SELinux root directory:         /etc/selinux
7   Loaded policy name:             targeted
8   Current mode:                   enforcing
9   Mode from config file:          enforcing
10  Policy MLS status:              enabled
11  Policy deny_unknown status:     allowed
12  Memory protection checking:     actual (secure)
13  Max kernel policy version:      33
14  [root@demo devops]# semanage permissive -l
15  bash: semanage: command not found
16  [root@demo devops]#
```

after execution

```
1   $ ssh devops@demo.example.com
2   [devops@demo ~]$ sudo su
3   [root@demo devops]# sestatus
4   SELinux status:                 enabled
5   SELinuxfs mount:                /sys/fs/selinux
6   SELinux root directory:         /etc/selinux
7   Loaded policy name:             targeted
8   Current mode:                   enforcing
9   Mode from config file:          enforcing
10  Policy MLS status:              enabled
11  Policy deny_unknown status:     allowed
12  Memory protection checking:     actual (secure)
13  Max kernel policy version:      33
14  [root@demo devops]# semanage permissive -l
15  Builtin Permissive Types
16  Customized Permissive Types
17  httpd_t
```

```
18   [root@demo devops]# reboot
19   Connection to demo.example.com closed by remote host.
20   Connection to demo.example.com closed.
21   ansible-pilot $ ssh devops@demo.example.com
22   [devops@demo ~]$ sudo su
23   [root@demo devops]# sestatus
24   SELinux status:                  enabled
25   SELinuxfs mount:                 /sys/fs/selinux
26   SELinux root directory:          /etc/selinux
27   Loaded policy name:              targeted
28   Current mode:                    enforcing
29   Mode from config file:           enforcing
30   Policy MLS status:               enabled
31   Policy deny_unknown status:      allowed
32   Memory protection checking:      actual (secure)
33   Max kernel policy version:       33
34   [root@demo devops]# semanage permissive -l
35   Builtin Permissive Types
36   Customized Permissive Types
37   httpd_t
38   [root@demo devops]#
```

Vulnerability Scanner/Detector Log4Shell Remote Code Execution Log4j (CVE-2021–44228) — Ansible log4j-cve-2021–44228

How to automate the Vulnerability Scanner/Detector provided by Red Hat RHSB-2021–009 Log4Shell — Remote Code Execution — log4j (CVE-2021–44228) with Ansible Playbook. Installation of dependency, GPG key verification, Vulnerability Scanner/Detector run, and result display on target Linux machine.

Log4Shell Remote Code Execution Log4j (CVE-2021–44228)

Remember 2014? Heartbleed was a bug in OpenSSL, the most popular open-source code library for Transport Layer Security (TLS) and Secure Sockets Layer (SSL) protocols usage in encrypting websites and software. At the time the flaw allowed to read confidential information allowing the hackers to trick a vulnerable web server with encryption keys.

Back to the present!

Log4j - the Java program compromised by the Log4Shell bug - is a widely used, multi-platform open-source Java logging framework library developed and maintained under the volunteer Apache Software Foundation. Log4j is widely used on servers to record users' activities to analyze later by security or development teams. Hackers could use the Log4Shell flaw to access sensitive information on a variety of devices, plant ransomware attacks, and take over machines to mine cryptocurrencies. The vulnerability was discovered almost by happenstance when Microsoft announced it had found suspicious activity in Minecraft: Java Edition, a popular video game it owns.

The flaw was officially founded by Chen Zhaojun of Alibaba's Cloud Security Team on the 24th of November 2021.

Some estimation to Wiz and EY, the vulnerability affected 93% of enterprise cloud environments. Affected commercial services include Amazon Web Services, Cloudflare, iCloud, Minecraft: Java Edition, Steam, Tencent QQ, and many others.

Links

- Log4Shell[82]
- CVE-2021-44228[83]

---

[82] https://en.wikipedia.org/wiki/Log4Shell
[83] https://cve.mitre.org/cgi-bin/cvename.cgi?name=CVE-2021-44228

- RHSB-2021-009[84]
- Inside the code: How the Log4Shell exploit works[85]

Red Hat detector

version 1.2 release 2021-12-20

- cve-2021-44228–2021-12-20-1836.sh[86]
- cve-2021-44228–2021-12-20-1836.sh.asc[87]

version 1.3 release 2022-01-10

- cve-2021-44228–2022-01-10-1242.sh[88]
- cve-2021-44228–2022-01-10-1242.sh.asc[89]

demo

A real-life demo of how to automate the Red Hat Detector Log4Shell Remote Code Execution Log4j (CVE-2021–44228) on Linux with Ansible playbook.

code

- vars.yml

---

[84] https://access.redhat.com/security/vulnerabilities/RHSB-2021-009
[85] https://news.sophos.com/en-us/2021/12/17/inside-the-code-how-the-log4shell-exploit-works/
[86] https://access.redhat.com/sites/default/files/cve-2021-44228--2021-12-20-1836.sh
[87] https://access.redhat.com/sites/default/files/cve-2021-44228--2021-12-20-1836.sh.asc
[88] https://access.redhat.com/sites/default/files/cve-2021-44228--2022-01-10-1242.sh
[89] https://access.redhat.com/sites/default/files/cve-2021-44228--2022-01-10-1242.sh.asc

```
# Red Hat detector: https://access.redhat.com/security/vu\
lnerabilities/RHSB-2021-009
sh_detector: "cve-2021-44228--2021-12-20-1836.sh"
sh_signature: 'cve-2021-44228--2021-12-20-1836.sh.asc'
detector_baseurl: 'https://access.redhat.com/sites/defaul\
t/files/'
detector_path: "/var/"
detector_dir: "/tmp/cve-2021-44228/"
detector_run_dir: 'tmp'
detector_options: '-n -d --no-progress --scan {{ detector\
_path }}'
gpg_keyid: '7514F77D8366B0D9'
gpg_public_key: 'gpg --keyserver pgp.mit.edu --recv {{ gp\
g_keyid }}'
clean_run_before: true
delete_after: false
verify_gpg: true
```

- log4j-cve-2021–44228.yml

```
---
- name: detector for Apache Log4j (CVE-2021-44228)
  hosts: all
  become: true
  tasks:
    - include_vars: vars.yml

    - name: dependency present
      ansible.builtin.package:
        name: unzip
        state: present
        update_cache: true

    - name: create detector directory
      ansible.builtin.file:
```

```yaml
16          path: '{{ detector_dir }}'
17          state: directory
18
19      - name: download detector file(s)
20        ansible.builtin.get_url:
21          url: "{{ detector_baseurl }}{{ item }}"
22          dest: "{{ detector_dir }}{{ item }}"
23          mode: '0755'
24          owner: root
25          group: root
26        with_items:
27          - '{{ sh_detector }}'
28          - '{{ sh_signature }}'
29
30      - name: gpg public key
31        ansible.builtin.shell: '{{ gpg_public_key }}'
32        when: verify_gpg == true
33
34      - name: gpg verify detector
35        ansible.builtin.shell: 'gpg --verify {{ detector_di\
36  r }}{{ sh_signature }} {{ detector_dir }}{{ sh_detector }\
37  }'
38        when: verify_gpg == true
39
40      - name: remove any detector run directory
41        ansible.builtin.file:
42          path: '{{ detector_dir }}{{ detector_run_dir }}'
43          state: absent
44        when: clean_run_before == true
45
46      - name: create detector run directory
47        ansible.builtin.file:
48          path: '{{ detector_dir }}{{ detector_run_dir }}'
49          state: directory
50
```

```
51      - name: run detector/scanner
52        ansible.builtin.shell: '{{ detector_dir }}{{ sh_det\
53  ector }} {{ detector_options }} --tmp {{ detector_dir }}{\
54  { detector_run_dir }}'
55
56      - name: files in detector run directory
57        ansible.builtin.find:
58          paths: '{{ detector_dir }}{{ detector_run_dir }}'
59        register: vulnerable
60
61      - name: print vulnerable path(s) found
62        ansible.builtin.debug:
63          var: vulnerable
64
65      - name: remove detector directory
66        ansible.builtin.file:
67          path: '{{ detector_dir }}'
68          state: absent
69        when: delete_after == true
```

code with ⬡ in GitHub[90]

execution

```
1   PLAY [detector for Apache Log4j (CVE-2021-44228)] *******\
2   ***********************
3   TASK [Gathering Facts] **********************************\
4   **********************
5   ok: [demo]
6   TASK [include_vars] *************************************\
7   **********************
8   ok: [demo]
9   TASK [dependency present] *******************************\
10  **********************
```

---

[90]https://github.com/lucab85/log4j-cve-2021-44228

```
11  ok: [demo]
12  TASK [create detector directory] **********************\
13  **********************
14  ok: [demo]
15  TASK [download detector file(s)] **********************\
16  **********************
17  ok: [demo] => (item=cve-2021-44228--2021-12-20-1836.sh)
18  ok: [demo] => (item=cve-2021-44228--2021-12-20-1836.sh.as\
19  c)
20  TASK [gpg public key] *********************************\
21  **********************
22  changed: [demo]
23  TASK [gpg verify detector] ****************************\
24  **********************
25  changed: [demo]
26  TASK [remove any detector run directory] **************\
27  **********************
28  changed: [demo]
29  TASK [create detector run directory] ******************\
30  **********************
31  changed: [demo]
32  TASK [run detector/scanner] ***************************\
33  **********************
34  changed: [demo]
35  TASK [files in detector run directory] ************
36  ok: [demo]
37  TASK [print vulnerable path(s) found] *****************\
38  **********************
39  ok: [demo] => {
40      "vulnerable": {
41          "changed": false,
42          "examined": 1,
43          "failed": false,
44          "files": [],
45          "matched": 0,
```

```
46          "msg": "All paths examined",
47          "skipped_paths": {}
48      }
49  }
50  TASK [remove detector directory] **********************\
51  *********************
52  skipping: [demo]
53  PLAY RECAP ************************************************\
54  *********************
55  demo                        : ok=12    changed=5     unreach\
56  able=0    failed=0    skipped=1    rescued=0    ignored=0
```

Ansible Galaxy role

Code also available as Ansible Galaxy role lucab85.ansible_role_-log4shell[91]:

```
1  ansible-galaxy install lucab85.ansible_role_log4shell
```

---

[91]https://galaxy.ansible.com/lucab85/ansible_role_log4shell

Ansible Playbook Code for RedHat-like systems

How to manage some RedHat-like specific configuration.

Register a system with Red Hat Subscription-Manager - Ansible module redhat_subscription

How to automate the registration of a machine RedHat Enterprise Linux 8 to subscription-manager using the access.redhat.com credential, assign a pool of entitlement, and install some packages.

Ansible register a system with Red Hat Subscription-Manager

- community.general.redhat_subscription
- Manage registration and subscriptions to RHSM using the subscription-manager command

Today we're talking about the Ansible module redhat_subscription. The full name is `community.general.redhat_subscription`, which means that is part of the collection `community.general` maintained by the Ansible community
Manage registration and subscriptions to RHSM using the subscription-manager command.
This module is specific for RedHat Enterprise Linux.

Parameters

- state string - present/absent
- username string - access.redhat.com or Satellite 6 username
- password string - access.redhat.com or Satellite 6 password
- auto_attach boolean - no/yes auto-consume available subscriptions
- pool_id list - subscription pool IDs to consume
- pool string - '^(Red Hat Enterprise Server|Red Hat Virtualization)$'
- consumer_id string - resume a previous registration

Let me summarize the main parameters.

The `state` parameter allows you to specify if you want to add or remove a registration from the target machine.

The username and password allow you to specify the `access.redhat.com` website credential or Satellite 6 credential.

Once the machine is registered you need to define which subscription to consume.

The `auto_attach` allows you to auto consume all the available subscriptions for the Machine.

Alternatively you can specify manually the ID in the `pool_id` list or a text with all the products that you want to add.

Another interesting option is the parameter `customer_id` to resume a previous registration.

demo

Live demo of how to register a system with Red Hat Subscription-Manager with Ansible playbook

code

- subscription-manager.yml

```
1   ---
2   - name: subscription-manager module demo
3     hosts: all
4     become: true
5     vars:
6       subscription_username: "username"
7       subscription_password: "password"
8     tasks:
9       - name: register with subscription-manager
10        community.general.redhat_subscription:
11          state: present
12          username: "{{ subscription_username }}"
13          password: "{{ subscription_password }}"
14          auto_attach: true
```

execution

```
1   $ ansible-playbook -i virtualmachines/demo/inventory regi\
2   ster\ RedHat\ subscription/subscription_manager.yml
3   PLAY [subscription-manager module demo] *****************\
4   ******************************************
5   TASK [Gathering Facts] *********************************\
6   ******************************************
7   ok: [demo.example.com]
8   TASK [register with subscription-manager] **************\
9   ******************************************
10  changed: [demo.example.com]
11  PLAY RECAP *********************************************\
12  ******************************************
13  demo.example.com           : ok=2    changed=1    unreach\
14  able=0    failed=0    skipped=0    rescued=0    ignored=0
```

before execution

```
$ ssh devops@demo.example.com
[devops@demo ~]$ sudo su
[root@demo devops]# cat /etc/redhat-release
Red Hat Enterprise Linux release 8.4 (Ootpa)
[root@demo devops]# dnf install nfs-utils
Updating Subscription Management repositories.
Unable to read consumer identity
This system is not registered to Red Hat Subscription Man\
agement. You can use subscription-manager to register.
Last metadata expiration check: 0:28:38 ago on Fri 26 Nov\
 2021 03:38:17 PM UTC.
No match for argument: nfs-utils
Error: Unable to find a match: nfs-utils
[root@demo devops]# subscription-manager status
+-------------------------------------------------+
System Status Details
+-------------------------------------------------+
Overall Status: Unknown
System Purpose Status: Unknown
[root@demo devops]# subscription-manager list
+-------------------------------------------------+
Installed Product Status
+-------------------------------------------------+
Product Name:   Red Hat Enterprise Linux for x86_64
Product ID:     479
Version:        8.4
Arch:           x86_64
Status:         Unknown
Status Details:
Starts:
Ends:
[root@demo devops]# subscription-manager list --available\
 --all
This system is not yet registered. Try 'subscription-mana\
ger register --help' for more information.
```

```
36  [root@demo devops]# subscription-manager refresh
37  This system is not yet registered. Try 'subscription-mana\
38  ger register --help' for more information.
39  [root@demo devops]#
```

after execution

```
1   $ ssh devops@demo.example.com
2   Last login: Fri Nov 26 16:09:35 2021 from 192.168.0.103
3   [devops@demo ~]$ sudo su
4   [root@demo devops]# subscription-manager status
5   +---------------------------------------------+
6   System Status Details
7   +---------------------------------------------+
8   Overall Status: Disabled
9   Content Access Mode is set to Simple Content Access. This\
10   host has access to content, regardless of subscription s\
11  tatus.
12  System Purpose Status: Disabled
13  [root@demo devops]# subscription-manager list
14  +---------------------------------------------+
15  Installed Product Status
16  +---------------------------------------------+
17  Product Name:    Red Hat Enterprise Linux for x86_64
18  Product ID:      479
19  Version:         8.4
20  Arch:            x86_64
21  Status:          Not Subscribed
22  Status Details:
23  Starts:
24  Ends:
25  [root@demo devops]# subscription-manager list --available\
26   --all
27  +---------------------------------------------+
28  Available Subscriptions
29  +---------------------------------------------+
```

```
30   SKU:                 xxxxxxx
31   Contract:            xxxxxxxx
32   Pool ID:             xxxxxxxxxxxxxxxxxxxxxxxxxxxxxxxxx
33   Provides Management: No
34   Available:           100
35   Suggested:           1
36   Service Type:        L1-L3
37   Roles:
38   Service Level:       Self-Support
39   Usage:
40   Add-ons:
41   Subscription Type:   Standard
42   Starts:              11/11/2021
43   Ends:                01/10/2022
44   Entitlement Type:    Physical
45   Subscription Name:   60 Day Product Trial of Red Hat Ansi\
46   ble Automation Platform, Self-Supported
47                        (100 Managed Nodes)
48   Provides:            dotNET on RHEL Beta (for RHEL Server)
49                        Red Hat Satellite
50                        Red Hat CodeReady Linux Builder for \
51   x86_64
52                        Red Hat Ansible Engine
53                        Red Hat Container Images Beta
54                        Red Hat Ansible Automation Platform
55                        Red Hat Enterprise Linux Atomic Host\
56    Beta
57                        Red Hat Container Images
58                        Red Hat Enterprise Linux High Availa\
59   bility for x86_64
60                        Red Hat Single Sign-On
61                        dotNET on RHEL (for RHEL Server)
62                        Red Hat CodeReady Linux Builder for \
63   x86_64 - Extended Update Support
64                        Red Hat Enterprise Linux Resilient S\
```

```
65   torage for x86_64 - Extended Update
66                       Support
67                       Red Hat Enterprise Linux High Availa\
68   bility for x86_64 - Extended Update
69                       Support
70                       Red Hat Enterprise Linux Resilient S\
71   torage for x86_64
72                       Red Hat Software Collections (for RH\
73   EL Server)
74                       Red Hat Satellite Capsule
75                       Red Hat Enterprise Linux Atomic Host
76                       Red Hat Developer Tools (for RHEL Se\
77   rver)
78                       Red Hat Software Collections Beta (f\
79   or RHEL Server)
80                       Red Hat Enterprise Linux Server
81                       Red Hat Developer Tools Beta (for RH\
82   EL Server)
83                       Red Hat Enterprise Linux for x86_64
84                       Red Hat Enterprise Linux for x86_64 \
85   - Extended Update Support
86                       Red Hat Developer Toolset (for RHEL \
87   Server)
88   SKU:                xxxxxxx
89   Contract:           xxxxxxxx
90   Pool ID:            xxxxxxxxxxxxxxxxxxxxxxxxxxxxxxxxx
91   Provides Management: No
92   Available:          100
93   Suggested:          1
94   Service Type:       L1-L3
95   Roles:
96   Service Level:      Self-Support
97   Usage:
98   Add-ons:
99   Subscription Type:  Standard
```

```
Starts:                 11/19/2021
Ends:                   01/18/2022
Entitlement Type:       Physical
[root@demo devops]# subscription-manager refresh
All local data refreshed
[root@demo devops]# dnf install nfs-utils
Updating Subscription Management repositories.
Last metadata expiration check: 0:02:31 ago on Fri 26 Nov\
 2021 04:09:10 PM UTC.
Dependencies resolved.
========================================================\
================================================
 Package                Arch            Version         \
 Repository                             Size
========================================================\
================================================
Installing:
 nfs-utils              x86_64          1:2.3.3-46.el8   \
 rhel-8-for-x86_64-baseos-rpms          500 k
Installing dependencies:
 gssproxy               x86_64          0.8.0-19.el8     \
 rhel-8-for-x86_64-baseos-rpms          119 k
 keyutils               x86_64          1.5.10-6.el8     \
 rhel-8-for-x86_64-baseos-rpms           63 k
 libverto-libevent      x86_64          0.3.0-5.el8      \
 rhel-8-for-x86_64-baseos-rpms           16 k
 python3-pyyaml         x86_64          3.12-12.el8      \
 rhel-8-for-x86_64-baseos-rpms          193 k
 quota                  x86_64          1:4.04-14.el8    \
 rhel-8-for-x86_64-baseos-rpms          214 k
 quota-nls              noarch          1:4.04-14.el8    \
 rhel-8-for-x86_64-baseos-rpms           95 k
 rpcbind                x86_64          1.2.5-8.el8      \
 rhel-8-for-x86_64-baseos-rpms           70 k
Transaction Summary
```

```
135  =================================================================\
136  =====================================================
137  Install   8 Packages
138  Total download size: 1.2 M
139  Installed size: 3.7 M
140  Is this ok [y/N]: n
141  Operation aborted.
142  [root@demo devops]# subscription-manager status
143  +--------------------------------------------+
144     System Status Details
145  +--------------------------------------------+
146  Overall Status: Disabled
147  Content Access Mode is set to Simple Content Access. This\
148   host has access to content, regardless of subscription s\
149  tatus.
150  System Purpose Status: Disabled
151  [root@demo devops]#
```

Install a package in RedHat like systems - Ansible module yum

How to install a package and a specific version of a package in RedHat-like systems: RedHat Enterprise Linux, CentOS, CentOS Stream, Fedora, ClearOS, Oracle Linux, EuroLinux, Fermi Linux, EulerOS, ROSA Linux, Springdale Linux, Asianux.

See also Install a package in Debian like systems - Ansible module apt

Ansible Install a package in RedHat-like systems

Let's talk about the Ansible module YUM and DNF.

The full names are ansible.builtin.yum and ansible.builtin.dnf, which means are part of the collection of modules "builtin" with ansible and shipped with it.

These modules are pretty stable and out for years.

They work on RedHat-like operating systems and Manages packages with the yum/DNF package manager.

For compatibility purpose you probably ended up using more the yum module than the DNF one, that is designed for modern operating systems.

Main Parameters

- name <u>string</u>
- state <u>string</u>
- update_cache <u>boolean</u>
- allow_downgrade <u>boolean</u>

The parameter list is pretty wide but this four are the most important options.

In the "name" parameter you are going to specify the name of the package or the specific version you would like to install.

The "state" specifies the action that we would like to perform. In our case for install is "present or installed".

I'd like to mention some additional parameters that might be useful for you.

For example "update_cache" forces to update the repository metadata before the installation. It could be useful to make sure that the repository is up-to-date.

"allow_downgrade" is an interesting option that allows you to install a previous version of a package currently installed (the downgrade process), default disabled.

Demo

How to install a package in RedHat-like systems with Ansible.

single package

- package install

```
1   ---
2   - name: yum module demo
3     hosts: all
4     become: true
5     tasks:
6       - name: install package
7         yum:
8           name: wget
9           state: present
```

specific package version

- specific package version

```
1   ---
2   - name: yum module demo
3     hosts: all
4     become: true
5     tasks:
6       - name: install package
7         yum:
8           name: wget-1.19.5-7.el8
9           state: present
10          allow_downgrade: true
```

Rolling Update RedHat like systems - Ansible module yum

Maintaining in a consistent state your fleet of machines is one of the most time-consuming tasks of the System Administrator.
I'm going to show you how to perform Rolling Update with Ansible in RedHat-like systems.

See also Install a package in Debian like systems - Ansible module apt

Ansible rolling update packages in RedHat-like systems

Let's talk about how to perform rolling updates in RedHat-like systems using Ansible module yum and DNF.
We already talked about these modules for installing packages but we would like to consider another use case.
Both manage packages with the yum/DNF package manager.

Parameters

- name <u>string</u>
- state <u>string</u>
- update_cache <u>boolean</u>
- bugfix <u>boolean</u>
- security <u>boolean</u>

The parameter list is pretty wide but today we are focus on these four options for our use case.

In the name could be a package or we could select all the packages of the system with the "*" (star symbol).

The state for this case needs to be "latest" so we target the latest version for every package.

The "update_cache" is useful to forces the update of repository metadata before the installation, default no.

Other very interesting options are "bugfix" and "security" which allow you to update only packages marked as bugfix or security-related

Demo

How to automate the rolling update in RedHat-like systems with Ansible Playbook.

- yum.yml

```
1   ---
2   - name: rolling update demo
3     hosts: all
4     become: true
5     tasks:
6       - name: ensure pkg updated
7         yum:
8           name: nginx
9           state: latest
10          update_cache: true
```

- yum-system.yml

```
1    ---
2    - name: rolling update demo
3      hosts: all
4      become: true
5      tasks:
6        - name: ensure system updated
7          yum:
8            name: "*"
9            state: latest
10           update_cache: true
```

Open firewall ports in RedHat like systems - Ansible module firewalld

How to open HTTP and HTTPS firewall ports in RedHat-like systems with firewalld and Ansible.

Ansible open firewall ports in RedHat-like systems

Today we're talking about the Ansible module `firewalld`.
The full name is `ansible.posix.firewalld`, which means that is part of the collection targeting POSIX platforms. This module requires Ansible 2.9+.
It works in RedHat-like systems with firewalld >= 0.2.11 and python firewalld bindings.
It manages arbitrary ports/services with firewalld.

Parameters

- **state** <u>string</u> - enabled / present / absent / disabled
- service <u>string</u> - firewall-cmd - get services

- port <u>string</u> - PORT/PROTOCOL or PORT-PORT/PROTOCOL
- permanent <u>boolean</u> - no/yes
- immediate <u>boolean</u> - **no**/yes

The parameter list is pretty wide but these are the most important options for our use case to open firewall ports.

The "state" parameter is mandatory and specifies to enable or disable a setting.

The options "enabled" accept and "disabled" reject connections for ports.

The options "present" and "absent" are for zone-level operations.

The "service" parameter specifies the name of a service to add/remove to/from firewalld. For the full list please use "firewall-cmd -get-services".

The "port" parameter specifies the name of a port or port range to add/remove to/from firewalld. The format is PORT/PROTOCOL so for example 80/TCP for HTTP connections. You could also specify a range with PORT-PORT/PROTOCOL.

The "permanent" parameter defines if the configuration should persist across reboots. Note that if "permanent" is no, "immediate" is assumed yes.

The "immediate" parameter applies immediately to the configuration of the system.

demo

Let's jump in a real-life demo about how to open firewall ports in RedHat-like systems with Ansible Playbook.

- verify-firewall.sh

```
1   # firewall-cmd --state
2   # systemctrl status firewalld
3   # firewall-cmd --list-all
4   # firewall-cmd --list-services
5   # dnf info nginx
```

- firewalld.yml

```
1   ---
2   - name: firewalld module demo
3     hosts: all
4     become: true
5     tasks:
6   - name: nginx installed
7         ansible.builtin.yum:
8           name: nginx
9           state: present
10  - name: firewalld rules
11        ansible.posix.firewalld:
12          service: "{{ item }}"
13          state: enabled
14          permanent: true
15          immediate: true
16        with_items:
17          - http
18          - https
```

Install Google Chrome in RedHat-like systems - Ansible module rpm_key, yum_repos

How to install the latest Google Chrome Stable on a RedHat-like workstation (RedHat Enterprise Linux, CentOS, CentOS Stream,

Fedora, etc.) verify software using the public GPG key and set up the Google repository. Code tested with RHEL 8.4.

Ansible install Google Chrome in RedHat-like systems

- Add Google Chrome key ⇒ ansible.builtin.rpm_key
- Add Google Chrome repository ⇒ ansible.builtin.yum_repository
- Update yum cache and install Google Chrome ⇒ ansible.builtin.yum

In order to install Google Chrome on a RedHat-like system, we need to perform three different steps.

The first step is to download the GPG signature key for the repository. You are going to use the `ansible.builtin.rpm_key` Ansible module.

This encrypted key verifies the genuinity of the packages and the repository and guarantees that the software is the same as Google releases.

The second step is to add the add Google Chrome repository to the distribution. It's an extra website where `yum/dnf`, your distribution package manager looks like for software.

You are going to use the `ansible.builtin.yum_repository` Ansible module.

The third step is to update the yum cache for the available packages and install Google Chrome using the `ansible.builtin.yum` Ansible module.

Parameters

- rpm_key key string — URL
- rpm_key state string — present/absent

- yum_repository name string — repository
- yum_repository baseurl string — URL
- yum_repository gpgcheck boolean — enable GPG
- yum_repository gpgkey string — GPG check and key URL
- yum name string — name or package-specific
- yum state string — latest/present/absent
- yum update_cache boolean — no/yes

For the `ansible.builtin.rpm_key` Ansible module I'm going to use two parameters: "key" and "state".

The "key" parameter specifies the URL or the key ID of the repository gpg signature key and the "state" verify that is present in our system after the execution.

For the `ansible.builtin.yum_repository` Ansible module I'm going to use four parameters: "name", "baseurl", "gpgcheck" and "gpgkey".

The "name" parameter specifies the repository parameters and the "baseurl" URL of it.

The "gpgcheck" parameter enables the gpg verification with the URL specified in "gpgkey" parameter.

For the `ansible.builtin.yum` Ansible module I'm going to use three parameters: "name", "state", and "update_cache".

The "name" parameter specifies the package name (Google Chrome in our use-case) and the "state" verify that is present in our system after the execution.

Before installing the package the "update_cache" performs an update of the yum cache to ensure that the latest version of the package is going to be downloaded.

demo

Install Google Chrome in RedHat-like systems with Ansible Playbook.

code

- install_chrome_redhat.yml

```
1   ---
2   - name: install Google Chrome
3     hosts: all
4     become: true
5     tasks:
6       - name: Add Yum signing key
7         rpm_key:
8           key: https://dl.google.com/linux/linux_signing_ke\
9   y.pub
10          state: present
11    - name: Add repository into repo.d list
12        yum_repository:
13          name: google-chrome
14          description: google-chrome repository
15          baseurl: http://dl.google.com/linux/chrome/rpm/st\
16  able/x86_64
17          enabled: true
18          gpgcheck: true
19          gpgkey: https://dl.google.com/linux/linux_signing\
20  _key.pub
21    - name: Install google-chrome-stable
22        yum:
23          name: "google-chrome-stable"
24          state: latest
25          update_cache: true
```

execution

output

```
$ ansible-playbook -i demo/inventory install\ chrome/redh\
at.yml
PLAY [install Google Chrome] ****************************\
*******************************************
TASK [Gathering Facts] *********************************\
*******************************************
ok: [demo.example.com]
TASK [Add Yum signing key] *****************************\
*******************************************
changed: [demo.example.com]
TASK [Add repository into repo.d list] *****************\
*******************************************
changed: [demo.example.com]
TASK [Install google-chrome-stable] ********************\
*******************************************
changed: [demo.example.com]
PLAY RECAP *********************************************\
*******************************************
demo.example.com           : ok=4    changed=3    unreach\
able=0    failed=0    skipped=0    rescued=0    ignored=0
```

verification

```
$ ssh devops@demo.example.com
$ sudo su -
# ls -l /etc/yum.repos.d/
total 420
-rw-r--r--. 1 root root   1485 Sep  4 17:28 epel-modular.\
repo
-rw-r--r--. 1 root root   1304 Sep  1 00:13 epel-playgrou\
nd.repo
-rw-r--r--. 1 root root   1564 Sep  4 17:28 epel-playgrou\
nd.repo.rpmnew
-rw-r--r--. 1 root root   1111 Sep  1 00:13 epel.repo
-rw-r--r--. 1 root root   1422 Sep  4 17:28 epel.repo.rpm\
new
```

```
14    -rw-r--r--. 1 root root    1584 Sep   4 17:28 epel-testing-\
15    modular.repo
16    -rw-r--r--. 1 root root    1258 Sep   1 00:13 epel-testing.\
17    repo
18    -rw-r--r--. 1 root root    1521 Sep   4 17:28 epel-testing.\
19    repo.rpmnew
20    -rw-r--r--. 1 root root     205 Oct 12 14:50 google-chrome\
21    .repo
22    -rw-r--r--. 1 root root 391942 Oct   8 10:54 redhat.repo
23    # cat /etc/yum.repos.d/google-chrome.repo
24    [google-chrome]
25    async = 1
26    baseurl = http://dl.google.com/linux/chrome/rpm/stable/x8\
27    6_64
28    enabled = 1
29    gpgcheck = 1
30    gpgkey = https://dl.google.com/linux/linux_signing_key.pub
31    name = google-chrome repository
32    # rpm -qa | grep google-chrome-stable
33    google-chrome-stable-94.0.4606.81-1.x86_64
34    [root@demo ~]# yum list installed google-chrome-stable
35    Updating Subscription Management repositories.
36    Installed Packages
37    google-chrome-stable.x86_64                       94.0.460\
38    6.81-1                          @google-chrome
```

Install Microsoft Edge in RedHat-like systems - Ansible module rpm_key, yum_repository and yum

How to install the latest Microsoft Edge Stable on a RedHat-like workstation verify software using the public GPG key and set up the Microsoft repository. Included code tested in Fedora 34.

Microsoft Edge on Linux

Microsoft Edge is available in the following channels:

- Stable Channel
- Beta Channel - Major update every 4 weeks
- Dev Channel - Updated weekly
- Canary Channel - Updated daily

More information https://www.microsoftedgeinsider.com/en-us/download/

Ansible install Microsoft Edge in RedHat-like systems

- Add Microsoft Edge key ⇒ ansible.builtin.rpm_key
- Add Microsoft Edge repository ⇒ ansible.builtin.yum_repository
- Update yum cache and install Microsoft Edge ⇒ ansible.builtin.yum

In order to install Microsoft Edge on a RedHat-like system, we need to perform three different steps.

The first step is to download the GPG signature key for the repository. You are going to use the `ansible.builtin.rpm_key` Ansible module.

This encrypted key verifies the genuinity of the packages and the repository and guarantees that the software is the same as Microsoft releases.

The second step is to add the add Microsoft Edge repository to the distribution. It's an extra website where `yum/dnf`, your distribution package manager looks like for software.

You are going to use the `ansible.builtin.yum_repository` Ansible module.

The third step is to update the yum cache for the available packages and install Microsoft Edge using the `ansible.builtin.yum` Ansible module.

Parameters

- rpm_key key string - URL
- rpm_key state string - present/absent
- yum_repository name string - repository
- yum_repository baseurl string - URL
- yum_repository gpgcheck boolean gpgkey string - GPG check and key URL
- yum name string - name or package-specific
- yum state string - latest/present/absent
- yum update_cache boolean - no/yes

For the `ansible.builtin.rpm_key` Ansible module I'm going to use two parameters: "key" and "state".

The "key" parameter specifies the URL or the key ID of the repository gpg signature key and the "state" verify that is present in our system after the execution.

For the `ansible.builtin.yum_repository` Ansible module I'm going to use four parameters: "name", "baseurl", "gpgcheck" and "gpgkey".

The "name" parameter specifies the repository parameters and the "baseurl" URL of it.

The "gpgcheck" parameter enables the GPG verification with the URL specified in "gpgkey" parameter.

For the `ansible.builtin.yum` Ansible module I'm going to use three parameters: "name", "state", and "update_cache".

The "name" parameter specifies the package name (Microsoft Edge in our use-case) and the "state" verify that is present in our system after the execution.

Before installing the package the "update_cache" performs an update of the apt cache to ensure that the latest version of the package is going to be downloaded.

demo

Let's jump in a real-life Ansible Playbook to install Microsoft Edge in RedHat-like systems.

code

- install_microsoft_edge_redhat.yml

```
1   ---
2   - name: install Microsoft Edge
3     hosts: all
4     become: true
5     tasks:
6       - name: Add Yum signing key
7         ansible.builtin.rpm_key:
8           key: "https://packages.microsoft.com/keys/microso\
9   ft.asc"
10          state: present
11  - name: Add repository into repo.d list
12        ansible.builtin.yum_repository:
13          name: microsoft-edge
14          description: microsoft-edge
15          baseurl: "https://packages.microsoft.com/yumrepos\
16  /edge/"
17          enabled: true
18          gpgcheck: true
19          gpgkey: "https://packages.microsoft.com/keys/micr\
20  osoft.asc"
21  - name: Install microsoft-edge-stable
```

```
22        ansible.builtin.yum:
23          name: "microsoft-edge-stable"
24          state: latest
25          update_cache: true
```

execution

```
1  $ ansible-playbook -i fedora/inventory install\ edge/redh\
2  at.yml
3
4  PLAY [install Microsoft Edge] ***************************\
5  *******************************************
6
7  TASK [Gathering Facts] *********************************\
8  *******************************************
9  ok: [fedora.example.com]
10
11 TASK [Add Yum signing key] *****************************\
12 *******************************************
13 changed: [fedora.example.com]
14
15 TASK [Add repository into repo.d list] *****************\
16 *******************************************
17 changed: [fedora.example.com]
18
19 TASK [Install microsoft-edge-stable] *******************\
20 *******************************************
21 changed: [fedora.example.com]
22
23 PLAY RECAP *********************************************\
24 *******************************************
25 fedora.example.com          : ok=4    changed=3    unreach\
26 able=0    failed=0    skipped=0    rescued=0    ignored=0
```

verification

```
$ ssh devops@fedora.example.com
[devops@demo ~]$ sudo su
[root@demo devops]# yum list installed microsoft-edge-sta\
ble
Installed Packages
microsoft-edge-stable.x86_64                      95.0.102\
0.40-1                            @microsoft-edge
[root@demo devops]# rpm -qa | grep microsoft-edge-stable
microsoft-edge-stable-95.0.1020.40-1.x86_64
[root@demo devops]# ls -al /etc/yum.repos.d/
total 40
drwxr-xr-x.  2 root root 4096 Nov  1 11:15 .
drwxr-xr-x. 77 root root 4096 Nov  1 11:16 ..
-rw-r--r--.  1 root root  728 Apr 12  2021 fedora-cisco-o\
penh264.repo
-rw-r--r--.  1 root root 1302 Apr 12  2021 fedora-modular\
.repo
-rw-r--r--.  1 root root 1239 Apr 12  2021 fedora.repo
-rw-r--r--.  1 root root 1349 Apr 12  2021 fedora-updates\
-modular.repo
-rw-r--r--.  1 root root 1286 Apr 12  2021 fedora-updates\
.repo
-rw-r--r--.  1 root root 1391 Apr 12  2021 fedora-updates\
-testing-modular.repo
-rw-r--r--.  1 root root 1344 Apr 12  2021 fedora-updates\
-testing.repo
-rw-r--r--.  1 root root  190 Nov  1 11:16 microsoft-edge\
.repo
[root@demo devops]# cat /etc/yum.repos.d/microsoft-edge.r\
epo
[microsoft-edge]
async = 1
baseurl = https://packages.microsoft.com/yumrepos/edge/
enabled = 1
gpgcheck = 1
```

```
36   gpgkey = https://packages.microsoft.com/keys/microsoft.asc
37   name = microsoft-edge
```

NFS Server - Export an NFS Share in RedHat-like systems: RHEL, CentOS, CentOS Stream, Fedora - Ansible modules yum, file, lineinfile, command, firewalld, service

How to automate the configuration of an NFS Server with Ansible in six tasks: install packages, create the NFS share directory, add share in the config, export shares, restart NFS service and enable on boot, and open firewall service ports on boot in a RedHat-like Linux target system.

Export an NFS Share in RedHat-like systems

- install packages ⇒ ansible.builtin.yum
- create directory ⇒ ansible.builtin.file
- share in config ⇒ ansible.builtin.lineinfile
- export shares ⇒ ansible.builtin.command
- restart service ⇒ ansible.builtin.service
- open firewall ⇒ ansible.posix.firewalld

Let's talk about how to export an NFS Share in RedHat-like Linux systems.

The full process requires six steps that you could automate with six different Ansible modules.

Firstly you need to install the `nfs-utils` package and dependency using the `ansible.builtin.yum` Ansible module.

Secondly, you need to create the share directory and assign the

permission using the `ansible.builtin.file` Ansible module.
Thirdly you need to add the share in the `/etc/exports` config file using the `ansible.builtin.lineinfile` Ansible module to add text lines in files.
Fourthly you need to export shares executing the `exportfs` command line utility via `ansible.builtin.command` Ansible module, unfortunately there is not a specific module, yet.
Fifthly you need to restart the `nfs-server` service and all the dependent using the `ansible.builtin.service` Ansible module.
Sixth you need to open the relevant firewall service-related ports using the `ansible.posix.firewalld` Ansible module.

demo

Export NFS Share in RedHat-like systems with Ansible Playbook.

code

- nfs_server_redhat.yml

```
1   ---
2   - name: nfs service demo
3     hosts: all
4     become: true
5     vars:
6       share: "/nfs/share"
7       options: "192.168.0.0/24(rw,sync,root_squash)"
8       permission: '0777'
9     tasks:
10      - name: NFS server installed
11        ansible.builtin.yum:
12          name:
13            - nfs-utils
14            - nfs4-acl-tools
```

```
15         state: present
16
17    - name: share directory exists
18      ansible.builtin.file:
19        path: "{{ share }}"
20        state: directory
21        mode: "{{ permission }}"
22        owner: root
23        group: root
24
25    - name: share in /etc/exports file
26      ansible.builtin.lineinfile:
27        path: /etc/exports
28        state: present
29        line: '{{ share }} {{ options }}'
30      notify: restart NFS server
31
32    - name: export share
33      ansible.builtin.command: "exportfs -rav"
34
35    - name: firewall enabled
36      ansible.posix.firewalld:
37        service: "{{ item }}"
38        state: enabled
39        permanent: true
40        immediate: true
41      with_items:
42        - nfs
43        - rpc-bind
44        - mountd
45
46  handlers:
47    - name: restart NFS server
48      ansible.builtin.service:
49        name: nfs-server
```

```
50          state: restarted
51          enabled: true
```

execution

```
 1  $ ansible-playbook -i virtualmachines/demo/inventory serv\
 2  ices/nfs_redhat.yml
 3  PLAY [nfs service demo] *********************************\
 4  *********************************************
 5  TASK [Gathering Facts] *********************************\
 6  *********************************************
 7  ok: [demo.example.com]
 8  TASK [NFS server installed] ****************************\
 9  *********************************************
10  changed: [demo.example.com]
11  TASK [share directory exists] **************************\
12  *********************************************
13  changed: [demo.example.com]
14  TASK [share in /etc/exports file] **********************\
15  *********************************************
16  changed: [demo.example.com]
17  TASK [export share] ************************************\
18  *********************************************
19  changed: [demo.example.com]
20  TASK [firewall enabled] ********************************\
21  *********************************************
22  changed: [demo.example.com] => (item=nfs)
23  changed: [demo.example.com] => (item=rpc-bind)
24  changed: [demo.example.com] => (item=mountd)
25  RUNNING HANDLER [restart NFS server] *******************\
26  *********************************************
27  changed: [demo.example.com]
28  PLAY RECAP *********************************************\
29  *********************************************
30  demo.example.com            : ok=7      changed=6      unreach\
31  able=0     failed=0    skipped=0    rescued=0    ignored=0
```

before execution

```
1   $ ssh devops@demo.example.com
2   [devops@demo ~]$ sudo su
3   [root@demo devops]# cat /etc/redhat-release
4   Red Hat Enterprise Linux release 8.4 (Ootpa)
5   [root@demo devops]# rpm -qa | grep nfs-utils
6   [root@demo devops]# systemctl status nfs-server.service
7   Unit nfs-server.service could not be found.
8   [root@demo devops]# exportfs -s
9   bash: exportfs: command not found
10  [root@demo devops]# cat /etc/exports
11  [root@demo devops]# ls -al /etc/exports
12  -rw-r--r--. 1 root root 0 Sep 10  2018 /etc/exports
13  [root@demo devops]# ls -al /nfs/share
14  ls: cannot access '/nfs/share': No such file or directory
15  [root@demo devops]# firewall-cmd --state
16  running
17  [root@demo devops]# firewall-cmd --list-services
18  cockpit dhcpv6-client ssh
19  [root@demo devops]# firewall-cmd --list-all
20  public (active)
21    target: default
22    icmp-block-inversion: no
23    interfaces: eth0 eth1
24    sources:
25    services: cockpit dhcpv6-client ssh
26    ports:
27    protocols:
28    masquerade: no
29    forward-ports:
30    source-ports:
31    icmp-blocks:
32    rich rules:
33  [root@demo devops]#
```

after execution

```
$ ssh devops@demo.example.com
Last login: Sun Nov 28 16:52:14 2021 from 192.168.0.103
[devops@demo ~]$ sudo su
[root@demo devops]# rpm -qa | grep nfs-utils
nfs-utils-2.3.3-46.el8.x86_64
[root@demo devops]# systemctl status nfs-server.service
☐ nfs-server.service - NFS server and services
   Loaded: loaded (/usr/lib/systemd/system/nfs-server.ser\
vice; enabled; vendor preset: disabled)
  Drop-In: /run/systemd/generator/nfs-server.service.d
           └─order-with-mounts.conf
   Active: active (exited) since Sun 2021-11-28 16:51:39 \
UTC; 1min 22s ago
  Process: 7484 ExecStart=/bin/sh -c if systemctl -q is-a\
ctive gssproxy; then systemctl reload gss>
  Process: 7472 ExecStart=/usr/sbin/rpc.nfsd (code=exited\
, status=0/SUCCESS)
  Process: 7471 ExecStartPre=/usr/sbin/exportfs -r (code=\
exited, status=0/SUCCESS)
 Main PID: 7484 (code=exited, status=0/SUCCESS)
Nov 28 16:51:39 demo.example.com systemd[1]: Starting NFS\
 server and services...
Nov 28 16:51:39 demo.example.com systemd[1]: Started NFS \
server and services.
[root@demo devops]# exportfs -s
/nfs/share  192.168.0.0/24(sync,wdelay,hide,no_subtree_ch\
eck,sec=sys,rw,secure,root_squash,no_all_squash)
[root@demo devops]# cat /etc/exports
/nfs/share 192.168.0.0/24(rw,sync,root_squash)
[root@demo devops]# ls -al /nfs/share
total 0
drwxrwxrwx. 2 root root  6 Nov 28 16:51 .
drwxrwxrwx. 3 root root 19 Nov 28 16:51 ..
[root@demo devops]# firewall-cmd --state
```

```
35   running
36   [root@demo devops]# firewall-cmd --list-services
37   cockpit dhcpv6-client mountd nfs rpc-bind ssh
38   [root@demo devops]# firewall-cmd --list-all
39   public (active)
40     target: default
41     icmp-block-inversion: no
42     interfaces: eth0 eth1
43     sources:
44     services: cockpit dhcpv6-client mountd nfs rpc-bind ssh
45     ports:
46     protocols:
47     masquerade: no
48     forward-ports:
49     source-ports:
50     icmp-blocks:
51     rich rules:
52   [root@demo devops]#
```

Deploy a web server apache httpd on RedHat-like systems - Ansible modules yum, copy, service firewalld

How to automate the deployment of a web server apache httpd on RedHat-like systems with custom web page taking care of downloading, installing, and enabling the service instantly and on boot and open the relevant firewall ports with Ansible modules yum, copy, service firewalld. RedHat Enterprise Linux, CentOS, CentOS Stream, Fedora, ClearOS, Oracle Linux, EuroLinux, Fermi Linux, EulerOS, ROSA Linux, Springdale Linux, Asianux.

Deploy a web server apache httpd on RedHat-like systems

- install packages ⇒ ansible.builtin.yum
- custom index.html ⇒ ansible.builtin.copy
- start service ⇒ ansible.builtin.service
- open firewall ⇒ ansible.posix.firewalld

Let's talk about how to Deploy a web server apache httpd on RedHat-like Linux systems.

The full process requires four steps that you could automate with different Ansible modules.

Firstly you need to install the `httpd` package and dependency using the `ansible.builtin.yum` Ansible module.

Secondly, you need to create the custom index.html with `ansible.builtin.copy` Ansible module. You could upgrade this step using the `template` module.

Thirsty you need to start the `httpd` service and enable on boot and all the dependant using the `ansible.builtin.service` Ansible module.

Fourthly you need to open the relevant firewall service-related ports using the `ansible.posix.firewalld` Ansible module.

demo

Deploy a web server apache httpd on RedHat-like systems with Ansible Playbook.

code

```
 1   ---
 2   - name: setup webserver
 3     hosts: all
 4     become: true
 5     tasks:
 6       - name: httpd installed
 7         ansible.builtin.yum:
 8           name: httpd
 9           state: latest
10       - name: custom index.html
11         ansible.builtin.copy:
12           dest: /var/www/html/index.html
13           content: |
14             Custom Web Page
15       - name: httpd service enabled
16         ansible.builtin.service:
17           name: httpd
18           enabled: true
19           state: started
20       - name: open firewall
21         ansible.posix.firewalld:
22           service: http
23           state: enabled
24           immediate: true
25           permanent: true
```

execution

```
1   ansible-pilot $ ansible-playbook -i virtualmachines/demo/\
2   inventory services/httpd_redhat.yml
3   PLAY [setup webserver] *******************************\
4   *********************************************
5   TASK [Gathering Facts] *******************************\
6   *********************************************
7   ok: [demo.example.com]
8   TASK [httpd installed] *******************************\
9   *********************************************
10  changed: [demo.example.com]
11  TASK [custom index.html] *****************************\
12  *********************************************
13  changed: [demo.example.com]
14  TASK [httpd service enabled] *************************\
15  *********************************************
16  changed: [demo.example.com]
17  TASK [open firewall] *********************************\
18  *********************************************
19  changed: [demo.example.com]
20  PLAY RECAP ******************************************\
21  *********************************************
22  demo.example.com           : ok=5    changed=4    unreach\
23  able=0    failed=0    skipped=0    rescued=0    ignored=0
24  ansible-pilot $
```

idempotency

```
ansible-pilot $ ansible-playbook -i virtualmachines/demo/\
inventory services/httpd_redhat.yml
PLAY [setup webserver] *********************************\
***********************************************
TASK [Gathering Facts] *********************************\
***********************************************
ok: [demo.example.com]
TASK [httpd installed] *********************************\
***********************************************
ok: [demo.example.com]
TASK [custom index.html] *********************************\
***********************************************
ok: [demo.example.com]
TASK [httpd service enabled] *********************************\
***********************************************
ok: [demo.example.com]
TASK [open firewall] *********************************\
***********************************************
ok: [demo.example.com]
PLAY RECAP *********************************\
***********************************************
demo.example.com               : ok=5    changed=0    unreach\
able=0    failed=0    skipped=0    rescued=0    ignored=0
ansible-pilot $
```

before execution

```
ansible-pilot $ ssh devops@demo.example.com
Last login: Sat Feb 12 10:08:51 2022 from 192.168.0.100
[devops@demo ~]$ sudo su
[root@demo devops]# cat /etc/os-release
NAME="Red Hat Enterprise Linux"
VERSION="8.5 (Ootpa)"
ID="rhel"
ID_LIKE="fedora"
VERSION_ID="8.5"
PLATFORM_ID="platform:el8"
PRETTY_NAME="Red Hat Enterprise Linux 8.5 (Ootpa)"
ANSI_COLOR="0;31"
CPE_NAME="cpe:/o:redhat:enterprise_linux:8::baseos"
HOME_URL="https://www.redhat.com/"
DOCUMENTATION_URL="https://access.redhat.com/documentatio\
n/red_hat_enterprise_linux/8/"
BUG_REPORT_URL="https://bugzilla.redhat.com/"
REDHAT_BUGZILLA_PRODUCT="Red Hat Enterprise Linux 8"
REDHAT_BUGZILLA_PRODUCT_VERSION=8.5
REDHAT_SUPPORT_PRODUCT="Red Hat Enterprise Linux"
REDHAT_SUPPORT_PRODUCT_VERSION="8.5"
[root@demo devops]# dnf list installed httpd
Updating Subscription Management repositories.
Error: No matching Packages to list
[root@demo devops]# rpm -qa | grep httpd
[root@demo devops]# cat /var/www/html/index.html
cat: /var/www/html/index.html: No such file or directory
[root@demo devops]# ls -al /var/www
ls: cannot access '/var/www': No such file or directory
[root@demo devops]#
```

after execution

```
1   ansible-pilot $ ssh devops@demo.example.com
2   Last login: Sat Feb 12 10:12:47 2022 from 192.168.0.100
3   [devops@demo ~]$ sudo su
4   [root@demo devops]# dnf list installed httpd
5   Updating Subscription Management repositories.
6   Installed Packages
7   httpd.x86_64          2.4.37-43.module+el8.5.0+13806+b30d9eec\
8   .1          @rhel-8-for-x86_64-appstream-rpms
9   [root@demo devops]# rpm -qa | grep httpd
10  httpd-tools-2.4.37-43.module+el8.5.0+13806+b30d9eec.1.x86\
11  _64
12  httpd-filesystem-2.4.37-43.module+el8.5.0+13806+b30d9eec.\
13  1.noarch
14  httpd-2.4.37-43.module+el8.5.0+13806+b30d9eec.1.x86_64
15  redhat-logos-httpd-84.5-1.el8.noarch
16  [root@demo devops]# cat /var/www/html/index.html
17  Custom Web Page
18  [root@demo devops]#
```

Custom Web Page

web server apache httpd on RedHat-like system

Recap

Now you know how to deploy a web server apache httpd on RedHat-like systems with Ansible.

Deploy a proxy server squid on RedHat-like systems - Ansible modules yum, template, service and firewalld

How to automate the configuration of squid proxy server on Red Hat like target Linux system installing the packages, set the configuration files, run the service immediately and after boot and open the relevant firewall port. RedHat Enterprise Linux, CentOS, CentOS Stream, Fedora, ClearOS, Oracle Linux, EuroLinux, Fermi Linux, EulerOS, ROSA Linux, Springdale Linux, Asianux.

Deploy a proxy server squid on RedHat-like

- install packages ⇒ `ansible.builtin.yum`
- configuration ⇒ `ansible.builtin.template`
- start service ⇒ `ansible.builtin.service`
- open firewall ⇒ `ansible.posix.firewalld`

How to deploy a proxy server squid on RedHat-like Linux system? The full process requires four steps that you could automate with different Ansible modules.

Firstly you need to install the `squid` package and dependency using the `ansible.builtin.yum` Ansible module.

Secondly, you need to create the custom configuration with the `ansible.builtin.template` Ansible module.

Thirsty you need to start the `squid` service and enable it on boot and all the dependant using the `ansible.builtin.service` Ansible module.

Fourthly you need to open the relevant firewall service-related ports using the `ansible.posix.firewalld` Ansible module.

demo

Deploy a proxy server squid on RedHat-like with Ansible Playbook.

code

- proxy_redhat.yml

```
 1   ---
 2   - name: setup proxy
 3     hosts: all
 4     become: true
 5     vars:
 6       squid_port: 3128
 7       localnet: "192.168.0.0/24"
 8     tasks:
 9       - name: squid installed
10         ansible.builtin.yum:
11           name: squid
12           state: latest
13       - name: squid configuration
14         ansible.builtin.template:
15           src: "templates/squid.conf.j2"
16           dest: "/etc/squid/squid.conf"
17       - name: squid service enabled
18         ansible.builtin.service:
19           name: squid
20           enabled: true
```

```
21          state: started
22      - name: open firewall
23        ansible.posix.firewalld:
24          port: "{{ squid_port }}/tcp"
25          state: enabled
26          immediate: true
27          permanent: true
```

- templates/squid.conf.j2

```
 1  acl localnet src {{ localnet }}
 2  acl SSL_ports port 443
 3  acl CONNECT method CONNECT
 4  acl Safe_ports port 21
 5  acl Safe_ports port 80
 6  acl Safe_ports port 443
 7  http_access deny !Safe_ports
 8  http_access deny CONNECT !SSL_ports
 9  http_access allow localhost manager
10  http_access deny manager
11  http_access allow localnet
12  http_access allow localhost
13  http_access deny all
14  http_port {{ squid_port }}
15  coredump_dir /var/spool/squid 10000 16 256
16  refresh_pattern ^ftp:   1440 20% 10080
17  refresh_pattern ^gopher: 1440 0% 1440
18  refresh_pattern -i (/cgi-bin/|\?) 0 0% 0
19  refresh_pattern .   0 20% 4320
```

execution

```
ansible-pilot $ ansible-playbook -i virtualmachines/proxy\
/inventory services/proxy_redhat.yml
PLAY [setup proxy] ************************************\
******************************************
TASK [Gathering Facts] *******************************\
******************************************
ok: [proxy.example.com]
TASK [squid installed] *******************************\
******************************************
changed: [proxy.example.com]
TASK [squid configuration] ***************************\
******************************************
changed: [proxy.example.com]
TASK [squid service enabled] *************************\
******************************************
changed: [proxy.example.com]
TASK [open firewall] *********************************\
******************************************
changed: [proxy.example.com]
PLAY RECAP ***********************************************\
******************************************
proxy.example.com              : ok=5     changed=4     unreach\
able=0     failed=0     skipped=0     rescued=0     ignored=0
ansible-pilot $
```

idempotency

```
ansible-pilot $ ansible-playbook -i virtualmachines/proxy\
/inventory services/proxy_redhat.yml
PLAY [setup proxy] **************************************\
*******************************************
TASK [Gathering Facts] *********************************\
*******************************************
ok: [proxy.example.com]
TASK [squid installed] *********************************\
*******************************************
ok: [proxy.example.com]
TASK [squid configuration] *****************************\
*******************************************
ok: [proxy.example.com]
TASK [squid service enabled] ***************************\
*******************************************
ok: [proxy.example.com]
TASK [open firewall] ***********************************\
*******************************************
ok: [proxy.example.com]
PLAY RECAP *********************************************\
*******************************************
proxy.example.com          : ok=5    changed=0    unreach\
able=0    failed=0    skipped=0    rescued=0    ignored=0
ansible-pilot $
```

before execution

```
1   ansible-pilot $ ssh devops@proxy.example.com
2   Last login: Fri Feb 18 11:25:15 2022 from 192.168.0.59
3   [devops@proxy ~]$ sudo su
4   [root@proxy devops]# cat /etc/os-release
5   NAME="Red Hat Enterprise Linux"
6   VERSION="8.5 (Ootpa)"
7   ID="rhel"
8   ID_LIKE="fedora"
9   VERSION_ID="8.5"
10  PLATFORM_ID="platform:el8"
11  PRETTY_NAME="Red Hat Enterprise Linux 8.5 (Ootpa)"
12  ANSI_COLOR="0;31"
13  CPE_NAME="cpe:/o:redhat:enterprise_linux:8::baseos"
14  HOME_URL="https://www.redhat.com/"
15  DOCUMENTATION_URL="https://access.redhat.com/documentatio\
16  n/red_hat_enterprise_linux/8/"
17  BUG_REPORT_URL="https://bugzilla.redhat.com/"
18  REDHAT_BUGZILLA_PRODUCT="Red Hat Enterprise Linux 8"
19  REDHAT_BUGZILLA_PRODUCT_VERSION=8.5
20  REDHAT_SUPPORT_PRODUCT="Red Hat Enterprise Linux"
21  REDHAT_SUPPORT_PRODUCT_VERSION="8.5"
22  [root@proxy devops]# dnf list installed squid
23  Waiting for process with pid 5699 to finish.
24  Error: No matching Packages to list
25  [root@proxy devops]# rpm -qa | grep squid
26  [root@proxy devops]# cat /etc/squid/squid.conf
27  cat: /etc/squid/squid.conf: No such file or directory
28  [root@proxy devops]# exit
29  exit
30  [devops@proxy ~]$ exit
31  logout
32  Connection to proxy.example.com closed.
33  ansible-pilot $ curl -O -L "https://www.ansiblepilot.com/\
34  index.html" -x "proxy.example.com:3128"
35    % Total    % Received % Xferd  Average Speed   Time    \
```

```
36  Time         Time   Current
37                                      Dload  Upload   Total   \
38  Spent    Left  Speed
39    0      0     0       0      0      0       0       0 --:--:-- --\
40  :--:-- --:--:--     0
41  curl: (7) Failed to connect to proxy.example.com port 312\
42  8: Connection refused
43  ansible-pilot $
```

after execution

```
1   ansible-pilot $ ssh devops@proxy.example.com
2   Last login: Fri Feb 18 11:29:25 2022 from 192.168.0.59
3   [devops@proxy ~]$ sudo su
4   [root@proxy devops]# cat /etc/os-release
5   NAME="Red Hat Enterprise Linux"
6   VERSION="8.5 (Ootpa)"
7   ID="rhel"
8   ID_LIKE="fedora"
9   VERSION_ID="8.5"
10  PLATFORM_ID="platform:el8"
11  PRETTY_NAME="Red Hat Enterprise Linux 8.5 (Ootpa)"
12  ANSI_COLOR="0;31"
13  CPE_NAME="cpe:/o:redhat:enterprise_linux:8::baseos"
14  HOME_URL="https://www.redhat.com/"
15  DOCUMENTATION_URL="https://access.redhat.com/documentatio\
16  n/red_hat_enterprise_linux/8/"
17  BUG_REPORT_URL="https://bugzilla.redhat.com/"
18  REDHAT_BUGZILLA_PRODUCT="Red Hat Enterprise Linux 8"
19  REDHAT_BUGZILLA_PRODUCT_VERSION=8.5
20  REDHAT_SUPPORT_PRODUCT="Red Hat Enterprise Linux"
21  REDHAT_SUPPORT_PRODUCT_VERSION="8.5"
22  [root@proxy devops]# dnf list installed squid
23  Updating Subscription Management repositories.
24  Installed Packages
25  squid.x86_64              7:4.15 1.module+el8.5.0+11469+24c223d\
```

```
26  9          @rhel-8-for-x86_64-appstream-rpms
27  [root@proxy devops]# rpm -qa | grep squid
28  squid-4.15-1.module+el8.5.0+11469+24c223d9.x86_64
29  [root@proxy devops]# cat /etc/squid/squid.conf
30  acl localnet src 192.168.0.0/24
31  acl SSL_ports port 443
32  acl CONNECT method CONNECT
33  acl Safe_ports port 21
34  acl Safe_ports port 80
35  acl Safe_ports port 443
36  http_access deny !Safe_ports
37  http_access deny CONNECT !SSL_ports
38  http_access allow localhost manager
39  http_access deny manager
40  http_access allow localnet
41  http_access allow localhost
42  http_access deny all
43  http_port 3128
44  coredump_dir /var/spool/squid 10000 16 256
45  refresh_pattern ^ftp:   1440 20% 10080
46  refresh_pattern ^gopher: 1440 0% 1440
47  refresh_pattern -i (/cgi-bin/|\?) 0 0% 0
48  refresh_pattern .   0 20% 4320
49  [root@proxy devops]# ls -al /var/spool/squid/
50  total 0
51  drwxr-x---. 2 squid squid  6 Jun 18  2021 .
52  drwxr-xr-x. 9 root  root  97 Feb 18 11:17 ..
53  [root@proxy devops]# exit
54  exit
55  [devops@proxy ~]$ exit
56  logout
57  Connection to proxy.example.com closed.
58  ansible-pilot $ curl -O -L "https://www.ansiblepilot.com/\
59  index.html" -x "proxy.example.com:3128"
60    % Total    % Received % Xferd  Average Speed   Time    \
```

```
61   Time       Time  Current
62                               Dload  Upload   Total    \
63   Spent    Left  Speed
64   100 49405    0 49405    0     0   49306       0 --:--:-- 0\
65   :00:01 --:--:-- 49306
66   ansible-pilot $ less index.html
67   ansible-pilot $ rm index.html
68   ansible-pilot $ ssh devops@proxy.example.com
69   Last login: Fri Feb 18 11:29:54 2022 from 192.168.0.59
70   [devops@proxy ~]$ sudo su
71   [root@proxy devops]# cat /var/log/squid/access.log
72   1645183932.399   1002 192.168.0.59 TCP_TUNNEL/200 53662 C\
73   ONNECT www.ansiblepilot.com:443 - HIER_DIRECT/172.67.206.\
74   66 -
75   [root@proxy devops]#
```

Deploy a web server apache httpd virtualhost on RedHat-like systems - Ansible modules yum, file, copy, template, service and firewalld

How to automate the deployment of a web server apache httpd virtual host "example.com" on RedHat-like systems with custom web page taking care of downloading, installing, and enabling the service instantly and on boot and open the relevant firewall ports with Ansible modules yum, file, copy, template, service, and firewalld. CentOS, Fedora, RockyLinux, AlmaLinux, Amazon Linux all the similar distributions.

Deploy a web server apache httpd virtualhost on RedHat-like systems

- install packages ⇒ `ansible.builtin.yum`
- document root ⇒ `ansible.builtin.file`
- custom index.html ⇒ `ansible.builtin.copy`
- Apache virtualhost ⇒ `ansible.builtin.template`
- start service ⇒ `ansible.builtin.service`
- open firewall ⇒ `ansible.posix.firewalld`

Today we're talking about how to Deploy a web server apache httpd on RedHat-like Linux systems.

The full process requires six steps that you could automate with different Ansible modules.

Firstly you need to install the `httpd` package and dependency using the `ansible.builtin.yum` Ansible module.

Secondly, you need to create the document root with the right permission with the `ansible.builtin.file` module.

Thirsty, you need to create the custom index.html with `ansible.builtin.copy` Ansible module. You could upgrade this step using the `template` module.

Fourthly, you need to set up Apache configuration for the specific virtual host using the `ansible.builtin.template` module.

Fifthly, you need to start the `httpd` service and enable it on boot and all the dependant using the `ansible.builtin.service` Ansible module.

Sixthly you need to open the relevant firewall service-related ports using the `ansible.posix.firewalld` Ansible module.

demo

Deploy a web server apache httpd virtual host on RedHat-like systems with Ansible Playbook.

code

- httpd_redhat_vhost.yml

```yaml
1   ---
2   - name: setup webserver with vhost
3     hosts: all
4     become: true
5     vars:
6       app_user: "apache"
7       http_host: "example.com"
8       http_conf: "example.com.conf"
9       http_port: "80"
10    tasks:
11      - name: httpd installed
12        ansible.builtin.yum:
13          name: httpd
14          state: latest
15
16      - name: document root exist
17        ansible.builtin.file:
18          path: "/var/www/{{ http_host }}"
19          state: directory
20          owner: "{{ app_user }}"
21          mode: '0755'
22          setype: "httpd_sys_content_t"
23
24      - name: custom index.html
25        ansible.builtin.copy:
26          dest: "/var/www/{{ http_host }}/index.html"
27          content: |
28            Custom Web Page
29
30      - name: setup Apache virtualhost
31        ansible.builtin.template:
```

```
32          src: "templates/httpd.conf.j2"
33          dest: "/etc/httpd/conf.d/{{ http_conf }}"
34
35      - name: httpd service enabled
36        ansible.builtin.service:
37          name: httpd
38          enabled: true
39          state: restarted
40
41      - name: open firewall
42        ansible.posix.firewalld:
43          service: http
44          state: enabled
45          immediate: true
46          permanent: true
```

- templates/httpd.conf.j2

```
1   <VirtualHost *:{{ http_port }}>
2     ServerAdmin webmaster@localhost
3     ServerName {{ http_host }}
4     ServerAlias www.{{ http_host }}
5     ErrorLog /var/log/httpd/error.log
6     CustomLog /var/log/httpd/access.log combined
7     DocumentRoot "/var/www/{{ http_host }}"
8   </VirtualHost>
```

execution

```
ansible-pilot $ ansible-playbook -i virtualmachines/demo/\
inventory services/httpd_redhat_vhost.yml
PLAY [setup webserver with vhost] **********************\
********************************************
TASK [Gathering Facts] ********************************\
********************************************
ok: [demo.example.com]
TASK [httpd installed] ********************************\
********************************************
changed: [demo.example.com]
TASK [document root exist] ****************************\
********************************************
changed: [demo.example.com]
TASK [custom index.html] ******************************\
********************************************
changed: [demo.example.com]
TASK [setup Apache virtualhost] ***********************\
********************************************
changed: [demo.example.com]
TASK [httpd service enabled] **************************\
********************************************
changed: [demo.example.com]
TASK [open firewall] **********************************\
********************************************
changed: [demo.example.com]
PLAY RECAP ************************************************\
********************************************
demo.example.com                 : ok=7     changed=6     unreach\
able=0    failed=0    skipped=0    rescued=0    ignored=0
ansible-pilot $
```

idempotency

```
ansible-pilot $ ansible-playbook -i virtualmachines/demo/\
inventory services/httpd_redhat_vhost.yml
PLAY [setup webserver with vhost] ********************\
*******************************************
TASK [Gathering Facts] ******************************\
*******************************************
ok: [demo.example.com]
TASK [httpd installed] ******************************\
*******************************************
ok: [demo.example.com]
TASK [document root exist] **************************\
*******************************************
ok: [demo.example.com]
TASK [custom index.html] ****************************\
*******************************************
ok: [demo.example.com]
TASK [setup Apache virtualhost] *********************\
*******************************************
ok: [demo.example.com]
TASK [httpd service enabled] ************************\
*******************************************
ok: [demo.example.com]
TASK [open firewall] ********************************\
*******************************************
ok: [demo.example.com]
PLAY RECAP **********************************************\
*******************************************
demo.example.com              : ok=7     changed=0     unreach\
able=0     failed=0     skipped=0     rescued=0     ignored=0
ansible-pilot $
```

before execution

1   TODO

after execution

```
1    ansible-pilot $ ssh devops@demo.example.com
2    Last login: Tue Mar  1 15:44:18 2022 from 192.168.0.59
3    [devops@demo ~]$ sudo su
4    [root@demo devops]# dnf list httpd
5    Updating Subscription Management repositories.
6    Last metadata expiration check: 0:01:21 ago on Tue 01 Mar\
7     2022 03:43:25 PM UTC.
8    Installed Packages
9    httpd.x86_64        2.4.37-43.module+el8.5.0+13806+b30d9eec\
10   .1         @rhel-8-for-x86_64-appstream-rpms
11   [root@demo devops]# rpm -qa | grep httpd
12   httpd-tools-2.4.37-43.module+el8.5.0+13806+b30d9eec.1.x86\
13   _64
14   redhat-logos-httpd-84.5-1.el8.noarch
15   httpd-filesystem-2.4.37-43.module+el8.5.0+13806+b30d9eec.\
16   1.noarch
17   httpd-2.4.37-43.module+el8.5.0+13806+b30d9eec.1.x86_64
18   [root@demo devops]# cat /etc/httpd/conf.d/example.com.conf
19   <VirtualHost *:80>
20     ServerAdmin webmaster@localhost
21     ServerName example.com
22     ServerAlias www.example.com
23     ErrorLog /var/log/httpd/error.log
24     CustomLog /var/log/httpd/access.log combined
25     DocumentRoot "/var/www/example.com"
26   </VirtualHost>
27   [root@demo devops]# cat /var/www/example.com/index.html
28   Custom Web Page
29   [root@demo devops]# ls -al /var/www/example.com/
30   total 4
31   drwxr-xr-x. 2 apache root 24 Mar  1 15:43 .
32   drwxr-xr-x. 5 root   root 52 Mar  1 15:43 ..
```

```
33  -rw-r--r--. 1 root    root 16 Mar  1 15:43 index.html
34  [root@demo devops]# ls -alZ /var/www/example.com/
35  total 4
36  drwxr-xr-x. 2 apache root unconfined_u:object_r:httpd_sys\
37  _content_t:s0 24 Mar  1 15:43 .
38  drwxr-xr-x. 5 root    root system_u:object_r:httpd_sys_con\
39  tent_t:s0     52 Mar  1 15:43 ..
40  -rw-r--r--. 1 root    root system_u:object_r:httpd_sys_con\
41  tent_t:s0     16 Mar  1 15:43 index.html
42  [root@demo devops]# systemctl status httpd
43  ▯ httpd.service - The Apache HTTP Server
44     Loaded: loaded (/usr/lib/systemd/system/httpd.service;\
45   enabled; vendor preset: disabled)
46     Active: active (running) since Tue 2022-03-01 15:43:39\
47  UTC; 2min 20s ago
48       Docs: man:httpd.service(8)
49  Main PID: 7516 (httpd)
50     Status: "Running, listening on: port 80"
51      Tasks: 213 (limit: 4952)
52     Memory: 25.0M
53     CGroup: /system.slice/httpd.service
54             ├─7516 /usr/sbin/httpd -DFOREGROUND
55             ├─7517 /usr/sbin/httpd -DFOREGROUND
56             ├─7518 /usr/sbin/httpd -DFOREGROUND
57             ├─7519 /usr/sbin/httpd -DFOREGROUND
58             └─7520 /usr/sbin/httpd -DFOREGROUND
59  Mar 01 15:43:38 demo.example.com systemd[1]: Starting The\
60   Apache HTTP Server...
61  Mar 01 15:43:39 demo.example.com systemd[1]: Started The \
62  Apache HTTP Server.
63  Mar 01 15:43:39 demo.example.com httpd[7516]: Server conf\
64  igured, listening on: port 80
65  [root@demo devops]# firewall-cmd --list-all
66  public (active)
67    target: default
```

```
 68    icmp-block-inversion: no
 69    interfaces: eth0 eth1
 70    sources:
 71    services: cockpit dhcpv6-client http ssh
 72    ports:
 73    protocols:
 74    forward: no
 75    masquerade: no
 76    forward-ports:
 77    source-ports:
 78    icmp-blocks:
 79    rich rules:
 80    [root@demo devops]# cat /var/log/httpd/access.log
 81    192.168.0.59 - - [01/Mar/2022:16:03:58 +0000] "GET / HT\
 82 TP/1.1" 200 17 "-" "Mozilla/5.0 (Macintosh; Intel Mac OS \
 83 X 10_15_7) AppleWebKit/605.1.15 (KHTML, like Gecko) Versi\
 84 on/15.1 Safari/605.1.15"
 85    192.168.0.59 - - [01/Mar/2022:16:03:58 +0000] "GET /fav\
 86 icon.ico HTTP/1.1" 404 196 "http://demo.example.com/" "Mo\
 87 zilla/5.0 (Macintosh; Intel Mac OS X 10_15_7) AppleWebKit\
 88 /605.1.15 (KHTML, like Gecko) Version/15.1 Safari/605.1.1\
 89 5"
 90    192.168.0.59 - - [01/Mar/2022:16:04:02 +0000] "GET / HT\
 91 TP/1.1" 304 - "-" "Mozilla/5.0 (Macintosh; Intel Mac OS X\
 92  10_15_7) AppleWebKit/605.1.15 (KHTML, like Gecko) Versio\
 93 n/15.1 Safari/605.1.15"
 94    192.168.0.59 - - [01/Mar/2022:16:04:10 +0000] "GET /fav\
 95 icon.ico HTTP/1.1" 404 196 "http://demo.example.com/" "Mo\
 96 zilla/5.0 (Macintosh; Intel Mac OS X 10_15_7) AppleWebKit\
 97 /605.1.15 (KHTML, like Gecko) Version/15.1 Safari/605.1.1\
 98 5"
 99    192.168.0.59 - - [01/Mar/2022:16:04:55 +0000] "GET / HT\
100 TP/1.1" 304 - "-" "Mozilla/5.0 (Macintosh; Intel Mac OS X\
101  10_15_7) AppleWebKit/605.1.15 (KHTML, like Gecko) Versio\
102 n/15.1 Safari/605.1.15"
```

```
103    192.168.0.59 - - [01/Mar/2022:16:04:57 +0000] "-" 408 -\
104    "-" "-"
```

Custome Web Page

web server apache httpd virtual host on RedHat-like system

Ansible Playbook Code for Debian-like systems

How to manage some Debian-like specific configuration.

Install a package in Debian like systems - Ansible module apt

Some real-life examples of how to install a package in Debian-like systems: Debian, Ubuntu, Linux Mint, MX Linux, Deepin, AntiX, PureOS, Kali Linux, Parrot OS, Devuan, Knoppix, AV Linux Linux.

Ansible Install a package in Debian-like systems

Let's talk about the Ansible module APT.
The full name is "ansible.builtin.apt" which means is part of the collection of modules "builtin" with ansible and shipped with it.
This module is pretty stable and out for years.
It works on Debian-like operating systems and Manages packages with the apt package manager.
It's similar to the yum or DNF module for RedHat-like operating systems.

See also Install a package in RedHat like systems - Ansible module yum

Main Parameters

- name <u>string</u>
- state <u>string</u>
- update_cache <u>boolean</u>

The parameter list is pretty wide but this three are the most important options.

In the "name" parameter you are going to specify the name of the package or the specific version you would like to install.

The state specifies the action that we would like to perform. In our case for install is "present".

"update_cache" forces to update the repository metadata before the installation. It could be useful to make sure that the repository is up-to-date.

Demo

How to install a package in Debian-like systems with Ansible.

```
1  ---
2  - name: module apt demo
3    hosts: all
4    become: true
5    tasks:
6      - name: install package
7        apt:
8          name: curl
9          state: present
```

Rolling Update Debian-like systems - Ansible module apt

Maintaining in a consistent state your fleet of machines is one of the most time-consuming tasks of the System Administrator.
I'm going to show you how to perform Rolling Update with Ansible in Debian-like systems.

 See also Install a package in RedHat like systems - Ansible module yum

Ansible Rolling Update packages in Debian-like systems

Let's talk about rolling updates on Debian-like systems using Ansible module apt.

We already talked about this module for installing packages but we would like to consider another use case.

This module allows you to manage packages with the apt package manager.

Parameters

- name string
- state string
- update_cache boolean
- upgrade no/safe/full/dist

The parameter list is pretty wide but today we are focus on these four options for our use case.

The "name" parameter could be a package or we could select all the packages of the system with the "*" star symbol.

The state for this case needs to be "latest" so we target the latest version for every package.

The "update_cache" is useful to forces the update of repository metadata before the installation.

Another useful option is "upgrade" with four alternatives:

- default is a no,
- if safe, performs an aptitude safe-upgrade,
- if full, performs an aptitude full-upgrade,
- if dist performs an apt-get dist-upgrade.

Demo

How to automate rolling update on Debian-like systems with Ansible Playbook.

- apt-nginx.yml

```yaml
---
- name: rolling update demo
  hosts: all
  become: true
  tasks:
    - name: ensure pkg updated
      ansible.builtin.apt:
        name: nginx
        state: latest
        update_cache: true
```

- apt-system.yml

```
1   ---
2   - name: rolling update demo
3     hosts: all
4     become: true
5     tasks:
6       - name: ensure system updated
7         ansible.builtin.apt:
8           name: "*"
9           state: latest
10          update_cache: true
```

Open firewall ports in Debian like systems - Ansible module ufw

How to open firewall HTTP and HTTPS ports in Debian-like systems using Ansible and ufw, the Uncomplicated Firewall.

Ansible open firewall ports in Debian-like systems

Let's talk about the Ansible module UFW.
The full name is `community.general.ufw`, which means that is part of the collection supported by the Ansible community. This module requires Ansible 2.9+.
It works in Debian-like systems so distributions like Debian, Ubuntu, and Mint with `ufw` firewall, the Uncomplicated Firewall. This module manages the firewall with UFW.

Parameters

The parameter list is pretty wide but this are the most important options for our use case to open firewall ports.

The first set of parameters controls UFW program and the second the single rules.

UFW program parameters

- default <u>string</u> (policy) - allow / deny / reject
- logging <u>string</u> - on / off / low / medium / high /full
- **state** <u>string</u> - enabled / present / absent / disabled

Let's start with three UFW program parameters.

The "default" parameter, also called as "policy", change the default policy for incoming or outgoing traffic.

The "logging" parameter toggles UFW logging. Logged packets use the LOG_KERN syslog facility.

The "state" parameter specify to enable or disable firewall. Four options are possible:

- "enabled" reloads firewall and enables firewall on boot,
- "disabled" unloads firewall and disables firewall on boot,
- "reloaded" reloads firewall,
- "reset" disables and resets firewall to installation defaults.

rule-specific parameters

- rule <u>string</u> - allow / deny / limit / reject
- name <u>string</u> (app) - `/etc/ufw/applications.d`
- port <u>string</u> (to_port) - destination port
- proto <u>string</u> - any / tcp / udp / ipv6 / esp / ah/ gre /igmp

Now let's move to four rule-specific parameters.

The "rule" parameter adds a firewall rule with four options available: "allow" / "deny" / "limit" / "reject".

The "name" parameter, also called "app", uses a profile located in `/etc/ufw/applications.d`.

The "to_port" parameter, also called "port", specifies the destination port. It could be a single port or a range for example (60000:61000). The "proto" parameter specifies the destination protocol.

demo

Let's jump in a real-life demo about how to
open firewall ports in Debian-like systems with Ansible Playbook.

- verify-firewall.sh

```
1   # apt list nginx
2   # sudo ufw status
3   # sudo ufw status verbose
```

- ufw.yml

```
1   ---
2   - name: ufw module demo
3     hosts: all
4     become: true
5     tasks:
6   - name: nginx installed
7       ansible.builtin.apt:
8         name: "nginx"
9         state: "present"
10        update_cache: true
11  - name: ufw enabled
12      community.general.ufw:
13        state: "enabled"
14        policy: "deny"
15        logging: "on"
```

```
16    - name: ufw rules
17        community.general.ufw:
18          rule: "allow"
19          port: "{{ item }}"
20          proto: "tcp"
21        with_items:
22          - "22"
23          - "80"
24          - "443"
```

Install Google Chrome in Debian-like systems - Ansible module apt_key, apt_repos

How to install the latest Google Chrome Stable on a Debian-like workstation (Debian, Ubuntu, Linux Mint, MX Linux, Deepin, AntiX, PureOS, Kali Linux, Parrot OS, Devuan, Knoppix, AV Linux Linux) verify software using the public GPG key and set up the Google repository. Included demo in Ubuntu 20.04 LTS.

Ansible install Google Chrome in Debian-like systems

- Add Google Chrome key ⇒ `ansible.builtin.apt_key`
- Add Google Chrome repository ⇒ `ansible.builtin.apt_-repository`
- Update apt cache and install Google Chrome ⇒ `ansible.builtin.apt`

In order to install Google Chrome on a Debian-like system, we need to perform three different steps.

The first step is to download the gpg signature key for the repository.

You are going to use the `ansible.builtin.apt_key` Ansible module. This encrypted key verifies the genuinity of the packages and the repository and guarantees that the software is the same as Google releases.

The second step is to add the add Google Chrome repository to the distribution. It's an extra website were `apt`, your distribution Package Manager looks like for software.

You are going to use the `ansible.builtin.apt_repository` Ansible module.

The third step is to update the apt cache for the available packages and install Google Chrome using the `ansible.builtin.apt` Ansible module.

Parameters

- apt-key url string - URL
- apt-key state string - present/absent
- apt_repository repo string - repository
- apt_repository state string - present/absent
- apt name string - name or package-specific
- apt state string - latest/present/absent
- apt update_cache boolean - no/yes

For the `ansible.builtin.apt_key` Ansible module I'm going to use two parameters: "url" and "state".

The "url" parameter specifies the URL of the repository gpg signature key and the "state" verify that is present in our system after the execution.

For the `ansible.builtin.apt_repository` Ansible module I'm going to use two parameters: "repo" and "state".

The "repo" parameter specifies the repository parameters and the "state" verify that is present in our system after the execution.

For the `ansible.builtin.apt` Ansible module I'm going to use three parameters: "name", "state", and "update_cache".

The "name" parameter specifies the package name (Google Chrome in our use-case) and the "state" verify that is present in our system after the execution.

Before installing the package the "update_cache" performs an update of the apt-cache to ensure that the latest version of the package is going to be downloaded.

demo

Install Google Chrome in Debian-like systems with Ansible Playbook.

code

- install_chrome_debian.yml

```
1   ---
2   - name: install Google Chrome
3     hosts: all
4     become: true
5     tasks:
6       - name: Install apt-transport-https
7         ansible.builtin.apt:
8           state: latest
9           update_cache: true
10  - name: Add Apt signing key
11        ansible.builtin.apt_key:
12          url: "https://dl.google.com/linux/linux_signing_k\
13  ey.pub"
14          state: present
15  - name: Add repository into sources list
16        ansible.builtin.apt_repository:
17          repo: deb [arch=amd64] http://dl.google.com/linux\
18  /chrome/deb/ stable main
```

```
19          state: present
20          filename: google-chrome
21   - name: Install google-chrome-stable
22       ansible.builtin.apt:
23         name: "google-chrome-stable"
24         state: latest
25         update_cache: true
```

execution

```
1  $ ansible-playbook -i ubuntu/inventory install\ chrome/de\
2  bian.yml
3  PLAY [install Google Chrome] ****************************\
4  *******************************************
5  TASK [Gathering Facts] *********************************\
6  *******************************************
7  ok: [ubuntu.example.com]
8  TASK [Install apt-transport-https] *********************\
9  *******************************************
10 changed: [ubuntu.example.com]
11 TASK [Add Apt signing key] *****************************\
12 *******************************************
13 changed: [ubuntu.example.com]
14 TASK [Add repository into sources list] ****************\
15 *******************************************
16 changed: [ubuntu.example.com]
17 TASK [Install google-chrome-stable] ********************\
18 *******************************************
19 changed: [ubuntu.example.com]
20 PLAY RECAP *********************************************\
21 *******************************************
22 ubuntu.example.com          : ok=5    changed=4    unreach\
23 able=0    failed=0    skipped=0    rescued=0    ignored=0
```

verification

```
$ ssh devops@ubuntu.example.com
$ sudo su -
# apt-cache search google-chrome
google-chrome-beta - The web browser from Google
google-chrome-stable - The web browser from Google
google-chrome-unstable - The web browser from Google
# apt-cache show google-chrome-stable
Package: google-chrome-stable
Version: 94.0.4606.81-1
Architecture: amd64
Maintainer: Chrome Linux Team <chromium-dev@chromium.org>
Installed-Size: 276179
Pre-Depends: dpkg (>= 1.14.0)
Depends: ca-certificates, fonts-liberation, libasound2 (>\
= 1.0.16), libatk-bridge2.0-0 (>= 2.5.3), libatk1.0-0 (>=\
 2.2.0), libatspi2.0-0 (>= 2.9.90), libc6 (>= 2.17), libc\
airo2 (>= 1.6.0), libcups2 (>= 1.6.0), libcurl3-gnutls | \
libcurl3-nss | libcurl4 | libcurl3, libdbus-1-3 (>= 1.5.1\
2), libdrm2 (>= 2.4.38), libexpat1 (>= 2.0.1), libgbm1 (>\
= 8.1~0), libgcc1 (>= 1:3.0), libglib2.0-0 (>= 2.39.4), l\
ibgtk-3-0 (>= 3.9.10) | libgtk-4-1, libnspr4 (>= 2:4.9-2~\
), libnss3 (>= 2:3.22), libpango-1.0-0 (>= 1.14.0), libx1\
1-6 (>= 2:1.4.99.1), libxcb1 (>= 1.9.2), libxcomposite1 (\
>= 1:0.4.4-1), libxdamage1 (>= 1:1.1), libxext6, libxfixe\
s3, libxkbcommon0 (>= 0.4.1), libxrandr2, libxshmfence1, \
wget, xdg-utils (>= 1.0.2)
Recommends: libu2f-udev, libvulkan1
Provides: www-browser
Priority: optional
Section: web
Filename: pool/main/g/google-chrome-stable/google-chrome-\
stable_94.0.4606.81-1_amd64.deb
Size: 90229076
SHA256: bfe97cd8d9f941e4a1e73f53d9de6bb54e73a007ee4ce5d4e\
94a9a65ae2d7fb4
```

```
36   SHA1: 2dc4cbaa205ab61dbf10303400f23e3515fe6c4b
37   MD5sum: bd49a8b9956cef901657482050a88925
38   Description: The web browser from Google
39    Google Chrome is a browser that combines a minimal desig\
40   n with sophisticated technology to make the web faster, s\
41   afer, and easier.
42   Description-md5: a2d34067fc33f1c87253c33b9fd975f0
43   # ls -al /etc/apt/sources.list.d/
44   total 16
45   drwxr-xr-x 2 root root 4096 Oct 11 11:42 .
46   drwxr-xr-x 7 root root 4096 Oct 11 11:42 ..
47   -rw-r--r-- 1 root root   68 Oct 11 11:40 dl_google_com_li\
48   nux_chrome_deb.list
49   -rw-r--r-- 1 root root  189 Oct 11 11:42 google-chrome.li\
50   st
51   root@ubuntu:~# cat /etc/apt/sources.list.d/google-chrome.\
52   list
53   ### THIS FILE IS AUTOMATICALLY CONFIGURED ###
54   # You may comment out this entry, but any other modificat\
55   ions may be lost.
56   deb [arch=amd64] http://dl.google.com/linux/chrome/deb/ s\
57   table main
58   root@ubuntu:~# cat /etc/apt/sources.list.d/dl_google_com_\
59   linux_chrome_deb.list
60   deb [arch=amd64] http://dl.google.com/linux/chrome/deb/ s\
61   table main
62   # apt list google-chrome-stable
63   Listing... Done
64   google-chrome-stable/stable,now 94.0.4606.81-1 amd64 [ins\
65   talled]
```

Install Google Chrome in Debian-like systems - Ansible module apt_key, apt_repos

How to install the latest Google Chrome Stable on a Debian-like workstation (Debian, Ubuntu, Linux Mint, MX Linux, Deepin, AntiX, PureOS, Kali Linux, Parrot OS, Devuan, Knoppix, AV Linux Linux) verify software using the public GPG key and set up the Google repository. Included demo in Ubuntu 20.04 LTS.

Ansible install Google Chrome in Debian-like systems

- Add Google Chrome key ⇒ `ansible.builtin.apt_key`
- Add Google Chrome repository ⇒ `ansible.builtin.apt_-repository`
- Update apt cache and install Google Chrome ⇒ `ansible.builtin.apt`

In order to install Google Chrome on a Debian-like system, we need to perform three different steps.

The first step is to download the gpg signature key for the repository. You are going to use the `ansible.builtin.apt_key` Ansible module. This encrypted key verifies the genuinity of the packages and the repository and guarantees that the software is the same as Google releases.

The second step is to add the add Google Chrome repository to the distribution. It's an extra website were `apt`, your distribution Package Manager looks like for software.

You are going to use the `ansible.builtin.apt_repository` Ansible module.

The third step is to update the apt cache for the available packages and install Google Chrome using the `ansible.builtin.apt` Ansible module.

Parameters

- apt-key url string - URL
- apt-key state string - present/absent
- apt_repository repo string - repository
- apt_repository state string - present/absent
- apt name string - name or package-specific
- apt state string - latest/present/absent
- apt update_cache boolean - no/yes

For the `ansible.builtin.apt_key` Ansible module I'm going to use two parameters: "url" and "state".

The "url" parameter specifies the URL of the repository gpg signature key and the "state" verify that is present in our system after the execution.

For the `ansible.builtin.apt_repository` Ansible module I'm going to use two parameters: "repo" and "state".

The "repo" parameter specifies the repository parameters and the "state" verify that is present in our system after the execution.

For the `ansible.builtin.apt` Ansible module I'm going to use three parameters: "name", "state", and "update_cache".

The "name" parameter specifies the package name (Google Chrome in our use-case) and the "state" verify that is present in our system after the execution.

Before installing the package the "update_cache" performs an update of the apt-cache to ensure that the latest version of the package is going to be downloaded.

demo

Install Google Chrome in Debian-like systems with Ansible Playbook.

code

- install_chrome_debian.yml

```
1   ---
2   - name: install Google Chrome
3     hosts: all
4     become: true
5     tasks:
6       - name: Install apt-transport-https
7         ansible.builtin.apt:
8           state: latest
9           update_cache: true
10  - name: Add Apt signing key
11        ansible.builtin.apt_key:
12          url: "https://dl.google.com/linux/linux_signing_k\
13  ey.pub"
14          state: present
15  - name: Add repository into sources list
16        ansible.builtin.apt_repository:
17          repo: deb [arch=amd64] http://dl.google.com/linux\
18  /chrome/deb/ stable main
19          state: present
20          filename: google-chrome
21  - name: Install google-chrome-stable
22        ansible.builtin.apt:
23          name: "google-chrome-stable"
24          state: latest
25          update_cache: true
```

execution

```
$ ansible-playbook -i ubuntu/inventory install\ chrome/de\
bian.yml
PLAY [install Google Chrome] ***************************\
*********************************************
TASK [Gathering Facts] ********************************\
*********************************************
ok: [ubuntu.example.com]
TASK [Install apt-transport-https] ********************\
*********************************************
changed: [ubuntu.example.com]
TASK [Add Apt signing key] ****************************\
*********************************************
changed: [ubuntu.example.com]
TASK [Add repository into sources list] ***************\
*********************************************
changed: [ubuntu.example.com]
TASK [Install google-chrome-stable] *******************\
*********************************************
changed: [ubuntu.example.com]
PLAY RECAP ********************************************\
*********************************************
ubuntu.example.com              : ok=5     changed=4     unreach\
able=0     failed=0     skipped=0     rescued=0     ignored=0
```

verification

```
$ ssh devops@ubuntu.example.com
$ sudo su -
# apt-cache search google-chrome
google-chrome-beta - The web browser from Google
google-chrome-stable - The web browser from Google
google-chrome-unstable - The web browser from Google
# apt-cache show google-chrome-stable
Package: google-chrome-stable
Version: 94.0.4606.81-1
Architecture: amd64
Maintainer: Chrome Linux Team <chromium-dev@chromium.org>
Installed-Size: 276179
Pre-Depends: dpkg (>= 1.14.0)
Depends: ca-certificates, fonts-liberation, libasound2 (>\
= 1.0.16), libatk-bridge2.0-0 (>= 2.5.3), libatk1.0-0 (>=\
 2.2.0), libatspi2.0-0 (>= 2.9.90), libc6 (>= 2.17), libc\
airo2 (>= 1.6.0), libcups2 (>= 1.6.0), libcurl3-gnutls | \
libcurl3-nss | libcurl4 | libcurl3, libdbus-1-3 (>= 1.5.1\
2), libdrm2 (>= 2.4.38), libexpat1 (>= 2.0.1), libgbm1 (>\
= 8.1~0), libgcc1 (>= 1:3.0), libglib2.0-0 (>= 2.39.4), l\
ibgtk-3-0 (>= 3.9.10) | libgtk-4-1, libnspr4 (>= 2:4.9-2~\
), libnss3 (>= 2:3.22), libpango-1.0-0 (>= 1.14.0), libx1\
1-6 (>= 2:1.4.99.1), libxcb1 (>= 1.9.2), libxcomposite1 (\
>= 1:0.4.4-1), libxdamage1 (>= 1:1.1), libxext6, libxfixe\
s3, libxkbcommon0 (>= 0.4.1), libxrandr2, libxshmfence1, \
wget, xdg-utils (>= 1.0.2)
Recommends: libu2f-udev, libvulkan1
Provides: www-browser
Priority: optional
Section: web
Filename: pool/main/g/google-chrome-stable/google-chrome-\
stable_94.0.4606.81-1_amd64.deb
Size: 90229076
SHA256: bfe97cd8d9f941e4a1e73f53d9de6bb54e73a007ee4ce5d4e\
94a9a65ae2d7fb4
```

```
36   SHA1: 2dc4cbaa205ab61dbf10303400f23e3515fe6c4b
37   MD5sum: bd49a8b9956cef901657482050a88925
38   Description: The web browser from Google
39    Google Chrome is a browser that combines a minimal desig\
40   n with sophisticated technology to make the web faster, s\
41   afer, and easier.
42   Description-md5: a2d34067fc33f1c87253c33b9fd975f0
43   # ls -al /etc/apt/sources.list.d/
44   total 16
45   drwxr-xr-x 2 root root 4096 Oct 11 11:42 .
46   drwxr-xr-x 7 root root 4096 Oct 11 11:42 ..
47   -rw-r--r-- 1 root root   68 Oct 11 11:40 dl_google_com_li\
48   nux_chrome_deb.list
49   -rw-r--r-- 1 root root  189 Oct 11 11:42 google-chrome.li\
50   st
51   root@ubuntu:~# cat /etc/apt/sources.list.d/google-chrome.\
52   list
53   ### THIS FILE IS AUTOMATICALLY CONFIGURED ###
54   # You may comment out this entry, but any other modificat\
55   ions may be lost.
56   deb [arch=amd64] http://dl.google.com/linux/chrome/deb/ s\
57   table main
58   root@ubuntu:~# cat /etc/apt/sources.list.d/dl_google_com_\
59   linux_chrome_deb.list
60   deb [arch=amd64] http://dl.google.com/linux/chrome/deb/ s\
61   table main
62   # apt list google-chrome-stable
63   Listing... Done
64   google-chrome-stable/stable,now 94.0.4606.81-1 amd64 [ins\
65   talled]
```

Deploy a web server apache httpd on Debian-like systems - Ansible modules apt, copy, service and ufw

How to automate the deployment of a web server apache httpd on Debian-like systems with custom web page taking care of downloading, installing, and enabling the service instantly and on boot and open the relevant firewall ports with Ansible modules yum, copy, service ufw. Debian, Ubuntu all the similar distributions.

Deploy a web server apache httpd on Debian-like systems

- install packages ⇒ `ansible.builtin.apt`
- custom index.html ⇒ `ansible.builtin.copy`
- start service ⇒ `ansible.builtin.service`
- open firewall ⇒ `community.general.ufw`

Let's talk about how to deploy a web server apache httpd on Debian-like Linux systems.

The full process requires six steps that you could automate with different Ansible modules.

Firstly you need to install the `apache2` package and dependency using the `ansible.builtin.apt` Ansible module.

Secondly, you need to create the custom index.html with `ansible.builtin.copy` Ansible module. You could upgrade this step using the `template` module.

Thirsty you need to start the `apache2` service and enable it on boot and all the dependant using the `ansible.builtin.service` Ansible module.

Fourthly you need to open the relevant firewall service-related ports using the `community.general.ufw` Ansible module.

demo

How to deploy a web server apache httpd on Debian-like systems with Ansible Playbook.

code

```
1    ---
2    - name: setup webserver
3      hosts: all
4      become: true
5      tasks:
6        - name: apache installed
7          ansible.builtin.apt:
8            name: apache2
9            update_cache: true
10           state: latest
11       - name: custom index.html
12         ansible.builtin.copy:
13           dest: "/var/www/html/index.html"
14           content: |
15             Custom Web Page
16       - name: apache2 service enabled
17         ansible.builtin.service:
18           name: apache2
19           enabled: true
20           state: started
21       - name: open firewall
22         community.general.ufw:
23           rule: allow
24           port: 80
25           proto: tcp
```

execution

```
ansible-pilot $ ansible-playbook -i virtualmachines/ubunt\
u/inventory services/httpd_debian.yml
PLAY [setup webserver] ********************************\
*******************************************
TASK [Gathering Facts] ********************************\
*******************************************
ok: [ubuntu.example.com]
TASK [apache installed] *******************************\
*******************************************
changed: [ubuntu.example.com]
TASK [custom index.html] ******************************\
*******************************************
changed: [ubuntu.example.com]
TASK [apache2 service enabled] ************************\
*******************************************
ok: [ubuntu.example.com]
TASK [open firewall] **********************************\
*******************************************
changed: [ubuntu.example.com]
PLAY RECAP ********************************************\
*******************************************
ubuntu.example.com          : ok=5    changed=3    unreach\
able=0    failed=0    skipped=0    rescued=0    ignored=0
ansible-pilot $
```

idempotency

```
ansible-pilot $ ansible-playbook -i virtualmachines/ubunt\
u/inventory services/httpd_debian.yml
PLAY [setup webserver] ***********************************\
*****************************************
TASK [Gathering Facts] ***********************************\
*****************************************
ok: [ubuntu.example.com]
TASK [apache installed] **********************************\
*****************************************
ok: [ubuntu.example.com]
TASK [custom index.html] *********************************\
*****************************************
ok: [ubuntu.example.com]
TASK [apache2 service enabled] ***************************\
*****************************************
ok: [ubuntu.example.com]
TASK [open firewall] *************************************\
*****************************************
ok: [ubuntu.example.com]
PLAY RECAP ***********************************************\
*****************************************
ubuntu.example.com         : ok=5    changed=0    unreach\
able=0    failed=0    skipped=0    rescued=0    ignored=0
ansible-pilot $
```

before execution

```
ansible-pilot $ ssh devops@ubuntu.example.com
The authenticity of host 'ubuntu.example.com (192.168.0.1\
91)' can't be established.
ECDSA key fingerprint is SHA256:SLtrfIjRKhuJtdTxjJ4V9yk+o\
/gO3MZi59KHehOQ3Ao.
Are you sure you want to continue connecting (yes/no/[fin\
gerprint])? yes
Warning: Permanently added 'ubuntu.example.com,192.168.0.\
191' (ECDSA) to the list of known hosts.
The programs included with the Ubuntu system are free sof\
tware;
the exact distribution terms for each program are describ\
ed in the
individual files in /usr/share/doc/*/copyright.
Ubuntu comes with ABSOLUTELY NO WARRANTY, to the extent p\
ermitted by
applicable law.
$ sudo su
root@ubuntu:/home/devops# cat /etc/os-release
NAME="Ubuntu"
VERSION="20.04.3 LTS (Focal Fossa)"
ID=ubuntu
ID_LIKE=debian
PRETTY_NAME="Ubuntu 20.04.3 LTS"
VERSION_ID="20.04"
HOME_URL="https://www.ubuntu.com/"
SUPPORT_URL="https://help.ubuntu.com/"
BUG_REPORT_URL="https://bugs.launchpad.net/ubuntu/"
PRIVACY_POLICY_URL="https://www.ubuntu.com/legal/terms-an\
d-policies/privacy-policy"
VERSION_CODENAME=focal
UBUNTU_CODENAME=focal
root@ubuntu:/home/devops# apt list apache2
Listing... Done
apache2/focal-updates 2.4.41-4ubuntu3.8 amd64
```

```
36  apache2/focal-updates 2.4.41-4ubuntu3.8 i386
37  root@ubuntu:/home/devops# apt list apache2 --installed
38  Listing... Done
39  root@ubuntu:/home/devops# dpkg -l | grep apache2
40  root@ubuntu:/home/devops# cat /var/www/html/index.html
41  cat: /var/www/html/index.html: No such file or directory
42  root@ubuntu:/home/devops# ls -al /var/www
43  ls: cannot access '/var/www': No such file or directory
44  root@ubuntu:/home/devops#
```

after execution

```
1   ansible-pilot $ ssh devops@ubuntu.example.com
2   Last login: Mon Feb 14 14:26:02 2022 from 192.168.0.101
3   $ sudo su
4   root@ubuntu:/home/devops# apt list apache2
5   Listing... Done
6   apache2/focal-updates,focal-security,now 2.4.41-4ubuntu3.\
7   9 amd64 [installed]
8   apache2/focal-updates,focal-security 2.4.41-4ubuntu3.9 i3\
9   86
10  root@ubuntu:/home/devops# dpkg -l | grep apache2
11  ii  apache2                      2.4.41-4ubuntu3.\
12  9                  amd64        Apache HTTP Server
13  ii  apache2-bin                  2.4.41-4ubuntu3.\
14  9                  amd64        Apache HTTP Server (mo\
15  dules and other binary files)
16  ii  apache2-data                 2.4.41-4ubuntu3.\
17  9                  all          Apache HTTP Server (co\
18  mmon files)
19  ii  apache2-utils                2.4.41-4ubuntu3.\
20  9                  amd64        Apache HTTP Server (ut\
21  ility programs for web servers)
22  root@ubuntu:/home/devops# systemctl status apache2
23  □ apache2.service - The Apache HTTP Servers
24       Loaded. loaded (/lib/systemd/system/apache2.service;\
```

```
25  enabled; vendor preset: enabled)
26      Active: active (running) since Mon 2022-02-14 14:25:\
27  31 UTC; 1min 20s ago
28        Docs: https://httpd.apache.org/docs/2.4/
29    Main PID: 3182 (apache2)
30       Tasks: 55 (limit: 1071)
31      Memory: 5.1M
32      CGroup: /system.slice/apache2.service
33              ├─3182 /usr/sbin/apache2 -k start
34              ├─3185 /usr/sbin/apache2 -k start
35              └─3186 /usr/sbin/apache2 -k start
36  Feb 14 14:25:31 ubuntu systemd[1]: Starting The Apache HT\
37  TP Server...
38  Feb 14 14:25:31 ubuntu systemd[1]: Started The Apache HTT\
39  P Server.
40  root@ubuntu:/home/devops# cat /var/www/html/index.html
41  Custom Web Page
42  root@ubuntu:/home/devops# ls -al /var/www/
43  total 12
44  drwxr-xr-x  3 root root 4096 Feb 14 14:25 .
45  drwxr-xr-x 14 root root 4096 Feb 14 14:25 ..
46  drwxr-xr-x  2 root root 4096 Feb 14 14:25 html
47  root@ubuntu:/home/devops#
```

web server apache httpd on Debian-like system

Deploy a web server apache httpd virtual host on Debian-like systems - Ansible modules apt, file, copy, template, command, ufw and service

How to automate the deployment of a web server apache httpd virtual host "example.com" on Debian-like systems with custom web page taking care of downloading, installing, and enabling the service instantly and on boot and open the relevant firewall ports with Ansible modules apt, file, copy, template, command, ufw, and service. Debian, Ubuntu all the similar distributions.

Deploy a web server apache httpd virtual host on Debian-like systems

- install packages ⇒ ansible.builtin.apt
- document root ⇒ ansible.builtin.file
- custom index.html ⇒ ansible.builtin.copy
- Apache virtualhost ⇒ ansible.builtin.template
- enable new site ⇒ ansible.builtin.command
- open firewall ⇒ community.general.ufw
- reload service ⇒ ansible.builtin.service

Today we're talking about how to Deploy a web server apache httpd on Debian-like Linux systems.
The full process requires seven steps that you could automate with different Ansible modules.
Firstly you need to install the `apache2` package and dependency using the `ansible.builtin.apt` Ansible module.
Secondly, you need to create the document root with the right

permission with the `ansible.builtin.file` module.

Thirsty, you need to create the custom index.html with the `ansible.builtin.copy` Ansible module. You could upgrade this step using the `template` module.

Fourthly, you need to set up Apache configuration for the specific virtual host using the `ansible.builtin.template` module.

Fifty, you need to enable a new site using the `a2ensite` via the `ansible.builtin.command` module.

Sixty, you need to start the `apache2` service and enable it on boot and all the dependant using the `ansible.builtin.service` Ansible module.

Seventy you need to open the relevant firewall service-related ports using the `community.general.ufw` Ansible module.

demo

How to automate the deployment of a web server apache httpd virtual host on Debian-like systems with Ansible Playbook.

code

- httpd_debian_vhost.yml

```yaml
---
- name: setup webserver vhost
  hosts: all
  become: true
  vars:
    app_user: "www-data"
    http_host: "example.com"
    http_conf: "example.com.conf"
    http_port: "80"
    disable_default: true
  tasks:
```

```
12        - name: apache installed
13          ansible.builtin.apt:
14            name: apache2
15            update_cache: true
16            state: latest
17
18        - name: document root exist
19          ansible.builtin.file:
20            path: "/var/www/{{ http_host }}"
21            state: directory
22            owner: "{{ app_user }}"
23            mode: '0755'
24
25        - name: custom index.html
26          ansible.builtin.copy:
27            dest: "/var/www/{{ http_host }}/index.html"
28            content: |
29              Custom Web Page
30
31        - name: set up Apache virtualhost
32          ansible.builtin.template:
33            src: "templates/apache.conf.j2"
34            dest: "/etc/apache2/sites-available/{{ http_conf \
35    }}"
36
37        - name: enable new site
38          ansible.builtin.command: "/usr/sbin/a2ensite {{ htt\
39    p_conf }}"
40          notify: reload Apache
41
42        - name: disable default Apache site
43          ansible.builtin.command: "/usr/sbin/a2dissite 000-d\
44    efault.conf"
45          when: disable_default
46          notify: reload Apache
```

```
47
48     - name: open firewall
49       community.general.ufw:
50         rule: allow
51         port: "{{ http_port }}"
52         proto: tcp
53
54   handlers:
55     - name: reload Apache
56       ansible.builtin.service:
57         name: apache2
58         state: reloaded
```

- apache.conf.j2

```
1   <VirtualHost *:{{ http_port }}>
2     ServerAdmin webmaster@localhost
3     ServerName {{ http_host }}
4     ServerAlias www.{{ http_host }}
5     ErrorLog ${APACHE_LOG}/error.log
6     CustomLog ${APACHE_LOG}/access.log combined
7     DocumentRoot "/var/www/{{ http_host }}"
8   </VirtualHost>
```

execution

```
ansible-pilot $ ansible-playbook -i virtualmachines/ubunt\
u/inventory services/httpd_debian_vhost.yml
PLAY [setup webserver] ********************************\
*******************************************
TASK [Gathering Facts] *******************************\
*******************************************
ok: [ubuntu.example.com]
TASK [apache installed] ******************************\
*******************************************
changed: [ubuntu.example.com]
TASK [document root exist] ***************************\
*******************************************
changed: [ubuntu.example.com]
TASK [custom index.html] *****************************\
*******************************************
changed: [ubuntu.example.com]
TASK [set up Apache virtualhost] *********************\
*******************************************
changed: [ubuntu.example.com]
TASK [enable new site] *******************************\
*******************************************
changed: [ubuntu.example.com]
TASK [disable default Apache site] *******************\
*******************************************
changed: [ubuntu.example.com]
TASK [open firewall] *********************************\
*******************************************
ok: [ubuntu.example.com]
RUNNING HANDLER [reload Apache] **********************\
*******************************************
changed: [ubuntu.example.com]
PLAY RECAP *******************************************\
*******************************************
ubuntu.example.com          : ok=9    changed=7    unreach\
able=0    failed=0    skipped=0    rescued=0    ignored=0
```

```
36   ansible-pilot $
```

(almost) idempotency

```
1    ansible-pilot $ ansible-playbook -i virtualmachines/ubunt\
2    u/inventory services/httpd_debian_vhost.yml
3    PLAY [setup webserver] *********************************\
4    ********************************************
5    TASK [Gathering Facts] *********************************\
6    ********************************************
7    ok: [ubuntu.example.com]
8    TASK [apache installed] ********************************\
9    ********************************************
10   ok: [ubuntu.example.com]
11   TASK [document root exist] *****************************\
12   ********************************************
13   ok: [ubuntu.example.com]
14   TASK [custom index.html] *******************************\
15   ********************************************
16   ok: [ubuntu.example.com]
17   TASK [set up Apache virtualhost] ***********************\
18   ********************************************
19   ok: [ubuntu.example.com]
20   TASK [enable new site] *********************************\
21   ********************************************
22   changed: [ubuntu.example.com]
23   TASK [disable default Apache site] *********************\
24   ********************************************
25   changed: [ubuntu.example.com]
26   TASK [open firewall] ***********************************\
27   ********************************************
28   ok: [ubuntu.example.com]
29   RUNNING HANDLER [reload Apache] ************************\
30   ********************************************
31   changed: [ubuntu.example.com]
32   PLAY RECAP ********************************************\
```

```
33  *******************************************
34  ubuntu.example.com          : ok=9      changed=3      unreach\
35  able=0      failed=0      skipped=0      rescued=0      ignored=0
36  ansible-pilot $
```

before execution

```
1   ansible-pilot $ ssh devops@ubuntu.example.com
2   Last login: Thu Feb 24 11:21:41 2022 from 192.168.76.111
3   $ sudo su
4   root@ubuntu:/home/devops# cat /etc/os-release
5   NAME="Ubuntu"
6   VERSION="20.04.3 LTS (Focal Fossa)"
7   ID=ubuntu
8   ID_LIKE=debian
9   PRETTY_NAME="Ubuntu 20.04.3 LTS"
10  VERSION_ID="20.04"
11  HOME_URL="https://www.ubuntu.com/"
12  SUPPORT_URL="https://help.ubuntu.com/"
13  BUG_REPORT_URL="https://bugs.launchpad.net/ubuntu/"
14  PRIVACY_POLICY_URL="https://www.ubuntu.com/legal/terms-an\
15  d-policies/privacy-policy"
16  VERSION_CODENAME=focal
17  UBUNTU_CODENAME=focal
18  root@ubuntu:/home/devops# apt list apache2
19  Listing... Done
20  apache2/focal-updates,focal-security 2.4.41-4ubuntu3.9 am\
21  d64
22  apache2/focal-updates,focal-security 2.4.41-4ubuntu3.9 i3\
23  86
24  root@ubuntu:/home/devops# apt list apache2 --installed
25  Listing... Done
26  root@ubuntu:/home/devops# dpkg -l | grep apache
27  root@ubuntu:/home/devops# cat /etc/apache2/sites-availabl\
28  e/example.com.conf
29  cat: /etc/apache2/sites-available/example.com.conf: No su\
```

```
30  ch file or directory
31  root@ubuntu:/home/devops# ls -al /var/www/example.com
32  ls: cannot access '/var/www/example.com': No such file or\
33   directory
34  root@ubuntu:/home/devops# cat /var/www/example.com/index.\
35  html
36  cat: /var/www/example.com/index.html: No such file or dir\
37  ectory
38  root@ubuntu:/home/devops# systemctl status apache2
39  Unit apache2.service could not be found.
40  root@ubuntu:/home/devops# ufw status verbose
41  Status: active
42  Logging: on (low)
43  Default: deny (incoming), allow (outgoing), disabled (rou\
44  ted)
45  New profiles: skip
46  To                         Action      From
47  --                         ------      ----
48  80/tcp                     ALLOW IN    Anywhere                \
49
50  22/tcp (OpenSSH)           ALLOW IN    Anywhere                \
51
52  80/tcp (v6)                ALLOW IN    Anywhere (v6)           \
53
54  22/tcp (OpenSSH (v6))      ALLOW IN    Anywhere (v6)
55  root@ubuntu:/home/devops#
```

after execution

```
ansible-pilot $ ssh devops@ubuntu.example.com
Last login: Thu Feb 24 11:37:49 2022 from 192.168.76.111
$ sudo su
root@ubuntu:/home/devops# apt list apache2
Listing... Done
apache2/focal-updates,focal-security,now 2.4.41-4ubuntu3.\
9 amd64 [installed]
apache2/focal-updates,focal-security 2.4.41-4ubuntu3.9 i3\
86
root@ubuntu:/home/devops# apt list apache2 --installed
Listing... Done
apache2/focal-updates,focal-security,now 2.4.41-4ubuntu3.\
9 amd64 [installed]
N: There is 1 additional version. Please use the '-a' swi\
tch to see it
root@ubuntu:/home/devops# apt list apache2 --installed -a
Listing... Done
apache2/focal-updates,focal-security,now 2.4.41-4ubuntu3.\
9 amd64 [installed]
apache2/focal 2.4.41-4ubuntu3 amd64
root@ubuntu:/home/devops# dpkg -l | grep apache2
ii  apache2                      2.4.41-4ubuntu3.\
9                   amd64        Apache HTTP Server
ii  apache2-bin                  2.4.41-4ubuntu3.\
9                   amd64        Apache HTTP Server (mo\
dules and other binary files)
ii  apache2-data                 2.4.41-4ubuntu3.\
9                   all          Apache HTTP Server (co\
mmon files)
ii  apache2-utils                2.4.41-4ubuntu3.\
9                   amd64        Apache HTTP Server (ut\
ility programs for web servers)
root@ubuntu:/home/devops# cat /etc/apache2/sites-availabl\
e/example.com.conf
<VirtualHost *:80>
```

```
36     ServerAdmin webmaster@localhost
37     ServerName example.com
38     ServerAlias www.example.com
39     DocumentRoot /var/www/example.com
40     ErrorLog ${APACHE_LOG_DIR}/error.log
41     CustomLog ${APACHE_LOG_DIR}/access.log combined
42 </VirtualHost>root@ubuntu:/home/devops# ls -al /var/www/e\
43 xample.com/
44 total 12
45 drwxr-xr-x 2 www-data root 4096 Feb 24 11:37 .
46 drwxr-xr-x 4 root     root 4096 Feb 24 11:37 ..
47 -rw-r--r-- 1 root     root   16 Feb 24 11:37 index.html
48 root@ubuntu:/home/devops# cat /var/www/example.com/index.\
49 html
50 Custom Web Page
51 root@ubuntu:/home/devops# systemctl status apache2
52 ▯ apache2.service - The Apache HTTP Server
53      Loaded: loaded (/lib/systemd/system/apache2.service;\
54  enabled; vendor preset: enabled)
55      Active: active (running) since Thu 2022-02-24 11:37:\
56 04 UTC; 2min 41s ago
57        Docs: https://httpd.apache.org/docs/2.4/
58     Process: 4191 ExecReload=/usr/sbin/apachectl graceful\
59  (code=exited, status=0/SUCCESS)
60    Main PID: 2318 (apache2)
61       Tasks: 55 (limit: 1071)
62      Memory: 5.7M
63      CGroup: /system.slice/apache2.service
64              ├─2318 /usr/sbin/apache2 -k start
65              ├─4195 /usr/sbin/apache2 -k start
66              └─4228 /usr/sbin/apache2 -k start
67 Feb 24 11:37:04 ubuntu systemd[1]: Starting The Apache HT\
68 TP Server...
69 Feb 24 11:37:04 ubuntu systemd[1]: Started The Apache HTT\
70 P Server.
```

```
71  Feb 24 11:37:12 ubuntu systemd[1]: Reloading The Apache H\
72  TTP Server.
73  Feb 24 11:37:13 ubuntu systemd[1]: Reloaded The Apache HT\
74  TP Server.
75  Feb 24 11:37:50 ubuntu systemd[1]: Reloading The Apache H\
76  TTP Server.
77  Feb 24 11:37:50 ubuntu systemd[1]: Reloaded The Apache HT\
78  TP Server.
79  root@ubuntu:/home/devops# ufw status verbose
80  Status: active
81  Logging: on (low)
82  Default: deny (incoming), allow (outgoing), disabled (rou\
83  ted)
84  New profiles: skip
85  To                         Action         From
86  --                         ------         ----
87  80/tcp                     ALLOW IN       Anywhere                  \
88
89  22/tcp (OpenSSH)           ALLOW IN       Anywhere                  \
90
91  80/tcp (v6)                ALLOW IN       Anywhere (v6)             \
92
93  22/tcp (OpenSSH (v6))      ALLOW IN       Anywhere (v6)
94  root@ubuntu:/home/devops# cat /var/log/apache2/access.log
95  192.168.76.111 - - [24/Feb/2022:11:41:21 +0000] "GET / HT\
96  TP/1.1" 200 299 "-" "Mozilla/5.0 (Macintosh; Intel Mac OS\
97   X 10_15_7) AppleWebKit/605.1.15 (KHTML, like Gecko) Vers\
98  ion/15.1 Safari/605.1.15"
99  192.168.76.111 - - [24/Feb/2022:11:41:23 +0000] "GET / HT\
100 TP/1.1" 200 299 "-" "Mozilla/5.0 (Macintosh; Intel Mac OS\
101  X 10_15_7) AppleWebKit/605.1.15 (KHTML, like Gecko) Vers\
102 ion/15.1 Safari/605.1.15"
103 192.168.76.111 - - [24/Feb/2022:11:41:23 +0000] "GET /fav\
104 icon.ico HTTP/1.1" 404 497 "http://ubuntu.example.com/" "\
105 Mozilla/5.0 (Macintosh; Intel Mac OS X 10_15_7) AppleWebK\
```

```
106  it/605.1.15 (KHTML, like Gecko) Version/15.1 Safari/605.1\
107  .15"
108  192.168.76.111 - - [24/Feb/2022:11:41:23 +0000] "GET /app\
109  le-touch-icon-precomposed.png HTTP/1.1" 404 497 "-" "Safa\
110  ri/16612.2.9.1.30 CFNetwork/1240.0.4 Darwin/20.6.0"
111  192.168.76.111 - - [24/Feb/2022:11:41:23 +0000] "GET /app\
112  le-touch-icon.png HTTP/1.1" 404 496 "-" "Safari/16612.2.9\
113  .1.30 CFNetwork/1240.0.4 Darwin/20.6.0"
114  192.168.76.111 - - [24/Feb/2022:11:41:49 +0000] "GET / HT\
115  TP/1.1" 200 299 "-" "Mozilla/5.0 (Macintosh; Intel Mac OS\
116   X 10_15_7) AppleWebKit/605.1.15 (KHTML, like Gecko) Vers\
117  ion/15.1 Safari/605.1.15"
118  192.168.76.111 - - [24/Feb/2022:11:41:49 +0000] "GET /fav\
119  icon.ico HTTP/1.1" 404 492 "http://192.168.76.32/" "Mozil\
120  la/5.0 (Macintosh; Intel Mac OS X 10_15_7) AppleWebKit/60\
121  5.1.15 (KHTML, like Gecko) Version/15.1 Safari/605.1.15"
122  192.168.76.111 - - [24/Feb/2022:11:42:14 +0000] "-" 408 0\
123   "-" "-"
124  192.168.76.111 - - [24/Feb/2022:11:42:17 +0000] "GET / HT\
125  TP/1.1" 304 180 "-" "Mozilla/5.0 (Macintosh; Intel Mac OS\
126   X 10_15_7) AppleWebKit/605.1.15 (KHTML, like Gecko) Vers\
127  ion/15.1 Safari/605.1.15"
128  root@ubuntu:/home/devops#
```

Custom Web Page

web server apache httpd virtual host on Debian-like system

Ansible Playbook Code for Suse-like systems

How to manage some Suse-like specific configuration.

Install a package in Suse-like systems - Ansible module zypper

A real-life example of how to install a package in Suse-like systems: SUSE Linux Enterprise Server and openSUSE.

How to Install a package with Ansible in Suse-like systems?

Let's talk about the Ansible module `zypper`.
The full name is `community.general.zypper` which means is part of the `Community General Collection` so maintained by the Ansible Community contributors.
It works on Syse-like operating systems and Manages packages on SUSE and openSUSE via the zypper package manager.
It's similar to the yum or DNF module for RedHat-like operating systems or the apt module for Debian-like operating systems.

Parameters

- name <u>string</u> - name or package specific
- state <u>string</u> - present / absent / latest
- type <u>string</u> - package / patch / pattern / product / srcpackage / application

- update_cache <u>boolean</u> - no/yes

The parameter list is pretty wide but these four are the most important options.

In the "name" parameter you are going to specify the name of the package or the specific version you would like to install.

The state specifies the action that we would like to perform. In our case for install is "present".

The type of package to be operated on package / patch / pattern / product / srcpackage / application. "update_cache" forces to update the repository metadata before the installation. It could be useful to make sure that repositories are up-to-date. The equivalent of console commandzypper refresh.

demo

Let's jump in a real-life playbook to install a package in Suse-like systems with Ansible.

code

- zypper.yml

```yaml
---
- name: zypper module demo
  hosts: all
  become: true
  tasks:
    - name: install package
      community.general.zypper:
        name: dos2unix
        state: present
```

execution

output

```
$ ansible-playbook -i suse/inventory install\ a\ package\\
 in\ Suse-like\ systems/zypper.yml
PLAY [zypper module demo] *******************************\
********************************************
TASK [Gathering Facts] **********************************\
********************************************
[WARNING]: Platform linux on host suse.example.com is usi\
ng the discovered Python interpreter at
/usr/bin/python, but future installation of another Pytho\
n interpreter could change the meaning of
that path. See https://docs.ansible.com/ansible-
core/2.11/reference_appendices/interpreter_discovery.html\
 for more information.
ok: [suse.example.com]
TASK [install package] **********************************\
********************************************
changed: [suse.example.com]
PLAY RECAP **********************************************\
********************************************
suse.example.com               : ok=2    changed=1    unreach\
able=0    failed=0    skipped=0    rescued=0    ignored=0
```

verification

```
$ ssh devops@suse.example.com
devops@suse:~> sudo su -
suse:~ # zypper se -i dos2unix
Loading repository data...
Warning: Repository 'openSUSE-Leap-42.3-Update' appears t\
o be outdated. Consider using a different mirror or serve\
r.
Warning: Repository 'openSUSE-Leap-42.3-Update-Non-Oss' a\
ppears to be outdated. Consider using a different mirror \
or server.
Reading installed packages...
S | Name      | Summary                                  \
  | Type
---+----------+-----------------------------------------\
---+--------
i+ | dos2unix | Text converters to and from DOS/MAC to UN\
IX | package
```

Install Google Chrome in Suse-like systems - Ansible module rpm_key, zypper_repo

How to install the latest Google Chrome Stable on a Suse-like workstation (SUSE Linux Enterprise Server and openSUSE) verify software using the public GPG key and set up the Google repository.

Ansible install Google Chrome in Suse-like systems

- Add Google Chrome key ⇒ ansible.builtin.rpm_key

- Add Google Chrome repository ⇒ community.general.zypper_repository
- Update yum cache and install Google Chrome ⇒ community.general.zypper

In order to install Google Chrome on a Suse-like system, we need to perform three different steps.

The first step is to download the GPG signature key for the repository. You are going to use the `ansible.builtin.rpm_key` Ansible module.

This encrypted key verifies the genuinity of the packages and the repository and guarantees that the software is the same as Google releases.

The second step is to add the add Google Chrome repository to the distribution. It's an extra website where `zypper`, your distribution package manager, looks like for software.

You are going to use the `community.general.zypper_repository` Ansible module.

The third step is to refresh the zypper cache for the available packages and install Google Chrome using the `community.general.zypper` Ansible module.

Parameters

- rpm_key key string - URL
- rpm_key state string - present/absent

For the `ansible.builtin.rpm_key` Ansible module I'm going to use two parameters: "key" and "state".

The "key" parameter specifies the URL or the key ID of the repository GPG signature key and the "state" verify that is present in our system after the execution.

- zypper_repository name string

- zypper_repository description string - repository
- zypper_repository repo string - URL
- zypper_repository auto_import_keys boolean - GPG signature

For the `community.general.zypper_repository` Ansible module I'm going to use four parameters: "name"/"description", "repo", and "auto_import_keys".
The "name" and "description" parameters specify the repository name in the Suse system and the "repo" URL of it.
The "auto_import_keys" parameter enables the GPG verification and imports of the suitable keys.

- zypper name string - name or package-specific
- zypper state string - latest/present/absent
- zypper update_cache boolean - no/yes

For the `community.general.zypper` Ansible module I'm going to use three parameters: "name", "state" and "update_cache".
The "name" parameter specifies the package name (Google Chrome in our use-case) and the "state" verify that is present in our system after the execution.
Before installing the package the "update_cache" performs a refresh of the zypper cache to ensure that the latest version of the package is going to be downloaded.

demo

Let's jump into a real-life Ansible Playbook to install Google Chrome in Suse-like systems.

code

- install_chrome_suse.yml

```yaml
---
- name: install Google Chrome
  hosts: all
  become: true
  tasks:
    - name: Add rpm signing key
      ansible.builtin.rpm_key:
        key: https://dl.google.com/linux/linux_signing_ke\
y.pub
        state: present
- name: Add repository into repo list
    community.general.zypper_repository:
      name: google-chrome
      description: google-chrome repository
      repo: http://dl.google.com/linux/chrome/rpm/stabl\
e/x86_64
      auto_import_keys: true
      state: present
      runrefresh: true
      enable: true
- name: Install google-chrome-stable
    community.general.zypper:
      name: "google-chrome-stable"
      state: latest
      update_cache: true
```

execution

```
$ ansible-playbook -i suse/inventory install\ chrome/suse\
.yml
PLAY [install Google Chrome] ****************************\
*******************************************
TASK [Gathering Facts] *********************************\
*******************************************
ok: [suse.example.com]
TASK [Add Yum signing key] *****************************\
*******************************************
changed: [suse.example.com]
TASK [Add repository into repo.d list] *****************\
*******************************************
changed: [suse.example.com]
TASK [Install google-chrome-stable] ********************\
*******************************************
changed: [suse.example.com]
PLAY RECAP *********************************************\
*******************************************
suse.example.com            : ok=4    changed=3    unreach\
able=0    failed=0    skipped=0    rescued=0    ignored=0
```

before Ansible execution

```
$ ssh devops@suse.example.com
devops@suse:~> sudo su -
suse:~ # zypper se -i google-chrome-stable
Loading repository data...
Warning: Repository 'openSUSE-Leap-42.3-Update' appears t\
o be outdated. Consider using a different mirror or serve\
r.
Warning: Repository 'openSUSE-Leap-42.3-Update-Non-Oss' a\
ppears to be outdated. Consider using a different mirror \
or server.
Reading installed packages...
No matching items found.
```

```
13  suse:~ # zypper repos
14  Repository priorities are without effect. All enabled rep\
15  ositories share the same priority.
16  # | Alias                                    | Name           \
17                           | Enabled | GPG Check | Refresh
18  --+-----------------------------------------+------------------\
19  -----------------+---------+-----------+--------
20  1 | openSUSE-Leap-42.3-Non-Oss              | openSUSE-Leap-42.\
21  3-Non-Oss            | Yes     | (r ) Yes  | No
22  2 | openSUSE-Leap-42.3-Oss                  | openSUSE-Leap-42.\
23  3-Oss                | Yes     | (r ) Yes  | No
24  3 | openSUSE-Leap-42.3-Update               | openSUSE-Leap-42.\
25  3-Update             | Yes     | (r ) Yes  | No
26  4 | openSUSE-Leap-42.3-Update-Non-Oss | openSUSE-Leap-42.\
27  3-Update-Non-Oss | Yes        | (r ) Yes  | No
```

after Ansible execution

```
1   $ ssh devops@suse.example.com
2   devops@suse:~> sudo su -
3   suse:~ # zypper se -i google-chrome-stable
4   Loading repository data...
5   Warning: Repository 'openSUSE-Leap-42.3-Update' appears t\
6   o be outdated. Consider using a different mirror or serve\
7   r.
8   Warning: Repository 'openSUSE-Leap-42.3-Update-Non-Oss' a\
9   ppears to be outdated. Consider using a different mirror \
10  or server.
11  Reading installed packages...
12  S  | Name                 | Summary         | Type
13  ---+----------------------+-----------------+--------
14  i+ | google-chrome-stable | Google Chrome   | package
15  suse:~ # zypper repos
16  Repository priorities are without effect. All enabled rep\
17  ositories share the same priority.
```

```
18  # | Alias                                     | Name                  \
19                     | Enabled | GPG Check | Refresh
20  --+----------------------------------+-------------------\
21  ----------------+---------+-----------+--------
22  1 | google-chrome                             | google-chrome rep\
23  ository            | Yes     | (r ) Yes  | Yes
24  2 | openSUSE-Leap-42.3-Non-Oss                | openSUSE-Leap-42.\
25  3-Non-Oss          | Yes     | (r ) Yes  | No
26  3 | openSUSE-Leap-42.3-Oss                    | openSUSE-Leap-42.\
27  3-Oss              | Yes     | (r ) Yes  | No
28  4 | openSUSE-Leap-42.3-Update                 | openSUSE-Leap-42.\
29  3-Update           | Yes     | (r ) Yes  | No
30  5 | openSUSE-Leap-42.3-Update-Non-Oss | openSUSE-Leap-42.\
31  3-Update-Non-Oss | Yes       | (r ) Yes  | No
32  suse:~ # zypper se -s google-chrome-stable
33  Loading repository data...
34  Warning: Repository 'openSUSE-Leap-42.3-Update' appears t\
35  o be outdated. Consider using a different mirror or serve\
36  r.
37  Warning: Repository 'openSUSE-Leap-42.3-Update-Non-Oss' a\
38  ppears to be outdated. Consider using a different mirror \
39  or server.
40  Reading installed packages...
41  S | Name                   | Type     | Version         | Ar\
42  ch   | Repository
43  ---+------------------------+---------+----------------+---\
44  -----+------------------------
45  i+ | google-chrome-stable | package | 94.0.4606.81-1 | x8\
46  6_64 | google-chrome repository
```

Ansible Troubleshooting The Most Common Errors

The most commons Ansible errors, how to troubleshoot and fix.

Ansible troubleshooting - connection failed

Connection failed errors are one of the most common Ansible problems.

The root cause of these types of problems rely directly on the networking. So jump on the ssh command line and troubleshoot like an ssh connection error.

In the following example the `Operation timed out` was caused by the virtual machine that doesn't have network card enabled.

Links

- Network Debug and Troubleshooting Guide[92]

demo

The best way of talking about Ansible troubleshooting is to jump in a live demo to show you practically the connection failed error and how to solve it!

---

[92]https://docs.ansible.com/ansible/latest/network/user_guide/network_debug_troubleshooting.html

error

Ansible relies on an SSH connection to the target machine. Let's try manually:

```
1  $ ssh username@hostname
2  Failed to connect to the host via ssh: ssh: connecto to h\
3  ost hostname port 22: Operation timed out
```

You need to verify the network connection between the source and the target machine.

fix

Once the network connection is fixed you could successfully connect to the target machine.

```
1  $ ssh username@hostname
2  username@hostname:~$
```

Ansible troubleshooting - macOS fork error

How to troubleshoot and fix the macOS fork error that might happen since macOS 10.13 High Sierra.

demo

The best way of talking about Ansible troubleshooting is to jump in a live demo to show you practically the macOS fork error and how to solve it!

error

- error

```
1  objc[22868]: +[__NSCFConstantString initialize] may have \
2  been in progress in another thread when fork() was called\
3  .
4  objc[22868]: +[__NSCFConstantString initialize] may have \
5  been in progress in another thread when fork() was called\
6  . We cannot safely call it or ignore it in the fork() chi\
7  ld process. Crashing instead. Set a breakpoint on objc_in\
8  itializeAfterForkError to debug.
```

fix current session

- fix - current session only

```
1  export "OBJC_DISABLE_INITIALIZE_FORK_SAFETY=YES"
```

fix all future sessions

- fix - for all future sessions

```
1  echo "OBJC_DISABLE_INITIALIZE_FORK_SAFETY=YES" >> .bash_p\
2  rofile
```

You could verify the environment of the terminal with the following command:

```
1  $ env
2  [...]
3  OBJC_DISABLE_INITIALIZE_FORK_SAFETY=YES
```

Ansible troubleshooting - indentation error

Indentation errors are one of the most common Ansible problems. In a live demo, we are going to troubleshoot starting from the error message. We are going to investigate the root cause of the problem and fix it.

Demo

The best way of talking about Ansible troubleshooting is to jump in a live demo to show you practically the error and how to solve it!

Error

```
1   ---
2   - name: blockinfile module demo
3     hosts: all
4     become: true
5     tasks:
6   - name: Generate /etc/hosts file
7     ansible.builtin.blockinfile:
8       state: present
9       dest: /etc/hosts
10      content: |
11        192.168.0.200 demo demo.example.com
```

Fix

```yaml
1  ---
2  - name: blockinfile module demo
3    hosts: all
4    become: true
5    tasks:
6    - name: Generate /etc/hosts file
7        ansible.builtin.blockinfile:
8          state: present
9          dest: /etc/hosts
10         content: |
11            192.168.0.200 demo demo.example.com
```

Ansible troubleshooting - syntax error

Let's troubleshoot together the Ansible fatal error "Syntax Error while loading YAML" to find the offending lines in our playbook code, the root cause, fix a missing quote, and verify the resolution is working.

demo

The best way of talking about Ansible troubleshooting is to jump in a live demo to show you practically the syntax error and how to solve it!

error code

- report.txt

```
1    test report.txt
```

- syntax_error.yml

```
1    ---
2    - name: win_copy module demo
3      hosts: all
4      become: false
5      gather_facts: false
6      vars:
7        source: "report.txt"
8        destination: "Desktop/report.txt"
9      tasks:
10       - name: copy report.txt
11         ansible.windows.win_copy:
12           src: "{{ source }}"
13           dest: "{{ destination }}
```

error execution

```
1    $ ansible-playbook -i win/inventory troubleshooting/synta\
2    x_error.yml
3    ERROR! We were unable to read either as JSON nor YAML, th\
4    ese are the errors we got from each:
5    JSON: Expecting value: line 1 column 1 (char 0)
6
7    Syntax Error while loading YAML.
8    found unexpected end of stream
9
10   The error appears to be in 'ansible-pilot/troubleshooting\
11   /syntax_error.yml': line 14, column 1, but may
12   be elsewhere in the file depending on the exact syntax pr\
13   oblem.
14
15   The offending line appears to be:
```

```
16
17   src: "{{ source }}"
18   dest: "{{ destination }}
19   ^ here
20   We could be wrong, but this one looks like it might be an\
21     issue with
22   missing quotes. Always quote template expression brackets\
23     when they
24   start a value. For instance:
25
26   with_items:
27   - {{ foo }}
28
29   Should be written as:
30
31   with_items:
32   - "{{ foo }}"
```

fix code

- syntax_fix.yml

```
1    ---
2    - name: win_copy module demo
3      hosts: all
4      become: false
5      gather_facts: false
6      vars:
7        source: "report.txt"
8        destination: "Desktop/report.txt"
9      tasks:
10       - name: copy report.txt
11         ansible.windows.win_copy:
12           src: "{{ source }}"
13           dest: "{{ destination }}"
```

fix execution

output:

```
1   $ ansible-playbook -i win/inventory troubleshooting/synta\
2   x_fix.yml
3
4   PLAY [win_copy module demo] *****************************\
5   *******************************************
6
7   TASK [copy report.txt] *********************************\
8   *******************************************
9   ok: [WindowsServer]
10
11  PLAY RECAP *********************************************\
12  *******************************************
13  WindowsServer              : ok=1    changed=0    unreach\
14  able=0    failed=0    skipped=0    rescued=0    ignored=0
```

Ansible troubleshooting - undefined variable

How to reproduce the undefined variable error in Ansible, troubleshooting, and fix to be able to successfully print the value of a variable on screen.

demo

The best way of talking about Ansible troubleshooting is to jump in a live demo to show you practically the undefined variable error and how to solve it!

error code

- underfinedvariable_error.yml

```
1   ---
2   - name: debug module demo
3     hosts: all
4     tasks:
5       - name: debug message
6         ansible.builtin.debug:
7           msg: "{{ fruit }}"
```

error execution

```
1   $ ansible-playbook troubleshooting/undefinedvariable_erro\
2   r.yml
3
4   PLAY [file module demo] ********************************\
5   ******************************************
6
7   TASK [Gathering Facts] ********************************\
8   ******************************************
9   ok: [demo.example.com]
10
11  TASK [debug message] **********************************\
12  ******************************************
13  fatal: [demo.example.com]: FAILED! => {"msg": "The task i\
14  ncludes an option with an undefined variable. The error w\
15  as: 'fruit' is undefined\n\nThe error appears to be in '/\
16  Users/lberton/prj/github/ansible-pilot/troubleshooting/un\
17  definedvariable_error.yml': line 5, column 7, but may\nbe\
18   elsewhere in the file depending on the exact syntax prob\
19  lem.\n\nThe offending line appears to be:\n\n  tasks:\n  \
20    - name: debug message\n        ^ here\n"}
21
```

```
22  PLAY RECAP ***********************************************\
23  ****************************************
24  demo.example.com            : ok=1    changed=0    unreach\
25  able=0     failed=1    skipped=0    rescued=0    ignored=0
```

fix code

- underfinedvariable_fix.yml

```
1   ---
2   - name: debug module demo
3     hosts: all
4     vars:
5       fruit: "apple"
6     tasks:
7       - name: debug message
8         ansible.builtin.debug:
9           msg: "{{ fruit }}"
```

fix execution

```
1   $ ansible-playbook troubleshooting/undefinedvariable_fix.\
2   yml
3
4   PLAY [debug module demo] ********************************\
5   ****************************************
6
7   TASK [Gathering Facts] *********************************\
8   ****************************************
9   ok: [demo.example.com]
10
11  TASK [debug message] ***********************************\
12  ****************************************
13  ok: [demo.example.com] => {
14  "msg": "apple"
```

```
15    }
16
17    PLAY RECAP ******************************************\
18    *****************************************
19    demo.example.com            : ok=2     changed=0     unreach\
20    able=0     failed=0     skipped=0    rescued=0     ignored=0
```

Ansible troubleshooting - invalid argument

How to reproduce the `invalid argument` error of the Ansible module file, troubleshooting, and fix to be able to successfully.

See also Create a symbolic link (also symlink or soft link) in Linux - Ansible module file.

demo

The best way of talking about Ansible troubleshooting is to jump in a live demo to show you practically the missing module parameter and how to solve
it!

error code

- invalidargument_error.yml

```
1   ---
2   - name: file module demo
3     hosts: all
4     vars:
5       mylink: "~/example"
6       mysrc: "/proc/cpuinfo"
7     tasks:
8       - name: Creating a symlink
9         ansible.builtin.file:
10          path: "{{ mylink }}"
11          dest: "{{ mysrc }}"
12          state: link
```

error execution

```
1   $ ansible-playbook -i virtualmachines/demo/inventory trou\
2   bleshooting/invalidargument_error.yml
3   PLAY [file module demo] **********************************\
4   ***********************
5   TASK [Gathering Facts] **********************************\
6   ***********************
7   ok: [demo.example.com]
8   TASK [Creating a symlink] *******************************\
9   ***********************
10  An exception occurred during task execution. To see the f\
11  ull traceback, use -vvv. The error was: OSError: [Errno 2\
12  2] Invalid argument: b'/proc/cpuinfo'
13  fatal: [demo.example.com]: FAILED! => {"changed": false, \
14  "module_stderr": "Shared connection to 192.168.0.190 clos\
15  ed.\r\n", "module_stdout": "Traceback (most recent call l\
16  ast):\r\n  File \"/home/devops/.ansible/tmp/ansible-tmp-1\
17  637075583.2696111-7687-94302336849468/AnsiballZ_file.py\"\
18  , line 100, in <module>\r\n    _ansiballz_main()\r\n  Fil\
19  e \"/home/devops/.ansible/tmp/ansible-tmp-1637075583.2696\
20  111-7687-94302336849468/AnsiballZ_file.py\", line 92, in \
21  _ansiballz_main\r\n    invoke_module(zipped_mod, temp_pat\
```

```
22  h, ANSIBALLZ_PARAMS)\r\n  File \"/home/devops/.ansible/tm\
23  p/ansible-tmp-1637075583.2696111-7687-94302336849468/Ansi\
24  ballZ_file.py\", line 41, in invoke_module\r\n    run_nam\
25  e='__main__', alter_sys=True)\r\n  File \"/usr/lib64/pyth\
26  on3.6/runpy.py\", line 205, in run_module\r\n    return _\
27  run_module_code(code, init_globals, run_name, mod_spec)\r\
28  \n  File \"/usr/lib64/python3.6/runpy.py\", line 96, in _\
29  run_module_code\r\n    mod_name, mod_spec, pkg_name, scri\
30  pt_name)\r\n  File \"/usr/lib64/python3.6/runpy.py\", lin\
31  e 85, in _run_code\r\n    exec(code, run_globals)\r\n  Fi\
32  le \"/tmp/ansible_ansible.builtin.file_payload_7ktwrx3h/a\
33  nsible_ansible.builtin.file_payload.zip/ansible/modules/f\
34  ile.py\", line 966, in <module>\r\n  File \"/tmp/ansible_\
35  ansible.builtin.file_payload_7ktwrx3h/ansible_ansible.bui\
36  ltin.file_payload.zip/ansible/modules/file.py\", line 954\
37  , in main\r\n  File \"/tmp/ansible_ansible.builtin.file_p\
38  ayload_7ktwrx3h/ansible_ansible.builtin.file_payload.zip/\
39  ansible/modules/file.py\", line 688, in ensure_symlink\r\\
40  nOSError: [Errno 22] Invalid argument: b'/proc/cpuinfo'\r\
41  \n", "msg": "MODULE FAILURE\nSee stdout/stderr for the ex\
42  act error", "rc": 1}
43  PLAY RECAP *******************************************\
44  *********************
45  demo.example.com            : ok=1    changed=0    unreach\
46  able=0    failed=1    skipped=0    rescued=0    ignored=0
```

high verbose execution (-vvv)

```
$ ansible-playbook -i virtualmachines/demo/inventory trou\
bleshooting/invalidargument_error.yml -vvv
ansible-playbook [core 2.11.6]
  config file = None
  configured module search path = ['/Users/lberton/.ansib\
le/plugins/modules', '/usr/share/ansible/plugins/modules'\
]
  ansible python module location = /usr/local/Cellar/ansi\
ble/4.8.0/libexec/lib/python3.10/site-packages/ansible
  ansible collection location = /Users/lberton/.ansible/c\
ollections:/usr/share/ansible/collections
  executable location = /usr/local/bin/ansible-playbook
  python version = 3.10.0 (default, Oct 13 2021, 06:45:00\
) [Clang 13.0.0 (clang-1300.0.29.3)]
  jinja version = 3.0.2
  libyaml = True
No config file found; using defaults
host_list declined parsing /Users/lberton/prj/github/ansi\
ble-pilot/virtualmachines/demo/inventory as it did not pa\
ss its verify_file() method
script declined parsing /Users/lberton/prj/github/ansible\
-pilot/virtualmachines/demo/inventory as it did not pass \
its verify_file() method
auto declined parsing /Users/lberton/prj/github/ansible-p\
ilot/virtualmachines/demo/inventory as it did not pass it\
s verify_file() method
Parsed /Users/lberton/prj/github/ansible-pilot/virtualmac\
hines/demo/inventory inventory source with ini plugin
Skipping callback 'default', as we already have a stdout \
callback.
Skipping callback 'minimal', as we already have a stdout \
callback.
Skipping callback 'oneline', as we already have a stdout \
callback.
PLAYBOOK: invalidargument_error.yml ********************\
```

```
36  ***********************
37  1 plays in troubleshooting/invalidargument_error.yml
38  PLAY [file module demo] *******************************\
39  ***********************
40  TASK [Gathering Facts] ********************************\
41  ***********************
42  task path: /Users/lberton/prj/github/ansible-pilot/troubl\
43  eshooting/invalidargument_error.yml:2
44  <192.168.0.190> ESTABLISH SSH CONNECTION FOR USER: devops
45  <192.168.0.190> SSH: EXEC ssh -C -o ControlMaster=auto -o\
46   ControlPersist=60s -o StrictHostKeyChecking=no -o 'Ident\
47  ityFile="/Users/lberton/prj/github/ansible-pilot/demo/id_\
48  rsa"' -o KbdInteractiveAuthentication=no -o PreferredAuth\
49  entications=gssapi-with-mic,gssapi-keyex,hostbased,public\
50  key -o PasswordAuthentication=no -o 'User="devops"' -o Co\
51  nnectTimeout=10 -o ControlPath=/Users/lberton/.ansible/cp\
52  /bf202c4314 192.168.0.190 '/bin/sh -c '"'"'echo ~devops &\
53  & sleep 0'"'"''
54  <192.168.0.190> (0, b'/home/devops\n', b'')
55  <192.168.0.190> ESTABLISH SSH CONNECTION FOR USER: devops
56  <192.168.0.190> SSH: EXEC ssh -C -o ControlMaster=auto -o\
57   ControlPersist=60s -o StrictHostKeyChecking=no -o 'Ident\
58  ityFile="/Users/lberton/prj/github/ansible-pilot/demo/id_\
59  rsa"' -o KbdInteractiveAuthentication=no -o PreferredAuth\
60  entications=gssapi-with-mic,gssapi-keyex,hostbased,public\
61  key -o PasswordAuthentication=no -o 'User="devops"' -o Co\
62  nnectTimeout=10 -o ControlPath=/Users/lberton/.ansible/cp\
63  /bf202c4314 192.168.0.190 '/bin/sh -c '"'"'( umask 77 && \
64  mkdir -p "` echo /home/devops/.ansible/tmp `"&& mkdir "` \
65  echo /home/devops/.ansible/tmp/ansible-tmp-1637075611.201\
66  921-7700-238727032540101 `" && echo ansible-tmp-163707561\
67  1.201921-7700-238727032540101="` echo /home/devops/.ansib\
68  le/tmp/ansible-tmp-1637075611.201921-7700-238727032540101\
69   `" ) && sleep 0'"'"''
70  <192.168.0.190> (0, b'ansible-tmp-1637075611.201921-7700-\
```

```
238727032540101=/home/devops/.ansible/tmp/ansible-tmp-163\
7075611.201921-7700-238727032540101\n', b'')
<demo.example.com> Attempting python interpreter discovery
<192.168.0.190> ESTABLISH SSH CONNECTION FOR USER: devops
<192.168.0.190> SSH: EXEC ssh -C -o ControlMaster=auto -o\
 ControlPersist=60s -o StrictHostKeyChecking=no -o 'Ident\
ityFile="/Users/lberton/prj/github/ansible-pilot/demo/id_\
rsa"' -o KbdInteractiveAuthentication=no -o PreferredAuth\
entications=gssapi-with-mic,gssapi-keyex,hostbased,public\
key -o PasswordAuthentication=no -o 'User="devops"' -o Co\
nnectTimeout=10 -o ControlPath=/Users/lberton/.ansible/cp\
/bf202c4314 192.168.0.190 '/bin/sh -c '"'"'echo PLATFORM;\
 uname; echo FOUND; command -v '"'"'"'"'"'"'"'"'/usr/bin/\
python'"'"'"'"'"'"'"'"'; command -v '"'"'"'"'"'"'"'"'pyth\
on3.9'"'"'"'"'"'"'"'"'; command -v '"'"'"'"'"'"'"'"'pytho\
n3.8'"'"'"'"'"'"'"'"'; command -v '"'"'"'"'"'"'"'"'python\
3.7'"'"'"'"'"'"'"'"'; command -v '"'"'"'"'"'"'"'"'python3\
.6'"'"'"'"'"'"'"'"'; command -v '"'"'"'"'"'"'"'"'python3.\
5'"'"'"'"'"'"'"'"'; command -v '"'"'"'"'"'"'"'"'python2.7\
'"'"'"'"'"'"'"'"'; command -v '"'"'"'"'"'"'"'"'python2.6'\
'"'"'"'"'"'"'"'"'; command -v '"'"'"'"'"'"'"'"'/usr/libexe\
c/platform-python'"'"'"'"'"'"'"'"'; command -v '"'"'"'"'\
'"'"'"'/usr/bin/python3'"'"'"'"'"'"'"'"'; command -v '"'"'\
'"'"'"'"'"'python'"'"'"'"'"'"'"'"'; echo ENDFOUND && sl\
eep 0'"'"''
<192.168.0.190> (0, b'PLATFORM\nLinux\nFOUND\n/usr/bin/py\
thon3.6\n/usr/libexec/platform-python\n/usr/bin/python3\n\
ENDFOUND\n', b'')
<192.168.0.190> ESTABLISH SSH CONNECTION FOR USER: devops
<192.168.0.190> SSH: EXEC ssh -C -o ControlMaster=auto -o\
 ControlPersist=60s -o StrictHostKeyChecking=no -o 'Ident\
ityFile="/Users/lberton/prj/github/ansible-pilot/demo/id_\
rsa"' -o KbdInteractiveAuthentication=no -o PreferredAuth\
entications=gssapi-with-mic,gssapi-keyex,hostbased,public\
key -o PasswordAuthentication=no -o 'User="devops"' -o Co\
```

```
nnectTimeout=10 -o ControlPath=/Users/lberton/.ansible/cp\
/bf202c4314 192.168.0.190 '/bin/sh -c '"'"'/usr/bin/pytho\
n3.6 && sleep 0'"'"''
<192.168.0.190> (0, b'{"platform_dist_result": ["redhat",\
 "8.4", "Ootpa"], "osrelease_content": "NAME=\\"Red Hat E\
nterprise Linux\\"\\nVERSION=\\"8.4 (Ootpa)\\"\\nID=\\"rh\
el\\"\\nID_LIKE=\\"fedora\\"\\nVERSION_ID=\\"8.4\\"\\nPLA\
TFORM_ID=\\"platform:el8\\"\\nPRETTY_NAME=\\"Red Hat Ente\
rprise Linux 8.4 (Ootpa)\\"\\nANSI_COLOR=\\"0;31\\"\\nCPE\
_NAME=\\"cpe:/o:redhat:enterprise_linux:8.4:GA\\"\\nHOME_\
URL=\\"https://www.redhat.com/\\"\\nDOCUMENTATION_URL=\\"\
https://access.redhat.com/documentation/red_hat_enterpris\
e_linux/8/\\"\\nBUG_REPORT_URL=\\"https://bugzilla.redhat\
.com/\\"\\n\\nREDHAT_BUGZILLA_PRODUCT=\\"Red Hat Enterpri\
se Linux 8\\"\\nREDHAT_BUGZILLA_PRODUCT_VERSION=8.4\\nRED\
HAT_SUPPORT_PRODUCT=\\"Red Hat Enterprise Linux\\"\\nREDH\
AT_SUPPORT_PRODUCT_VERSION=\\"8.4\\"\\n"}\n', b'')
Using module file /usr/local/Cellar/ansible/4.8.0/libexec\
/lib/python3.10/site-packages/ansible/modules/setup.py
<192.168.0.190> PUT /Users/lberton/.ansible/tmp/ansible-l\
ocal-7697iluh4khz/tmpjxztg1jt TO /home/devops/.ansible/tm\
p/ansible-tmp-1637075611.201921-7700-238727032540101/Ansi\
ballZ_setup.py
<192.168.0.190> SSH: EXEC sftp -b - -C -o ControlMaster=a\
uto -o ControlPersist=60s -o StrictHostKeyChecking=no -o \
'IdentityFile="/Users/lberton/prj/github/ansible-pilot/de\
mo/id_rsa"' -o KbdInteractiveAuthentication=no -o Preferr\
edAuthentications=gssapi-with-mic,gssapi-keyex,hostbased,\
publickey -o PasswordAuthentication=no -o 'User="devops"'\
 -o ConnectTimeout=10 -o ControlPath=/Users/lberton/.ansi\
ble/cp/bf202c4314 '[192.168.0.190]'
<192.168.0.190> (0, b'sftp> put /Users/lberton/.ansible/t\
mp/ansible-local-7697iluh4khz/tmpjxztg1jt /home/devops/.a\
nsible/tmp/ansible-tmp-1637075611.201921-7700-23872703254\
0101/AnsiballZ_setup.py\n', b'')
```

```
141  <192.168.0.190> ESTABLISH SSH CONNECTION FOR USER: devops
142  <192.168.0.190> SSH: EXEC ssh -C -o ControlMaster=auto -o\
143   ControlPersist=60s -o StrictHostKeyChecking=no -o 'Ident\
144  ityFile="/Users/lberton/prj/github/ansible-pilot/demo/id_\
145  rsa"' -o KbdInteractiveAuthentication=no -o PreferredAuth\
146  entications=gssapi-with-mic,gssapi-keyex,hostbased,public\
147  key -o PasswordAuthentication=no -o 'User="devops"' -o Co\
148  nnectTimeout=10 -o ControlPath=/Users/lberton/.ansible/cp\
149  /bf202c4314 192.168.0.190 '/bin/sh -c '"'"'chmod u+x /hom\
150  e/devops/.ansible/tmp/ansible-tmp-1637075611.201921-7700-\
151  238727032540101/ /home/devops/.ansible/tmp/ansible-tmp-16\
152  37075611.201921-7700-238727032540101/AnsiballZ_setup.py &\
153  & sleep 0'"'"''
154  <192.168.0.190> (0, b'', b'')
155  <192.168.0.190> ESTABLISH SSH CONNECTION FOR USER: devops
156  <192.168.0.190> SSH: EXEC ssh -C -o ControlMaster=auto -o\
157   ControlPersist=60s -o StrictHostKeyChecking=no -o 'Ident\
158  ityFile="/Users/lberton/prj/github/ansible-pilot/demo/id_\
159  rsa"' -o KbdInteractiveAuthentication=no -o PreferredAuth\
160  entications=gssapi-with-mic,gssapi-keyex,hostbased,public\
161  key -o PasswordAuthentication=no -o 'User="devops"' -o Co\
162  nnectTimeout=10 -o ControlPath=/Users/lberton/.ansible/cp\
163  /bf202c4314 -tt 192.168.0.190 '/bin/sh -c '"'"'/usr/libex\
164  ec/platform-python /home/devops/.ansible/tmp/ansible-tmp-\
165  1637075611.201921-7700-238727032540101/AnsiballZ_setup.py\
166   && sleep 0'"'"''
167  <192.168.0.190> (0, b'\r\n{"ansible_facts": {"ansible_pyt\
168  hon": {"version": {"major": 3, "minor": 6, "micro": 8, "r\
169  eleaselevel": "final", "serial": 0}, "version_info": [3, \
170  6, 8, "final", 0], "executable": "/usr/libexec/platform-p\
171  ython", "has_sslcontext": true, "type": "cpython"}, "ansi\
172  ble_system": "Linux", "ansible_kernel": "4.18.0-305.el8.x\
173  86_64", "ansible_kernel_version": "#1 SMP Thu Apr 29 08:5\
174  4:30 EDT 2021", "ansible_machine": "x86_64", "ansible_pyt\
175  hon_version": "3.6.8", "ansible_fqdn": "demo.example.com"\
```

, "ansible_hostname": "demo", "ansible_nodename": "demo.e\
xample.com", "ansible_domain": "example.com", "ansible_us\
erspace_bits": "64", "ansible_architecture": "x86_64", "a\
nsible_userspace_architecture": "x86_64", "ansible_machin\
e_id": "e03fdda4378049efaa08f0a40eeb3df7", "ansible_iscsi\
_iqn": "", "ansible_user_id": "devops", "ansible_user_uid\
": 1001, "ansible_user_gid": 10, "ansible_user_gecos": ""\
, "ansible_user_dir": "/home/devops", "ansible_user_shell\
": "/bin/bash", "ansible_real_user_id": 1001, "ansible_ef\
fective_user_id": 1001, "ansible_real_group_id": 10, "ans\
ible_effective_group_id": 10, "ansible_cmdline": {"BOOT_I\
MAGE": "(hd0,msdos1)/vmlinuz-4.18.0-305.el8.x86_64", "roo\
t": "/dev/mapper/rhel_rhel8-root", "ro": true, "no_timer_\
check": true, "crashkernel": "auto", "resume": "/dev/mapp\
er/rhel_rhel8-swap", "rd.lvm.lv": "rhel_rhel8/swap", "bio\
sdevname": "0", "net.ifnames": "0", "rhgb": true, "quiet"\
: true}, "ansible_proc_cmdline": {"BOOT_IMAGE": "(hd0,msd\
os1)/vmlinuz-4.18.0-305.el8.x86_64", "root": "/dev/mapper\
/rhel_rhel8-root", "ro": true, "no_timer_check": true, "c\
rashkernel": "auto", "resume": "/dev/mapper/rhel_rhel8-sw\
ap", "rd.lvm.lv": ["rhel_rhel8/root", "rhel_rhel8/swap"],\
 "biosdevname": "0", "net.ifnames": "0", "rhgb": true, "q\
uiet": true}, "ansible_distribution": "RedHat", "ansible_\
distribution_release": "Ootpa", "ansible_distribution_ver\
sion": "8.4", "ansible_distribution_major_version": "8", \
"ansible_distribution_file_path": "/etc/redhat-release", \
"ansible_distribution_file_variety": "RedHat", "ansible_d\
istribution_file_parsed": true, "ansible_distribution_fil\
e_search_string": "Red Hat", "ansible_os_family": "RedHat\
", "ansible_is_chroot": false, "ansible_ssh_host_key_rsa_\
public": "AAAAB3NzaC1yc2EAAAADAQABAAABgQDAW9MaZgK1RHLUfi5\
920uH7iVdSr4QrxH66r2b4QcZDa1ormtbb/zyiX0by71MYTutyfATE2rJ\
Ls+eWbdUppAr3AfLK8ZOdC6mypN6vD3SAmIToQq2LA/UtNFSr49Rbi4JB\
KYGrrJayRdVSg/I7fupYDmoEryW5/RMzpLfEUdeFfIw3AMVnPxOaMTH1I\
n2hEUplgexVIgKQXaS9gLFrxUrjZh4KYIbfrvPRdMifU1psUwdK/AHEXu\

```
c4aNpQXI55+bKHkWUhNd4bsLnAxfmjUTqe+hLzOIXVxqR9vNE4tmJm0V2\
oo6Dqn1jv17enQ/4kTpotJTvSpddxoAYNE1V+RiBXqzmZ/U2fNith41Pv\
dPRoVuU6vAdMeONbqt6HSYueMZggayRSnJBdpNL1z2mhEYLaqOPCAoT6e\
UynFGD3d2+g805mDx9Aib6dxj0KKdQ7EqsRt/v/BSnG1onUimfeOq3UK8\
zZaZ8c9jEBL4xpFRh11vXn/PqAW6yfvlXzYR186E=", "ansible_ssh_\
host_key_rsa_public_keytype": "ssh-rsa", "ansible_ssh_hos\
t_key_ecdsa_public": "AAAAE2VjZHNhLXNoYTItbmlzdHAyNTYAAAA\
IbmlzdHAyNTYAAABBBD191gzPfk8M293CUSfpDqIyYeCZ/CTkBhnfssDc\
17hTjglDv2+bk286IYXW8MWDvsrBDNnD3obro23X7rPUm6k=", "ansib\
le_ssh_host_key_ecdsa_public_keytype": "ecdsa-sha2-nistp2\
56", "ansible_ssh_host_key_ed25519_public": "AAAAC3NzaC1l\
ZDI1NTE5AAAAIC0jh56hNupL4dEEY70XwEovfX3VmxdIEg1tDXdvsizO"\
, "ansible_ssh_host_key_ed25519_public_keytype": "ssh-ed2\
5519", "ansible_selinux_python_present": true, "ansible_s\
elinux": {"status": "enabled", "policyvers": 33, "config_\
mode": "enforcing", "mode": "enforcing", "type": "targete\
d"}, "ansible_date_time": {"year": "2021", "month": "11",\
 "weekday": "Tuesday", "weekday_number": "2", "weeknumber\
": "46", "day": "16", "hour": "15", "minute": "13", "seco\
nd": "32", "epoch": "1637075612", "date": "2021-11-16", "\
time": "15:13:32", "iso8601_micro": "2021-11-16T15:13:32.\
116130Z", "iso8601": "2021-11-16T15:13:32Z", "iso8601_bas\
ic": "20211116T151332116130", "iso8601_basic_short": "202\
11116T151332", "tz": "UTC", "tz_dst": "UTC", "tz_offset":\
 "+0000"}, "ansible_system_capabilities_enforced": "True"\
, "ansible_system_capabilities": [""], "ansible_dns": {"s\
earch": ["example.com"], "nameservers": ["10.0.2.3", "192\
.168.0.1"]}, "ansible_virtualization_role": "guest", "ans\
ible_virtualization_type": "virtualbox", "ansible_virtual\
ization_tech_guest": ["virtualbox"], "ansible_virtualizat\
ion_tech_host": [], "ansible_processor": ["0", "GenuineIn\
tel", "Intel(R) Core(TM) i7-9750H CPU @ 2.60GHz"], "ansib\
le_processor_count": 1, "ansible_processor_cores": 1, "an\
sible_processor_threads_per_core": 1, "ansible_processor_\
vcpus": 1, "ansible_processor_nproc": 1, "ansible_memtota\
```

l_mb": 809, "ansible_memfree_mb": 231, "ansible_swaptotal\
_mb": 2107, "ansible_swapfree_mb": 2106, "ansible_memory_\
mb": {"real": {"total": 809, "used": 578, "free": 231}, "\
nocache": {"free": 615, "used": 194}, "swap": {"total": 2\
107, "free": 2106, "used": 1, "cached": 0}}, "ansible_bio\
s_date": "12/01/2006", "ansible_bios_vendor": "innotek Gm\
bH", "ansible_bios_version": "VirtualBox", "ansible_board\
_asset_tag": "NA", "ansible_board_name": "VirtualBox", "a\
nsible_board_serial": "NA", "ansible_board_vendor": "Orac\
le Corporation", "ansible_board_version": "1.2", "ansible\
_chassis_asset_tag": "NA", "ansible_chassis_serial": "NA"\
, "ansible_chassis_vendor": "Oracle Corporation", "ansibl\
e_chassis_version": "NA", "ansible_form_factor": "Other",\
 "ansible_product_name": "VirtualBox", "ansible_product_s\
erial": "NA", "ansible_product_uuid": "NA", "ansible_prod\
uct_version": "1.2", "ansible_system_vendor": "innotek Gm\
bH", "ansible_devices": {"dm-1": {"virtual": 1, "links": \
{"ids": ["dm-name-rhel_rhel8-swap", "dm-uuid-LVM-zC6A0QsB\
DrGwKwxZtr1rcyTIPcBHeh3GT17wXnKVT0iabIr6cIdgtij0sxe1yQl9"\
], "uuids": ["7e5dc044-a7d1-4384-8a2e-e5d829e31945"], "la\
bels": [], "masters": []}, "vendor": null, "model": null,\
 "sas_address": null, "sas_device_handle": null, "removab\
le": "0", "support_discard": "0", "partitions": {}, "rota\
tional": "1", "scheduler_mode": "", "sectors": "4317184",\
 "sectorsize": "512", "size": "2.06 GB", "host": "", "hol\
ders": []}, "dm-0": {"virtual": 1, "links": {"ids": ["dm-\
name-rhel_rhel8-root", "dm-uuid-LVM-zC6A0QsBDrGwKwxZtr1rc\
yTIPcBHeh3Grwodyj91WNUBFX1nPY4UW5GbWxigVvff"], "uuids": [\
"a3dfbd25-503a-413a-a281-45cfaad69feb"], "labels": [], "m\
asters": []}, "vendor": null, "model": null, "sas_address\
": null, "sas_device_handle": null, "removable": "0", "su\
pport_discard": "0", "partitions": {}, "rotational": "1",\
 "scheduler_mode": "", "sectors": "146800640", "sectorsiz\
e": "512", "size": "70.00 GB", "host": "", "holders": []}\
, "sda": {"virtual": 1, "links": {"ids": ["ata-VBOX_HARDD\

ISK_VBcff81b56-ec300eaa", "scsi-0ATA_VBOX_HARDDISK_VBcff8\
1b56-ec300eaa", "scsi-1ATA_VBOX_HARDDISK_VBcff81b56-ec300\
eaa", "scsi-SATA_VBOX_HARDDISK_VBcff81b56-ec300eaa"], "uu\
ids": [], "labels": [], "masters": []}, "vendor": "ATA", \
"model": "VBOX HARDDISK", "sas_address": null, "sas_devic\
e_handle": null, "removable": "0", "support_discard": "0"\
, "partitions": {"sda2": {"links": {"ids": ["ata-VBOX_HAR\
DDISK_VBcff81b56-ec300eaa-part2", "lvm-pv-uuid-g7SkxV-RYr\
T-JL47-mMcA-qBOB-Zjjk-mdaQSN", "scsi-0ATA_VBOX_HARDDISK_V\
Bcff81b56-ec300eaa-part2", "scsi-1ATA_VBOX_HARDDISK_VBcff\
81b56-ec300eaa-part2", "scsi-SATA_VBOX_HARDDISK_VBcff81b5\
6-ec300eaa-part2"], "uuids": [], "labels": [], "masters":\
 ["dm-0", "dm-1"]}, "start": "2099200", "sectors": "26633\
6256", "sectorsize": 512, "size": "127.00 GB", "uuid": nu\
ll, "holders": ["rhel_rhel8-swap", "rhel_rhel8-root"]}, "\
sda1": {"links": {"ids": ["ata-VBOX_HARDDISK_VBcff81b56-e\
c300eaa-part1", "scsi-0ATA_VBOX_HARDDISK_VBcff81b56-ec300\
eaa-part1", "scsi-1ATA_VBOX_HARDDISK_VBcff81b56-ec300eaa-\
part1", "scsi-SATA_VBOX_HARDDISK_VBcff81b56-ec300eaa-part\
1"], "uuids": ["ae6c1777-c1c9-42a1-8fcf-513077aac39b"], "\
labels": [], "masters": []}, "start": "2048", "sectors": \
"2097152", "sectorsize": 512, "size": "1.00 GB", "uuid": \
"ae6c1777-c1c9-42a1-8fcf-513077aac39b", "holders": []}}, \
"rotational": "1", "scheduler_mode": "mq-deadline", "sect\
ors": "268435456", "sectorsize": "512", "size": "128.00 G\
B", "host": "IDE interface: Intel Corporation 82371AB/EB/\
MB PIIX4 IDE (rev 01)", "holders": []}}, "ansible_device_\
links": {"ids": {"sda1": ["ata-VBOX_HARDDISK_VBcff81b56-e\
c300eaa-part1", "scsi-0ATA_VBOX_HARDDISK_VBcff81b56-ec300\
eaa-part1", "scsi-1ATA_VBOX_HARDDISK_VBcff81b56-ec300eaa-\
part1", "scsi-SATA_VBOX_HARDDISK_VBcff81b56-ec300eaa-part\
1"], "sda2": ["ata-VBOX_HARDDISK_VBcff81b56-ec300eaa-part\
2", "lvm-pv-uuid-g7SkxV-RYrT-JL47-mMcA-qBOB-Zjjk-mdaQSN",\
 "scsi-0ATA_VBOX_HARDDISK_VBcff81b56-ec300eaa-part2", "sc\
si-1ATA_VBOX_HARDDISK_VBcff81b56-ec300eaa-part2", "scsi-S\

```
ATA_VBOX_HARDDISK_VBcff81b56-ec300eaa-part2"], "sda": ["a\
ta-VBOX_HARDDISK_VBcff81b56-ec300eaa", "scsi-0ATA_VBOX_HA\
RDDISK_VBcff81b56-ec300eaa", "scsi-1ATA_VBOX_HARDDISK_VBc\
ff81b56-ec300eaa", "scsi-SATA_VBOX_HARDDISK_VBcff81b56-ec\
300eaa"], "dm-1": ["dm-name-rhel_rhel8-swap", "dm-uuid-LV\
M-zC6A0QsBDrGwKwxZtr1rcyTIPcBHeh3GT17wXnKVT0iabIr6cIdgtij\
0sxe1yQl9"], "dm-0": ["dm-name-rhel_rhel8-root", "dm-uuid\
-LVM-zC6A0QsBDrGwKwxZtr1rcyTIPcBHeh3Grwodyj91WNUBFX1nPY4U\
W5GbWxigVvff"]}, "uuids": {"dm-1": ["7e5dc044-a7d1-4384-8\
a2e-e5d829e31945"], "dm-0": ["a3dfbd25-503a-413a-a281-45c\
faad69feb"], "sda1": ["ae6c1777-c1c9-42a1-8fcf-513077aac3\
9b"]}, "labels": {}, "masters": {"sda2": ["dm-0", "dm-1"]\
}}, "ansible_uptime_seconds": 15365, "ansible_mounts": [{\
"mount": "/", "device": "/dev/mapper/rhel_rhel8-root", "f\
stype": "xfs", "options": "rw,seclabel,relatime,attr2,ino\
de64,logbufs=8,logbsize=32k,noquota", "size_total": 75125\
227520, "size_available": 71803695104, "block_size": 4096\
, "block_total": 18341120, "block_available": 17530199, "\
block_used": 810921, "inode_total": 36700160, "inode_avai\
lable": 36624744, "inode_used": 75416, "uuid": "a3dfbd25-\
503a-413a-a281-45cfaad69feb"}, {"mount": "/boot", "device\
": "/dev/sda1", "fstype": "xfs", "options": "rw,seclabel,\
relatime,attr2,inode64,logbufs=8,logbsize=32k,noquota", "\
size_total": 1063256064, "size_available": 863862784, "bl\
ock_size": 4096, "block_total": 259584, "block_available"\
: 210904, "block_used": 48680, "inode_total": 524288, "in\
ode_available": 523979, "inode_used": 309, "uuid": "ae6c1\
777-c1c9-42a1-8fcf-513077aac39b"}], "ansible_local": {}, \
"ansible_hostnqn": "", "ansible_fibre_channel_wwn": [], "\
ansible_lsb": {}, "ansible_service_mgr": "systemd", "ansi\
ble_interfaces": ["eth1", "lo", "eth0"], "ansible_eth0": \
{"device": "eth0", "macaddress": "08:00:27:dc:e4:34", "mt\
u": 1500, "active": true, "module": "e1000", "type": "eth\
er", "pciid": "0000:00:03.0", "speed": 1000, "promisc": f\
alse, "ipv4": {"address": "10.0.2.15", "broadcast": "10.0\
```

```
.2.255", "netmask": "255.255.255.0", "network": "10.0.2.0\
"}, "features": {"rx_checksumming": "off", "tx_checksummi\
ng": "on", "tx_checksum_ipv4": "off [fixed]", "tx_checksu\
m_ip_generic": "on", "tx_checksum_ipv6": "off [fixed]", "\
tx_checksum_fcoe_crc": "off [fixed]", "tx_checksum_sctp":\
 "off [fixed]", "scatter_gather": "on", "tx_scatter_gathe\
r": "on", "tx_scatter_gather_fraglist": "off [fixed]", "t\
cp_segmentation_offload": "on", "tx_tcp_segmentation": "o\
n", "tx_tcp_ecn_segmentation": "off [fixed]", "tx_tcp_man\
gleid_segmentation": "off", "tx_tcp6_segmentation": "off \
[fixed]", "generic_segmentation_offload": "on", "generic_\
receive_offload": "on", "large_receive_offload": "off [fi\
xed]", "rx_vlan_offload": "on", "tx_vlan_offload": "on [f\
ixed]", "ntuple_filters": "off [fixed]", "receive_hashing\
": "off [fixed]", "highdma": "off [fixed]", "rx_vlan_filt\
er": "on [fixed]", "vlan_challenged": "off [fixed]", "tx_\
lockless": "off [fixed]", "netns_local": "off [fixed]", "\
tx_gso_robust": "off [fixed]", "tx_fcoe_segmentation": "o\
ff [fixed]", "tx_gre_segmentation": "off [fixed]", "tx_gr\
e_csum_segmentation": "off [fixed]", "tx_ipxip4_segmentat\
ion": "off [fixed]", "tx_ipxip6_segmentation": "off [fixe\
d]", "tx_udp_tnl_segmentation": "off [fixed]", "tx_udp_tn\
l_csum_segmentation": "off [fixed]", "tx_gso_partial": "o\
ff [fixed]", "tx_tunnel_remcsum_segmentation": "off [fixe\
d]", "tx_sctp_segmentation": "off [fixed]", "tx_esp_segme\
ntation": "off [fixed]", "tx_udp_segmentation": "off [fix\
ed]", "tx_gso_list": "off [fixed]", "rx_gro_list": "off",\
 "tls_hw_rx_offload": "off [fixed]", "fcoe_mtu": "off [fi\
xed]", "tx_nocache_copy": "off", "loopback": "off [fixed]\
", "rx_fcs": "off", "rx_all": "off", "tx_vlan_stag_hw_ins\
ert": "off [fixed]", "rx_vlan_stag_hw_parse": "off [fixed\
]", "rx_vlan_stag_filter": "off [fixed]", "l2_fwd_offload\
": "off [fixed]", "hw_tc_offload": "off [fixed]", "esp_hw\
_offload": "off [fixed]", "esp_tx_csum_hw_offload": "off \
[fixed]", "rx_udp_tunnel_port_offload": "off [fixed]", "t\
```

```
386  ls_hw_tx_offload": "off [fixed]", "rx_gro_hw": "off [fixe\
387  d]", "tls_hw_record": "off [fixed]"}, "timestamping": [],\
388   "hw_timestamp_filters": []}, "ansible_eth1": {"device": \
389  "eth1", "macaddress": "08:00:27:85:5a:fe", "mtu": 1500, "\
390  active": true, "module": "e1000", "type": "ether", "pciid\
391  ": "0000:00:08.0", "speed": 1000, "promisc": false, "ipv4\
392  ": {"address": "192.168.0.190", "broadcast": "192.168.0.2\
393  55", "netmask": "255.255.255.0", "network": "192.168.0.0"\
394  }, "ipv6": [{"address": "fe80::a00:27ff:fe85:5afe", "pref\
395  ix": "64", "scope": "link"}], "features": {"rx_checksummi\
396  ng": "off", "tx_checksumming": "on", "tx_checksum_ipv4": \
397  "off [fixed]", "tx_checksum_ip_generic": "on", "tx_checks\
398  um_ipv6": "off [fixed]", "tx_checksum_fcoe_crc": "off [fi\
399  xed]", "tx_checksum_sctp": "off [fixed]", "scatter_gather\
400  ": "on", "tx_scatter_gather": "on", "tx_scatter_gather_fr\
401  aglist": "off [fixed]", "tcp_segmentation_offload": "on",\
402   "tx_tcp_segmentation": "on", "tx_tcp_ecn_segmentation": \
403  "off [fixed]", "tx_tcp_mangleid_segmentation": "off", "tx\
404  _tcp6_segmentation": "off [fixed]", "generic_segmentation\
405  _offload": "on", "generic_receive_offload": "on", "large_\
406  receive_offload": "off [fixed]", "rx_vlan_offload": "on",\
407   "tx_vlan_offload": "on [fixed]", "ntuple_filters": "off \
408  [fixed]", "receive_hashing": "off [fixed]", "highdma": "o\
409  ff [fixed]", "rx_vlan_filter": "on [fixed]", "vlan_challe\
410  nged": "off [fixed]", "tx_lockless": "off [fixed]", "netn\
411  s_local": "off [fixed]", "tx_gso_robust": "off [fixed]", \
412  "tx_fcoe_segmentation": "off [fixed]", "tx_gre_segmentati\
413  on": "off [fixed]", "tx_gre_csum_segmentation": "off [fix\
414  ed]", "tx_ipxip4_segmentation": "off [fixed]", "tx_ipxip6\
415  _segmentation": "off [fixed]", "tx_udp_tnl_segmentation":\
416   "off [fixed]", "tx_udp_tnl_csum_segmentation": "off [fix\
417  ed]", "tx_gso_partial": "off [fixed]", "tx_tunnel_remcsum\
418  _segmentation": "off [fixed]", "tx_sctp_segmentation": "o\
419  ff [fixed]", "tx_esp_segmentation": "off [fixed]", "tx_ud\
420  p_segmentation": "off [fixed]", "tx_gso_list": "off [fixe\
```

```
d]", "rx_gro_list": "off", "tls_hw_rx_offload": "off [fix\
ed]", "fcoe_mtu": "off [fixed]", "tx_nocache_copy": "off"\
, "loopback": "off [fixed]", "rx_fcs": "off", "rx_all": "\
off", "tx_vlan_stag_hw_insert": "off [fixed]", "rx_vlan_s\
tag_hw_parse": "off [fixed]", "rx_vlan_stag_filter": "off\
 [fixed]", "l2_fwd_offload": "off [fixed]", "hw_tc_offloa\
d": "off [fixed]", "esp_hw_offload": "off [fixed]", "esp_\
tx_csum_hw_offload": "off [fixed]", "rx_udp_tunnel_port_o\
ffload": "off [fixed]", "tls_hw_tx_offload": "off [fixed]\
", "rx_gro_hw": "off [fixed]", "tls_hw_record": "off [fix\
ed]"}, "timestamping": [], "hw_timestamp_filters": []}, "\
ansible_lo": {"device": "lo", "mtu": 65536, "active": tru\
e, "type": "loopback", "promisc": false, "ipv4": {"addres\
s": "127.0.0.1", "broadcast": "", "netmask": "255.0.0.0",\
 "network": "127.0.0.0"}, "features": {"rx_checksumming":\
 "on [fixed]", "tx_checksumming": "on", "tx_checksum_ipv4\
": "off [fixed]", "tx_checksum_ip_generic": "on [fixed]",\
 "tx_checksum_ipv6": "off [fixed]", "tx_checksum_fcoe_crc\
": "off [fixed]", "tx_checksum_sctp": "on [fixed]", "scat\
ter_gather": "on", "tx_scatter_gather": "on [fixed]", "tx\
_scatter_gather_fraglist": "on [fixed]", "tcp_segmentatio\
n_offload": "on", "tx_tcp_segmentation": "on", "tx_tcp_ec\
n_segmentation": "on", "tx_tcp_mangleid_segmentation": "o\
n", "tx_tcp6_segmentation": "on", "generic_segmentation_o\
ffload": "on", "generic_receive_offload": "on", "large_re\
ceive_offload": "off [fixed]", "rx_vlan_offload": "off [f\
ixed]", "tx_vlan_offload": "off [fixed]", "ntuple_filters\
": "off [fixed]", "receive_hashing": "off [fixed]", "high\
dma": "on [fixed]", "rx_vlan_filter": "off [fixed]", "vla\
n_challenged": "on [fixed]", "tx_lockless": "on [fixed]",\
 "netns_local": "on [fixed]", "tx_gso_robust": "off [fixe\
d]", "tx_fcoe_segmentation": "off [fixed]", "tx_gre_segme\
ntation": "off [fixed]", "tx_gre_csum_segmentation": "off\
 [fixed]", "tx_ipxip4_segmentation": "off [fixed]", "tx_i\
pxip6_segmentation": "off [fixed]", "tx_udp_tnl_segmentat\
```

ion": "off [fixed]", "tx_udp_tnl_csum_segmentation": "off\
 [fixed]", "tx_gso_partial": "off [fixed]", "tx_tunnel_re\
mcsum_segmentation": "off [fixed]", "tx_sctp_segmentation\
": "on", "tx_esp_segmentation": "off [fixed]", "tx_udp_se\
gmentation": "off [fixed]", "tx_gso_list": "off [fixed]",\
 "rx_gro_list": "off", "tls_hw_rx_offload": "off [fixed]"\
, "fcoe_mtu": "off [fixed]", "tx_nocache_copy": "off [fix\
ed]", "loopback": "on [fixed]", "rx_fcs": "off [fixed]", \
"rx_all": "off [fixed]", "tx_vlan_stag_hw_insert": "off [\
fixed]", "rx_vlan_stag_hw_parse": "off [fixed]", "rx_vlan\
_stag_filter": "off [fixed]", "l2_fwd_offload": "off [fix\
ed]", "hw_tc_offload": "off [fixed]", "esp_hw_offload": "\
off [fixed]", "esp_tx_csum_hw_offload": "off [fixed]", "r\
x_udp_tunnel_port_offload": "off [fixed]", "tls_hw_tx_off\
load": "off [fixed]", "rx_gro_hw": "off [fixed]", "tls_hw\
_record": "off [fixed]"}, "timestamping": [], "hw_timesta\
mp_filters": []}, "ansible_default_ipv4": {"gateway": "10\
.0.2.2", "interface": "eth0", "address": "10.0.2.15", "br\
oadcast": "10.0.2.255", "netmask": "255.255.255.0", "netw\
ork": "10.0.2.0", "macaddress": "08:00:27:dc:e4:34", "mtu\
": 1500, "type": "ether", "alias": "eth0"}, "ansible_defa\
ult_ipv6": {}, "ansible_all_ipv4_addresses": ["10.0.2.15"\
, "192.168.0.190"], "ansible_all_ipv6_addresses": ["fe80:\
:a00:27ff:fe85:5afe"], "ansible_fips": false, "ansible_ap\
parmor": {"status": "disabled"}, "ansible_env": {"LS_COLO\
RS": "rs=0:di=38;5;33:ln=38;5;51:mh=00:pi=40;38;5;11:so=3\
8;5;13:do=38;5;5:bd=48;5;232;38;5;11:cd=48;5;232;38;5;3:o\
r=48;5;232;38;5;9:mi=01;05;37;41:su=48;5;196;38;5;15:sg=4\
8;5;11;38;5;16:ca=48;5;196;38;5;226:tw=48;5;10;38;5;16:ow\
=48;5;10;38;5;21:st=48;5;21;38;5;15:ex=38;5;40:*.tar=38;5\
;9:*.tgz=38;5;9:*.arc=38;5;9:*.arj=38;5;9:*.taz=38;5;9:*.\
lha=38;5;9:*.lz4=38;5;9:*.lzh=38;5;9:*.lzma=38;5;9:*.tlz=\
38;5;9:*.txz=38;5;9:*.tzo=38;5;9:*.t7z=38;5;9:*.zip=38;5;\
9:*.z=38;5;9:*.dz=38;5;9:*.gz=38;5;9:*.lrz=38;5;9:*.lz=38\
;5;9:*.lzo=38;5;9:*.xz=38;5;9:*.zst=38;5;9:*.tzst=38;5;9:\

```
*.bz2=38;5;9:*.bz=38;5;9:*.tbz=38;5;9:*.tbz2=38;5;9:*.tz=\
38;5;9:*.deb=38;5;9:*.rpm=38;5;9:*.jar=38;5;9:*.war=38;5;\
9:*.ear=38;5;9:*.sar=38;5;9:*.rar=38;5;9:*.alz=38;5;9:*.a\
ce=38;5;9:*.zoo=38;5;9:*.cpio=38;5;9:*.7z=38;5;9:*.rz=38;\
5;9:*.cab=38;5;9:*.wim=38;5;9:*.swm=38;5;9:*.dwm=38;5;9:*\
.esd=38;5;9:*.jpg=38;5;13:*.jpeg=38;5;13:*.mjpg=38;5;13:*\
.mjpeg=38;5;13:*.gif=38;5;13:*.bmp=38;5;13:*.pbm=38;5;13:\
*.pgm=38;5;13:*.ppm=38;5;13:*.tga=38;5;13:*.xbm=38;5;13:*\
.xpm=38;5;13:*.tif=38;5;13:*.tiff=38;5;13:*.png=38;5;13:*\
.svg=38;5;13:*.svgz=38;5;13:*.mng=38;5;13:*.pcx=38;5;13:*\
.mov=38;5;13:*.mpg=38;5;13:*.mpeg=38;5;13:*.m2v=38;5;13:*\
.mkv=38;5;13:*.webm=38;5;13:*.ogm=38;5;13:*.mp4=38;5;13:*\
.m4v=38;5;13:*.mp4v=38;5;13:*.vob=38;5;13:*.qt=38;5;13:*.\
nuv=38;5;13:*.wmv=38;5;13:*.asf=38;5;13:*.rm=38;5;13:*.rm\
vb=38;5;13:*.flc=38;5;13:*.avi=38;5;13:*.fli=38;5;13:*.fl\
v=38;5;13:*.gl=38;5;13:*.dl=38;5;13:*.xcf=38;5;13:*.xwd=3\
8;5;13:*.yuv=38;5;13:*.cgm=38;5;13:*.emf=38;5;13:*.ogv=38\
;5;13:*.ogx=38;5;13:*.aac=38;5;45:*.au=38;5;45:*.flac=38;\
5;45:*.m4a=38;5;45:*.mid=38;5;45:*.midi=38;5;45:*.mka=38;\
5;45:*.mp3=38;5;45:*.mpc=38;5;45:*.ogg=38;5;45:*.ra=38;5;\
45:*.wav=38;5;45:*.oga=38;5;45:*.opus=38;5;45:*.spx=38;5;\
45:*.xspf=38;5;45:", "SSH_CONNECTION": "192.168.0.105 564\
48 192.168.0.190 22", "_": "/usr/libexec/platform-python"\
, "LANG": "en_US.UTF-8", "S_COLORS": "auto", "XDG_SESSION\
_ID": "9", "USER": "devops", "SELINUX_ROLE_REQUESTED": ""\
, "PWD": "/home/devops", "HOME": "/home/devops", "LC_CTYP\
E": "C.UTF-8", "SSH_CLIENT": "192.168.0.105 56448 22", "S\
ELINUX_LEVEL_REQUESTED": "", "SSH_TTY": "/dev/pts/0", "SH\
ELL": "/bin/bash", "TERM": "xterm-256color", "SELINUX_USE\
_CURRENT_RANGE": "", "SHLVL": "2", "LOGNAME": "devops", "\
DBUS_SESSION_BUS_ADDRESS": "unix:path=/run/user/1001/bus"\
, "XDG_RUNTIME_DIR": "/run/user/1001", "PATH": "/home/dev\
ops/.local/bin:/home/devops/bin:/usr/local/bin:/usr/bin:/\
usr/local/sbin:/usr/sbin", "HISTSIZE": "100000", "LESSOPE\
N": "||/usr/bin/lesspipe.sh %s"}, "ansible_pkg_mgr": "dnf\
```

```
526  ", "gather_subset": ["all"], "module_setup": true}, "invo\
527  cation": {"module_args": {"gather_subset": ["all"], "gath\
528  er_timeout": 10, "filter": [], "fact_path": "/etc/ansible\
529  /facts.d"}}}\r\n', b'Shared connection to 192.168.0.190 c\
530  losed.\r\n')
531  <192.168.0.190> ESTABLISH SSH CONNECTION FOR USER: devops
532  <192.168.0.190> SSH: EXEC ssh -C -o ControlMaster=auto -o\
533   ControlPersist=60s -o StrictHostKeyChecking=no -o 'Ident\
534  ityFile="/Users/lberton/prj/github/ansible-pilot/demo/id_\
535  rsa"' -o KbdInteractiveAuthentication=no -o PreferredAuth\
536  entications=gssapi-with-mic,gssapi-keyex,hostbased,public\
537  key -o PasswordAuthentication=no -o 'User="devops"' -o Co\
538  nnectTimeout=10 -o ControlPath=/Users/lberton/.ansible/cp\
539  /bf202c4314 192.168.0.190 '/bin/sh -c '"'"'rm -f -r /home\
540  /devops/.ansible/tmp/ansible-tmp-1637075611.201921-7700-2\
541  38727032540101/ > /dev/null 2>&1 && sleep 0'"'"''
542  <192.168.0.190> (0, b'', b'')
543  ok: [demo.example.com]
544  META: ran handlers
545  TASK [Creating a symlink] ******************************\
546  **********************
547  task path: /Users/lberton/prj/github/ansible-pilot/troubl\
548  eshooting/invalidargument_error.yml:8
549  <192.168.0.190> ESTABLISH SSH CONNECTION FOR USER: devops
550  <192.168.0.190> SSH: EXEC ssh -C -o ControlMaster=auto -o\
551   ControlPersist=60s -o StrictHostKeyChecking=no -o 'Ident\
552  ityFile="/Users/lberton/prj/github/ansible-pilot/demo/id_\
553  rsa"' -o KbdInteractiveAuthentication=no -o PreferredAuth\
554  entications=gssapi-with-mic,gssapi-keyex,hostbased,public\
555  key -o PasswordAuthentication=no -o 'User="devops"' -o Co\
556  nnectTimeout=10 -o ControlPath=/Users/lberton/.ansible/cp\
557  /bf202c4314 192.168.0.190 '/bin/sh -c '"'"'echo ~devops &\
558  & sleep 0'"'"''
559  <192.168.0.190> (0, b'/home/devops\n', b'')
560  <192.168.0.190> ESTABLISH SSH CONNECTION FOR USER: devops
```

```
<192.168.0.190> SSH: EXEC ssh -C -o ControlMaster=auto -o\
 ControlPersist=60s -o StrictHostKeyChecking=no -o 'Ident\
ityFile="/Users/lberton/prj/github/ansible-pilot/demo/id_\
rsa"' -o KbdInteractiveAuthentication=no -o PreferredAuth\
entications=gssapi-with-mic,gssapi-keyex,hostbased,public\
key -o PasswordAuthentication=no -o 'User="devops"' -o Co\
nnectTimeout=10 -o ControlPath=/Users/lberton/.ansible/cp\
/bf202c4314 192.168.0.190 '/bin/sh -c '"'"'( umask 77 && \
mkdir -p "` echo /home/devops/.ansible/tmp `"&& mkdir "` \
echo /home/devops/.ansible/tmp/ansible-tmp-1637075612.284\
926-7710-266273776232000 `" && echo ansible-tmp-163707561\
2.284926-7710-266273776232000="` echo /home/devops/.ansib\
le/tmp/ansible-tmp-1637075612.284926-7710-266273776232000\
 `" ) && sleep 0'"'"''
<192.168.0.190> (0, b'ansible-tmp-1637075612.284926-7710-\
266273776232000=/home/devops/.ansible/tmp/ansible-tmp-163\
7075612.284926-7710-266273776232000\n', b'')
Using module file /usr/local/Cellar/ansible/4.8.0/libexec\
/lib/python3.10/site-packages/ansible/modules/file.py
<192.168.0.190> PUT /Users/lberton/.ansible/tmp/ansible-l\
ocal-7697iluh4khz/tmp6r_9w7_f TO /home/devops/.ansible/tm\
p/ansible-tmp-1637075612.284926-7710-266273776232000/Ansi\
ballZ_file.py
<192.168.0.190> SSH: EXEC sftp -b - -C -o ControlMaster=a\
uto -o ControlPersist=60s -o StrictHostKeyChecking=no -o \
'IdentityFile="/Users/lberton/prj/github/ansible-pilot/de\
mo/id_rsa"' -o KbdInteractiveAuthentication=no -o Preferr\
edAuthentications=gssapi-with-mic,gssapi-keyex,hostbased,\
publickey -o PasswordAuthentication=no -o 'User="devops"'\
 -o ConnectTimeout=10 -o ControlPath=/Users/lberton/.ansi\
ble/cp/bf202c4314 '[192.168.0.190]'
<192.168.0.190> (0, b'sftp> put /Users/lberton/.ansible/t\
mp/ansible-local-7697iluh4khz/tmp6r_9w7_f /home/devops/.a\
nsible/tmp/ansible-tmp-1637075612.284926-7710-26627377623\
2000/AnsiballZ_file.py\n', b'')
```

```
<192.168.0.190> ESTABLISH SSH CONNECTION FOR USER: devops
<192.168.0.190> SSH: EXEC ssh -C -o ControlMaster=auto -o\
 ControlPersist=60s -o StrictHostKeyChecking=no -o 'Ident\
ityFile="/Users/lberton/prj/github/ansible-pilot/demo/id_\
rsa"' -o KbdInteractiveAuthentication=no -o PreferredAuth\
entications=gssapi-with-mic,gssapi-keyex,hostbased,public\
key -o PasswordAuthentication=no -o 'User="devops"' -o Co\
nnectTimeout=10 -o ControlPath=/Users/lberton/.ansible/cp\
/bf202c4314 192.168.0.190 '/bin/sh -c '"'"'chmod u+x /hom\
e/devops/.ansible/tmp/ansible-tmp-1637075612.284926-7710-\
266273776232000/ /home/devops/.ansible/tmp/ansible-tmp-16\
37075612.284926-7710-266273776232000/AnsiballZ_file.py &&\
 sleep 0'"'"''
<192.168.0.190> (0, b'', b'')
<192.168.0.190> ESTABLISH SSH CONNECTION FOR USER: devops
<192.168.0.190> SSH: EXEC ssh -C -o ControlMaster=auto -o\
 ControlPersist=60s -o StrictHostKeyChecking=no -o 'Ident\
ityFile="/Users/lberton/prj/github/ansible-pilot/demo/id_\
rsa"' -o KbdInteractiveAuthentication=no -o PreferredAuth\
entications=gssapi-with-mic,gssapi-keyex,hostbased,public\
key -o PasswordAuthentication=no -o 'User="devops"' -o Co\
nnectTimeout=10 -o ControlPath=/Users/lberton/.ansible/cp\
/bf202c4314 -tt 192.168.0.190 '/bin/sh -c '"'"'/usr/libex\
ec/platform-python /home/devops/.ansible/tmp/ansible-tmp-\
1637075612.284926-7710-266273776232000/AnsiballZ_file.py \
&& sleep 0'"'"''
<192.168.0.190> (1, b'Traceback (most recent call last):\\
r\n  File "/home/devops/.ansible/tmp/ansible-tmp-16370756\
12.284926-7710-266273776232000/AnsiballZ_file.py", line 1\
00, in <module>\r\n    _ansiballz_main()\r\n  File "/home\
/devops/.ansible/tmp/ansible-tmp-1637075612.284926-7710-2\
66273776232000/AnsiballZ_file.py", line 92, in _ansiballz\
_main\r\n    invoke_module(zipped_mod, temp_path, ANSIBAL\
LZ_PARAMS)\r\n  File "/home/devops/.ansible/tmp/ansible-t\
mp-1637075612.284926-7710-266273776232000/AnsiballZ_file.\
```

```
631  py", line 41, in invoke_module\r\n    run_name=\'__main__\
632  \', alter_sys=True)\r\n  File "/usr/lib64/python3.6/runpy\
633  .py", line 205, in run_module\r\n    return _run_module_c\
634  ode(code, init_globals, run_name, mod_spec)\r\n  File "/u\
635  sr/lib64/python3.6/runpy.py", line 96, in _run_module_cod\
636  e\r\n    mod_name, mod_spec, pkg_name, script_name)\r\n  \
637  File "/usr/lib64/python3.6/runpy.py", line 85, in _run_co\
638  de\r\n    exec(code, run_globals)\r\n  File "/tmp/ansible\
639  _ansible.builtin.file_payload_gvofg1m0/ansible_ansible.bu\
640  iltin.file_payload.zip/ansible/modules/file.py", line 966\
641  , in <module>\r\n  File "/tmp/ansible_ansible.builtin.fil\
642  e_payload_gvofg1m0/ansible_ansible.builtin.file_payload.z\
643  ip/ansible/modules/file.py", line 954, in main\r\n  File \
644  "/tmp/ansible_ansible.builtin.file_payload_gvofg1m0/ansib\
645  le_ansible.builtin.file_payload.zip/ansible/modules/file.\
646  py", line 688, in ensure_symlink\r\nOSError: [Errno 22] I\
647  nvalid argument: b\'/proc/cpuinfo\'\r\n', b'Shared connec\
648  tion to 192.168.0.190 closed.\r\n')
649  <192.168.0.190> Failed to connect to the host via ssh: Sh\
650  ared connection to 192.168.0.190 closed.
651  <192.168.0.190> ESTABLISH SSH CONNECTION FOR USER: devops
652  <192.168.0.190> SSH: EXEC ssh -C -o ControlMaster=auto -o\
653   ControlPersist=60s -o StrictHostKeyChecking=no -o 'Ident\
654  ityFile="/Users/lberton/prj/github/ansible-pilot/demo/id_\
655  rsa"' -o KbdInteractiveAuthentication=no -o PreferredAuth\
656  entications=gssapi-with-mic,gssapi-keyex,hostbased,public\
657  key -o PasswordAuthentication=no -o 'User="devops"' -o Co\
658  nnectTimeout=10 -o ControlPath=/Users/lberton/.ansible/cp\
659  /bf202c4314 192.168.0.190 '/bin/sh -c '"'"'rm -f -r /home\
660  /devops/.ansible/tmp/ansible-tmp-1637075612.284926-7710-2\
661  66273776232000/ > /dev/null 2>&1 && sleep 0'"'"''
662  <192.168.0.190> (0, b'', b'')
663  The full traceback is:
664  Traceback (most recent call last):
665    File "/home/devops/.ansible/tmp/ansible-tmp-1637075612.\
```

```
284926-7710-266273776232000/AnsiballZ_file.py", line 100,\
 in <module>
    _ansiballz_main()
  File "/home/devops/.ansible/tmp/ansible-tmp-1637075612.\
284926-7710-266273776232000/AnsiballZ_file.py", line 92, \
in _ansiballz_main
    invoke_module(zipped_mod, temp_path, ANSIBALLZ_PARAMS)
  File "/home/devops/.ansible/tmp/ansible-tmp-1637075612.\
284926-7710-266273776232000/AnsiballZ_file.py", line 41, \
in invoke_module
    run_name='__main__', alter_sys=True)
  File "/usr/lib64/python3.6/runpy.py", line 205, in run_\
module
    return _run_module_code(code, init_globals, run_name,\
 mod_spec)
  File "/usr/lib64/python3.6/runpy.py", line 96, in _run_\
module_code
    mod_name, mod_spec, pkg_name, script_name)
  File "/usr/lib64/python3.6/runpy.py", line 85, in _run_\
code
    exec(code, run_globals)
  File "/tmp/ansible_ansible.builtin.file_payload_gvofg1m\
0/ansible_ansible.builtin.file_payload.zip/ansible/module\
s/file.py", line 966, in <module>
  File "/tmp/ansible_ansible.builtin.file_payload_gvofg1m\
0/ansible_ansible.builtin.file_payload.zip/ansible/module\
s/file.py", line 954, in main
  File "/tmp/ansible_ansible.builtin.file_payload_gvofg1m\
0/ansible_ansible.builtin.file_payload.zip/ansible/module\
s/file.py", line 688, in ensure_symlink
OSError: [Errno 22] Invalid argument: b'/proc/cpuinfo'
fatal: [demo.example.com]: FAILED! => {
    "changed": false,
    "module_stderr": "Shared connection to 192.168.0.190 \
closed.\r\n",
```

```
    "module_stdout": "Traceback (most recent call last):\\
r\n  File \"/home/devops/.ansible/tmp/ansible-tmp-1637075\
612.284926-7710-266273776232000/AnsiballZ_file.py\", line\
 100, in <module>\r\n    _ansiballz_main()\r\n  File \"/h\
ome/devops/.ansible/tmp/ansible-tmp-1637075612.284926-771\
0-266273776232000/AnsiballZ_file.py\", line 92, in _ansib\
allz_main\r\n    invoke_module(zipped_mod, temp_path, ANS\
IBALLZ_PARAMS)\r\n  File \"/home/devops/.ansible/tmp/ansi\
ble-tmp-1637075612.284926-7710-266273776232000/AnsiballZ_\
file.py\", line 41, in invoke_module\r\n    run_name='__m\
ain__', alter_sys=True)\r\n  File \"/usr/lib64/python3.6/\
runpy.py\", line 205, in run_module\r\n    return _run_mo\
dule_code(code, init_globals, run_name, mod_spec)\r\n  Fi\
le \"/usr/lib64/python3.6/runpy.py\", line 96, in _run_mo\
dule_code\r\n    mod_name, mod_spec, pkg_name, script_nam\
e)\r\n  File \"/usr/lib64/python3.6/runpy.py\", line 85, \
in _run_code\r\n    exec(code, run_globals)\r\n  File \"/\
tmp/ansible_ansible.builtin.file_payload_gvofg1m0/ansible\
_ansible.builtin.file_payload.zip/ansible/modules/file.py\
\", line 966, in <module>\r\n  File \"/tmp/ansible_ansibl\
e.builtin.file_payload_gvofg1m0/ansible_ansible.builtin.f\
ile_payload.zip/ansible/modules/file.py\", line 954, in m\
ain\r\n  File \"/tmp/ansible_ansible.builtin.file_payload\
_gvofg1m0/ansible_ansible.builtin.file_payload.zip/ansibl\
e/modules/file.py\", line 688, in ensure_symlink\r\nOSErr\
or: [Errno 22] Invalid argument: b'/proc/cpuinfo'\r\n",
    "msg": "MODULE FAILURE\nSee stdout/stderr for the exa\
ct error",
    "rc": 1
}
PLAY RECAP *********************************************\
**********************
demo.example.com           : ok=1    changed=0    unreach\
able=0    failed=1    skipped=0    rescued=0    ignored=0
```

- ansible.builtin.file official documentation

https://docs.ansible.com/ansible/latest/collections/ansible/builtin/file_-module.html

fix code

- invalidargument_fix.yml

```
1   ---
2   - name: file module demo
3     hosts: all
4     vars:
5       mylink: "~/example"
6       mysrc: "/proc/cpuinfo"
7     tasks:
8       - name: Creating a symlink
9         ansible.builtin.file:
10          src: "{{ mysrc }}"
11          dest: "{{ mylink }}"
12          state: link
```

fix execution

```
1   $ ansible-playbook -i virtualmachines/demo/inventory trou\
2   bleshooting/invalidargument_fix.yml
3   PLAY [file module demo] ********************************\
4   *******************************************
5   TASK [Gathering Facts] ********************************\
6   *******************************************
7   ok: [demo.example.com]
8   TASK [Creating a symlink] *****************************\
9   *******************************************
10  ok: [demo.example.com]
11  PLAY RECAP ********************************************\
12  *******************************************
```

```
13   demo.example.com              : ok=2     changed=0     unreach\
14   able=0     failed=0     skipped=0     rescued=0     ignored=0
```

Ansible troubleshooting - privilege escalation error

Privilege escalation errors are one of the most common Ansible problems.

It happens when the connection user Ansible doesn't have the permission to perform the operation. The solution is simply to switch to the user with administrative rights. In Ansible you perform this operation enabling the become statement.

Behind the scenes Ansible is connecting to the target host using the normal user, switching to the administrative user and then executing the playbook code.

The standard privilege escalation method is sudo but more are available for example su, pfexec, doas, pbrun, dzdo, ksu, runas, machinectl, Centrify, etc.

Links

- Understanding privilege escalation: become[93]

demo

The best way of talking about Ansible troubleshooting is to jump in a live demo to show you practically the privilege escalation error and how to solve it!

error

---

[93]https://docs.ansible.com/ansible/latest/user_guide/become.html

```
1   ---
2   - name: yum module demo
3     hosts: all
4     become: false
5     tasks:
6       - name: install package
7         yum:
8           name: git
9           state: present
```

fix

```
1   ---
2   - name: yum module demo
3     hosts: all
4     become: true
5     tasks:
6       - name: install package
7         yum:
8           name: git
9           state: present
```

Ansible troubleshooting - missing sudo password and incorrect sudo password

How to reproduce the fatal errors `missing sudo password` and `incorrect sudo password` and how to solve it!

demo

The best way of talking about Ansible troubleshooting is to jump in a live demo to show you practically the missing sudo password and incorrect sudo password and how to solve it!

error code

- missingsudopassword_error.yml

```
1   ---
2   - name: debug module demo
3     hosts: all
4     become: true
5     tasks:
6       - name: root test
7         ansible.builtin.debug:
8           msg: "privilege escalation successful"
```

error execution

```
1   $ ansible-playbook -i demo/inventory troubleshooting/miss\
2   ingsudopassword_error.yml
3
4   PLAY [debug module demo] ********************************\
5   ***************************************************
6
7   TASK [Gathering Facts] *********************************\
8   ***************************************************
9   fatal: [demo.example.com]: FAILED! => {"msg": "Missing su\
10  do password"}
11
12  PLAY RECAP *********************************************\
13  ***************************************************
14  demo.example.com            : ok=0    changed=0    unreach\
15  able=0    failed=1    skipped=0    rescued=0    ignored=0
```

troubleshoot

```
$ ansible-playbook --help
usage: ansible-playbook [-h] [--version] [-v] [-k] [--pri\
vate-key PRIVATE_KEY_FILE] [-u REMOTE_USER]
[...]
Privilege Escalation Options:
control how and which user you become as on target hosts

--become-method BECOME_METHOD
privilege escalation method to use (default=sudo), use `a\
nsible-doc -t become
-l` to list valid choices.
--become-user BECOME_USER
run operations as this user (default=root)
-K, --ask-become-pass
ask for privilege escalation password
-b, --become              run operations with become (does no\
t imply password prompting)
ansible-pilot $ ansible-playbook -i demo/inventory troubl\
eshooting/missingsudopassword_error.yml -bK
BECOME password:

PLAY [debug module demo] *******************************\
****************************************

TASK [Gathering Facts] *********************************\
***************************************
fatal: [demo.example.com]: FAILED! => {"msg": "Incorrect \
sudo password"}

PLAY RECAP *********************************************\
***************************************
demo.example.com                : ok=0    changed=0    unreach\
able=0    failed=1    skipped=0    rescued=0    ignored=0
```

verification

```
$ ssh devops@demo.example.com
Last login: Mon Nov  8 10:24:10 2021 from 192.168.43.5
[devops@demo ~]$ sudo su

We trust you have received the usual lecture from the loc\
al System
Administrator. It usually boils down to these three thing\
s:

#1) Respect the privacy of others.
#2) Think before you type.
#3) With great power comes great responsibility.

[sudo] password for devops:
Sorry, try again.
[sudo] password for devops:
Sorry, try again.
[sudo] password for devops:
sudo: 2 incorrect password attempts
[devops@demo ~]$ su -
Password:
Last login: Mon Nov  8 09:44:37 UTC 2021 on pts/0
[root@demo ~]# ls -al /etc/sudo
sudo.conf        sudoers          sudoers.d/        sudo-ldap\
.conf
[root@demo ~]# ls -al /etc/sudoers.d/
total 16
drwxr-x---.  2 root root   21 Nov  8 09:06 .
drwxr-xr-x. 87 root root 8192 Nov  8 09:14 ..
-r--r-----.  1 root root   45 Sep  1 00:19 vagrant
[root@demo ~]# vim /etc/sudoers.d/devops
[root@demo ~]# cat /etc/sudoers.d/devops
devops ALL=(ALL) NOPASSWD: ALL
[root@demo ~]# exit
logout
```

```
36   [devops@demo ~]$ whoami
37   devops
38   [devops@demo ~]$ sudo su
39   [root@demo devops]# whoami
40   root
41   [root@demo devops]# exit
42   exit
43   [devops@demo ~]$ exit
44   logout
45   Connection to demo.example.com closed.
```

fix

- /etc/sudoers.d/devops

```
1   devops ALL=(ALL) NOPASSWD: ALL
```

fix execution

```
1   $ ansible-playbook -i demo/inventory troubleshooting/miss\
2   ingsudopassword_error.yml
3
4   PLAY [debug module demo] ********************************\
5   ************************************************
6
7   TASK [Gathering Facts] *********************************\
8   ************************************************
9   ok: [demo.example.com]
10
11  TASK [root test] **************************************\
12  ************************************************
13  ok: [demo.example.com] => {
14  "msg": "privilege escalation successful"
15  }
16
```

```
17  PLAY RECAP ******************************************\
18  **********************************************
19  demo.example.com            : ok=2    changed=0    unreach\
20  able=0    failed=0    skipped=0    rescued=0    ignored=0
```

Ansible troubleshooting - missing module parameter

A mispelled parameter name lead you to the `missing module parameter` fatal error. Sometimes it's difficult troubleshoot and find the wrong typo.

demo

The best way of talking about Ansible troubleshooting is to jump in a live demo to show you practically the missing module parameter and how to solve it!

error code

- missingparam_error.yml

```
1   ---
2   - name: service module demo
3     hosts: all
4     become: true
5     tasks:
6       - name: sshd restart
7         ansible.builtin.service:
8           nme: sshd
9           state: restarted
10          enabled: true
```

In this example the parameter `nme` doesn't exist, causing a fatal error for Ansible. The solution is simple, just a typo!

fix code

- missingparam_fix.yml

```
1    ---
2    - name: service module demo
3      hosts: all
4      become: true
5      tasks:
6        - name: sshd restart
7          ansible.builtin.service:
8            name: sshd
9            state: restarted
10           enabled: true
```

Ansible troubleshooting - failure downloading

Downloading content from the internet sometimes you might receive the `failure downloading` error. The root cause is usually a misspelled URL or a content moved by the website. This error is most of the time caused by the HTTP 404 error. Double check the URL in your browser before using it in Ansible.

demo

A wrong (HTTP 404 error) URL lead to the Ansible error `failure downloading`.

 See also Extract an archive - Ansible module unarchive.

code

- failuredownloading_error.yml

```
1    ---
2    - name: unarchive module demo
3      hosts: all
4      become: false
5      vars:
6        myurl: "https://github.com/lucab85/ansible-pilot/arch\
7    ive/refs/master.zip"
8      tasks:
9        - name: extract archive
10         ansible.builtin.unarchive:
11           src: "{{ myurl }}"
12           dest: "/home/devops/"
13           remote_src: true
14           validate_certs: true
```

- failuredownloading_fix.yml

```yaml
1  ---
2  - name: unarchive module demo
3    hosts: all
4    become: false
5    vars:
6      myurl: "https://github.com/lucab85/ansible-pilot/arch\
7  ive/refs/heads/master.zip"
8    tasks:
9      - name: extract archive
10       ansible.builtin.unarchive:
11         src: "{{ myurl }}"
12         dest: "/home/devops/"
13         remote_src: true
14         validate_certs: true
```

Ansible troubleshooting - chgrp failed

When you try to change permission to file your Ansible Playbook might end up with "chgrp failed" error. Let's investigate together why this error happens and how to solve it!

See also:

- Ansible changes the User Primary Group on Linux
- Ansible adds a user to a secondary group(s)

demo

The best way of talking about Ansible troubleshooting is to jump
in a live demo to show you practically the chgrp failed error and
how to solve it!

code

- fix_permission.sh

```
1   # groups devops
2   devops : wheel
3   # useradd -a -G users devops
4   # groups devops
5   devops : wheel users
6   # id devops
7   uid=1001(devops) gid=10(wheel) groups=10(wheel),100(users)
```

Ansible troubleshooting - not a valid attribute for a Play error

How to reproduce, troubleshoot, and fix the "not a valid attribute
for a Play" error.

demo

The best way of talking about Ansible troubleshooting is to jump
in a live demo to show you practically the not a valid attribute
for a Play error and how to solve it!

error code

- invalid_play_attribute_error.yml

```
1    ---
2    - name: file module demo
3      hosts: all
4      vars:
5        myfile: "~/example.txt"
6      task:
7        - name: Creating an empty
8          ansible.builtin.file:
9            path: "{{ myfile }}"
10           state: touch
```

error execution

- output

```
1    $ ansible-playbook -i demo/inventory troubleshooting/inva\
2    lid_play_attribute_fix.yml
3    ERROR! 'task' is not a valid attribute for a Play
4    The error appears to be in 'ansible-pilot/troubleshooting\
5    /invalid_play_attribute_error.yml': line 2, column 3, but\
6      may
7    be elsewhere in the file depending on the exact syntax pr\
8    oblem.
9    The offending line appears to be:
10     - -
11   - name: file module demo
12     ^ here
```

fix code

- invalid_play_attribute_fix.yml

```
1   ---
2   - name: file module demo
3     hosts: all
4     vars:
5       myfile: "~/example.txt"
6     tasks:
7       - name: Creating an empty
8         ansible.builtin.file:
9           path: "{{ myfile }}"
10          state: touch
```

fix execution

```
1   $ ansible-playbook -i demo/inventory troubleshooting/inva\
2   lid_play_attribute_fix.yml
3   PLAY [file module demo] ********************************\
4   ***********************************
5   TASK [Gathering Facts] ********************************\
6   ***********************************
7   ok: [demo.example.com]
8   TASK [Creating an empty file] *************************\
9   ***********************************
10  changed: [demo.example.com]
11  PLAY RECAP ********************************************\
12  ***********************************
13  demo.example.com : ok=2 changed=1 unreachable=0 failed=0 \
14  skipped=0 rescued=0 ignored=0
```

Ansible troubleshooting - fatal template error while templating string

How to reproduce, troubleshoot, and fix the "FATAL template error while templating string" Ansible runtime error.

demo

The best way of talking about Ansible troubleshooting is to jump in a live demo to show you practically the `not a valid attribute for a Play` error and how to solve it!

error code

- template_error_string_error.yml

```yaml
---
- name: file module demo
  hosts: all
  vars:
    myfile: "{{ ~/example.txt }}"
  tasks:
    - name: Creating an empty file
      ansible.builtin.file:
        path: "{{ myfile }}"
        state: touch
```

error execution

- output

```
$ ansible-playbook -i demo/inventory troubleshooting/temp\
late_error_string_error.yml
PLAY [file module demo] *********************************\
*********************************************************\
*********************************************************\
************************
TASK [Gathering Facts] *********************************\
*********************************************************\
*********************************************************\
************************
ok: [demo.example.com]
TASK [Creating an empty file] **************************\
*********************************************************\
*********************************************************\
************************
fatal: [demo.example.com]: FAILED! => {"msg": "An unhandl\
ed exception occurred while templating '{{ ~/example.txt \
}}'. Error was a <class 'ansible.errors.AnsibleError'>, o\
riginal message: template error while templating string: \
unexpected '~'. String: {{ ~/example.txt }}"}
PLAY RECAP *********************************************\
*********************************************************\
*********************************************************\
************************
demo.example.com             : ok=1    changed=0    unreach\
able=0    failed=1    skipped=0    rescued=0    ignored=0
```

fix code

- template_error_string_fix.yml

```yaml
1   ---
2   - name: file module demo
3     hosts: all
4     vars:
5       myfile: "~/example.txt"
6     tasks:
7       - name: Creating an empty file
8         ansible.builtin.file:
9           path: "{{ myfile }}"
10          state: touch
```

fix execution

- output

```
1   $ ansible-playbook -i demo/inventory troubleshooting/temp\
2   late_error_string_fix.yml
3   PLAY [file module demo] ********************************\
4   ******************************************************\
5   ******************************************************\
6   ***********************
7   TASK [Gathering Facts] ********************************\
8   ******************************************************\
9   ******************************************************\
10  ***********************
11  ok: [demo.example.com]
12  TASK [Creating an empty file] *************************\
13  ******************************************************\
14  ******************************************************\
15  ***********************
16  changed: [demo.example.com]
17  PLAY RECAP ********************************************\
18  ******************************************************\
19  ******************************************************\
20  ***********************
```

```
21  demo.example.com              : ok=2     changed=1      unreach\
22  able=0
23  failed=0     skipped=0     rescued=0     ignored=0
```

Ansible troubleshooting - PowerShell incompatible with the sudo become plugin

How to reproduce, troubleshoot, and fix the PowerShell shell family is incompatible with the sudo become plugin Ansible runtime error.

 See also: Reboot Windows hosts - Ansible module win_reboot

demo

The following code reproduce the practically "the PowerShell shell family is incompatible with the sudo become plugin" error and how to solve it!

error code

- incompatiblesudo_error.yml

```
1   ---
2   - name: win_reboot module demo
3     hosts: all
4     become: true
5     tasks:
6       - name: reboot host(s)
7           ansible.windows.win_reboot:
```

error execution

```
1   $ ansible-playbook -i win/inventory troubleshooting/incom\
2   patiblesudo_error.yml
3   PLAY [win_reboot module demo] ***************************\
4   ******************************************
5   TASK [Gathering Facts] *********************************\
6   ******************************************
7   fatal: [WindowsServer]: FAILED! => {"msg": "The powershel\
8   l shell family is incompatible with the sudo become plugi\
9   n"}
10  PLAY RECAP *********************************************\
11  ******************************************
12  WindowsServer                  : ok=0    changed=0    unreach\
13  able=0    failed=1    skipped=0    rescued=0    ignored=0
```

fix code

- incompatiblesudo_fix.yml

```
1   ---
2   - name: win_reboot module demo
3     hosts: all
4     become: false
5     tasks:
6       - name: reboot host(s)
7           ansible.windows.win_reboot:
```

fix execution

```
1   $ ansible-playbook -i win/inventory troubleshooting/incom\
2   patiblesudo_fix.yml
3   PLAY [win_reboot module demo] ***************************\
4   ******************************************
5   TASK [Gathering Facts] *********************************\
6   ******************************************
7   ok: [WindowsServer]
8   TASK [reboot host(s)] **********************************\
9   ******************************************
10  changed: [WindowsServer]
11  PLAY RECAP *********************************************\
12  ******************************************
13  WindowsServer              : ok=2    changed=1    unreach\
14  able=0    failed=0    skipped=0    rescued=0    ignored=0
```

Ansible troubleshooting - passwordless account

How to reproduce the "usermod: unlocking the user's password would result in a passwordless account." error and how to solve it!

 See also Enable user account - Ansible module user.

demo

The best way of talking about Ansible troubleshooting is to jump in a live demo to show you practically the `usermod: unlocking the user's password would result in a passwordless account.` error and how to solve it!

error code

- passwordless_error.yml

```yaml
---
- name: user module demo
  hosts: all
  become: true
  vars:
    myuser: "example"
  tasks:
    - name: create a disabled user
      ansible.builtin.user:
        name: "{{ myuser }}"
        state: present
        password_lock: true
- name: enable user
      ansible.builtin.user:
        name: "{{ myuser }}"
        state: present
        password_lock: false
```

error verification

verify no user example in the target system:

```
$ ssh devops@demo.example.com
Last login: Tue Oct  5 09:35:24 2021 from 192.168.0.100
[devops@demo ~]$ sudo su -
Last login: Tue Oct  5 09:34:55 UTC 2021 on pts/0
[root@demo ~]# getent passwd | grep example
[root@demo ~]# exit
logout
[devops@demo ~]$ exit
logout
```

error execution

output

```
$ ansible-playbook -i demo/inventory troubleshooting/pass\
wordless_error.yml
PLAY [user module demo] ********************************\
********************************************
TASK [Gathering Facts] ********************************\
********************************************
ok: [demo.example.com]
TASK [create a disabled user] *************************\
********************************************
changed: [demo.example.com]
TASK [enable user] ************************************\
********************************************
fatal: [demo.example.com]: FAILED! => {"changed": false, \
"msg": "usermod: unlocking the user's password would resu\
lt in a passwordless account.\nYou should set a password \
with usermod -p to unlock this user's password.\n", "name\
": "example", "rc": 1}
PLAY RECAP ********************************************\
********************************************
demo.example.com             : ok=2    changed=1    unreach\
able=0    failed=1    skipped=0    rescued=0    ignored=
```

fix code

- passwordless_fix.yml

```yaml
1    ---
2    - name: user module demo
3      hosts: all
4      become: true
5      vars:
6        myuser: "example"
7        mypassword: "password"
8      tasks:
9        - name: create a disabled user
10         ansible.builtin.user:
11           name: "{{ myuser }}"
12           state: present
13           password_lock: true
14   - name: enable user
15         ansible.builtin.user:
16           name: "{{ myuser }}"
17           password: "{{ mypassword | password_hash('sha512'\
18   ) }}"
19           state: present
20           password_lock: false
```

fix execution

output

```
1   $ ansible-playbook -i demo/inventory troubleshooting/pass\
2   wordless_fix.yml
3   PLAY [user module demo] ********************************\
4   ********************************************
5   TASK [Gathering Facts] ********************************\
6   ********************************************
7   ok: [demo.example.com]
8   TASK [create a disabled user] *************************\
9   ********************************************
10  ok: [demo.example.com]
11  TASK [enable user] ***********************************\
12  ********************************************
13  changed: [demo.example.com]
14  PLAY RECAP ********************************************\
15  ********************************************
16  demo.example.com              : ok=3    changed=1    unreach\
17  able=0    failed=0    skipped=0    rescued=0    ignored=0
```

fix verification

```
1   $ ssh devops@demo.example.com
2   Last login: Tue Oct  5 09:37:07 2021 from 192.168.0.100
3   [devops@demo ~]$ sudo su -
4   Last login: Tue Oct  5 09:35:42 UTC 2021 on pts/0
5   [root@demo ~]# getent passwd | grep example
6   example:x:1002:1002::/home/example:/bin/bash
7   [root@demo ~]# passwd -S example
8   example PS 2021-10-05 0 99999 7 -1 (Password set, SHA512 \
9   crypt.)
10  [root@demo ~]# grep example /etc/shadow
11  example:$6$kg63VBL5Hw3AwjQt$GSn.Z7h3/ipgaY2p0ypSrymLN/2.1\
12  hZnMeONjkiaYc5o7R6TkfHtPJyXmKqoW3IQxw6Udxb2khiJ8NCVo4QKM1\
13  :18905:0:99999:7:::
```

Ansible troubleshooting - user module password_expiry_min bug

How to reproduce the `password_expiry_min` bug of the module user, triage, read the GitHub report, and workaround!

Demo

The best way of talking about Ansible troubleshooting is to jump in a live demo to show you practically the user module bug triage and possible workaround!

error code

- userbug_error.yml

```yaml
1   ---
2   - name: user module demo
3     hosts: all
4     become: true
5     vars:
6       myuser: "example"
7     tasks:
8       - name: password expiration
9         ansible.builtin.user:
10          name: "{{ myuser }}"
11          password_expire_min: 7
12          password_expire_max: 90
```

error execution

```
$ ansible-playbook -i demo/inventory troubleshooting/user\
bug_error.yml.yml
PLAY [user module demo] ********************************\
****************************************************
TASK [Gathering Facts] ********************************\
****************************************************
ok: [demo.example.com]
TASK [password expiration] ****************************\
****************************************************
changed: [demo.example.com]
PLAY RECAP ********************************************\
****************************************************
demo.example.com              : ok=2    changed=1    unreach\
able=0    failed=0    skipped=0    rescued=0    ignored=0
ansible-pilot $ ansible-playbook -i demo/inventory user\ \
expiration/user.yml
PLAY [user module demo] ********************************\
****************************************************
TASK [Gathering Facts] ********************************\
****************************************************
ok: [demo.example.com]
TASK [password expiration] ****************************\
****************************************************
ok: [demo.example.com]
PLAY RECAP ********************************************\
****************************************************
demo.example.com              : ok=2    changed=0    unreach\
able=0    failed=0    skipped=0    rescued=0    ignored=0
ansible-pilot $ ssh devops@demo.example.com
Last login: Mon Nov  8 17:09:16 2021 from 192.168.43.5
[devops@demo ~]$ sudo su
[root@demo devops]# chage -l example
Last password change        : Nov 08, 2021
Password expires      : Feb 06, 2022
Password inactive      : never
```

```
36   Account expires          : never
37   Minimum number of days between password change  : 0
38   Maximum number of days between password change  : 90
39   Number of days of warning before password expires : 7
```

We expected a 7 value for `Minimum number of days between password change` but we obtain 0.

Troubleshoot

- bug report - user module can't handle password expiration parameters correctly #75017[94]
- pull request - user module password expiration fixes #75390[95]

Workaround

- userbug_workaround.yml

```
1    ---
2    - name: user module demo
3      hosts: all
4      become: true
5      vars:
6        myuser: "example"
7      tasks:
8        - name: password min expiration
9          ansible.builtin.user:
10           name: "{{ myuser }}"
11           password_expire_min: 7
12     - name: password max expiration
13         ansible.builtin.user:
14           name: "{{ myuser }}"
15           password_expire_max: 90
```

---

[94]https://github.com/ansible/ansible/issues/75017
[95]https://github.com/ansible/ansible/pull/75390

Workaround execution

```
$ ansible-playbook -i demo/inventory troubleshooting/user\
bug_workaround.yml
PLAY [user module demo] ********************************\
*************************************************
TASK [Gathering Facts] ********************************\
*************************************************
ok: [demo.example.com]
TASK [password min expiration] ************************\
*************************************************
changed: [demo.example.com]
TASK [password max expiration] ************************\
*************************************************
ok: [demo.example.com]
PLAY RECAP ********************************************\
*************************************************
demo.example.com            : ok=3    changed=1    unreach\
able=0    failed=0    skipped=0    rescued=0    ignored=0
ansible-pilot $ ssh devops@demo.example.com
Last login: Wed Nov 10 10:38:59 2021 from 192.168.43.5
[devops@demo ~]$ sudo su
[root@demo devops]# chage -l example
Last password change     : Nov 08, 2021
Password expires      : Feb 06, 2022
Password inactive     : never
Account expires       : never
Minimum number of days between password change  : 7
Maximum number of days between password change  : 90
Number of days of warning before password expires : 7
```

Ansible troubleshooting - urlopen error

How to reproduce the urlopen error in Ansible, troubleshooting, and fix to be able to successfully open an URL in your playbook. Wrong or mispelled URL lead to the `urlopen error`.

See also:

- Submit a GET request to a REST API endpoint - Interact with web services - Ansible module uri
- Token-Based Authentication in REST API - Interact with webservice - Ansible module uri - Authentication request using the REST API token

demo

The best way of talking about Ansible troubleshooting is to jump in a live demo to show you practically the `urlopen error` and how to solve it!

error code

- urlopen_error.yml

```
1   ---
2   - name: uri module demo
3     hosts: all
4     become: false
5     vars:
6       server: "https://reqres.it"
7       endpoint: "/api/users?page=2"
8     tasks:
9       - name: list users
10        ansible.builtin.uri:
11          url: "{{ server }}{{ endpoint }}"
12          method: GET
13          status_code: 200
14          timeout: 30
15        register: result
16
17      - name: debug
18        ansible.builtin.debug:
19          var: result.json.data
```

error execution

```
1   $ ansible-playbook -i virtualmachines/demo/inventory trou\
2   bleshooting/urlopen_error.yml
3   PLAY [uri module demo] ********************************\
4   *********************
5   TASK [Gathering Facts] ********************************\
6   *********************
7   ok: [demo.example.com]
8   TASK [list users] ********************************\
9   *********************
10  fatal: [demo.example.com]: FAILED! => {"changed": false, \
11  "elapsed": 15, "msg": "Status code was -1 and not [200]: \
12  Request failed: <urlopen error [Errno -2] Name or service\
13   not known>", "redirected": false, "status": -1, "url": "\
14  https://reqres.it/api/users?page=2"]
```

```
15    PLAY RECAP ******************************************\
16    **********************
17    demo.example.com              : ok=1    changed=0    unreach\
18    able=0    failed=1    skipped=0    rescued=0    ignored=0
```

fix code

- urlopen_fix.yml

```yaml
1    ---
2    - name: uri module demo
3      hosts: all
4      become: false
5      vars:
6        server: "https://reqres.in"
7        endpoint: "/api/users?page=2"
8      tasks:
9        - name: list users
10         ansible.builtin.uri:
11           url: "{{ server }}{{ endpoint }}"
12           method: GET
13           status_code: 200
14           timeout: 30
15         register: result
16
17       - name: debug
18         ansible.builtin.debug:
19           var: result.json.data
```

fix execution

```
$ ansible-playbook -i virtualmachines/demo/inventory trou\
bleshooting/urlopen_fix.yml
PLAY [uri module demo] ********************************\
********************************************
TASK [Gathering Facts] ********************************\
********************************************
ok: [demo.example.com]
TASK [list users] ************************************\
********************************************
ok: [demo.example.com]
TASK [debug] *****************************************\
******************************************
ok: [demo.example.com] => {
    "result.json.data": [
        {
                "avatar": "https://reqres.in/img/faces/7-imag\
e.jpg",
                "email": "michael.lawson@reqres.in",
                "first_name": "Michael",
                "id": 7,
                "last_name": "Lawson"
        },
        {
                "avatar": "https://reqres.in/img/faces/8-imag\
e.jpg",
                "email": "lindsay.ferguson@reqres.in",
                "first_name": "Lindsay",
                "id": 8,
                "last_name": "Ferguson"
        },
        {
                "avatar": "https://reqres.in/img/faces/9-imag\
e.jpg",
                "email": "tobias.funke@reqres.in",
                "first_name": "Tobias",
```

```
36                "id": 9,
37                "last_name": "Funke"
38            },
39            {
40                "avatar": "https://reqres.in/img/faces/10-ima\
41  ge.jpg",
42                "email": "byron.fields@reqres.in",
43                "first_name": "Byron",
44                "id": 10,
45                "last_name": "Fields"
46            },
47            {
48                "avatar": "https://reqres.in/img/faces/11-ima\
49  ge.jpg",
50                "email": "george.edwards@reqres.in",
51                "first_name": "George",
52                "id": 11,
53                "last_name": "Edwards"
54            },
55            {
56                "avatar": "https://reqres.in/img/faces/12-ima\
57  ge.jpg",
58                "email": "rachel.howell@reqres.in",
59                "first_name": "Rachel",
60                "id": 12,
61                "last_name": "Howell"
62            }
63        ]
64  }
65  PLAY RECAP *******************************************\
66  *****************************************
67  demo.example.com           : ok=3     changed=0     unreach\
68  able=0     failed=0     skipped=0     rescued=0     ignored=0
```

Ansible troubleshooting - destination does not exist

How to reproduce the destination does not exist error in Ansible, troubleshooting, and fix to be able to successfully download a file from an URL in a home directory with your Ansible playbook.

Local path in `dest` parameter lead to `destination does not exist` error.

See also: Download a file - Ansible module get_url.

demo

The best way of talking about Ansible troubleshooting is to jump in a live demo to show you practically the `destination does not exist error` and how to solve it!

error code

- destinationdoesnotexist_error.yml

```
1   ---
2   - name: get_url module demo
3     hosts: all
4     become: false
5     vars:
6       myurl: "https://releases.ansible.com/ansible/ansible-\
7   2.9.25.tar.gz"
8       mycrc: "sha256:https://releases.ansible.com/ansible/a\
9   nsible-2.9.25.tar.gz.sha"
10      mydest: "ansible-2.9.25.tar.gz"
11    tasks:
12      name: download file
```

```
13      ansible.builtin.get_url:
14        url: "{{ myurl }}"
15        dest: "{{ mydest }}"
16        checksum: "{{ mycrc }}"
17        mode: '0644'
```

error execution

```
1   $ ansible-playbook -i virtualmachines/demo/inventory trou\
2   bleshooting/destinationdoesnotexist_error.yml
3
4   PLAY [get_url module demo] *******************************\
5   **********************************
6
7   TASK [Gathering Facts] **********************************\
8   **********************************
9   ok: [demo.example.com]
10
11  TASK [download file] ************************************\
12  **********************************
13  fatal: [demo.example.com]: FAILED! => {"changed": false, \
14  "checksum_dest": null, "checksum_src": "574e24659f555fe37\
15  0571167d3d44704671f1773", "dest": "ansible-2.9.25.tar.gz"\
16  , "elapsed": 3, "msg": "Destination  does not exist", "sr\
17  c": "/home/devops/.ansible/tmp/ansible-tmp-1640555219.326\
18  019-1431-267536126421544/tmpmx_ra0hd", "url": "https://re\
19  leases.ansible.com/ansible/ansible-2.9.25.tar.gz"}
20
21  PLAY RECAP **********************************************\
22  **********************************
23  demo.example.com              : ok=1    changed=0    unreach\
24  able=0    failed=1    skipped=0    rescued=0    ignored=0\
25
```

fix code

- destinationdoesnotexist_fix.yml

```
1    ---
2    - name: get_url module demo
3      hosts: all
4      become: false
5      vars:
6        myurl: "https://releases.ansible.com/ansible/ansible-\
7    2.9.25.tar.gz"
8        mycrc: "sha256:https://releases.ansible.com/ansible/a\
9    nsible-2.9.25.tar.gz.sha"
10       mydest: "ansible-2.9.25.tar.gz"
11     tasks:
12       - name: download file
13         ansible.builtin.get_url:
14           url: "{{ myurl }}"
15           dest: "./{{ mydest }}"
16           checksum: "{{ mycrc }}"
17           mode: '0644'
```

fix execution

```
1    $ ansible-playbook -i virtualmachines/demo/inventory trou\
2    bleshooting/destinationdoesnotexist_fix.yml
3
4    PLAY [get_url module demo] *****************************\
5    ***********************************
6
7    TASK [Gathering Facts] ********************************\
8    ***********************************
9    ok: [demo.example.com]
10
11   TASK [download file] *********************************\
```

```
12    ************************************
13    changed: [demo.example.com]
14
15    PLAY RECAP ***********************************************\
16    ************************************
17    demo.example.com          : ok=2    changed=1    unreach\
18    able=0    failed=0    skipped=0    rescued=0    ignored=0\
19
```

verification

```
1    $ ssh devops@demo.example.com
2    [devops@demo ~]$ ls -al
3    total 13964
4    drwx------. 4 devops wheel        140 Dec 26 21:47 .
5    drwxr-xr-x. 5 root   root          50 Dec 15 13:00 ..
6    drwx------. 3 devops wheel         17 Dec 15 13:00 .ansible
7    -rw-------. 1 devops wheel        322 Dec 26 21:46 .bash_hi\
8    story
9    -rw-r--r--. 1 devops wheel         18 Jul 26 09:51 .bash_lo\
10   gout
11   -rw-r--r--. 1 devops wheel        141 Jul 26 09:51 .bash_pr\
12   ofile
13   -rw-r--r--. 1 devops wheel        376 Jul 26 09:51 .bashrc
14   drwx------. 2 devops wheel         29 Dec 15 13:00 .ssh
15   -rw-r--r--. 1 devops wheel 14280306 Dec 26 21:47 ansible-\
16   2.9.25.tar.gz
```

Ansible troubleshooting - "role not found" error

How to solve the "role not found" error using ansible-galaxy command-line utility and requirements.yml file to download and use "lucab85.ansible_role_log4shell" Ansible Role from Ansible Galaxy.

demo

The best way of talking about Ansible troubleshooting is to jump in a live demo to show you practically the `role not found errror` and how to solve it!

error code

- role.yml

```
1    ---
2    - name: role demo
3      hosts: all
4      become: true
5      roles:
6        - role: lucab85.ansible_role_log4shell
7          detector_path: "/var"
```

error execution

```
1    $ ansible-playbook -i virtualmachines/demo/inventory trou\
2    bleshooting/role/role.yml
3    ERROR! the role 'lucab85.ansible_role_log4shell' was not \
4    found in /Users/lberton/prj/github/ansible-pilot/troubles\
5    hooting/role/roles:/Users/lberton/.ansible/roles:/usr/sha\
6    re/ansible/roles:/etc/ansible/roles:/Users/lberton/prj/gi\
7    thub/ansible-pilot/troubleshooting/role
8    The error appears to be in '/Users/lberton/prj/github/ans\
9    ible-pilot/troubleshooting/role/role.yml': line 6, column\
10    7, but may
11   be elsewhere in the file depending on the exact syntax pr\
```

```
12   oblem.
13   The offending line appears to be:
14   roles:
15       - role: lucab85.ansible_role_log4shell
16         ^ here
17   ansible-pilot $ ls -al ~/.ansible/roles
18   total 0
19   drwxr-xr-x  2 lberton  staff   64 Jan  7 08:19 .
20   drwxr-xr-x  8 lberton  staff  256 Jan  7 08:19 ..
21   ansible-pilot $
```

fix code

- requirements.yml

```
1   ---
2   roles:
3     - name: lucab85.ansible_role_log4shell
```

fix execution

```
1   $ ansible-galaxy install -r troubleshooting/role/requirem\
2   ents.yml
3   Starting galaxy role install process
4   - downloading role 'ansible_role_log4shell', owned by luc\
5   ab85
6   - downloading role from https://github.com/lucab85/ansibl\
7   e-role-log4shell/archive/v0.6.1.tar.gz
8   - extracting lucab85.ansible_role_log4shell to /Users/lbe\
9   rton/.ansible/roles/lucab85.ansible_role_log4shell
10  - lucab85.ansible_role_log4shell (v0.6.1) was installed s\
11  uccessfully
12  ansible-pilot $ ls -al ~/.ansible/roles
13  total 0
14  drwxr-xr-x   3 lberton  staff   96 Jan  7 08:24 .
```

```
drwxr-xr-x    8 lberton   staff   256 Jan   7 08:19 ..
drwxr-xr-x   12 lberton   staff   384 Jan   7 08:24 lucab85.a\
nsible_role_log4shell
ansible-pilot $ ls -al ~/.ansible/roles/lucab85.ansible_r\
ole_log4shell
total 32
drwxr-xr-x   12 lberton   staff   384 Jan   7 08:24 .
drwxr-xr-x    3 lberton   staff    96 Jan   7 08:24 ..
-rw-rw-r--    1 lberton   staff    96 Jan   6 11:22 .ansible\
-lint
drwxr-xr-x    5 lberton   staff   160 Jan   7 08:24 .github
-rw-rw-r--    1 lberton   staff   121 Jan   6 11:22 .yamllint
-rw-rw-r--    1 lberton   staff  1068 Jan   6 11:22 LICENSE
-rw-rw-r--    1 lberton   staff  3739 Jan   6 11:22 README.md
drwxr-xr-x    3 lberton   staff    96 Jan   7 08:24 defaults
drwxr-xr-x    4 lberton   staff   128 Jan   7 08:24 meta
drwxr-xr-x    3 lberton   staff    96 Jan   7 08:24 molecule
drwxr-xr-x    3 lberton   staff    96 Jan   7 08:24 tasks
drwxr-xr-x    3 lberton   staff    96 Jan   7 08:24 vars
ansible-pilot $ ls -al ~/.ansible/roles/lucab85.ansible_r\
ole_log4shell/*
-rw-rw-r-- 1 lberton  staff  1068 Jan  6 11:22 /Users/lb\
erton/.ansible/roles/lucab85.ansible_role_log4shell/LICEN\
SE
-rw-rw-r-- 1 lberton  staff  3739 Jan  6 11:22 /Users/lb\
erton/.ansible/roles/lucab85.ansible_role_log4shell/READM\
E.md
/Users/lberton/.ansible/roles/lucab85.ansible_role_log4sh\
ell/defaults:
total 8
drwxr-xr-x   3 lberton   staff    96 Jan   7 08:24 .
drwxr-xr-x  12 lberton   staff   384 Jan   7 08:24 ..
-rw-rw-r--   1 lberton   staff   528 Jan   6 11:22 main.yml
/Users/lberton/.ansible/roles/lucab85.ansible_role_log4sh\
ell/meta:
```

```
50  total 16
51  drwxr-xr-x   4 lberton   staff    128 Jan   7 08:24 .
52  drwxr-xr-x  12 lberton   staff    384 Jan   7 08:24 ..
53  -rw-r--r--   1 lberton   staff     55 Jan   7 08:24 .galaxy_\
54  install_info
55  -rw-rw-r--   1 lberton   staff   1002 Jan   6 11:22 main.yml
56  /Users/lberton/.ansible/roles/lucab85.ansible_role_log4sh\
57  ell/molecule:
58  total 0
59  drwxr-xr-x   3 lberton   staff     96 Jan   7 08:24 .
60  drwxr-xr-x  12 lberton   staff    384 Jan   7 08:24 ..
61  drwxr-xr-x   4 lberton   staff    128 Jan   7 08:24 default
62  /Users/lberton/.ansible/roles/lucab85.ansible_role_log4sh\
63  ell/tasks:
64  total 8
65  drwxr-xr-x   3 lberton   staff     96 Jan   7 08:24 .
66  drwxr-xr-x  12 lberton   staff    384 Jan   7 08:24 ..
67  -rw-rw-r--   1 lberton   staff   2209 Jan   6 11:22 main.yml
68  /Users/lberton/.ansible/roles/lucab85.ansible_role_log4sh\
69  ell/vars:
70  total 8
71  drwxr-xr-x   3 lberton   staff     96 Jan   7 08:24 .
72  drwxr-xr-x  12 lberton   staff    384 Jan   7 08:24 ..
73  -rw-rw-r--   1 lberton   staff    722 Jan   6 11:22 main.yml
74  ansible-pilot $ ansible-playbook -i virtualmachines/demo/\
75  inventory troubleshooting/role/role.yml
76  PLAY [role not found demo] ****************************\
77  ****************************************
78  TASK [Gathering Facts] *******************************\
79  ****************************************
80  ok: [demo.example.com]
81  TASK [lucab85.ansible_role_log4shell : print information]\
82   ****************************************
83  ok: [demo.example.com] => {
84      "msg": "Ansible Playbook tested with detector version\
```

```
85   1.2 released 2021-12-20.\nIf a 404 error occur please ad\
86   just the URL with the latest version available\nfor detec\
87   tor URL.\nPlease refer to the Red Hat Security Bullettin \
88   for up-to-date information and\nadjust the playbook varia\
89   bles accordingly.\nhttps://access.redhat.com/security/vul\
90   nerabilities/RHSB-2021-009.\n"
91   }
92   TASK [lucab85.ansible_role_log4shell : dependency present\
93   s] ************************************
94   ok: [demo.example.com]
95   TASK [lucab85.ansible_role_log4shell : create detector di\
96   rectory] ******************************
97   changed: [demo.example.com]
98   TASK [lucab85.ansible_role_log4shell : download detector \
99   file] *********************************
100  changed: [demo.example.com]
101  TASK [lucab85.ansible_role_log4shell : download detector \
102  signature] ****************************
103  skipping: [demo.example.com]
104  TASK [lucab85.ansible_role_log4shell : gpg public key] **\
105  *********************************************
106  skipping: [demo.example.com]
107  TASK [lucab85.ansible_role_log4shell : gpg verify detecto\
108  r] ************************************
109  skipping: [demo.example.com]
110  TASK [lucab85.ansible_role_log4shell : remove any detecto\
111  r run directory] **********************
112  ok: [demo.example.com]
113  TASK [lucab85.ansible_role_log4shell : create detector ru\
114  n directory] **************************
115  changed: [demo.example.com]
116  TASK [lucab85.ansible_role_log4shell : run detector/scann\
117  er] ***********************************
118  changed: [demo.example.com]
119  TASK [lucab85.ansible_role_log4shell : files in detector \
```

```
120   run directory] **************************
121   ok: [demo.example.com]
122   TASK [lucab85.ansible_role_log4shell : print vulnerable p\
123   ath(s) found] **************************
124   ok: [demo.example.com] => {
125       "vulnerable": {
126           "changed": false,
127           "examined": 1,
128           "failed": false,
129           "files": [],
130           "matched": 0,
131           "msg": "All paths examined",
132           "skipped_paths": {}
133       }
134   }
135   TASK [lucab85.ansible_role_log4shell : remove detector di\
136   rectory] ******************************
137   changed: [demo.example.com]
138   PLAY RECAP *********************************************\
139   ****************************************
140   demo.example.com           : ok=11    changed=5    unreach\
141   able=0    failed=0    skipped=3    rescued=0    ignored=0
142   ansible-pilot $
```

Ansible troubleshooting - permission denied Errno 13

How to troubleshoot the Permission denied Errno 13 Ansible fatal error and workaround the problem using the privilege escalation on Ansible Playbook.

Let's talk about Ansible troubleshooting, specifically about permission denied [Errno 13].

See also: Permanently Set Remote System Wide Environment Variables on Linux - /etc/environment - Ansible module lineinfile

demo

How to troubleshoot the Ansible fatal error[Errno 13] Permission denied and fix in Ansible Playbook code.

error code

```
1   ---
2   - name: set environment demo
3     hosts: all
4     gather_facts: false
5     vars:
6       os_environment:
7         - key: EDITOR
8           value: vi
9     tasks:
10      - name: customize /etc/environment
11        ansible.builtin.lineinline:
12          dest: "/etc/environment"
13          state: present
14          regexp: "^{{ item.key }}="
15          line: "{{ item.key }}={{ item.value }}"
16        with_items: "{{ os_environment }}"
```

error execution

```
ansible-pilot $ ansible-playbook -i virtualmachines/demo/\
inventory troubleshooting/permissiondenied_error.yml
PLAY [set environment demo] ******************************\
********************************************
TASK [customize /etc/environment] ***********************\
********************************************
An exception occurred during task execution. To see the f\
ull traceback, use -vvv. The error was: PermissionError: \
[Errno 13] Permission denied: b'/home/devops/.ansible/tmp\
/ansible-tmp-1645543127.772594-89712-144540003805636/tmpv\
hoh4q83' -> b'/etc/environment'
failed: [demo.example.com] (item={'key': 'EDITOR', 'value\
': 'vi'}) => {"ansible_facts": {"discovered_interpreter_p\
ython": "/usr/libexec/platform-python"}, "ansible_loop_va\
r": "item", "changed": false, "item": {"key": "EDITOR", "\
value": "vi"}, "msg": "The destination directory (/etc) i\
s not writable by the current user. Error was: [Errno 13]\
 Permission denied: b'/etc/.ansible_tmp_hwdwg3denvironmen\
t'"}
PLAY RECAP **********************************************\
********************************************
demo.example.com           : ok=0    changed=0    unreach\
able=0    failed=1    skipped=0    rescued=0    ignored=0
ansible-pilot $
```

fix code

```
1   ---
2   - name: set environment demo
3     hosts: all
4     gather_facts: false
5     become: true
6     vars:
7       os_environment:
8         - key: EDITOR
9           value: vi
10    tasks:
11      - name: customize /etc/environment
12        ansible.builtin.lineinline:
13          dest: "/etc/environment"
14          state: present
15          regexp: "^{{ item.key }}="
16          line: "{{ item.key }}={{ item.value }}"
17        with_items: "{{ os_environment }}"
```

fix execution

```
1   ansible-pilot $ ansible-playbook -i virtualmachines/demo/\
2   inventory troubleshooting/permissiondenied_fix.yml
3   PLAY [set environment demo] ****************************\
4   ******************************************
5   TASK [customize /etc/environment] *********************\
6   ******************************************
7   changed: [demo.example.com] => (item={'key': 'EDITOR', 'v\
8   alue': 'vi'})
9   PLAY RECAP ********************************************\
10  ******************************************
11  demo.example.com            : ok=1    changed=1    unreach\
12  able=0    failed=0    skipped=0    rescued=0    ignored=0
13  ansible-pilot $
```

Ansible troubleshooting - VARIABLE IS NOT DEFINED! ansible_hostname

Root cause analysis when the variable is not misspelled or not defined using the ansible_hostname internal variable and gather_facts boolean.

Most of the time the root cause is a misspelled variable or a variable really not defined. This use case is special about the `ansible_hostname` internal variable.

demo

The best way of talking about Ansible troubleshooting is to jump in a live demo to show you practically the VARIABLE IS NOT DEFINED! and how to solve it!

error code

```
1  ---
2  - name: hostname demo
3    hosts: all
4    gather_facts: false
5    tasks:
6      - name: print hostname
7        ansible.builtin.debug:
8          var: ansible_hostname
```

error execution

```
1    ansible-pilot $ ansible-playbook -i virtualmachines/demo/\
2    inventory troubleshooting/variablenotdefined_error.yml
3    PLAY [hostname demo] ************************************\
4    ********************************************
5    TASK [print hostname] ************************************\
6    ********************************************
7    ok: [demo.example.com] => {
8    "ansible_hostname": "VARIABLE IS NOT DEFINED!"
9    }
10   PLAY RECAP ***********************************************\
11   ********************************************
12   demo.example.com           : ok=1    changed=0      unreach\
13   able=0     failed=0     skipped=0     rescued=0    ignored=0
14   ansible-pilot $
```

fix code

```
1    ---
2    - name: hostname demo
3      hosts: all
4      gather_facts: true
5      tasks:
6        - name: print hostname
7          ansible.builtin.debug:
8            var: ansible_hostname
```

fix execution

```
ansible-pilot $ ansible-playbook -i virtualmachines/demo/\
inventory troubleshooting/variablenotdefined_fix.yml
PLAY [hostname demo] ************************************\
*********************************************
TASK [Gathering Facts] *********************************\
*********************************************
ok: [demo.example.com]
TASK [print hostname] **********************************\
*********************************************
ok: [demo.example.com] => {
    "ansible_hostname": "demo"
}
PLAY RECAP *********************************************\
*********************************************
demo.example.com              : ok=2    changed=0    unreach\
able=0    failed=0    skipped=0    rescued=0    ignored=0
ansible-pilot $
```

Ansible troubleshooting - This command has to be run under the root user

Permission error messages are annoying Ansible problems. In a live demo, we are going to troubleshoot starting from the error message. We are going to investigate the root cause of the problem and fix using the package module.

This fatal error message happens when we are trying to execute a module that requires more privilege during module execution. These circumstances are usually related to Ansible Playbook or Ansible configuration.

demo

The best way of talking about Ansible troubleshooting is to jump
in a live demo to show you practically the "This command has to
be run under the root user" and how to solve it!
This demo is going to try to install the "rsync" package on our target
system.

error code

```
1   ---
2   - name: troubleshooting under the root user
3     hosts: all
4     become: false
5     tasks:
6       - name: rsync installed
7         ansible.builtin.package:
8           name: rsync
9           state: present
```

error execution

```
1   ansible-pilot $ ansible-playbook -i virtualmachines/demo/\
2   inventory troubleshooting/under_root_user_error.yml
3   PLAY [troubleshooting under the root user] *************\
4   ****************************************
5   TASK [Gathering Facts] ********************************\
6   ****************************************
7   ok: [demo.example.com]
8   TASK [rsync installed] ********************************\
9   ****************************************
10  fatal: [demo.example.com]: FAILED! => {"changed": false, \
11  "msg": "This command has to be run under the root user.",\
12   "results": []}
13  PLAY RECAP ********************************************\
14  ****************************************
```

```
15  demo.example.com              : ok=1      changed=0      unreach\
16  able=0     failed=1     skipped=0     rescued=0     ignored=0
17  ansible-pilot $
```

fix code

```
1   ---
2   - name: troubleshooting under the root user
3     hosts: all
4     become: true
5     tasks:
6       - name: rsync installed
7         ansible.builtin.package:
8           name: rsync
9           state: present
```

fix execution

```
1   ansible-pilot $ ansible-playbook -i virtualmachines/demo/\
2   inventory troubleshooting/under_root_user_fix.yml
3   PLAY [troubleshooting under the root user] *************\
4   ******************************************
5   TASK [Gathering Facts] ********************************\
6   ******************************************
7   ok: [demo.example.com]
8   TASK [rsync installed] ********************************\
9   ******************************************
10  ok: [demo.example.com]
11  PLAY RECAP ********************************************\
12  ******************************************
13  demo.example.com              : ok=2      changed=0      unreach\
14  able=0     failed=0     skipped=0     rescued=0     ignored=0
15  ansible-pilot $
```

Thank you

Let me remind yourself that Ansible is a Red Hat evolving product.

In this book we covered the most useful day-to-day code and activities in the most used Operating Systems.

Use this book as a guidance in your day-to-day life but feel free to use your creativity to invent new automation workflow.

This is where the Ansible starts becoming truly fun, but this is also where ths book's story ends and others' begin.

For pointers on where to turn after this book, see the list on reccomended follow-up text in the Preface.

Good luck with your journey.

And of course, "Always look on the bright side of Life!"

www.ingramcontent.com/pod-product-compliance
Lightning Source LLC
Chambersburg PA
CBHW051804150726
47998CB00001B/17